Treasury of the True Dharma Eye

Dōgen's *Shōbōgenzō*

Treasury of the True Dharma Eye
Dōgen's *Shōbōgenzō*

Volume VII

Supplementary Chapters
and Variant Texts

An annotated translation
by the Sōtō Zen Text Project

Sōtōshū Shūmuchō
Tokyo

University of Hawai'i Press
Honolulu

© 2023 by Sōtōshū Shūmuchō
The Administrative Headquarters of Sōtō Zen Buddhism
All rights reserved.
Printed in China

Treasury of the True Dharma Eye: Dōgen's *Shōbōgenzō*
Volume VII: Supplementary Chapters and Variant Texts

Published in Japan by Sōtōshū Shūmuchō, Tokyo
ISBN: 978-4-911061-00-8

Published for the rest of the world by University of Hawai'i Press, Honolulu

Library of Congress Cataloging-in-Publication Data

Names: Dōgen, 1200–1253, author. | Sōtō Zen Text Project, translator.

Title: Treasury of the true dharma eye : Dōgen's Shōbōgenzō / an
annotated translation by the Sōtō Zen Text Project.

Other titles: Shōbō genzō. English

Description: Honolulu : University of Hawai'i Press, [2024] | Published in
Japan by Sōtōshū Shūmuchō, 2023. | Includes bibliographical
references and index. | Contents: v. 7. Supplementary chapters and variant texts

Identifiers: LCCN 2024004760 (print) | LCCN 2024004761 (ebook) | ISBN
9780824899172 (v. 1 ; paperback) | ISBN 9780824899189 (v. 2 ; paperback)
| ISBN 9780824899196 (v. 3 ; paperback) | ISBN 9780824899202 (v. 4 ;
paperback) | ISBN 9780824899219 (v. 5 ; paperback) | ISBN 9780824899226
(v. 6 ; paperback) | ISBN 9780824899233 (v. 7 ; paperback) | ISBN
9780824899240 (v. 8 ; paperback) | ISBN 9780824899257 (paperback) | ISBN
9798880700264 (v. 1 ; pdf) | ISBN 9798880700271 (v. 2 ; pdf) | ISBN
9798880700288 (v. 3 ; pdf) | ISBN 9798880700295 (v. 4 ; pdf) | ISBN
9798880700301 (v. 5 ; pdf) | ISBN 9798880700318 (v. 6 ; pdf) | ISBN
9798880700325 (v. 7 ; pdf) | ISBN 9798880700332 (v. 8 ; pdf)

Subjects: LCSH: Sōtōshū—Doctrines—Early works to 1800.

Classification: LCC BQ9449.D653 E5 2024 (print) | LCC BQ9449.D653 (ebook)
| DDC 294.3/85—-dc23/eng/20240318

LC record available at https://lccn.loc.gov/2024004760
LC ebook record available at https://lccn.loc.gov/2024004761

Cover art: Eihei Dōgen Zenji Gyōjōzu scroll, courtesy of Rev. Ōtani Tetsuo
Cover design by Urs App

University of Hawai'i Press books are printed on acid-free paper and meet the
guidelines for permanence and durability of the Council on Library Resources.
Printer-ready copy has been provided by Sōtōshū Shūmuchō

CONTENTS

VOLUME VII

SUPPLEMENTARY CHAPTERS AND VARIANT TEXTS

Conventions iii

Abbreviations v

SUPPLEMENTARY CHAPTERS

Introduction to the Supplementary Chapters 2

S1. Talk on Pursuing the Way *Bendōwa* 辦道話 5

S2. Procedures for the Hall of Gathered Clouds
Jūundō shiki 重雲堂式 49

S3. The *Lotus* Turns the *Lotus Hokke ten Hokke* 法華轉法華 59

S4. The Mind Cannot Be Got *Shin fukatoku* 心不可得 99

S5. The Four Attractions of the Bodhisattva
Bodaisatta shishōbō 菩提薩埵四攝法 121

S6. Instructions to the Administration Cloister *Ji kuin mon* 示庫院文 ... 133

S7. Only Buddhas with Buddhas *Yui butsu yo butsu* 唯佛與佛 141

S8. Birth and Death *Shōji* 生死 159

S9. The Way of the Buddhas *Butsudō* 佛道 165

VARIANT TEXTS

Introduction to the Variant Texts 173

V1. Talk on Pursuing the Way *Bendōwa* 辦道話 175

V2. The Inheritance Certificate *Shisho* 嗣書 215

V3. Beyond the Buddha *Butsu kōjō ji* 佛向上事 239

V4. Washing the Face *Senmen* 洗面 261

V5. Extensive Study *Henzan* 遍參 285

V6. Great Awakening *Daigo* 大悟 299

V7. Karma of the Three Times *Sanji gō* 三時業 331

Conventions

This publication is an annotated translation, in seven volumes, of one hundred three texts of Dōgen's Japanese *Shōbōgenzō,* plus an additional volume containing an introduction, supplementary notes, appendices, and list of works cited. The translation is based on the edition of the *Shōbōgenzō* published in Kawamura Kōdō 河村孝道, ed., *Dōgen zenji zenshū* 道元禅師全集, vols. 1-2 (Tokyo: Shunjūsha, 1991, 1993), cited herein as DZZ.1 and DZZ.2; volume and page numbers of this edition are noted in braces at the corresponding locations in the translation.

The Japanese text accompanying the translation here follows the punctuation and *kanazukai* of the Kawamura edition; for ease of reference to premodern sources, Kawamura's modern Japanese kanji have been replaced with traditional forms. Also, for ease of reference, the sections into which the texts of the Kawamura edition are divided have been assigned numbers in square brackets by the translators. The translation of Kawamura's longer sections is sometimes broken into separate paragraphs, and transitions to new topics between sections are sometimes marked by a string of asterisks.

Though primarily written in Japanese, the *Shōbōgenzō* includes many passages of Chinese, ranging from long quotations of texts to short phrases inserted into the Japanese sentences. Since this inclusion of Chinese is a prominent linguistic feature of the original texts, the translation seeks to indicate such passages by the use of oblique font. The reader is warned that, given the ubiquity in the Japanese language of expressions adopted from Chinese, the identification of the shorter phrases as Chinese, rather than Japanese, is often rather arbitrary.

Much of the *Shōbōgenzō* is devoted to comment on material in other texts. The translation uses quotation marks to indicate terms and passages on which Dōgen is commenting. Here, again, the reader is warned that the distinction between use and mention can often be difficult to draw.

Sanskrit, Chinese, and Japanese terms appearing in the *Oxford English Dictionary* (3rd edition) are considered to have been adopted into English; other such terms are treated as foreign words and rendered in italics. Romanization of all such terms, whether treated as foreign or English, is given with diacritics.

With some exceptions, Chinese transliterations of Sanskrit terms are rendered as romanized Sanskrit. Indic proper nouns, whether transliterated or translated in the Chinese, are rendered as their presumed originals where possible; the reader is warned that some such reconstructions are unattested and speculative.

The proper noun "Zen" is used in reference to (a) the tradition that Dōgen calls the "buddhas and ancestors," and (b) the Japanese instantiation of that tradition; the Chinese name "Chan" is used in reference to the Chinese instantiation of the tradition.

Romanized readings of the Japanese text given in the notes follow wherever possible the ruby in Kawamura's text; readings not provided by Kawamura are based on *Zengaku daijiten* 禅学大辞典 (1978) and/or Katō Shūkō 加藤宗厚, *Shōbōgenzō yōgo sakuin* 正法眼藏用語索引 (1962).

Citations of T (*Taishō shinshū daizōkyō* 大正新脩大藏經) are from the *SAT Daizōkyō Text Database* (https://21dzk.l.u-tokyo.ac.jp/SAT). Citations of ZZ (*Dainihon zokuzōkyō* 大日本續藏經) are from the *CBETA Hanwen dazangjing* 漢文大藏經 (http://tripitaka.cbeta.org). Citations of KR are from *Kanripo* 漢リポ *Kanseki Repository* (https://www.kanripo.org).

The Kawamura edition provides colophons from several sources, some following the relevant chapter, some in the head notes of the chapter, some in the collation notes (*honbun kōi* 本文校異) for that chapter in the end matter of DZZ.1 and DZZ.2. For the convenience of the reader, this translation collects these colophons (and occasionally others omitted by Kawamura) at the end of each chapter. Colophons without attribution are assumed to have been written by Dōgen.

ABBREVIATIONS

C   Chinese language

DZZ   *Dōgen zenji zenshū* 道元禅師全集, Kagamishima Genryū 鏡島元隆 et al., compilers. 7 vols. Tokyo: Shunjūsha, 1988–1993.

ESST *Eihei Shōbōgenzō shūsho taisei* 永平正法眼蔵蒐書大成, Kawamura Kōdō 河村孝道, ed. 27 vols. Tokyo: Taishūkan Shoten, 1974-1982.

J   Japanese language

KR   Kanseki Repository (Kanseki Ripo 漢籍リポ). Online: https://www.kanripo.org

M   *Dai kanwa jiten* 大漢和辞典, Morohashi Tetsuji 諸橋轍次, ed. 13 vols. (plus 2-vol. supplement). Tokyo: Taishūkan Shoten, 1955-1960.

S   Sanskrit

SCZ   *Shōbōgenzō chūkai zensho* 正法眼藏註解全書, Jinbo Nyoten 神保如天 and Andō Bun'ei 安藤文英, eds. 11 vols. Reprint Tokyo: Nihon Bussho Kankōkai, 1956-1957.

SZ   *Sōtōshū zensho* 曹洞宗全書. 20 vols. Tokyo: Kōmeisha, 1929-1938.

T   *Taishō shinshū daizōkyō* 大正新脩大藏經, Takakusu Junjirō 高楠順次郎 and Watanabe Kaikyoku 渡邊海旭, eds. 100 vols. Tokyo: Daizōkyōkai, 1924–1935.

ZT   *Zengaku taikei* 禪學大系. 8 vols. Tokyo: Kokusho Kankōkai, 1952 (orig. publ. 1910-11).

ZTS   *Zengaku tenseki sōkan* 禅学典籍叢刊, Yanagida Seizan 柳田聖山 and Shiina Kōyū 椎名宏雄, eds. 12 vols. Kyoto: Rinsen Shoten, 1999-2001.

ZZ   *Dainihon zokuzōkyō* 大日本続藏經. 150 vols. Kyoto: Bussho Kankōkai, 1905-1912.

Supplementary Chapters
of the *Shōbōgenzō*

Introduction to the Supplementary Chapters

of the *Shōbōgenzō*

The nine titles in this collection of supplementary chapters represent works included in the 1815 ninety-five-chapter Honzan edition of the Shōbōgenzō that are not found in either the seventy-five- or twelve-chapter compilations. The inclusion of these extra chapters in the Honzan edition is the result of an effort within the Sōtōshū to create the most comprehensive possible *Shōbōgenzō*, an effort that began at least as early as the beginning of the fifteenth century.

In 1419, Taiyō Bonsei 太容梵清 (who in 1422 would become abbot of Sōjiji 総持寺) produced a *Shōbōgenzō* in eighty-four chapters, consisting of the basic seventy-five-chapter version plus a supplement of nine additional chapters found in the sixty-chapter compilation. Of our titles translated below, two (numbers S3 and S5) were among these additional chapters. Bonsei's original manuscript still exists, although it was heavily damaged by fire in 1814. Over the centuries, his work served as the model for subsequent attempts to compile a comprehensive *Shōbōgenzō*.

Over two and a half centuries later, in 1686, Manzan Dōhaku 卍山道白 (1636–1714) created an eighty-nine chapter compilation, based on Bonsei's eighty-four chapters, renumbered and put into a rough chronological order, plus a new supplemental section of five additional chapters. Two of these works are found in the twelve-chapter *Shōbōgenzō* (though Manzan's source for them is uncertain); two (numbers S2 and S6 below) are brief monastic regulations not originally associated with the *Shōbōgenzō*. The fifth text added by Menzan (S1 below) is the famous "Bendōwa" 辨道話, a previously little-known work from a manuscript of unknown provenance.

A few years later, in 1693, Handō Kōzen 版橈晃全 (1625–1693), an abbot at Eiheiji 永平寺, expanded Manzan's *Shōbōgenzō* to ninety-six chapters, adding six works discovered among the manuscripts in the so-called *Himitsu* 秘密 collection of twenty-eight texts belonging to Eiheiji. (He also included one additional work, entitled "Shinzo" 陞座 ["Ascending the Seat"], that was subsequently deemed spurious and omitted from the ninety-five-chapter Honzan edition.) Kōzen integrated the supplemental chapters into a single chronological sequence, an arrangement subsequently followed by the 1815 Honzan edition. Of the six works added from the *Himitsu* collection, two have counterparts in the twelve-chapter *Shōbōgenzō* (numbers T7 and T10), while four are unique to the *Himitsu* collection and are translated here below (numbers S4, S7, S8, and S9).

The nine supplemental chapters in this section correspond to the chapters in the 1815 Honzan edition as follows:

Supplementary chapters	Honzan chapters
S1	1
S2	5
S3	17
S4	19
S5	45
S6	81
S7	91
S8	92
S9	93

TREASURY OF THE TRUE DHARMA EYE
SUPPLEMENTARY CHAPTER 1

Talk on Pursuing the Way
Bendōwa
辧道話

Talk on Pursuing the Way

Bendōwa

INTRODUCTION

The "Bendōwa" represents the first chapter of the Honzan edition of the *Shōbōgenzō*; but this celebrated work, often regarded as the introduction to the *Shōbōgenzō*, was almost certainly not originally composed with that collection in mind and, indeed, was not included in any of the premodern compilations of the *Shōbōgenzō*. According to its colophon, it was written in the autumn of 1231, only four years after Dōgen's return from China and a year before he opened his Kōshōji and began work on the *Shōbōgenzō*.

Rather like his earlier *Fukan zazen gi* 普勸坐禪儀, the "Bendōwa" seeks to introduce to a Japanese audience the practice of seated meditation that its author had experienced on the mainland. Unlike that earlier text, carefully crafted in elegant Chinese, this work is written in the vernacular language used for informal Buddhist homiletic literature. The work is divided into two parts: (a) an introductory essay (represented by the first fourteen sections here) extolling seated meditation as the Buddha's "samādhi of self-enjoyment," recounting the author's quest for the dharma in Japan and China, and rehearsing the history of the transmission of the Zen tradition; and (b) a set of eighteen questions and answers about the practice. In both parts, we see the young Dōgen writing in a style and addressing themes more common to the Japanese Buddhism of his day than is the more technical Zen discourse of the representative *Shōbōgenzō* essays.

The version of the "Bendōwa" given below translates the Honzan text, which is based on a woodblock print published in 1788 by Gentō Sokuchū 玄透即中 (1729–1807). The work is also extant in a variant version, preserved in the Shōbōji 正法寺 manuscript (dated 1332, recopied 1515), the translation of which can be found below, as Variant Text 1.

正法眼藏別輯一

Treasury of the True Dharma Eye
Supplementary Chapter 1

辨道話

Talk on Pursuing the Way

(玄透開版本)

(Gentō printed text)

[S1:1] {2:460}

諸佛如來、ともに妙法を單傳して、阿耨菩提を證するに、最上無爲の妙術あり。これ、ただほとけ、佛にさづけてよこしまなることなきは、すなはち自受用三昧、その標準なり。この三昧に遊化するに、端坐參禪を正門とせり。

The buddhas, the tathāgatas, all have a wondrous skill, supreme and unconditioned, for uniquely transmitting the wondrous dharma and verifying *anuttara-bodhi*. That it is bestowed only from buddha to buddha without error is because the samādhi of self-enjoyment is its standard.[1] To disport oneself in this samādhi, studying Zen in upright sitting, is considered the main gateway.[2]

[S1:2]

この法は、人人の分上にゆたかにそなはれりといへども、いまだ修せざるにはあらはれず、證せざるにはうることなし。はなてば、てにみてり、一多のきはならむや。かたれば、くちにみつ、縦横、きはまりなし。諸佛の、つねにこのなかに住持たる、各各の方面に知覺をのこさず。群生の、とこしなへにこのなかに使用する、各各の知覺に方面あらはれず。

Although this dharma is abundantly allotted to each person, when we have not practiced it, it does not appear, and when we do not verify it, it is not attained.[3] Let it go, and it fills the hand — how could it be bounded by one or many? Speak of it, and it fills the mouth — vertically and

---

1 **samādhi of self-enjoyment is its standard** (*ji juyū zanmai, sono hyōjun nari* 自受用三昧、その標準なり): I.e., the concentration in which the buddhas experience their own awakening is the standard by which is measured the transmission of their "wondrous dharma."

2 **main gateway** (*shōmon* 正門): Or "the correct, or primary, approach"; a term treated below, sections 17 and 18, but not otherwise common in the *Shōbōgenzō*.

3 **this dharma** (*kono hō* この法): Presumably, the antecedent is the "wondrous dharma" marked by "the samādhi of self-enjoyment."

8 DŌGEN'S *SHŌBŌGENZŌ* VOLUME VII

horizontally without limit. The buddhas are always within it, dwelling in and maintaining it, without leaving perception of it in any of its quarters; living beings are continuously within it, making use of it, without its quarters appearing in any of their perceptions.[4]

[S1:3]

いまをしふる功夫辦道は、證上に萬法をあらしめ、出路に一如を行ずるなり。その超關脱落のとき、この節目にかかはらむや。

The concentrated effort in pursuit of the way that I teach here brings the myriad dharmas into existence based on verification and practices their oneness on the path leading out.[5] When we pass beyond those barriers and slough them off, how could we be concerned with these particulars?[6]

* * * * *

[S1:4] {2:461}

予、發心求法よりこのかた、わが朝の遍方に知識をとぶらひき。ちなみに建仁の全公をみる。あひしたがふ霜華、すみやかに九廻をへたり。いささか臨濟の家風をきく。全公は、祖師西和尚の上足として、ひとり無上の佛法を正傳せり、あへて餘輩のならぶべきにあらず。予、かさねて大宋國におもむき、知識を兩浙にとぶらひ、家風を五門にきく。つひに太白峰の淨禪師に參じて、一生參學の大事、ここにをはりぬ。

---

4 **The buddhas are always within it, dwelling in and maintaining it** (*shobutsu no, tsune ni kono naka ni jūji taru* 諸佛の、つねにこのなかに住持たる): This sentence might be paraphrased, "The buddhas reside in this dharma without being self-conscious of it; we are also living in this dharma but are oblivious of it."

5 **brings the myriad dharmas into existence based on verification and practices their oneness on the path leading out** (*shōjō ni manbō o arashime, shutsuro ni ichinyo o gyōzuru* 證上に萬法をあらしめ、出路に一如を行ずる): Perhaps meaning something like, "revealing all things as they are to the awakened consciousness, practices on the path to liberation in the light of their ultimate unity." The term *shutsuro* 出路 (rendered here "path leading out") is not common in Dōgen's writing; it is taken here as roughly synonymous with his more common *katsuro* 活路 ("path to survival"; "lifesaving route").

6 **When we pass beyond those barriers and slough them off** (*sono chōkan datsuraku no toki* その超關脱落のとき): The antecedent of "those" (*sono* その) here is not entirely obvious: it could be taken as the distinction between "verification" (*shōjō* 證上) and "the path leading out" (*shutsuro* 出路); or, perhaps, between "the myriad dharmas" (*manbō* 萬法) and their "oneness" (*ichinyo* 一如). The following "these particulars" (or, perhaps, "this division"; *kono setsumoku* この節目) presumably refers to the same distinction. For the use of "slough off" (*datsuraku* 脱落), see Supplementary Notes, s.v. "Slough off."

S1. Talk on Pursuing the Way *Bendōwa* 辨道話

From the time that I brought forth the mind [of bodhi] and sought the dharma, I inquired of wise friends throughout our kingdom. Thus, I met the Honorable Zen of Kennin.[7] Frosts and flowers, one after another, swiftly passed nine rounds, as I heard something of the house style of Linji.[8] The Honorable Zen, the foremost disciple of the Ancestral Master Reverend Sai, alone received the direct transmission of the unsurpassed buddha dharma; none of the others could compare.[9]

Thereafter, journeying to the Land of the Great Song, I called on wise friends in the Two Zhes and heard of the house styles at the five gates.[10] Finally, I went to study under Chan Master Jing of Taibai Peak, and here the great matter of my entire life's study was resolved.[11]

[S1:5]

それよりのち、大宋紹定のはじめ、本郷にかへりし、すなはち弘法救生を
おもひとせり、なほ重擔をかたにおけるがごとし。しかあるに、弘通のこ
ころを放下せん激揚のときをまつゆえに、しばらく雲遊萍寄して、まさに
先哲の風をきこえんとす。

Thereafter, at the beginning of Shaoding in the Great Song, I returned to my native land, with the intention of spreading the dharma and saving beings.[12] It was just as if I had shouldered a heavy burden. Nevertheless, I put aside my thoughts of propagation and, in order to wait for a time

---

7 **the Honorable Zen of Kennin** (*Kennin no Zen kō* 建仁の全公): I.e., Myōzen 明全 (1184–1225), a dharma heir in the Rinzai 臨濟 lineage of Eisai 榮西 (1141–1215), founder of Kenninji 建仁寺.

8 **Frosts and flowers** (*sōka* 霜華): I.e., autumn frosts and spring flowers; the seasons of the year. The "nine rounds" (*kue* 九廻) here represents the years from 1217, when Dōgen first met Myōzen, to 1225, when the latter died while Dōgen was accompanying him on pilgrimage to China.

9 **the Ancestral Master Reverend Sai** (*soshi Sai oshō* 祖師西和尚): I.e., Eisai 榮西. In fact, he had a number of prominent disciples, including Taikō Gyōyū 退耕行勇 (1162-1241), who succeeded him as abbot of Kenninji.

10 **I called on wise friends in the Two Zhes and heard of the house styles at the five gates** (*chishiki o Ryōsetsu ni toburai, kafū o gomon ni kiku* 知識を兩浙にとぶらひ、家風を五門にきく): I.e., Dōgen sought out teachers in the Districts of Zhedong (*Settō* 浙東) and Zhexi (*Sessai* 浙西) (in present-day Jiangsu and Zhejiang) and learned the teachings of the five houses (*goke* 五家) of Chan.

11 **Chan Master Jing of Taibai Peak** (*Taihakuhō no Jō zenji* 太白峰の淨禪師): I.e., Tiantong Rujing 天童如淨 (1162–1227). Taibai Peak (*Taihakuhō* 太白峰) is the mountain, near Ningbo, in present-day Zhejiang, at which Rujing's Tiantong 天童 monastery was located.

12 **at the beginning of Shaoding in the Great Song** (*Daisō Jōtei no hajime* 大宋紹定のはじめ). The first year of the Shaoding era corresponds to 1228 CE in the Gregorian calendar.

when I could fully devote myself to it, I *drifted like a cloud and floated like a water plant*, seeking to convey the style of the former wise men.[13]

[S1:6]

ただし、おのづから名利にかかはらず、道念をさきとせん眞實の參學あらんか、いたづらに邪師にまどはされて、みだりに正解をおほひ、むなしく自狂にえふて、ひさしく迷鄉にしづまん。なにによりてか般若の正種を長じ、得道の時をえん。貧道は、いま雲遊萍寄をこととすれば、いづれの山川をか、とぶらはん。これをあはれむゆえに、まのあたり大宋國にして、禪林の風規を見聞し、知識の玄旨を裏持せしを、しるしあつめて、參學閑道の人にのこして、佛家の正法をしらしめんとす。これ眞訣ならむかも。

Still, there could occasionally be a few genuine students, unconcerned with fame or profit and giving priority to thoughts of the way.[14] Led astray in vain by false teachers, rashly obscuring the correct understanding and worthlessly drunk on their own delusions, they may sink into the land of delusion. How could they nurture the true seed of prajñā and reach a time when they gain the way? If this humble wayfarer is now *drifting like a cloud and floating like a water plant*, what mountains and rivers will they visit?[15] Out of pity for them, compiling these teachings of what I personally experienced of the customs and rules of the Chan groves and what I received of the dark import of the wise friends while I was in the Land of the Great Song, I leave them for those who would study and master the way, that they may know the true dharma of the house of the buddhas.[16] This indeed is the true arcanum.

[S1:7]

いはく、大師釋尊、靈山會上にして法を迦葉につけ、祖祖正傳して菩提達磨尊者にいたる。尊者、みづから神丹國におもむき、法を慧可大師につけき。これ東地の、佛法傳來のはじめなり。かくのごとく單傳して、おのづから六祖大鑑禪師にいたるごとき、眞實の佛法まさに東漢に流演して、節目にかかはらぬむねあらはれき。ときに、六祖に二位の神足ありき、南嶽

---

13 **Nevertheless** (*shika aru ni* しかあるに): Some readers suggest this should be taken in the sense "thus" (*shika areba* しかあれば).

drifted like a cloud and floated like a water plant (*unyū hyōki* 雲遊萍寄): A fixed expression for the life of the peripatetic monk.

14 **occasionally** (*onozukara* おのづから): Taking this in the sense *tama ni* たまに.

15 **what mountains and rivers will they visit?** (*izure no sansen o ka, toburawan* いづれの山川をか、とぶらはん): I.e., where can they go for instruction?

16 **those who would study and master the way** (*sangaku kandō no hito* 參學閑道の人): Taking *kan* 閑 in the sense *kanshū* 閑習 ("to learn"), as is often done here. The phrase may be a play with the opening line of the famous *Zhengdao ge* 證道歌, attributed to Yongjia Xuanjue 永嘉玄覺 (or Zenjue 眞覺, d. 713) (T.2014.48:395c9), which describes not the student in need of instruction, but one with nothing more to study:

絕學無爲閑道人。

A person at ease in the way, finished learning, with nothing to do.

S1. Talk on Pursuing the Way *Bendōwa* 辨道話   11

の懷讓と青原の行思となり。ともに佛印を傳持して、おなじく人天の導師
なり。その二派の流通するに、よく五門ひらけたり。いはゆる、法眼宗・
潙仰宗・曹洞宗・雲門宗・臨濟宗なり。見在大宋には臨濟宗のみ天下にあ
まねし。五家ことなれども、ただ一佛心印なり。

It is said that Great Master Śākya, the Honored One, at an assembly
on Vulture Peak, entrusted the dharma to Kāśyapa.[17] Directly transmitted by ancestor after ancestor, it reached Venerable Bodhidharma. The
Venerable himself traveled to the Land of Cīnasthāna and entrusted the
dharma to Great Master Huike. This was the start of the transmission
of the buddha dharma in the Eastern Earth. In this way, having been
uniquely transmitted, when it reached the Sixth Ancestor, Chan Master
Dajian, the genuine buddha dharma spread throughout Han in the East,
and its message, uninvolved in particulars, became apparent.[18] At the
time, the Sixth Ancestor had two superior disciples: Huairang of Nanyue
and Xingsi of Qingyuan.[19] Both received transmission of the buddha seal
and were equally the guides of humans and devas. As their two factions
spread, five gates were opened: the Fayan lineage, Weiyang lineage,
Caodong lineage, Yunmen lineage, and Linji lineage.[20] At present in the
Great Song, the Linji lineage alone is widespread throughout the land.
Although the five houses differ, they are but one buddha mind seal.

[S1:8] {2:462}

大宋國も、後漢よりこのかた、教籍、あとをたれて一天にしけりといへど
も、雌雄、いまださだめざりき。祖師西來ののち、直に葛藤の根源をき
り、純一の佛法ひろまれり。わがくにも、又しかあらむことを、こひねが
ふべし。

Even in the Land of the Great Song, although since the Later Han texts
of the teachings had spread and left their traces throughout the realm,
their strengths and weaknesses were still undetermined. After the An-

---

17   **at an assembly on Vulture Peak** (*Ryōzen e jō ni shite* 靈山會上にして): I.e., the
legendary gathering of the Buddha's community on Gṛdhrakūṭa-parvata (*Ryōjusen* 靈鷲
山), at which the Buddha is said to have held up a flower and wordlessly transmitted the
treasury of the true dharma eye to his disciple Mahākāśyapa; see Supplementary Notes,
s.v. "Treasury of the True Dharma Eye."

18   **the Sixth Ancestor, Chan Master Dajian** (*Rokuso Daikan zenji* 六祖大鑑禪師):
I.e., Caoxi Huineng 曹溪慧能.

Han in the East (*Tōkan* 東漢): Here, a reference to China, not the Eastern Han (or Later
Han) dynasty (25-220 CE).

19   **Huairang of Nanyue and Xingsi of Qingyuan** (*Nangaku no Ejō to Seigen no
Gyōshi* 南嶽の懷讓と青原の行思): I.e., Nanyue Huairang 南嶽懷讓 (677-744) and
Qingyuan Xingsi 青原行思 (d. 740), the two disciples of the Sixth Ancestor from whom
the lineages leading to the five houses were said to descend.

20   **five gates** (*gomon* 五門): I.e., the five houses (*goke* 五家) of Chan recognized in
Song-dynasty histories of the school.

12 DŌGEN'S *SHŌBŌGENZŌ* VOLUME VII

cestral Master came from the west, the roots of the tangled vines were immediately cut off, and the pure buddha dharma spread.[21] We should earnestly hope for the same in our land as well.

[S1:9]

いはく、佛法を住持せし諸祖ならびに諸佛、ともに自受用三昧に端坐依行するを、その開悟のまさしきみちとせり。西天東地、さとりをえし人、その風にしたがへり。これ、師資ひそかに妙術を正傳し、眞訣を稟持せしによりてなり。

It is said that the ancestors, along with the buddhas, who maintain the buddha dharma have all regarded practice that relies on upright sitting in the samādhi of self-enjoyment as the right path to the opening of awakening. From Sindh in the West to the Land of the East, those who have attained awakening have followed that style. This is because the masters and disciples privately transmitted directly the wondrous skill and received the true arcanum.

[S1:10]

宗門の正傳にいはく、この單傳正直の佛法は、最上のなかに最上なり。參見知識のはじめより、さらに燒香・禮拜・念佛・修懺・看經をもちいず、ただし打坐して身心脱落することをえよ。

In the direct transmission of our school, it is said, "This uniquely transmitted, true and direct buddha dharma is supreme among the supreme.[22] From the start of your consultation with a wise friend, without further need of burning incense, making bows, recollecting the buddha, practicing repentance or reading sūtras, just sit and attain the sloughing off of body and mind."

[S1:11]

もし人、一時なりといふとも、三業に佛印を標し、三昧に端坐するとき、遍法界みな佛印となり、盡虚空ことごとくさとりとなる。ゆえに、諸佛如來をしては、本地の法樂をまし、覺道の莊嚴をあらたにす。および十方法界・三途六道の群類、みなともに一時に身心明淨にして、大解脱地を證し、本來面目現ずるとき、諸法みな正覺を證會し、萬物ともに佛身を使用して、すみやかに證會の邊際を一超して、覺樹王に端坐し、一時に無等等の大法輪を轉じ、究竟無爲の深般若を開演す。

---

21 **tangled vines** (*kattō* 葛藤): Literally, "arrowroot and wisteria," twining plants commonly used as a metaphor for "entanglements," or "complications," especially of the Buddhist teachings or language in general; see Supplementary Notes, s.v. "Tangled vines."

22 **In the direct transmission of our school, it is said** (*shūmon no shōden ni iwaku* 宗門の正傳にいはく): Variation on a saying that Dōgen attributes elsewhere to Rujing 如淨; see Supplementary Notes, s.v. "Just sit."

S1. Talk on Pursuing the Way *Bendōwa* 辨道話

If someone, even once, marks the three modes of karma with the buddha seal and sits upright in samādhi, at that time, everything throughout the dharma realms becomes the buddha seal and everywhere in the entirety of empty space becomes awakening.[23] Therefore, for the buddhas, the tathāgatas, it increases the bliss of the dharma of their original ground and renews the adornments of their awakening to the way. Then, beings throughout the dharma realms in the ten directions, in the three roads and six paths, being bright and pure in body and mind, will all together simultaneously verify the ground of the great liberation and manifest their original face.[24] At that time, the dharmas, all realizing right awakening, and the myriad things, all using the buddha body, quickly transcending the boundaries of realization, sit upright at the king tree of awakening, simultaneously turn the great dharma wheel, equal to the unequalled, and proclaim the profound prajñā, ultimate and unconditioned.[25]

[S1:12] {2:463}

これらの等正覺、さらにかへりてしたしくあひ冥資するみちかよふがゆえに、この坐禪人、確爾として身心脱落し、從來雜穢の知見思量を截斷して、天眞の佛法に證會し、あまねく微塵際そこばくの諸佛如來の道場ごとに、佛事を助發し、ひろく佛向上の機にかうぶらしめて、よく佛向上の法を激揚す。このとき、十方法界の土地・草木・牆壁・瓦礫、みな佛事をなすをもて、そのおこすところの風水の利益にあづかるともがら、みな甚妙不可思議の佛化に冥資せられて、ちかきさとりをあらはす。この水火を受用するたぐひ、みな本證の佛化を周旋するゆえに、これらのたぐひと共住して同語するもの、またことごとくあひたがひに無窮の佛德そなはり、展轉廣作して、無盡、無間斷、不可思議、不可稱量の佛法を、遍法界の内外に流通するものなり。しかあれども、このもろもろの當人の知覺に昏ぜざらしむることは、靜中の無造作にして、直證なるをもてなり。もし、凡流のおもひのごとく、修證を兩段にあらせば、おのおのあひ覺知すべきなり。もし、覺知にまじはるは、證則にあらず、證則には、迷情およばざるがゆえに。

Because these perfectly awakened ones then return and follow the path of intimately providing mutual dark assistance, this person of seated meditation, definitely having body and mind sloughed off and severing previous confused and defiled knowledge and thinking, realizes the natural buddha dharma and, at every practice place of the buddhas, the tathāgatas, numerous as infinitesimal dust motes, furthers the buddha work and, widely providing for listeners beyond the buddha, vigorously

---

23 **marks the three modes of karma with the buddha seal** (*sangō ni butsu'in o hyō shi* 三業に佛印を標し): I.e., to express the acts of a buddha in body, speech, and mind.

24 **three roads and six paths** (*sanzu rokudō* 三途六道): I.e., the three evil destinies and the six destinies; see Supplementary Notes, s.v. "Six paths."

25 **king tree of awakening** (*kakujuō* 覺樹王): I.e., the bodhi tree, king of trees, under which Siddhārtha attained awakening.

14 DŌGEN'S *SHŌBŌGENZŌ* VOLUME VII

promotes the dharma beyond the buddha.[26] At this time, by all the lands, grasses and trees, fences and walls, tiles and pebbles of dharma realms in the ten directions engaging in the buddha work, all those enjoying the benefits of wind and water thereby produced, darkly assisted by the extremely wondrous inconceivable buddha conversion, manifest an intimate awakening.[27]

Because the ones who receive and use this water and fire all circulate the buddha conversion of original verification, those who dwell and speak with them are also ones who are all endowed together with inexhaustible buddha virtues, and who, gradually expanding their work, disseminate the inexhaustible, ceaseless, inconceivable, inestimable buddha dharma throughout the interior and exterior of the dharma realms.[28] The reason that, nevertheless, all these do not darken the perception of that person is that it is a direct verification, unconstructed in stillness.[29] If, as is thought by deluded people, practice and verification were located on two levels, each would perceive the other; but [for them] to be

---

26 **path of intimately providing mutual dark assistance** (*shitashiku ai myōshi suru michi* したしくあひ冥資するみち): I.e., the practice of unseen spiritual aid.

furthers the buddha work (*butsuji o jōhotsu shi* 佛事を助發し): I.e., "this person of seated meditation" contributes to the dissemination of the buddha dharma.

widely providing for listeners beyond the buddha (*hiroku butsu kōjō no ki ni kōburashimete* ひろく佛向上の機にかうぶらしめて): Taking *ki* 機 here as those being taught. Likely referring to audiences for whom the highest teaching — "the dharma beyond the buddha" (*butsu kōjō no hō* 佛向上の法) — is appropriate. See Supplementary Notes, s.v. "Beyond the buddha."

27 **benefits of wind and water** (*fū sui no riyaku* 風水の利益): I.e., the spiritual benefits of the preaching by "all the lands, grasses, and trees," etc. "Wind and water" (*fū sui* 風水) here, and "water and fire" (*sui ka* 水火) just below, likely represent synecdoches for the four elements (*shidai* 四大), of earth, water, fire, and wind, that make up the physical world of Buddhist cosmology. See Supplementary Notes, s.v. "Four elements and five aggregates."

28 **buddha conversion of original verification** (*honshō no bukke* 本證の佛化): Can be taken either as "the Buddha's teaching about original verification" or "the Buddha's teaching that is originally verified."

29 **The reason that, nevertheless, all these do not darken the perception of that person** (*shika aredomo, kono moromoro no tōnin no chikaku ni konzezarashimuru koto* しかあれども、このもろもろの當人の知覺に昏ぜざらしむること): Perhaps meaning something like, "the reason that all those involved in this dissemination of the buddha dharma nevertheless do not affect the mind of the person in the samādhi"; taking the antecedent of *moromoro* もろもろ ("all these") as the *mono* もの ("those who") of the previous sentence, and *tōnin* 當人 ("that person") as a reference to the *zazen nin* 坐禪人 ("person of seated meditation") in the opening sentence of this section.

it is a direct verification, unconstructed in stillness (*jōchū no muzōsa ni shite, jikishō naru* 靜中の無造作にして、直證なる): I.e., it is the immediate, unconstructed experience in their samādhi.

S1. Talk on Pursuing the Way *Bendōwa* 辨道話 15

mixed into [that] perception would not meet the standard of verification, for, in the standard of verification, deluded feelings do not extend to it.[30]

[S1:13] {2:464}

又、心・境ともに靜中の證入悟出あれども、自受用の境界なるをもて、一塵をうごかさず、一相をやぶらず、廣大の佛事、甚深微妙の佛化をなす。この化道のおよぶところの草木・土地、ともに大光明をはなち、深妙法をとくこと、きはまるときなし。草木・牆壁は、よく凡聖含靈のために宣揚し、凡聖含靈は、かつて草木・牆壁のために演暢す。自覺覺他の境界、もとより證相をそなへてかけたることなく、證則おこなはれておこたるときなからしむ。

Moreover, although, in the stillness, both mind and object enter verification and exit awakening, since it is the realm of self-enjoyment, without disturbing a single dust mote, without destroying a single aspect, one engages in the vast buddha work, the extremely profound and subtle buddha conversion.[31] All the grasses and trees and the lands reached by this guidance emit a great radiance, and their preaching of the profound, wondrous dharma is without end. The grasses and trees, fences and walls, proclaim it to commoners, sages, and all the animate; the commoners, sages, and all the animate in turn proclaim it to the grasses and trees, fences and walls.[32] The realm of self-awakening and awakening others is endowed from the start with the marks of verification, with nothing lacking, and carries out the standard of verification, leaving no time for negligence.

[S1:14]

ここをもて、わづかに一人一時の坐禪なりといへども、諸法とあひ冥し、諸時とまどかに通ずるがゆえに、無盡法界のなかに、去・來・現に、常恆の佛化道事をなすなり。彼彼ともに一等の同修なり、同證なり。ただ坐上の修のみにあらず、空をうちてひびきをなすこと、撞の前後に妙聲綿綿たるものなり。このきはのみにかぎらんや、百頭みな本面目に本修行をそなへて、はかりはかるべきにあらず。しるべし、たとひ十方無量恆河沙數の

---

30 **each would perceive the other** (*ono ono aikakuchi su beki nari* おのおのあひ覺知すべきなり): Presumably referring to those who are practicing and those who have verified, or, perhaps, those who are disseminating the buddha dharma and the person of zazen.

[for them] to be mixed into [that] perception (*kakuchi ni majiwaru wa* 覺知にまじはるは): Taking the unexpressed grammatical subject here to be "all these" (*ono ono* おのおの) and assuming that the perception in question belongs to "that person" (*tōnin* 當人).

31 **enter verification and exit awakening** (*shōnyū goshutsu* 證入悟出): An unusual expression, not encountered elsewhere; perhaps, meaning simply "verify and awaken."

32 **commoners, sages, and all the animate** (*bonshō ganrei* 凡聖含靈): A fixed expression for sentient beings, including ordinary humans and advanced Buddhist adepts; "the animate" renders *ganrei* 含靈, "those possessed of spirit."

16 DŌGEN'S *SHŌBŌGENZŌ* VOLUME VII

諸佛、ともにちからをはげまして、佛知慧をもて、一人坐禪の功德をはか
り、しりきはめんとすといふとも、あへてほとりをうることあらじ。

Accordingly, even if it is the seated meditation of merely one person
for one time, because it is imperceptibly one with the dharmas and perfectly penetrates the times, it carries out the constant work of the way
of buddha conversion within inexhaustible dharma realms in the past,
present, and future. For each and every one, it is equally the same practice, the same verification.[33] It is not just practice while seated: striking
the sky and making an echo has a wondrous sound that continues on and
on both before and after the strike.[34] How could it be limited just to this
time? The hundred heads, all endowed with the original practice by their
original faces, are not to be calculated or measured.[35] We should know
that, even if the buddhas of the ten directions, numerous as the incalculable sands of the Ganges, were to use their powers together, and by their
buddha wisdom, were to try to calculate and fully know the merit of the
seated meditation of a single person, they still would not be able to get
to the end of it.

* * * * *

[S1:15]
いま、この坐禪の功德、高大なることを、ききをはりぬ。

Now, we have heard how lofty and great are the merits of this seated
meditation.[36]

[S1:16]
おろかならん人、うたがふていはむ、佛法におほくの門あり、なにをもて
かひとへに坐禪をすすむるや。

Foolish people will doubt this, saying, "The buddha dharma has many
gates; why do you only recommend seated meditation?"[37]

---

33 **it is equally the same practice, the same verification** (*ittō no dōshu nari, dōshō
nari* 一等の同修なり、同證なり): A phrase that could also be read, "it is equally their
practice together, their verification together."

34 **striking the sky and making an echo** (*kū o uchite hibiki o nasu koto* 空をうちて
ひびきをなすこと): This phrase could also be read, "striking emptiness and making an
echo."

35 **The hundred heads** (*hyakutō* 百頭): Generally taken to mean "everyone."

36 **Now** (*ima* いま): A sentence presumably spoken by the fictive interlocutor in the
following question and answer portion of the text.

37 **Foolish people** (*oroka naran hito* おろかならん人): Question number 1.

S1. Talk on Pursuing the Way *Bendōwa* 辨道話

[S1:17] {2:465}

しめしていはく、これ佛法の正門なるをもてなり。

Answer: Because it is the main gate to the buddha dharma.

[S1:18]

とふていはく、なんぞひとり正門とする。しめしていはく、大師釋尊、まさしく得道の妙術を正傳し、又三世の如來、ともに坐禪より得道せり。このゆえに、正門なることをあひつたへたるなり。しかのみにあらず、西天東地の諸祖、みな坐禪より得道せるなり。ゆえに、いま正門を人天にしめす。

Question: Why do you take it alone as the main gate?[38]

Answer: Definitely, the Great Master, Śākya, the Honored One, directly transmitted this wondrous skill for gaining the way; also, the tathāgatas of the three times all gained the way by seated meditation. Therefore, they have handed down the fact that it is the main gate. Not only that, but the ancestors of Sindh in the West and the Land of the East all gained the way from seated meditation. Therefore, I now teach the main gate to humans and devas.

[S1:19]

とふていはく、あるいは如來の妙術を正傳し、または祖師のあとをたづぬるによらむ、まことに凡慮のおよぶにあらず。しかはあれども、讀經・念佛は、おのづからさとりの因縁となりぬべし。ただむなしく坐してなすところなからむ、なにによりてかさとりをうるたよりとならむ。

Question: Directly to transmit the wondrous technique of the tathāgatas, or to follow in the tracks of the ancestral masters, is certainly beyond the thought of the common person.[39] However, reading the sūtras or recollecting the buddhas can themselves be the causes of awakening. How can sitting idly without doing anything be the basis for attaining awakening?

[S1:20]

しめしていはく、なんぢいま、諸佛の三昧、無上の大法を、むなしく坐してなすところなし、とおもはむ、これを、大乘を謗ずる人、とす。まどひのいとふかき、大海のなかにいながら、水なし、といはむがごとし。すでにかたじけなく、諸佛自受用三昧に安坐せり。これ、廣大の功德をなすにあらずや。あはれむべし、まなこ、いまだひらけず、こころ、なほえひにあることを。

---

38 **Question: Why do you take it alone as the main gate?** (*tōte iwaku, nanzo hitori shōmon to suru* とうていはく、なんぞひとり正門とする): Question number 2.

39 **Question: Directly to transmit the wondrous technique of the tathāgatas** (*tōte iwaku, arui wa nyorai no myōjutsu o shōden shi* とうていはく、あるいは如來の妙術を正傳し): Question number 3.

18 DŌGEN'S *SHŌBŌGENZŌ* VOLUME VII

Answer: To think, as you do here, that the samādhi of the buddhas, their unsurpassed great dharma, is "sitting idly without doing anything" — this makes you a person who blasphemes the Great Vehicle. It is very deep delusion, like saying there is no water while being in a great ocean. Fortunately, the buddhas surely sat peacefully in the samādhi of self-enjoyment. Was this not creating vast merit? How pitiful you are, with your eyes still not open, and your mind still intoxicated.

[S1:21]

おほよそ諸佛の境界は、不可思議なり、心識のおよぶべきにあらず、いはむや不信劣智のしることをえむや。ただ正信の大機のみ、よくいることをうるなり。不信の人は、たとひをしふとも、うくべきことかたし。靈山に、なほ退亦佳矣のたぐひあり。おほよそ心に正信おこらば、修行し、參學すべし。しかあらずば、しばらくやむべし。むかしより法のうるほひなきことを、うらみよ。

In sum, the realm of the buddhas is inconceivable; it is beyond the reach of mind or consciousness, much less can it be known by those of no faith and deficient wisdom. Only one of great capacity for true faith can enter it; the person without faith cannot accept it even when taught about it. Even on Vulture Peak, there was the type [of which it was said,] "*it is just as well that they withdraw.*"[40] If true faith arises in the mind, we should practice and study; otherwise, we should stop for a while and regret the fact that we lack the moistening of the dharma from long ago.[41]

[S1:22]

又、讀經・念佛等のつとめにうるところの功德を、なんぢ、しるやいなや。ただ、したをうごかし、こえをあぐるを、佛事功德とおもへる、いとはかなし。佛法に擬するに、うたたとほく、いよいよはるかなり。又、經書をひらくことは、ほとけ、頓・漸修行の儀則ををしへおけるを、あきらめしり、教のごとく修行すれば、かならず證をとらしめむ、となり。いたづらに思量念度をつひやして、菩提をうる功德に擬せん、とにはあらぬなり。おろかに千萬誦の口業をしきりにして、佛道にいたらむとするは、なほこれ、ながえをきたにして、越にむかはむ、とおもはんがごとし。又、圓孔に方木をいれんとせん、とおなじ。文をみながら、修するみちにくらき、それ、醫方をみる人の、合藥をわすれん、なにの益かあらん。口聲をひまなくせる、春の田のかへるの、晝夜になくがごとし、つひに又、益な

---

40 **"it is just as well that they withdraw"** (*tai yaku kei i* 退亦佳矣): Words of Buddha Śākyamuni in the *Lotus Sūtra*, in reference to the five thousand members of his audience who withdrew upon hearing that he would preach a new doctrine of the one vehicle (*Miaofa lianhua jing* 妙法蓮華經, T.262.9:7a13):

舍利弗。如是增上慢人。退亦佳矣。

Śāriputra, arrogant ones like that, it is just as well that they withdraw.

41 **the moistening of the dharma from long ago** (*mukashi yori hō no uruoi* むかしより法のうるほひ): Presumably, the spiritual benefits of encounter with the buddha dharma in former lives.

S1. Talk on Pursuing the Way *Bendōwa* 辨道話

し。いはむやふかく名利にまどはさるるやから、これらのことをすてがた
し、それ利貪のこころ、はなはだふかきゆえに。むかしすでにありき、い
まのよになからむや、もともあはれむべし。

Furthermore, do you know the merit derived from the services of reading sūtras, recollecting the buddha, and the like? To think that merely
moving the tongue and raising the voice is the merit of the buddha work
is pure vanity. As an assessment of the buddha dharma, it is getting far
off, ever more distant. Again, opening the books of scripture is so that,
when we clarify the teachings left by the Buddha on the procedures of
the sudden and gradual practices, and we practice in accordance with
these teachings, we invariably gain verification of them; it is not so that,
wasting our thinking and calculating, we try in vain to assess their merit
for attaining bodhi. Trying to reach the way of the buddhas by foolishly
repeating the verbal acts of a thousand or ten thousand recitations is like
facing your cart thills north and thinking to head to Yue.[42] Again, it is
the same as trying to put a square peg in a round hole. Again, to read the
words while ignorant of how to practice them is like a person reading the
prescription who forgets to prepare the medicine: what benefit is there
in that? To vocalize ceaselessly is like the frog in the spring paddy fields
croaking day and night: again, in the end, there is no benefit. Not to
mention that it is hard to abandon these things for those who are deeply
deluded by fame and profit, for their greed is so deep.[43] They existed in
ancient times; how could they not exist today? How pitiful they are.

[S1:23]
ただまさにしるべし、七佛の妙法は、得道明心の宗匠に、契心證會の學人
あひしたがふて正傳すれば、的旨あらはれて稟持せらるるなり、文字習學
の法師の、しりおよぶべきにあらず。しかあればすなはち、この疑迷をや
めて、正師のをしへにより、坐禪辨道して諸佛自受用三昧を證得すべし。

We should know that the exact import of the wondrous dharma of the
seven buddhas appears and is instilled when students who have matched
their minds and verified their understanding follow and receive direct
transmission from lineage teachers who have gained the way and clar-

---

42 **like facing your cart thills north and thinking to head to Yue** (*nagae o kita
ni shite, Etsu ni mukawamu, to omowan ga gotoshi* ながえをきたにして、越にむか
はむ、とおもはんがごとし): I.e., to head in the opposite direction from your intended
destination ("Yue" 越 here referring to the territory south of China); a Japanese version
of the Chinese idiom *bei yuan shi yue* 北轅適楚. Dōgen uses the simile again in his
"Shōbōgenzō shōji" 正法眼藏生死.

43 **those who are deeply deluded by fame and profit** (*fukaku myōri ni madowasaruru
yakara* ふかく名利にまどはさるるやから): Perhaps a reference to those who gain a
reputation for piety through public recitation and/or to those who gain popularity by
preaching recitation as an alternative to ascetic and contemplative practices.

ified their minds.[44] This is not something that the dharma masters who study words and letters can know. Thus, putting an end to this doubt and delusion, and relying on the teachings of a true master, we should pursue the way in seated meditation and verify the samādhi of self-enjoyment of the buddhas.

[S1:24] {2:467}

とふていはく、いまわが朝につたはれるところの法華宗・華嚴教、ともに大乗の究竟なり。いはむや、眞言宗のごときは、毘盧遮那如來したしく金剛薩埵につたへて、師資みだりならず。その談ずるむね、即心是佛、是心作佛といふて、多劫の修行をふることなく、一座に五佛の正覺をとなふ、佛法の極妙といふべし。しかあるに、いまいふところの修行、なにのすぐれたることあれば、かれらをさしおきて、ひとへにこれをすすむるや。

Question: The Hokke school and Kegon teachings now transmitted to our kingdom are both the ultimate versions of the Great Vehicle.[45] Not to mention a school like Shingon, personally transmitted by Tathāgata Vairocana to Vajrasattva, with the line of masters and disciples undisrupted.[46] The gist of what they say is that "*this mind itself is the buddha*," "*this mind becomes the buddha*"; they proclaim that, without spending many kalpas of practice, one has the right awakening of the five buddhas in a single sitting.[47] This must be called the most wondrous expression of the buddha dharma. So, what is so superior in the practice you speak of here that you would set them aside and solely recommend it?

[S1:25]

しめしていはく、しるべし、佛家には、教の殊劣を對論することなく、法の淺深をえらばず、ただし修行の眞偽をしるべし。草華山水にひかれ

44　**students who have matched their minds and verified their understanding** (*kaishin shōe no gakunin* 契心證會の學人): I.e., students whose understanding accords with that of their master .

45　**Question: The Hokke school and Kegon teachings now transmitted to our kingdom** (*tōte iwaku, ima waga chō ni tsutawareru tokoro no Hokke shū Kegon kyō* とうていはく、いまわが朝につたはれるところの法華宗・華嚴教): Question number 4. Reference to the Tendai 天台 school, based on the *Lotus Sūtra*, and Kegon 華嚴 school, based on the *Avataṃsaka Sūtra*. In the hierarchy of Buddhist teachings widely accepted in Dōgen's Japan, these two represented the ultimate exoteric teachings (*kengyō* 顯教) of the Mahāyāna, "above" the more rudimentary teachings of the Hossō 法相 and Sanron 三論 schools, and "below" the esoteric teachings (*mikkyō* 密教) of the Shingon school 眞言宗.

46　**personally transmitted by Tathāgata Vairocana to Vajrasattva** (*Birushana nyorai shitashiku Kongōsatta ni tsutaete* 毘盧遮那如來したしく金剛薩埵につたへて): According to the tradition in Japanese Shingon that Buddha Mahāvairocana transmitted his teaching to Bodhisattva Vajrasattva (typically identified with Bodhisattva Samantabhadra).

47　**five buddhas** (*go butsu* 五佛): I.e., the buddhas of the four directions and the center of the *vajradhatu* (*kongō kai* 金剛界) maṇḍala.

S1. Talk on Pursuing the Way *Bendōwa* 辦道話

て、佛道に流入することありき、土石沙礫をにぎりて、佛印を禀持するこ
とあり。いはむや廣大の文字は、萬象にあまりて、なほゆたかなり、轉大
法輪、又一塵にをさまれり。しかあればすなはち、即心即佛のことば、な
ほこれ水中の月なり、即坐成佛のむね、さらに又、かがみのうちのかげな
り。ことばのたくみにかかはるべからず。いま直證菩提の修行をすすむる
に、佛祖單傳の妙道をしめして、眞實の道人とならしめん、となり。

Answer: We should know that, in the house of the buddhas, we do not
debate the superiority or inferiority of the teachings, nor distinguish the
dharmas as shallow or deep; we should just know whether the practice
is genuine or spurious. There have been cases of drifting onto the way
of the buddhas by being drawn to it by grass and flowers, mountains and
waters; there are cases of receiving the buddha seal by holding earth and
rocks, sand and pebbles.[48] Not to mention that the vast writings are even
more abundant than the myriad forms, and the turning of the great dharma wheel is contained within a single dust mote.[49] Thus, the words, "*this
mind itself is the buddha,*" are just the moon in the water; the message
of "*becoming a buddha in this very sitting*" is likewise the reflection in
the mirror. We should not have anything to do with clever talk. In rec-
ommending here the practice that directly verifies bodhi, I seek to make
you a true person of the way by teaching you the wondrous way uniquely
transmitted by the buddhas and ancestors.

---

48 **drawn to it by grass and flowers, mountains and waters** (*sōka sansui ni hikarete* 草
華山水にひかれて): Perhaps recalling famous Chan stories of those who were awakened
by the experience of nature; e.g., Lingyun Zhiqin 靈雲志勤 (dates unknown), whose insight upon seeing peach blossoms is recorded in Dōgen's *shinji Shōbōgenzō* 眞字正法
眼藏 (DZZ.5:206, case 155); or Xiangyan Zhixian 香嚴智閑 (d. 898), who famously
gained an understanding upon hearing a bit of debris strike a bamboo (*shinji Shōbōgenzō*
眞字正法眼藏, DZZ.5:134, case 17); or the poet Su Dongpo 蘇東坡, whose awakening
upon hearing the sound of a mountain stream Dōgen discusses in the "Shōbōgenzō keisei
sanshoku" 正法眼藏溪聲山色.

holding earth and rocks, sand and pebbles (*doseki sharyaku o nigirite* 土石沙礫をに
ぎりて): Perhaps recalling Śākyamuni's promise in the *Lotus Sūtra* (*Miaofa lianhua jing*
妙法蓮華經, T.262.9:8c23-25) that all who pile up earth to make stūpas, even children
who make stūpas while playing with sand, will have attained the way of the buddhas; or
the story of a prior life of King Aśoka, when, as a boy, he offered sand to the Buddha's
begging bowl and received the prediction that he would become a *cakravartin* (see, e.g.,
Ayu wang jing 阿育王經, T.2043.50:131c9-132b2).

49 **Not to mention that the vast writings are even more abundant than the myriad
forms** (*iwamuya kōdai no monji wa, manzō ni amarite, nao yutaka nari* いはむや廣大の
文字は、萬象にあまりて、なほゆたかなり): Presumably, meaning that the Buddhist
scriptures are more extensive than all the objects in the world (and yet, in the following clause, are all contained in even the tiniest object). See Supplementary Notes, s.v.
"Myriad forms."

[S1:26]

又、佛法を傳授することは、かならず證契の人を、その宗師とすべし。文字をかぞふる學者をもて、その導師とするにたらず、一盲の、衆盲をひかんがごとし。いまこの佛祖正傳の門下には、みな得道證契の哲匠をうやまひて、佛法を住持せしむ。かるがゆえに、冥陽の神道もきたり歸依し、證果の羅漢もきたり問法するに、おのおの心地を開明する手をさづけずといふことなし、餘門にいまだきかざるところなり、ただ、佛弟子は、佛法をならふべし。

Furthermore, in the transmitting of the buddha dharma, we should always take as our teacher a person who has verified and accorded [with the dharma]. It is not enough to take as one's guiding master a scholar who counts words and letters; this would be like the blind leading the blind. In this present tradition directly transmitted by the buddhas and ancestors, all venerate the wise instructors who have gained the way and verified and accorded [with the dharma] and have them maintain the buddha dharma. For this reason, when the deities of the dark and bright come to take refuge, and the arhats, who have verified the fruit, come to inquire about the dharma, [the masters] never fail to extend a hand that reveals the mind ground of each.[50] This is something never heard of in other traditions. Disciples of the Buddha should just study the buddha dharma.[51]

[S1:27] {2:468}

又しるべし、われらは、もとより無上菩提かけたるにあらず、とこしなへに受用すといへども、承當することをえざるゆえに、みだりに知見をおこすことをならひとして、これを物とおふによりて、大道いたづらに蹉過す。この知見によりて、空華まちまちなり。あるいは十二輪轉・二十五有の境界とおもひ、三乘・五乘、有佛・無佛の見、つくることなし。この知見をならうて、佛法修行の正道とおもふべからず。しかあるを、いまはまさしく佛印によりて萬事を放下し、一向に坐禪するとき、迷・悟情量のほとりをこえて、凡・聖のみちにかかはらず、すみやかに格外に逍遙し、大菩提を受用するなり。かの文字の筌罤にかかはるものの、かたをならぶるにおよばむや。

We should also know that, although from the beginning we have never lacked unsurpassed bodhi and have always been enjoying it, because we are unable to accede to it, we form the habit of mindlessly producing views and chasing after them as things, thereby pointlessly missing the great way. Based on these views, the sky flowers are varied: we may

---

50 **deities of the dark and bright** (*meiyō no shindō* 冥陽の神道): I.e., deities of realms invisible and visible to humans.

51 **Disciples of the Buddha should just study the buddha dharma** (*tada, butsu deshi wa, buppō o narau beshi* ただ、佛弟子は、佛法をならふべし): The implication would seem to be that Buddhist schools outside "this tradition directly transmitted by the buddhas and ancestors" are not the buddha dharma.

S1. Talk on Pursuing the Way *Bendōwa* 辨道話

think of the turning of the wheel of the twelve or the realms of the twenty-five forms of existence, or views of the three vehicles or five vehicles, of the existence of buddhas or the nonexistence of buddhas — there is no end to them.[52] Accustomed as we are to these views, we should not think them the correct path of the practice of the buddha dharma.

Now, however, when, based on the buddha seal, we truly cast aside the myriad affairs and single-mindedly sit in meditation, transcending the bounds of the feelings of delusion and awakening, without regard for the paths of the commoner and sage, we quickly wander beyond the norm and enjoy the great bodhi. How could those caught up in the traps and snares of words and letters stand shoulder to shoulder with us?

[S1:28]

とふていはく、三學のなかに定學あり、六度のなかに禪度あり。ともにこれ一切の菩薩の、初心よりまなぶところ、利・鈍をわかず修行す。いまの坐禪も、そのひとつなるべし。なにによりてか、このなかに、如來の正法あつめたりといふや。

Question: Among the three disciplines is the discipline of concentration; within the six perfections is the perfection of meditation.[53] These are both studied by all bodhisattvas from their first thought [of awakening] and practiced without distinction of sharp or dull [faculties]. The seated meditation here must be one of these. Why do you say that the true dharma of the tathāgatas is consolidated within it?

[S1:29] {2:469}

しめしていはく、いまこの如來一大事の正法眼藏無上の大法を、禪宗となづくるゆえに、この間、きたれり。しるべし、この禪宗の號は、神丹以東におこれり、竺乾にはきかず。

---

52 **sky flowers** (*kūge* 空華): S. *khapuṣpa*; spots appearing to the diseased eye; a standard metaphor in Buddhist texts for what is mere appearance without objective reality; see Supplementary Notes, s.v. "Clouded eyes and sky flowers."

wheel of the twelve (*jūni rin* 十二輪): I.e., the twelvefold chain of dependent origination (*jūni innen* 十二因緣).

twenty-five forms of existence (*nijūgo u* 二十五有): Divisions of the three realms (*sangai* 三界) of saṃsāra; see Supplementary Notes, s.v. "Three realms."

three vehicles or five vehicles (*sanjō gojō* 三乘・五乘): I.e., the vehicles of the śrāvaka, *pratyeka-buddha*, and bodhisattva; the "five vehicles" adds to the three vehicles the vehicles of humans and devas.

53 **Question: Among the three disciplines is the discipline of concentration; within the six perfections is the perfection of meditation** (*tōte iwaku, sangaku no naka ni jōgaku ari, rokudo no naka ni zendo ari* とうていはく、三學のなかに定學あり、六度のなかに禪度あり): Question number 5. The interlocutor assumes that Dōgen's seated meditation (*zazen* 坐禪) is merely the samādhi or dhyāna in these standard lists of Buddhist practices. The term *zen* 禪, of course, is a transliteration of the Sanskrit *dhyāna*.

24 DŌGEN'S *SHŌBŌGENZŌ* VOLUME VII

Answer: This question arises because this unsurpassed great dharma, the treasury of the true dharma eye that is "the one great matter" of the tathāgatas, has been called the "Zen school."[54] We should realize that this name, "Zen school," occurred in Cīnasthāna to the east and was never heard of in Sindhu.[55]

[S1:30]
はじめ達磨大師、嵩山の少林寺にして九年面壁のあひだ、道俗、いまだ佛正法をしらず、坐禪を宗とする婆羅門となづけき。のち代代の諸祖、みなつねに坐禪をもはらす。これをみるおろかなる俗家は、實をしらず、ひたたけて坐禪宗といひき。いまのよには、坐のことばを簡して、ただ禪宗といふなり。そのこころ、諸祖の廣語にあきらかなり。六度および三學の禪定にならつていふべきにあらず。

In the beginning, while Great Master Dharma spent nine years facing a wall at the Shaolin Monastery on Mount Song, the clerics and lay people, not yet knowing the true dharma of the buddhas, called him the "brahman who takes seated meditation as the essential point."[56] Thereafter, the ancestors of generation after generation took seated meditation as their main focus. Seeing this, foolish lay people, not knowing the reality of the matter, casually called them the "seated meditation school." Nowadays, the word "seated" has been dropped, and they just say, "the meditation [or *zen*] school." Its meaning is clear in the extensive records of the ancestors.[57] It is not to be equated with the meditations of the six perfections or three disciplines.

---

54 **"the one great matter"** (*ichidaiji* 一大事): A fixed idiom for the work of leading beings to supreme bodhi; best known from the famous passage in the *Lotus Sūtra*, in which Buddha Śākyamuni reveals that the buddhas come into this world only to lead beings to buddhahood. See Supplementary Notes, s.v. "Buddhas, the world-honored ones, appear in the world for the reason of one great matter alone."

55 **this name, "Zen school," occurred in Cīnasthāna to the east and was never heard of in Sindhu** (*kono zenshū no gō wa, Shintan itō ni okoreri, Chikuken ni wa kikazu* この禪宗の號は、神丹以東におこれり、竺乾にはきかず): The use of the term *Chanzong* 禪宗 (J. *Zenshū*; "Zen school," or "Zen lineage") in reference to the tradition of Bodhidharma seems to have begun in China in the ninth century.

56 **"brahman who takes seated meditation as the essential point"** (*zazen o shū to suru baramon to nazukeki* 坐禪を宗とする婆羅門となづけき): Or, depending on how one interprets the term *shū* 宗 here, "the brahman who makes a school of seated meditation." Dōgen likely has in mind here a passage in the *Linjian lu* 林間錄, by Juefan Huihong 覺範慧洪 (1071-1128), that he quotes in the "Shōbōgenzō gyōji" 正法眼藏行持 and "Shōbōgenzō butsudō" 正法眼藏佛道. See Supplementary Notes, s.v. "Practitioner of dhyāna."

57 **Its meaning is clear in the extensive records of the ancestors** (*sono kokoro, shoso no kōgo ni akiraka nari* そのこころ、諸祖の廣語にあきらかなり): I.e., the meaning of "seated meditation" is obvious in the sayings of the Chan masters.

S1. Talk on Pursuing the Way *Bendōwa* 辨道話 25

[S1:31]

この佛法の相傳の嫡意なること、一代にかくれなし。如來、むかし靈山會上にして、正法眼藏涅槃妙心無上の大法をもて、ひとり迦葉尊者にのみ付法せし儀式は、現在して上界にある天衆、まのあたりにみしもの存せり、うたがふべきにたらず。おほよそ佛法は、かの天衆、とこしなへに護持するものなり、その功、いまだふりず。まさにしるべし、これは佛法の全道なり、ならべていふべきものなし。

The fact that this buddha dharma is the legitimately inherited intent of the transmission has never been hidden for a single generation.[58] There are those at present among the host of devas in the higher realms who personally witnessed the ceremony long ago at the assembly on Vulture Peak in which the Tathāgata bequeathed the unsurpassed great dharma of the treasury of the true dharma eye, the wondrous mind of nirvāṇa, to Venerable Kāśyapa. It is not to be doubted. Those deva hosts forever protect the buddha dharma, and their efforts never flag. We should know that this is the entire way of the buddha dharma; nothing else can compare with it.

[S1:32]

とふていはく、佛家、なにによりてか、四儀のなかに、ただし坐にのみおほせて禪定をすすめて證入をいふや。

Question: In saying that it recommends meditation for entering verification, among the four deportments, on what basis does the house of the buddhas solely pursue sitting?[59]

[S1:33]

しめしていはく、むかしよりの諸佛、あひつぎて修行し證入せるみち、きはめしりがたし。ゆえをたづねば、ただ佛家のもちいるところをゆえとしるべし、このほかにたづぬべからず。ただし、祖師ほめていはく、坐禪はすなはち安樂の法門なり。はかりしりぬ、四儀のなかに安樂なるゆえか。いはむや、一佛・二佛の修行のみちにあらず、諸佛諸祖にみなこのみちあり。

Answer: It is impossible to know fully the ways by which the buddhas one after another from ancient times practiced and entered verification. If we ask for the reason, we should know that the reason is just that it is what is used by the house of the buddhas; we should not ask anything

---

58 **the legitimately inherited intent of the transmission** (*sōden no tekii* 相傳の嫡意): Taking the unusual term *tekii* 嫡意 to mean something like "the intent (or meaning) handed down in legitimate succession."

59 **among the four deportments, on what basis does the house of the buddhas solely pursue sitting?** (*bukke, nani ni yorite ka, shigi no naka ni, tadashi za ni nomi oosete* 佛家、なにによりてか、四儀のなかに、ただし坐にのみおほせて): Question number 6. The four deportments (*shigi* 四儀) are walking, standing, sitting, and reclining (*gyōjūza-ga* 行住坐臥).

other than this.[60] Still, the ancestral masters praise it, saying, "seated meditation is the dharma gate of ease and joy."[61] We can assume that the reason may be that, among the four deportments, it is the one of "ease and joy." Not to mention that it is the way of practice of not just one or two buddhas; all the buddhas and ancestors have this way.

[S1:34] {2:470}

とふていはく、この坐禪の行は、いまだ佛法を證會せざらんものは、坐禪辦道してその證をとるべし。すでに佛正法をあきらめえん人は、坐禪なにのまつところかあらむ。

Question: Regarding this practice of seated meditation, someone who has yet to verify an understanding of the buddha dharma should get that verification by pursuing the way in seated meditation; but what can someone who has already been able to clarify the true dharma of the Buddha expect from seated meditation?[62]

[S1:35]

しめしていはく、癡人のまへにゆめをとかず、山子の手には舟棹をあたへがたしといへども、さらに訓をたるべし。

Answer: "One does not tell dreams in front of a fool"; "one cannot put an oar in the hands of a woodsman."[63] Nevertheless, I shall give you some instruction.

[S1:36]

それ、修・證はひとつにあらずとおもへる、すなはち外道の見なり。佛法には、修證これ一等なり。いまも證上の修なるゆえに、初心の辦道すなはち本證の全體なり。かるがゆえに、修行の用心をさづくるにも、修のほかに證をまつおもひなかれ、とをしふ、直指の本證なるがゆえなるべし。

---

60 **If we ask for the reason** (*yue o tazuneba* ゆえをたづねば): I.e., the reason why sitting is emphasized.

61 **the ancestral masters praise it** (*soshi homete* 祖師ほめて): Or, perhaps, "an ancestral master has praised it." Likely recalling a line in the *Zuochan yi* 坐禪儀, by Changlu Zongze 長蘆宗賾 (dates unknown) (*Chixiu Baizhang qinggui* 勅修百丈清規, T.2025.48:1143a14-15) that Dōgen quotes in his *Fukan zazen gi* 普勸坐禪儀:

坐禪乃安樂法門。

Seated meditation is the dharma gate of ease and joy.

62 **Question** (*tōte iwaku* とうていはく): Question number 7.

63 **"One does not tell dreams in front of a fool"** (*chinin no mae ni yume o tokazu* 癡人のまへにゆめをとかず); **"one cannot put an oar in the hands of a woodsman"** (*sansu no te ni wa shūtō o ataegatashi* 山子の手には舟棹をあたへがたし): Japanese versions of two Chinese proverbs said to originate with the Jin-dynasty poet Tao Yuanming 陶淵明 (365-427): *chiren mianqian bude shuo meng* 癡人面前不可説夢; *shanzi shou buke yu zhouzhao* 山子手不可與舟棹.

S1. Talk on Pursuing the Way *Bendōwa* 辨道話

Now, to think that practice and verification are not one is a view of other paths. In the buddha dharma, practice and verification are identical. Even now, because it is practice based on verification, the pursuit of the way by the beginner is the complete embodiment of original verification.[64] For this reason, in giving cautionary advice on practice as well, it is taught not to expect verification outside of practice, which must be because it is the original verification directly pointed at.[65]

[S1:37]

すでに修の證なれば、證にきはなく、證の修なれば、修にはじめなし。こ
こをもて、釋迦如來・迦葉尊者、ともに證上の修に受用せられ、達磨大
師・大鑑高祖、おなじく證上の修に引轉せらる。佛法住持のあと、みなか
くのごとし。すでに證をはなれぬ修あり、われらさいはひに一分の妙修を
單傳せる、初心の辨道すなはち一分の本證を無爲の地にうるなり。

Since it is the verification of practice, verification has no limit; since it is the practice of verification, practice has no beginning. Hence, Tathāgata Śākya and Venerable Kāśyapa both enjoyed practice based on verification; Great Master Dharma and the Eminent Ancestor Dajian were similarly pulled along by practice based on verification.[66] The traces of those who have maintained the buddha dharma are all like this. There being a practice already inseparable from verification, and we fortunately having been uniquely transmitted one share of wondrous practice, our beginner's pursuit of the way attains one share of original verification at the ground of the unconditioned.[67]

[S1:38] {2:471}

しるべし、修をはなれぬ證を染汚せざらしめんがために、佛祖、しきりに
修行のゆるくすべからざるとをしふ。妙修を放下すれば、本證、手の中に
みてり、本證を出身すれば、妙修、通身におこなはる。

We should know that, in order to avoid defiling the verification inseparable from practice, the buddhas and ancestors repeatedly teach us not

---

64 **the beginner** (*shoshin* 初心): More technically, "one who has brought forth the initial thought [of bodhi at the beginning of the bodhisattva path]." See Supplementary Notes, s.v. "Beginner's mind."

65 **it is the original verification directly pointed at** (*jikishi no honshō naru* 直指の本證なる): I.e., practice is itself the inherent realization directly indicated by Zen teachers.

66 **the Eminent Ancestor Dajian** (*Daikan kōso* 大鑑高祖): I.e., the Sixth Ancestor, Huineng 慧能.

67 **one share of wondrous practice** (*ichibun no myōshu* 一分の妙修); **one share of original verification** (*ichibun no honshō* 一分の本證): A tentative translation. It might be better to take *ichibun* 一分 here in the sense "our own full measure."

the ground of the unconditioned (*mui no chi* 無爲の地): In a soteriological sense, the stage of nirvāṇa, the final station on the bodhisattva's path; in a metaphysical sense, the absolute ground "beneath" conditioned existence.

28 DŌGEN'S *SHŌBŌGENZŌ* VOLUME VII

to relax our practice. When we cast aside wondrous practice, original verification fills our hands; when the body escapes from original verification, wondrous practice occurs in the body throughout.

[S1:39]

又、まのあたり大宋國にしてみしかば、諸方の禪院みな坐禪堂をかまへて、五百六百、および一二千僧を安じて、日夜に坐禪をすすめき。その席主とせる傳佛心印の宗師に、佛法の大意をとぶらひしかば、修證の、兩段にあらぬむねを、きこえき。

Moreover, as I personally saw in the Land of the Great Song, the Chan cloisters of all quarters had all built halls for seated meditation, occupied by five or six hundred, up to one or two thousand, monks, engaged in seated meditation day and night. When I asked the teachers who transmit the buddha mind seal who were regarded as seat holders there about the great meaning of the buddha dharma, they taught me the message that practice and verification are not on two different levels.[68]

S1:

このゆえに、門下の參學のみにあらず、求法の高流、佛法のなかに眞實をねがはむ人、初心・後心をえらばず、凡人・聖人を論ぜず、佛祖のをしへにより、宗匠の道をおふて、坐禪辨道すべし、とすすむ。

Therefore, we recommend that, not only students in our tradition, but eminent persons, persons seeking the truth within the buddha dharma, should pursue the way in seated meditation, following the path of a teacher according to the teachings of the buddhas and ancestors, without discriminating between beginner or advanced, without considerations of common person or sage.

[S1:41]

きかずや、祖師のいはく、修證はすなはちなきにあらず、染汚することはえじ。又いはく、道をみるもの、道を修す、と。しるべし、得道のなかに修行すべしといふことを。

Have you not heard that the ancestral masters have said, "It's not that it lacks practice and verification, but it can't be defiled by them."[69] And

---

68 **the teachers who transmit the buddha mind seal who were regarded as seat holders there** (*sono sekishu to seru den busshin'in no shūshi* 其の席主とせる傳佛心印の宗師): I.e., those teachers, authentic inheritors of the lineage, who were regarded as the leaders at these Chan monasteries.

69 **"It's not that it lacks practice and verification, but it can't be defiled by them"** (*shushō wa sunawachi naki ni arazu, zenna suru koto wa eji* 修證はすなはちなきにあらず、染汚することはえじ): Japanese rendering of words, much loved by Dōgen, attributed to Nanyue Huairang 南嶽懷讓, in the famous dialogue with his teacher, the Sixth Ancestor, Huineng 慧能 (see, e.g., *shinji Shōbōgenzō* 眞字正法眼藏, DZZ.5:178, case 101). Upon receiving Nanyue, the Ancestor asked, "What thing is it that comes

S1. Talk on Pursuing the Way *Bendōwa* 辨道話

they have said, "One who sees the way practices the way."[70] We should know that this means we should practice within gaining the way.

[S1:42]

とふていはく、わが朝の先代に、教をひろめし諸師、ともにこれ入唐傳法せしとき、なんぞこのむねをさしおきて、ただ教をのみつたへし。

Question: Why is it that all the masters who spread the teachings in our kingdom in former ages, when they entered the Tang and transmitted the dharma, set aside this message and only transmitted the teachings?[71]

[S1:43]

しめしていはく、むかしの人師、この法をつたへざりしことは、時節のいまだいたらざりしゆえなり。

Answer: The fact that the teachers of humans in the past did not transmit this dharma is because the occasion had not yet arrived.[72]

[S1:44]

とふていはく、かの上代の師、この法を會得せりや。

Question: Did those masters of antiquity understand this dharma?[73]

---

like this?" Nanyue replied, "To say it's like any thing wouldn't hit it." The Ancestor continued,

> 還假修證否。師曰、修證即不無、染汚即不得。
>
> "Then does it depend on practice and verification?"
>
> The Master [Nanyue] said, "It's not that it lacks practice and verification, but it can't be defiled by them."

For the full dialogue, see Supplementary Notes, s.v. "What thing is it that comes like this?"

70 **"One who sees the way practices the way"** (*dō o miru mono, dō o shusu* 道をみるもの、道を修す): Japanese version of the first lines of a verse by Sikong Benjing 司空本淨 (667-761) (*Jingde chuandeng lu* 景德傳燈錄, T.2076.51:243a23-24) that actually raises a question about the need for practice:

> 見道方修道、不見復何修。道性如虚空、虚空何所修。
>
> One who sees the way practices the way;
> But, for one who doesn't see it, what's the practice?
> The nature of the way is like empty space;
> What's there to practice in empty space?

71 **Question** (*tōte iwaku* とうていはく): Question number 8.

72 **Answer** (*shimeshite iwaku* しめしていはく): C.f. the answer given in section 35 of the sixty-chapter *Shōbōgenzō* text:

> 示曰、昔の人師、此の法を傳へざりし事、昔の人に問ふべし。我は今の人なり。
>
> Answer: Why the teachers of humans in the past did not transmit this dharma, you should ask the people of the past. I am a person of the present.

73 **Question** (*tōte iwaku* とうていはく): Question number 9.

30 DŌGEN'S *SHŌBŌGENZŌ* VOLUME VII

[S1:45] {2:472}
しめしていはく、會せば通じてむ。

Answer: If they had understood it, they would have communicated it.

[S1:46]
とふていはく、あるがいはく、生死をなげくことなかれ、生死を出離する
に、いとすみやかなるみちあり、いはゆる、心性の常住なることわりをし
るなり、そのむねたらく、この身體は、すでに生あればかならず滅にうつ
されゆくことありとも、この心性は、あへて滅する事なし、よく、生滅に
うつされぬ心性わが身にあることをしりぬれば、これを本來の性とするが
ゆえに、身はこれかりのすがたなり、死此生彼さだまりなし、心はこれ常
住なり、去・來・現在かはるべからず、かくのごとくしるを、生死をはな
れたりとはいふなり、このむねをしるものは、從來の生死ながくたえて、
この身、をはるとき、性海にいる、性海に朝宗するとき、諸佛如來のごと
く、妙德、まさにそなはる、いまはたとひしるといへども、前世の安業に
なされたる身體なるがゆえに、諸聖とひとしからず、いまだこのむねをし
らざるものは、ひさしく生死にめぐるべし、しかあればすなはち、ただい
そぎて心性の常住なるむねを了知すべし、いたづらに閑坐して一生をすぐ
さん、なにのまつところかあらむ。かくのごとくいふむね、これはまこと
に諸佛諸祖の道にかなへりや、いかむ。

Question: Some say,[74]

Do not lament birth and death. There is a very quick path to escape
from birth and death: it is to know the principle that the nature of the
mind is permanent. The point is that, while this body, having been
born, inevitably moves on to extinction, the nature of the mind is never
extinguished. When we have understood that the nature of the mind
that does not move from birth to extinction is within us, insofar as
we take it as our original nature, our body is a temporary form, dying here, born there, indefinitely; our mind is permanent, unchanging
across past, present, and future.[75] To understand in this way is said to
have escaped from birth and death. For those who know this doctrine,
the birth and death up till now cease forever, and, when this body ends,
they enter the ocean of the nature. When they flow into the ocean of the
nature, they are endowed with wondrous virtues, like those of the buddhas, the tathāgatas; for now, though they know [the doctrine], since
their bodies are made from the deluded karma of former lives, they are

---

74 **Question: Some say** (*tōte iwaku, aru ga iwaku* とうていはく、あるがいはく):
Question number 10. It may well be that only the first two sentences of the following
description are intended as a quotation of what "some say," while the remainder, beginning with "the basic doctrine is that" (*sono mune taraku* そのむねたらく) represents the
interlocutor's explanation.

75 **dying here, born there** (*shi shi shō hi* 死此生彼): A fixed expression for the process
of death in one life and rebirth in another.

S1. Talk on Pursuing the Way *Bendōwa* 辨道話

not equivalent to the sages.[76] Those who do not know this doctrine will long revolve in birth and death. Thus, we should just quickly recognize the doctrine that the nature of the mind is permanent. What can one expect from spending one's life idly sitting in vain?

What about such a doctrine? Does it truly conform to the way of the buddhas and ancestors?

[S1:47]

しめしていはく、いまいふところの見、またく佛法にあらず、先尼外道が見なり。いはく、かの外道の見は、わが身、うちにひとつの靈知あり、かの知、すなはち縁にあふところに、よく好惡をわきまへ、是非をわきまふ、痛痒をしり、苦樂をしる、みなかの靈知のちからなり、しかあるに、かの靈性は、この身の滅するとき、もぬけてかしこにむまるるゆえに、ここに滅すとみゆれども、かしこの生あれば、ながく滅せずして常住なり、といふなり。かの外道が見、かくのごとし。

Answer: The view you describe here is definitely not the buddha dharma; it is the view of the other path of Śreṇika.[77] The view of that other path holds that, within our body, there is a numinous awareness, and that, upon encountering objects, this awareness distinguishes likes and dislikes, distinguishes right and wrong, feels pains and itches, feels suffering and joy — all these due to the powers of that numinous awareness. Yet, when this body perishes, that numinous awareness withdraws and is born elsewhere; hence, though it appears to perish here, since it is born elsewhere, it is forever unchanging and permanent. Such is the view of that other path.

[S1:48] {2:473}

しかあるを、この見をならふて佛法とせむ、瓦礫をにぎつて金寶とおもはんよりもなほおろかなり、癡迷のはづべき、たとふるにものなし。大唐國の慧忠國師、ふかくいましめたり。いま心常相滅の邪見を計して、諸佛の妙法にひとしめ、生死の本因をおこして、生死をはなれたりとおもはん、おろかなるにあらずや、もともあはれむべし。ただこれ、外道の邪見なりとしれ、みみにふるべからず。ことやむことをえず、いまなほあはれみを

---

76 **ocean of the nature** (*shōkai* 性海): I.e., the buddha nature (*busshō* 佛性) or dharma nature (*hosshō* 法性) likened to an ocean; a common term in East Asian Buddhist texts, perhaps especially associated with the Huayan literature, for the ultimate realm of suchness.

they are not equivalent to the sages (*shoshō to hitoshikarazu* 諸聖とひとしからず): I.e., they do not yet have the wondrous virtues of the advanced Buddhist adept.

77 **other path of Śreṇika** (*Senni gedō* 先尼外道): "Other path" here renders *gedō* 外道 (S. *tīrthika*), used in reference to non-Buddhist religions — especially, as in this case, Hinduism; "Śreṇika" represents a reconstruction of the Chinese *Xianni* 先尼, the name of a brahman appearing in the *Nirvāṇa Sūtra* (*Da banniepan jing* 大般涅槃經, T.374.12:594a14-596b10), who argues for a self that transmigrates from body to body. Dōgen refers to this view in several texts of the *Shōbōgenzō*.

たれて、なんぢが邪見をすくはば、しるべし、佛法には、もとより身心一
如にして、性相不二なりと談ずる、西天東地おなじくしれるところ、あへ
てたがふべからず。いはむや、常住を談ずる門には、萬法みな常住なり、
身と心とをわくことなし、寂滅を談ずる門には、諸法みな寂滅なり、性と
相とをわくことなし。しかあるを、なんぞ身滅心常といはむ、正理にそむ
かざらむや。しかのみならず、生死はすなはち涅槃なり、と覺了すべし、
いまだ生死のほかに涅槃を談ずることなし。いはむや、心は身をはなれて
常住なりと領解するをもて、生死をはなれたる佛智に妄計すといふとも、
この領解・智覺の心は、すなはちなほ生滅して、またく常住ならず、こ
れ、はかなきにあらずや。

Still, to study this view and take it as the buddha dharma is more foolish than grasping tiles and pebbles and thinking them to be gold and
jewels.[78] There is nothing to compare with such shameful delusion. The
National Teacher Huizhong of the Land of the Great Tang has strictly
warned against it.[79] Is it not foolish to treat the false view here that *the
mind is permanent while its attributes cease* as equivalent to the wondrous dharma of the buddhas, and to think that one is free from birth and
death even while creating the fundamental cause of birth and death? This
is most pathetic. We should just recognize this as the false view of other
paths and not give ear to it.

Yet the matter cannot be helped: if I am still to show you pity here
and save you from your false view, you should know that, in the buddha
dharma, from the start, we talk of body and mind as one and nature and
attribute as not two. This is something known in Sindh in the West and
the Land of the East alike, without any deviation. Moreover, in teachings
that talk of permanence, the myriad dharmas are all permanent, without
distinction between body and mind; and in teachings that talk of quiescence, the dharmas are all quiescent, without distinction between nature
and mark. Despite this, how can we say that the body perishes but the
mind is constant? Does this not go against reason? Not only that, but
we should realize that birth and death are themselves nirvāṇa; we never
speak of nirvāṇa apart from birth and death. Not to mention that, even
if, understanding that the mind is free from the body and is permanent,
one mistakes that for the buddha wisdom, free from birth and death, the
mind that has this understanding and awareness would itself still arise
and cease and in no sense be permanent. Is this not ludicrous?

---

78 **gold and jewels** (*kinpō* 金寶): Or, perhaps, "golden treasures."

79 **The National Teacher Huizhong** (*Echū kokushi* 慧忠國師): I.e., Nanyang Huizhong
南陽慧忠 (d. 775), disciple of the Sixth Ancestor. His warning against mistaking Śreṇika's
view as Buddhist can be found at *Jingde chuandeng lu* 景德傳燈錄, T.2076.51:437c17-
438a6; Dōgen quotes the passage in his "Shōbōgenzō soku shin ze butsu" 正法眼藏即
心是佛.

S1. Talk on Pursuing the Way *Bendōwa* 辨道話

[S1:49] {2:474}

嘗觀すべし、身心一如のむねは、佛法のつねの談ずるところなり。しかあるに、なんぞこの身の生滅せんとき、心ひとり身をはなれて、生滅せざらむ。もし、一如なるときあり、一如ならぬときあらば、佛説おのづから虚妄になりぬべし。又、生死はのぞくべき法ぞとおもへるは、佛法をいとふつみとなる。つつしまざらむや。

We should try to see that the teaching of the unity of body and mind is something always talked about in the buddha dharma. How, then, when the body arises and ceases, could the mind alone separate from the body and not arise or cease? If there are times when they are one and times when they are not one, the Buddha's preaching would become false. Moreover, to think that birth and death are dharmas to be eliminated amounts to the offense of despising the buddha dharma. Shouldn't we be more prudent?

[50]

しるべし、佛法に心性大總相の法門といふは、一大法界をこめて、性相をわかず、生滅をいふことなし。菩提・涅槃におよぶまで、心性にあらざるなし。一切諸法・萬象森羅、ともにただこれ一心にして、こめずかねざることなし。このもろもろの法門、みな平等一心なり。あへて異違なしと談ずる、これすなはち佛家の心性をしれる様子なり。しかあるを、この一法に身と心とを分別し、生死と涅槃とをわくことあらむや。すでに佛子なり、外道の見をかたる狂人のしたのひびきを、みみにふるることなかれ。

We should know that, in the buddha dharma, what is called the dharma gate of the great universal attribute of the nature of the mind collects the entire great dharma realm, without distinguishing nature and attribute, and does not speak of arising and ceasing.[80] There is nothing, even up to bodhi and nirvāṇa, that is not the nature of the mind. All the dharmas, the thicket of myriad forms, are all just this one mind, with nothing not included and unified.[81] The various dharma gates are all equally the one

---

80 **the dharma gate of the great universal attribute of the nature of the mind** (*shinshō daisōsō no hōmon* 心性大總相の法門): I.e., a teaching that treats the ultimate nature of the dharma realm as a whole. Perhaps, a reference to a doctrine of the *Dasheng qixin lun* 大乘起信論, which distinguishes two approaches to the mind: the gate of the true suchness of the mind (*xin zhenru men*; J. *shin shinnyo mon* 心眞如門), and the gate of the arising and ceasing of the mind (*xin shengmie men*; J. *shin shōmetsu mon* 心生滅門). Of the former, it is said (T.1666.32:576a8-9):

心眞如者、即是一法界大總相法門體。

The suchness of the mind is the substance of the dharma gate of the great universal attribute of the entire dharma realm. The nature of the mind does not arise and does not cease.

81 **thicket of myriad forms** (*manzō shinra* 萬象森羅): Also read *banzō shinra* 萬象森羅. A common expression for all things in the universe, based on the image of a dense stand of trees. See Supplementary Notes, s.v. "Myriad forms."

34 DŌGEN'S *SHŌBŌGENZŌ* VOLUME VII

mind. To talk of there being no differences — this is the sign that the house of the buddhas has understood the nature of the mind. Despite this, how could one differentiate this one dharma into body and mind and distinguish birth and death and nirvāṇa? Since we are children of the Buddha, do not give ear to the sounds of the tongues of crazy people who talk of the views of other paths.

[S1:51]

とふていはく、この坐禪をもはらせむ人、かならず戒律を嚴淨すべしや。

Question: Should the person who would exclusively practice seated meditation invariably observe the precepts in strict purity?[82]

[S1:52]

しめしていはく、持戒梵行は、すなはち禪門の規矩なり、佛祖の家風なり。いまだ戒をうけず、又、戒をやぶれるもの、その分なきにあらず。

Answer: Keeping the precepts and pure practice are the standards for the Zen gate and the house style of the buddhas and ancestors. But it is not the case that those who have not yet received the precepts or who have broken the precepts are disqualified.

[S1:53]

とふていはく、この坐禪をつとめん人、さらに眞言・止觀の行を、かね修せん、さまたげあるべからずや。

Question: Are there no obstacles to someone's performing this seated meditation who engages in dual cultivation with the practices of Shingon or Calming and Contemplation?[83]

[S1:54]

しめしていはく、在唐のとき、宗師に眞訣をききしちなみに、西天東地の古今に、佛印を正傳せし諸祖、いづれも、いまだ、しかのごときの行を、かね修すときかず、といひき。まことに、一事をこととせざれば、一智に達することなし。

Answer: When I was in the Tang, listening to the true arcanum of my teacher, he said that he had never heard of any of the ancestors who directly transmitted the buddha seal in Sindh in the West and the Land of the East, past or present, who engaged in the dual cultivation of such practices. Truly, when we do not devote ourselves to one thing, we do not master one wisdom.[84]

---

82 **Question** (*tōte iwaku* とうていはく): Question number 11.

83 **Question** (*tōte iwaku* とうていはく): Question number 12.

Shingon or Calming and Contemplation (*Shingon Shikan* 眞言・止觀): I.e., the esoteric teachings (*mikkyō* 密教) or the meditation teachings of the Tendai 天台 tradition.

84 **when we do not devote ourselves to one thing, we do not master one wisdom**

S1. Talk on Pursuing the Way *Bendōwa* 辨道話   35

[S1:55] {2:475}

とふていはく、この行は、在俗の男女もつとむべしや、ひとり出家人のみ
修するか。

Question: Is this practice something that lay men and women should also perform, or is it engaged in solely by those who have left home?[85]

[S1:56]

しめしていはく、祖師のいはく、佛法を會すること、男女・貴賤をえらぶ
べからず、ときこゆ。

Answer: The ancestral masters say that, in the understanding of the buddha dharma, we should not discriminate between male or female, noble or base.

[S1:57]

とふていはく、出家人は、諸縁すみやかにはなれて、坐禪辨道にさはりな
し。在俗の繁務は、いかにしてか一向に修行して、無爲の佛道にかなは
む。

Question: People who have left home, quickly escaping the various involvements, have no obstacles to pursuing the way in seated meditation; but how can the busy lay person practice single-mindedly and conform to the unconditioned way of the buddhas?[86]

[S1:58]

しめしていはく、おほよそ、佛祖あはれみのあまり、廣大の慈門をひら
きおけり。これ、一切衆生を證入せしめんがためなり、人天、たれかい
らざらむものや。ここをもて、むかし・いまをたづぬるに、その證、これ
おほし。しばらく、代宗・順宗の、帝位にして、萬機いとしげかりし、坐
禪辨道して佛祖の大道を會通す、李相國・防相國、ともに輔佐の臣位には
むべりて、一天の股肱たりし、坐禪辨道して佛祖の大道に證入す。ただこ
れ、こころざしのあり・なしによるべし、身の在家・出家には、かかはら
じ。又、ふかくことの殊劣をわきまふる人、おのづから信ずることあり。
いはむや、世務は佛法をさゆ、とおもへるものは、ただ、世中に佛法な
し、とのみしりて、佛中に世法なき事を、いまだしらざるなり。ちかごろ
大宋に、馮相公といふありき、祖道に長ぜりし大官なり、のちに詩をつく
りて、みづからをいふにいはく、公事之餘喜坐禪、少曾將脇到牀眠。雖然
現出宰官相、長老之名四海傳。これは、宦務にひまなかりし身なれども、

(*ichiji o koto to sezareba, ichichi ni tassuru koto nashi* 一事をこととせざれば、一智
に達することなし): Variation on a saying common in Chan texts, usually put, "If you
don't rely on one thing, you don't develop one wisdom" (*buyin yishi buchang yizhi* 不
因一事不長一智).

85 **Question** (*tōte iwaku* とうていはく): Question number 13.

86 **Question** (*tōte iwaku* とうていはく): Question number 14.

the unconditioned way of the buddhas (*mui no butsudō* 無爲の佛道): Or "the buddhas'
path of non-action."

36 DŌGEN'S *SHŌBŌGENZŌ* VOLUME VII

佛道にこころざしふかければ、得道せるなり。他をもてわれをかへりみ、むかしをもていまをかがみるべし。大宋國には、いまのよの國王・大臣・士俗・男女、ともに心を祖道にとどめずといふことなし。武門・文家、いづれも參禪學道をこころざせり。こころざすもの、かならず心地を開明することおほし。これ、世務の、佛法をさまたげざる、おのづからしられたり。國家に眞實の佛法弘通すれば、諸佛・諸天ひまなく衞護するがゆえに、王化太平なり、聖化太平なれば、佛法そのちからをうるものなり。又、釋尊の在世には、逆人邪見みちをえき。祖師の會下には、獦者・樵翁、さとりをひらく。いはむや、そのほかの人をや。ただ、正師の教道を、たづぬべし。

Answer: The buddhas and ancestors, with an overabundance of empathy, have opened this gate of compassion. It was in order to enable all living beings to enter verification; who among the humans and devas could not enter it? Hence, when we inquire into past and present, there are many who have had this verification. For the moment, [we might mention] Daizong and Shunzong, who, while serving as emperors and completely occupied with the myriad affairs of state, pursued the way in seated meditation and understood the great way of the buddhas and ancestors; or State Minister Li and State Minister Fang, who both served in ministerial posts as adjuncts and were the very arms and legs of the emperor, and who pursued the way in seated meditation and entered verification of the great way of the buddhas and ancestors.[87]

This must only depend on whether there is or is not the aspiration; it should have nothing to do with whether one's status is that of householder or renunciant. Again, the person who profoundly evaluates the value of things will naturally believe. Not to mention that those who think that worldly duties interfere with the buddha dharma know only that there is no buddha dharma within the worldly but do not yet recognize that there are no worldly dharmas within the buddha [dharma].

Recently, in the Great Song, there was a certain Ministerial Magistrate Feng, a high official advanced in the way of the ancestors.[88] Later, he

---

87 **Daizong and Shunzong** (*Daisō Junsō* 代宗・順宗): Daizong, eighth emperor of the Tang dynasty (r. 762-779), appears in Chan literature as a patron of Nanyang Huizhong 南陽慧忠 (see, e.g., *Jingde chuandeng lu* 景德傳燈錄, T.2076.51:244a11ff). Shunzong, briefly the tenth emperor of the Tang (r. 805), appears as an interlocutor in the sayings of Foguong Ruman 佛光如滿 (dates unknown) (*Jingde chuandeng lu* 景德傳燈錄, T.2076.51:249a3) and of Jingzhao Shili 京兆尸利 (dates unknown) (*Jingde chuandeng lu* 景德傳燈錄, T.2076.51:253a17-22).

State Minister Li and State Minister Fang (*Li shōkoku Bō shōkoku* 李相國・防相國): Identities uncertain. Traditionally, said to refer respectively to Li Ao 李翱 (772–841), a follower of Yaoshan Weiyan 藥山惟儼 (751-834), and Pei Xiu 裴休 (791–864), associated with Huangbo Xiyun 黃檗希運 (dates unknown).

88 **Ministerial Magistrate Feng** (*Hyō shōkō* 馮相公): I.e., Feng Ji 馮楫 (d. 1153),

S1. Talk on Pursuing the Way *Bendōwa* 辨道話

composed a verse in which he refers to himself, saying,

As official duties allow, I enjoy seated meditation,
Rarely reclining on a bed to sleep.
Though appointed to the Offices of the Secretariat,
My name as an elder is spread across the four seas.

Though he was someone without a break from his government duties, because his aspiration for the way of the buddhas was profound, he gained the way. We should use him to reflect on ourselves and use the past as a model for the present. In the Land of the Great Song today, the kings of the realm, the great ministers, the nobles, men and women — none fail to turn their minds to the way of the ancestors. Both military men and literati aspire to practice meditation and study the way. Of those who aspire, many are sure to clarify the mind ground. From this, we naturally recognize that worldly duties do not hinder the buddha dharma. When the genuine buddha dharma is spread throughout the realm, because the buddhas and devas constantly protect it, the royal influence brings great peace; and, when the sagely influence brings great peace, the buddha dharma gains strength. Moreover, when Śākya, the Honored One, was in the world, transgressive people and those with false views attained the way.[89] Within the assemblies of the ancestral masters, hunters and woodcutters opened awakening, not to mention the other people.[90] We should just seek the teaching of the way of a true master.

[S1:59] {2:476}
とふていはく、この行は、いま末代惡世にも、修行せば證をうべしや。

Question: If one cultivates this practice, can one attain verification even in the present evil world of the final age?[91]

---

styled Layman Budong 不動居士; a follower of Foyan Qingyuan 佛眼清遠 (1067-1120). His verse quoted here occurs at *Jiatai pudeng lu* 嘉泰普燈錄, ZZ.137:322b12-13.

89 **transgressive people and those with false views** (*gyakunin jaken* 逆人邪見): I.e., people who violate the precepts and people who hold erroneous beliefs.

90 **hunters and woodcutters** (*ryōsha shōō* 獦者・樵翁): Perhaps references respectively to Shigong Huizang 石鞏慧藏 (dates unknown), disciple of Mazu Daoyi 馬祖道一 (709-788), who had been a hunter in lay life; and the Sixth Ancestor, Huineng 慧能, who worked as a woodcutter as a layman.

91 **Question** (*tōte iwaku* とうていはく): Question number 15, reflecting the widespread belief among Dōgen's contemporaries that they were living at a time when awakening was no longer possible.

38　DŌGEN'S *SHŌBŌGENZŌ* VOLUME VII

[S1:60]

しめしていはく、教家に名相をこととせるに、なほ大乗實教には、正・像・末法をわくことなし、修すれば、みな得道すといふ。いはむや、この單傳の正法には、入法出身、おなじく自家の財珍を受用するなり。證の得否は、修せむものおのづからしらむこと、用水の人の、冷煖をみづからわきまふるがごとし。

Answer: In the teaching houses, even while focusing on names and forms, it is still said that, in the real teachings of the Great Vehicle, everyone who practices can gain the way, without distinction among the true, semblance, and final dharma.[92] How much more, then, in this uniquely transmitted true dharma, where, in entering the dharma and leaving the body, we all equally enjoy the precious assets of our own house.[93] Whether or not one has attained verification, those who practice know for themselves, just as people who use water can tell for themselves whether it is cold or hot.

[S1:61] {2:477}

とふていはく、あるがいはく、佛法には、即心是佛のむねを了達しぬるがごときは、くちに經典を誦せず、身に佛道を行ぜざれども、あへて佛法にかけたるところなし、ただ、佛法はもとより自己にありとしる、これを得道の全圓とす、このほかさらに、他人にむかひてもとむべきにあらず、いはむや、坐禪辦道をわづらはしくせむや。

Question: Some say that, in the buddha dharma, those who fully understand the teaching that "*this mind itself is the buddha*," though they neither recite scriptures with their mouths nor practice the way of the

---

92　**the real teachings of the Great Vehicle** (*daijō jikkyō* 大乗實教): No doubt reflecting the practice, common in Dōgen's day, of dividing the exoteric Mahayāna schools into "provisional" (*gon* 權) and "real" (*jitsu* 實); the latter were typically thought of as Tendai and Kegon.

true, semblance, and final dharma (*shō zō mappō* 正・像・末法): According to a common reckoning, the three stages in the degeneration of the dharma. The period of the "true dharma" (*shōbō* 正法) was most often taken as the first thousand years following the *parinirvāṇa* of the Buddha; the "semblance dharma" (*zōhō* 像法), during which there was practice but no longer attainment of awakening, was said to last an additional one thousand years; during the "final dharma" (*mappō* 末法), lasting ten thousand years, there was neither authentic practice nor awakening. Based on the traditional East Asian Buddhist reckoning of the date of Śākyamuni's *parinirvāṇa* as 949 BCE, the final dharma was thought have begun in 1052 CE.

93　**entering the dharma and leaving the body** (*nippō shusshin* 入法出身): An unusual combination, presumably meaning "from start to finish" of the practice. The expression *shusshin* 出身 can also mean to establish oneself as a teacher.

the precious assets of our own house (*jika no zaichin* 自家の財珍): Presumably, a metaphor for one's inherent spiritual riches.

S1. Talk on Pursuing the Way *Bendōwa* 辨道話 39

buddhas with their bodies, lack nothing of the buddha dharma.[94] Merely knowing that the buddha dharma is within oneself — this constitutes the entire perfection of gaining the way; aside from this, there is nothing further to seek from others, much less any need to pursue the way in seated meditation.

[S1:62]

しめしていはく、このことば、もともはかなし。もしなんぢがいふごとくならば、こころあらむもの、たれかこのむねををしへむに、しることなからむ。しるべし、佛法は、まさに自・他の見をやめて學するなり。もし、自己即佛、としるをもて得道とせば、釋尊、むかし化道にわづらはじ。しばらく古德の妙則をもて、これを證すべし。

Answer: These words are completely baseless. If it were as you say, how could anyone with a mind fail to know this teaching were someone to tell it to them? We should recognize that the buddha dharma is to study having quit views of self and other; if knowing that the self is buddha constitutes gaining the way, Śākya, the Honored One, would not have bothered long ago to teach the way. Here, let me verify this with a marvelous case of the old worthies.

[S1:63]

むかし、則公監院といふ僧、法眼禪師の會中にありしに、法眼禪師とうていはく、則監寺、なんぢわが會にありていくばくのときぞ。則公がいはく、われ師の會にはむべりて、すでに三年をへたり。禪師のいはく、なんぢはこれ後生なり、なんぞつねにわれに佛法をとはざる。則公がいはく、それがし、和尚をあざむくべからず。かつて青峰の禪師のところにありしとき、佛法におきて安樂のところを了達せり。禪師のいはく、なんぢいかなることばによりてか、いることをえし。則公がいはく、それがし、かつて青峰にとひき、いかなるかこれ學人の自己なる。青峰のいはく、丙丁童子來求火。法眼のいはく、よきことばなり。ただし、おそらくはなんぢ會せざらむことを。則公がいはく、丙丁は火に屬す、火をもてさらに火をもとむ、自己をもて自己をもとむるににたり、と會せり。禪師のいはく、まことにしりぬ、なんぢ會せざりけり。佛法、もしかくのごとくならば、けふまでつたはれじ。ここに則公、懊悶して、すなはちたちぬ。中路にいたりておもひき、禪師はこれ天下の善知識、又五百人の大導師なり、わが非をいさむる、さだめて長處あらむ。禪師のみもとにかへりて、懺悔禮謝してとふていはく、いかなるかこれ學人の自己なる。禪師のいはく、丙丁童子來求火、と。則公、このことばのしたに、おほきに佛法をさとりき。

Long ago, when a certain cleric, the monastic comptroller Honorable Ze, was in the assembly of Chan Master Fayan, Chan Master Fayan

---

94 **Question** (*tōte iwaku* とうていはく): Question number 16. "This mind itself is the buddha" (*soku shin ze butsu* 即心是佛) is a famous saying attributed to Mazu Daoyi 馬祖道一, cited in Dōgen's *shinji Shōbōgenzō* 眞字正法眼藏 (DZZ.5:266, case 278) and many other Chan sources; see Supplementary Notes.

40 DŌGEN'S *SHŌBŌGENZŌ* VOLUME VII

asked him, "Comptroller Ze, how long have you been in my assembly?"[95]

The Honorable Ze said, "I've served in the Master's assembly for three years already."

The Chan Master said, "You're my junior. Why don't you ever ask me about the buddha dharma?"

The Honorable Ze said, "I shouldn't deceive the Reverend. Previously, when I was with the Chan Master of Qingfeng, I fully understood what is ease and joy in the buddha dharma."[96]

The Chan Master said, "What words enabled you to enter it?"

The Honorable Ze said, "I once asked Qingfeng, 'What is this student's self?'[97] Qingfeng said, '*The bingding youth comes seeking fire.*'"[98]

Fayan said, "Good words. But I'm afraid you didn't understand them."

The Honorable Ze said, "*Bing* and *ding* belong to fire. I understood that seeking fire with fire is like seeking the self with the self."

The Chan Master said, "I knew it. You haven't understood it. If the buddha dharma were like this, it would never have come down to us today."

At this, the Honorable Ze was upset and immediately left. On the road, he thought, "The Chan Master is renowned everywhere as a wise friend; moreover, he is a great guide for five hundred people. Surely, his warning me of my error has merit."

---

95 **a certain cleric, the monastic comptroller Honorable Ze** (*Sokukō kannin to iu sō* 則公監院といふ僧): I.e, Baoen Xuanze 報恩玄則 (dates unknown). "Comptroller" (*kan'in* 監院) is one of the six traditional monastic offices (equivalent to *kanji* 監寺, appearing just below). This section represents a Japanese rendering of a Chinese dialogue found in Dōgen's *shinji Shōbōgenzō* 眞字正法眼藏 (DZZ.5:192, case 122); the source is thought to be the *Hongzhi chanshi guanglu* 宏智禪師廣錄 (T.2001.48:3a6-16).

Chan Master Fayan (*Hōgen zenji* 法眼禪師): I.e., Fayan Wenyi 法眼文益 (886–958).

96 **Chan Master of Qingfeng** (*Seihō no zenji* 青峰の禪師): Identity uncertain; sometimes said to refer to Baizhao Zhiyuan 白兆志圓 (dates unknown), after a suggestion at *Jingde chuandeng lu* 景德傳燈錄, T.2076.51:413b12.

97 **"'What is this student's self?'"** (*ikanaru ka kore gakunin no jiko naru* いかなるかこれ學人の自己なる): Variant versions of the story (e.g., at *Jingde chuandeng lu* 景德傳燈錄, T.2076.51:413b11-19, and *Biyan lu* 碧巖錄, T.2003.48:147b12-24) give Ze's question here as "What is a buddha?" (*ru he shi fo*; J. *nyo ka ze butsu* 如何是佛).

98 **"'The *bingding* youth comes seeking fire'"** (*byōjō dōji rai gu ka* 丙丁童子來求火): Also read *heitei dōji*. *Bing* 丙 and *ding* 丁 are the third and fourth celestial stems of the Chinese calendar, representing respectively the *yang* 陽 and *yin* 陰 aspects of fire (*huo* 火) among the five phases (*wuxing* 五行). "The *bingding* youth" (or "fire boy") has been variously understood, as a fire god, and as the boy in charge of the monastic lamps.

S1. Talk on Pursuing the Way *Bendōwa* 辨道話   41

He returned to the Chan Master, repented, made bows in apology, and asked, "What is this student's self?"

The Chan Master said, "*The bingding youth comes seeking fire.*"

At these words, the Honorable Ze had a great awakening to the buddha dharma.

[S1:64] {2:478}

あきらかにしりぬ、自己即佛の領解をもて、佛法をしれりといふにはあらず、といふことを。もし自己即佛の領解を佛法とせば、禪師、さきのことばをもてみちびかじ、又、しかのごとくいましむべからず。ただまさに、はじめ善知識をみむより、修行の儀則を咨問して、一向に坐禪辨道して、一知半解を心にとどむることなかれ。佛法の妙術、それむなしからじ。

We clearly see here that understanding that the self is the buddha does not mean that one has known the buddha dharma. If understanding that the self is the buddha were the buddha dharma, the Chan Master would not have guided him with the above words, nor would he have admonished him like this. From the time you first meet a wise friend, just inquire of the procedures for practice, single-mindedly pursue the way in seated meditation, and do not stop at a single knowledge and a half understanding.[99] The wondrous technique of the buddha dharma will not be in vain.

[S1:65]

とふていはく、乾唐の古今をきくに、あるいは、たけのこえをききて道をさとり、あるいは、はなのいろをみてこころをあきらむる物あり、いはむや、釋迦大師は、明星をみしとき道を證し、阿難尊者は、刹竿のたふれしところに法をあきらめし、のみならず、六代よりのち、五家のあひだに、一言半句のしたに、心地をあきらむるものおほし。かれらかならずしも、かつて坐禪辨道せるもののみならむや。

Question: We hear that in the past and present of Gandhāra and the Tang, there were those who awakened to the way upon hearing the sound of bamboo, or those who clarified the mind upon seeing the color of flowers; not to mention that Great Master Śākyamuni verified the way when he saw the dawn star, or that Venerable Ānanda clarified the dharma at the toppling of the flagpole.[100] And not only that but, after the sixth

---

99 **a single knowledge and a half understanding** (*itchi hange* 一知半解): A set phrase for little or shallow knowledge.

100 **Question** (*tōte iwaku* とうていはく): Question number 17.

Gandhāra and the Tang (*Ken Tō* 乾唐): I.e., India and China; an unusual expression, presumably derived from *Kendo* 乾土 ("Gandhāra," used metonymically for "India").

those who awakened to the way upon hearing the sound of bamboo, or those who clarified the mind upon seeing the color of flowers (*arui wa, take no koe o kikite dō o satori, arui wa hana no iro o mite kokoro o akiramuru mono ari* あるいは、たけの

42 DŌGEN'S *SHŌBŌGENZŌ* VOLUME VII

generation, among the five houses, there were many who clarified the mind ground at a single word or half a line. Were they invariably only those who had previously pursued the way in seated meditation?

[S1:66] {2:479}

しめしていはく、古今に見色明心し、聞聲悟道せし當人、ともに辨道に擬議量なく、直下に第二人なきことをしるべし。

Answer: We should know that those people who, in past and present, *saw the color and clarified the mind or heard the sound and awakened to the way* were all, without pondering or conjecturing in their pursuit of the way, right here, without a second person.[101]

[S1:67]

とふていはく、西天および神丹國は、人もとより質直なり。中華のしからしむるによりて、佛法を教化するに、いとはやく會入す。我朝は、むかしより人に仁智すくなくして、正種つもりがたし、蕃夷のしからしむる、うらみざらむや。又、このくにの出家人は、大國の在家人にもおとれり。擧

こえをききて道をさとり、あるいははなのいろをみてこころをあきらむる物あり): Likely recalling the stories, respectively, of Xiangyan Zhixian 香嚴智閑, who had an understanding upon hearing the sound of a bit of debris striking a bamboo (see Supplementary Notes, s.v. "A painted cake can't satisfy hunger"); and Lingyun Zhiqin 靈雲志勤, student of Dawei Lingyou 大潙靈祐 (771-853), who gained an understanding upon seeing peach trees in bloom (see Supplementary Notes, s.v. "Peach blossoms"). Dōgen cites these two anecdotes together elsewhere in the *Shōbōgenzō*.

Venerable Ānanda clarified the dharma at the toppling of the flagpole (*Anan sonja wa, sekkan no taureshi tokoro ni hō o akirameshi* 阿難尊者は、利竿のたふれしところに法をあきらめし): Reference to a dialogue between Mahākāsyapa and Ānanda recorded at *shinji Shōbōgenzō* 眞字正法眼藏, DZZ.5:212, case 169 (the source is thought to be the *Zongmen tongyao ji* 宗門統要集, ZTS.1:17a11-13):

二祖阿難尊者、問迦葉尊者曰、師兄傳佛金襴袈裟外、別傳箇什麼。迦葉召曰、阿難。阿難應諾。迦葉曰、倒却門前刹竿著。阿難大悟。

The Second Ancestor, Venerable Ānanda, asked Venerable Kāśyapa, "Elder brother, apart from the transmission of Buddha's gold brocade *kāṣāya*, what else was transmitted?"
Kāśyapa called, "Ānanda."
Ānanda answered.
Kāśyapa said, "Topple the flagpole in front of the gate."
Ānanda had a great awakening.

101 **without pondering or conjecturing** (*gigi ryō* 擬議量): A tentative translation of an unusual combination appearing elsewhere only in the "Shōbōgenzō jippō" 正法眼藏十方 chapter. *Gigi* 擬議 is a common term with the sense "to consider [saying something]," "to be on the verge of speaking"; the glyph *ryō* 量 ("measure") here might be taken as *shiryō* 思量 ("thinking") or, perhaps, *shōryō* 商量 ("deliberation").

right here, without a second person (*jikige ni daini nin naki* 直下に第二人なき): An expression, also appearing in the "Shōbōgenzō busshō" 正法眼藏佛性, that seems to reflect the Chinese of the *Fozhao chanshi zoudui lu* 佛照禪師奏對錄 (*Guzunsu yulu* 古尊宿語錄, ZZ.118:823a7): *zhixia geng wu dier ren* 直下更無第二人.

S1. Talk on Pursuing the Way *Bendōwa* 辨道話 43

世おろかにして、心量、狹少なり。ふかく有爲の功を執して、事相の善を
このむ。かくのごとくのやから、たとひ坐禪すといふとも、たちまちに佛
法を證得せむや。

Question: In Sindh in the West and in the Land of Cīnasthāna, people are fundamentally straightforward.[102] Being central cultures makes them so, and, as a result, when taught the buddha dharma, they are quick to understand it.[103] In our kingdom, from long ago, the benevolent and wise have been few, and the true seeds have been hard to accumulate.[104] Is it not regrettable that our being barbarians has made this so?[105] Moreover, the renunciants of this land are inferior to the householders of the great countries. Our whole world is stupid; our mentality, narrow and petty. Deeply attached to conditioned merit, we delight in superficial goods. Could such a people, even if they practice seated meditation, quickly verify the buddha dharma?

[S1:68]

しめしていはく、いふがごとし。わがくにの人、いまだ仁智あまねから
ず、人、また迂曲なり。たとひ正直の法をしめすとも、甘露かへりて毒
となりぬべし。名利にはおもむきやすく、惑執、とらけがたし。しかはあ
れども、佛法に證入すること、かならずしも人天の世智をもて出世の舟航
とするにはあらず。佛在世にも、てまりによりて四果を證し、袈裟をかけ
て大道をあきらめし、ともに愚暗のやから、癡狂の畜類なり。ただし、正
信のたすくるところ、まどひをはなるるみちあり。また、癡老の比丘、默
坐せしをみて、設齋の信女、さとりをひらきし、これ智によらず、文によ
らず、ことばをまたず、かたりをまたず、ただしこれ正信にたすけられた
り。

Answer: It is as you say. Benevolence and wisdom are not widespread, and the people are disingenuous. Even if we instruct them with the correct, straightforward dharma, the sweet nectar will become a poison. They easily turn toward fame and profit and find it hard to disperse their delusions and attachments.[106] Nevertheless, entering verification of the buddha dharma is not necessarily building a vessel to appear in

---

102 **Question** (*tōte iwaku* とうていはく): Question number 18.

103 **central cultures** (*chūka* 中華): A term typically used in reference only to China, it is unclear if it is intended to include India here.

104 **true seeds** (*shōshu* 正種): Or "correct seeds"; presumably, the karma, or spiritual potential, to understand the true dharma (or, perhaps, the people with such karma). The term appears again below (section 69) in the phrase "the true seeds of prajñā" (*hannya no shōshu* 般若の正種).

105 **barbarians** (*ban'i* 蕃夷): A Chinese term for the non-Han peoples living beyond the pale of Han civilization.

106 **delusions and attachments** (*wakushū* 惑執): Not a common term in the *Shōbō-genzō*; may be taken as *meiwaku shūjaku* 迷惑執著 or, possibly, *giwaku shūjaku* 疑惑執著 ("doubts and attachments").

44 DŌGEN'S *SHŌBŌGENZŌ* VOLUME VII

the world by the worldly wisdom of humans and devas. Even when the Buddha was in the world, both the one who verified the fourth fruit because of a handball and the one who clarified the great way by donning a *kāṣāya* were foolish and ignorant, deranged beasts.[107] Yet, where true faith saved them, they had a path to free themselves from their delusion. Again, upon seeing a stupid old bhikṣu sitting silently and offering him a meal, a woman of faith opened an awakening; this was not based on wisdom, not based on texts, did not depend on words, did not depend on explanations: she was just saved by true faith.[108]

[S1:69] {2:480}

また、釋教の、三千界にひろまること、わづかに二千餘年の前後なり。刹土のしなじななる、かならずしも仁智のくににあらず、人、またかならずしも利智聰明のみあらむや。しかあれども、如來の正法、もとより不思議の大功德力をそなへて、ときいたれば、その刹土にひろまる。人、まさに正信修行すれば、利・鈍をわかず、ひとしく得道するなり。わが朝は、仁智のくににあらず、人に知解おろかなりとして、佛法を會すべからず、とおもふことなかれ。いはむや、人みな般若の正種ゆたかなり。ただ承當することまれに、受用すること
いまだしきならし。

Moreover, the spread of the teachings of Śākya across the three chiliocosms has taken barely two thousand some years, more or less.[109] These lands are varied, not necessarily countries of benevolence and wisdom, their people also not necessarily sharp witted and clear. Nevertheless, when the time comes, the true dharma of the Tathāgata, endowed from

---

107 **one who verified the fourth fruit because of a handball** (*temari ni yorite shika o shō shi* てまりによりて四果を證し): Allusion to the story of an old monk who became an arhat, the fourth and final stage in the traditional *śravaka* path, when hit by a ball. The story, which is also alluded to in the Shinpukuji 真福寺 text of the "Shōbōgenzō daigo" 正法眼藏大悟, can be found in the *Saṃyukta-ratna-piṭaka-sūtra* (*Zabaozang jing* 雜寶藏經, T.203.4:494a22-b29).

one who clarified the great way by donning a *kāṣāya* (*kesa o kakete daidō o akirameshi* 袈裟をかけて大道をあきらめし): Allusion to the Buddha's disciple, the Bhikṣuṇī Utpalavarṇā, who became an arhat with the six spiritual powers because, in a previous life as a courtesan, she once wore the robe of a *bhikṣuṇī* as a joke. Her story is told in the *Dazhidu lun* 大智度論 (T.1509.25:161a27-b17), which Dōgen quotes in his "Shōbōgenzō kesa kudoku" 正法眼藏袈裟功德 and "Shōbōgenzō shukke kudoku" 正法眼藏出家功德.

108 **a woman of faith** (*shinnyo* 信女): Allusion to the story of a lay woman who invited an ignorant old bhikṣu for a meal, after which she asked for a teaching. She then closed her eyes and sat waiting, while the bhikṣu, having nothing to say, left without a word. Then the woman, sitting quietly, perceived for herself the three signs of conditioned dharmas and attained the first fruit of the *śrāvaka* path. See *Zabaozang jing* 雜寶藏經, T.203.4:494c1-16.

109 **three chiliocosms** (*sanzenkai* 三千界): Abbreviation of *sanzen daisen sekai* 三千大千世界 ("three-thousandfold great thousandfold world system"), equal to one billion Sumeru world systems; the extent of a buddha's domain.

S1. Talk on Pursuing the Way *Bendōwa* 辨道話

the start with the inconceivable power of great merit, spreads throughout these lands. When the people practice with true faith, they equally gain the way, whether they are sharp or dull. Do not think that, as our kingdom is not a land of benevolence and wisdom, and the intelligence of its people is stupid, they cannot understand the buddha dharma. Needless to say, people are all endowed with the true seeds of prajñā; they just rarely accede to it and have yet to enjoy it.

* * * * *

[S1:70]

さきの問答往來し、賓主相交すること、みだりがはし。いくばくか、はななきそらにはなをなさしむる。しかありとも、このくに、坐禪辨道におきて、いまだその宗旨つたはれず、しらむとところらざさむもの、かなしむべし。このゆえに、いささか異域の見聞をあつめ、明師の眞訣をしるしとどめて、參學のねがはむにきこえむとす。このほか、叢林の規範、および寺院の格式、いましめすにいとまあらず、又、草草にすべからず。

The preceding back and forth of questions and answers, with its alternation of guest and host, is rather random. It creates so many flowers in a flowerless sky. Nevertheless, in this land, the essential point of pursuit of the way in seated meditation has not been transmitted, and those who aspire to know it are to be pitied. For this reason, collecting something of what I saw and heard in the foreign regions, and recording the true arcanum of the illumined masters, I sought to inform those who wish to study them. Apart from this, I do not have time here to explain the rules and regulations of the monastic groves, or the customs and procedures of the temples and cloisters, which, moreover, should not be treated perfunctorily.

[S1:71]

おほよそ我朝は、龍海の以東にところして、雲煙はるかなれども、欽明・用明の前後より、秋方の佛法東漸する、これすなはち人のさいはひなり。しかあるを、名相事緣、しげくみだれて、修行のところにわづらふ。いまは、破衣綴盂を生涯として、青巖白石のほとりに茅をむすむで、端坐修練するに、佛向上の事たちまちにあらはれて、一生參學の大事すみやかに究竟するものなり。これすなはち龍牙の誠敕なり、鷄足の遺風なり。その坐禪の儀則は、すぎぬる嘉禄のころ撰集せし普勸坐禪儀に依行すべし。

In sum, our kingdom is located east of the dragon seas, far across the clouds and mist; yet, to the good fortune of its people, since around the time of Kinmei and Yōmei, the buddha dharma from the autumnal direction gradually came east.[110] However, matters of names and forms

---

110 **around the time of Kinmei and Yōmei** (*Kinmei Yōmei no zengo* 欽明・用明の前後): The Emperor Kinmei 欽明 reigned 531-571 (traditionally, 539-571), during which

46 DŌGEN'S *SHŌBŌGENZŌ* VOLUME VII

were seriously confused and created problems over the places of practice. Now, while we lead a life of torn robes and mended bowls, thatching reed roofs by green crags and white boulders, as we train ourselves sitting erect, the matter beyond the buddha immediately appears, and the great matter of a lifetime of study is quickly brought to completion. This is the admonition of Longya, the style bequeathed at Cock's Foot.[111] The procedures for its seated meditation should be carried out according to the *Universal Promotion of the Principles of Seated Meditation* that I composed during the preceding Karoku.[112]

[S1:72] {2:481}

それ、佛法を國中に弘通すること、王勅をまつべしといへども、ふたたび靈山の遺囑をおもへば、いま百萬億刹に現出せる王公相將、みなともにかたじけなく佛勅をうけて、夙生に佛法を護持する素懷をわすれず、生來せるものなり。その化をしくさかひ、いづれのところか佛國土にあらざらむ。このゆえに、佛祖の道を流通せむ、かならずしもところをえらび、縁をまつべきにあらず、ただ、けふをはじめとおもはむや。

While it may be that the propagation of the buddha dharma within a country should await a royal decree, when we recall once more the final bequest on Vulture Peak, the kings and dukes, magistrates and minis-

---

time it was said that Buddhism was imported to Japan; the Emperor Yōmei 用明, who reigned 585-587, was known as a strong early supporter of Buddhism.

autumnal direction (*shūhō* 秋方): I.e., the west, the direction associated with the autumn season.

111 **the admonition of Longya, the style bequeathed at Cock's Foot** (*kore sunawachi Ryūga no kaichoku nari, keisoku no ifū nari* これすなはち龍牙の誡敕なり、鶏足の遺風なり): "Cock's Foot" refers to Mount Kukkuṭapāda (*Keisokusen* 鶏足山), where legend has it that the First Ancestor, Mahākāśyapa, retired to practice and where he remains still today, waiting to transmit the robe of Buddha Śākyamuni to the future Buddha, Maitreya.

"The admonition of Longya" is traditionally thought to refer to the verses of Longya Judon 龍牙居遁 (835-923), especially his lines celebrating the reclusive life (see *Chanmen zhuzushi jisong* 禪門諸祖師偈頌, ZZ.116:923b14-15):

木食艸衣心似月。一生無念復無涯。時人若問居何處。渌水青山是我家。

Eating from trees and robed in grass, my mind like a mirror.
My whole life without a thought, without any horizon.
If someone were ever to ask where I live,
Clear waters and green mountains are my home.

112 *Universal Promotion of the Principles of Seated Meditation* **that I composed during the preceding Karoku** (*suginuru Karoku no koro senshū seshi Fukan zazen gi* すぎぬる嘉禄のころ撰集せし普勧坐禪儀): The Karoku era spanned the years 1225-1227. Since Dōgen only returned to Japan from China in 1227, the work mentioned here must have been composed almost immediately upon his return. The content of this work is unknown, since our earliest extant version of the *Fukan zazen gi* 普勧坐禪儀 is dated in the first year of the Tenpuku era (1233), after the composition of the "Bendōwa."

S1. Talk on Pursuing the Way *Bendōwa* 辨道話

ters who now appear in hundreds of myriads of *koṭis* of realms were all reborn having humbly accepted the Buddha's decree and not forgotten their cherished ideal from former lives to protect the buddha dharma. Which of the regions covered by their rule is not a buddha land? Therefore, in disseminating the way of the buddhas and ancestors, we need not necessarily choose the place nor await the circumstance: shall we simply think of today as the beginning?[113]

[S1:73]

しかあればすなはち、これをあつめて、佛法をねがはむ哲匠、あはせて道をとぶらひ雲遊萍寄せむ參學の眞流に、のこす。

Thus, compiling this, I leave it for teachers who desire the buddha dharma, as well as for the genuine stream of students who are like wandering clouds and floating weeds in search of the way.

ときに、寛喜辛卯中秋日、入宋傳法沙門道元記

On the mid-autumn day, in the junior metal year of the rabbit, in Kangi [12 September 1231], written by the Śramaṇa Dōgen, who entered the Song and transmitted the dharma[114]

辨道話

Talk on Pursuing the Way

---

113 **shall we simply think of today as the beginning?** (*tada, kyō o hajime to omowamuya* ただ、けふをはじめとおもはむや): A rhetorical question: i.e., we should recognize that our present dissemination of the buddha dharma is but a continuation of an age-old process.

114 **mid-autumn day** (*chūshū* 中秋): I.e., the Harvest Moon Festival, on the fifteenth of the eighth month.

TREASURY OF THE TRUE DHARMA EYE

SUPPLEMENTARY CHAPTER 2

Procedures for the Hall of Gathered Clouds
Jūundō shiki

重雲堂式

Procedures for the Hall of Gathered Clouds

Jūundō shiki

INTRODUCTION

This short work was not composed for the *Shōbōgenzō* and does not occur in the early manuscript traditions of that collection. Rather, it was first associated with the *Shōbōgenzō* chapters only in 1686, when Manzan Dōhaku 卍山道白 (1636–1714) included it in his eighty-nine-chapter *Shōbōgenzō* compilation; thereafter, it was reproduced in the ninety-five-chapter compilation by Handō Kōzen 版橈晃全 (1625–1693) and eventually published as number 5 in the 1815 Honzan edition. The version translated here is based on a manuscript preserved at the Kōfukuji 廣福寺 in Kumamoto Prefecture.

The text bears a colophon dated in the fourth month of 1239, near the start of the summer retreat, at Dōgen's newly established Kōshōji in Uji. This monastery was noteworthy for its introduction to Japan of the Chinese Chan practice of seated meditation on platforms in the saṃgha hall (*sōdō* 僧堂), or "cloud hall" (*undo* 雲堂). As its title indicates, the *Jūundō shiki* represents a set of guidelines for practice in this hall. Thus, although written in the vernacular, the subject matter of the work belongs with its author's more formal *kanbun* writings on monastic regulations collected in the *Eihei shingi* 永平清規.

正法眼藏別輯二
Treasury of the True Dharma Eye
Supplementary Chapter 2

觀音導利興聖護國寺
Kannon Dōri Kōshō Gokokuji

重雲堂式
Procedures for the Hall of Gathered Clouds

(廣福寺所藏本)
(Kōfukuji text)

[S2:1] {2:482}

道心ありて、名利をなげすてん人、いるべし、いたづらにまことなか
らんもの、いるべからず。あやまりていれりとも、かんがへていだす
べし。しるべし、道心ひそかにおこれば、名利たちどころに解脱する
ものなり。おほよそ大千界のうちに、正嫡の附嘱、まれなり。わがく
に、むかしよりいま、これを本源とせん、のちをあはれみても、いま
をおもくすべし。

Those with a mind of the way who have cast aside fame and profit should
be admitted; those not genuine should not be casually admitted. Those
admitted in error should be reconsidered and dismissed. We should understand that, when the mind of the way occurs within us, we are liberated from fame and profit on the spot. Generally speaking, within the
great chiliocosm, the bequest to a legitimate heir is rare. In our land from
ancient times to the present, this will be taken as the original source; in
consideration of those who follow, we should take the present seriously.[1]

---

1 **Kannon Dōri Kōshō Gokokuji** 觀音導利興聖護國寺: Better known as Kannon
Dōri Kōshō Hōrinji 觀音導利興聖寶林寺; the monastery at Fukakusa 深草, in Uji 宇治,
south of Heiankyō, where Dōgen taught during the period 1236-1243.

Procedures for the Hall of Gathered Clouds (*Jūundō shiki* 重雲堂式): More often
translated as "Rules for the Auxiliary Cloud Hall," after the suggestion by Manzan
Dōhaku 卍山道白 (1636–1714) that *jūundo* 重雲堂 here refers to a second saṃgha hall
built at Kōshōji 興聖寺 to accommodate the overflow of practitioners (though there does
not appear to be record of such a hall). In his notes to the text, Kawamura suggests that
jū 重 modifies *shiki* 式 ("procedures") and carries the sense "serious," "to be respected"
(*sonchō su beki* 尊重すべき) — hence, "major rules." This translation takes *jūun* 重雲

52
DŌGEN'S *SHŌBŌGENZŌ* VOLUME VII

[S2:2]

堂中の衆は、乳水のごとくに和合して、たがひに道業を一興すべし。いま
は、しばらく賓主なりといえども、のちには、ながく佛祖なるべし。しか
あればすなはち、おのおのともにあひがたきにあひて、おこなひがたきを
おこなふ、まことのおもひを、わすることなかれ。これを佛法の身心とい
ふ、かならず佛となり祖となる。すでに、いえをはなれ、さとをはなる。
くもをたのみ、みづをたのむ。みをたすけ、道をたすけむこと、この衆の
恩は、父母にもすぐるべし。父母は、しばらく生死のなかの親なり、この
衆は、ながく佛道のともにてあるべし。

The assembly in the hall should blend together like milk and water,
mutually supporting the work of the way. Although now, for a while, we
are guest and host, later, we shall forever be buddhas and ancestors.[2] So,
each of us is encountering what is hard to encounter and practicing what
is hard to practice; do not forget your genuine aspirations. This is called
the body and mind of the buddha dharma; it will definitely become a
buddha and become an ancestor. We have already left our homes and left
our villages; we rely on the clouds and rely on the waters.[3] In its support
of us and support of the way, our debt to this assembly is greater than
that to our fathers and mothers. Our fathers and mothers are parents for
a while in birth and death; this assembly will be our companions forever
on the way of the buddhas.

[S2:3] {2:483}

ありきを、このむべからず。たとひ切要には、一月に一度をばゆるす。む
かしの人、とほきやまにすみ、はるかなるはやしにおこなふし、人事、ま
れなるのみにあらず、萬緣、ともにすつ。韜光晦跡せしこころを、ならふ
べし。いまは、これ頭燃をはらふときなり、このときをもて、いたづらに
世緣にめぐらさん、なげかざらめや。無常たのみがたし、しらず、露命い
かなるみちのくさにかおちむ、まことにあはれむべし。

Do not enjoy going out. If it is absolutely necessary, once a month
is permitted. The ancients lived in distant mountains and practiced in
remote forests; not only were their human contacts rare but they abandoned the myriad involvements. We should learn from their attitude of

---

as a compound meaning "layered (or 'accumulated') clouds," in poetic reference to the
great assembly (*daishu* 大衆) of monks gathered in the cloud hall.

this will be taken as the original source (*kore o hongen to sen* これを本源とせん): The
antecedent of "this" (*kore* これ) here is unclear; often taken to be "this cloud hall" —
i.e., "this authentic Zen-style saṃgha hall will be recognized as the first in the history of
Buddhism in Japan." It is also possible to take it as a reference to Dōgen's introduction
to Japan of the lineage of the "legitimate heirs" of the Zen tradition.

2 **guest and host** (*hinju* 賓主): I.e., disciples and masters, respectively.

3 **we rely on the clouds and rely on the waters** (*kumo o tanomi, mizu o tanomu* くも
をたのみ、みづをたのむ): From the expression "clouds and water" (*unsui* 雲水) used
in reference to the Buddhist monk.

S2. Procedures for the Hall of Gathered Clouds *Jūundō shiki* 重雲堂式   53

"*hiding one's light and covering one's tracks.*"[4] Now is the time to "brush the fire from your head"; is it not deplorable to spend this time involved in worldly matters?[5] Unable to rely on the impermanent, not knowing on what wayside grass our dew-like life will fall — we are truly pitiful.

[S2:4]

堂のうちにて、たとひ禪冊なりとも、文字をみるべからず、消息もとりいるべからず。堂にしては、究理辦道すべし、明窓にむかふては、古教照心すべし。寸陰、すつることなかれ、専一に功夫すべし。

Do not read in the hall, even Zen books, and do not bring in correspondence. While in the hall, we should investigate the principle and pursue the way. We should "illumine the mind with the ancient teachings" when we are by the bright window.[6] Do not waste an inch of shadow; we should make single-minded effort.[7]

[S2:5]

おほよそ、よるも、ひるも、さらんところをば、堂主にしらすべし。ほしいままに、あそぶことなかれ、衆の規矩にかかはるべし。しらず、今生のをはりにてもあるらん、閑遊のなかに、いのちををえん、さだめて、のちにくやしからん。

In general, whether day or night, we should inform the hall chief where we are going. Do not wander off as you please; we should conform to the regulations of the assembly. We never know if this might be the end of this life; we would certainly regret it later if we were to end our life in idle wanderings.

---

4 **"hiding one's light and covering one's tracks"** (*tōkō kaiseki* 韜光晦跡): A Chinese idiom (also written 韜光晦蹟) for not exposing one's abilities. This and the following advice on "brushing the fire from your head" and "illumining the mind beneath the bright window" reflect the *Guijing wen* 龜鏡文 in the *Chanyuan qinggui* 禪苑清規 (ZZ.111:918a16-18):

> 手不把筆如救頭燃所以報書狀也。明窓淨案古教照心所以報藏主也。韜光晦迹不事追陪所以報知客也。
>
> Never touching the writing brush, [practicing] as if saving one's head from a fire, is to repay the secretary [of the monastery]. At the clean desk by the bright window, illumining the mind with the ancient teachings, is to repay the canon prefect. Hiding one's light and covering one's tracks, without engaging in excursions, is to repay the guest prefect.

5 **"brush the fire from your head"** (*zunen o harau* 頭燃をはらふ): A common expression for the urgency of Buddhist practice, appearing elsewhere in Dōgen's writing.

6 **bright window** (*meisō* 明窓): I.e., windows providing lighting in the sūtra reading halls (*kankindō* 看經堂) and common quarters (*shuryō* 衆寮), beneath which were located reading desks (*an* 案); see Supplementary Notes.

7 **an inch of shadow** (*sun'in* 寸陰): A literary expression for "a moment of time," occurring often in Dōgen's writings.

54 DŌGEN'S *SHŌBŌGENZŌ* VOLUME VII

[S2:6] {2:484}

他人のひゐに、てかくべからず。にくむこころにて、人の非をみるべからず。不見他非、我是自然の、むかしのことばあり。又、人の非をならぶべからず、わが德を修すべし。ほとけも、非を制することあれども、にくめ、とにはあらず。

Do not contribute to another's transgressions; do not look upon others' errors with hatred. There is an old saying, "When one does not see others in error and oneself in the right, naturally . . . ."[8] Also, do not imitate others' errors, but cultivate your own virtues. The Buddha proscribed errors but not out of hatred for them.

[S2:7]

大小の事、かならず堂主にふれて、おこなふべし。堂主にふれずして、ことをおこなはん人は、堂をいだすべし。賓主の禮みだれば、偏正あきらめがたし。

Matters both large and small should be conducted in consultation with the hall chief. Those who act without consulting the hall chief should be ejected. When the etiquette of guest and host is confused, inclined and upright cannot be clarified.[9]

[S2:8]

堂のうち、ならびにその近邊にて、こえをたくし、かしらをつどえて、ものいふべからず。堂主、これを制すべし。

Within the hall and in its vicinity, do not raise the voice or gather together to talk. The hall chief should prevent this.

[S2:9]

堂のうちにて、行道すべからず。

Do not circumambulate within the hall.[10]

---

8 **an old saying** (*mukashi no kotoba* むかしのことば): Quoting lines from a verse by Baiyang Fashun 白楊法順 (dates unknown; disciple of Longmen Qingyuan 龍門清遠, 1067-1120). Dōgen's version here seems to have been corrupted (or the source misread?); see, e.g., *Jiatai pudeng lu* 嘉泰普燈錄, ZZ.137:246b18:

不見他非我是、自然上敬下恭。

When one does not see others in error and oneself in the right,
Naturally, one is respected by superiors and admired by inferiors.

9 **inclined and upright** (*henshō* 偏正): Or "side and center"; terms used in Zen thought in reference to "relative and absolute" but here perhaps indicating something like "practice and principle." See Supplementary Notes, s.v. "Upright or inclined."

10 **circumambulate** (*gyōdō* 行道): Likely referring to the ritual practice of walking recitation.

S2. Procedures for the Hall of Gathered Clouds *Jūundō shiki* 重雲堂式　55

[S2:10]

堂のうちにて、數珠、もつべからず。てをたれて、いで・いりすべから
ず。

Do not carry counting beads in the hall.[11] Do not exit or enter the hall
with arms dangling.

[S2:11]

堂のうちにて、念誦・看經すべからず。檀那の、一會の看經を請せんは、
ゆるす。

Do not perform recitations or sūtra readings within the hall. When
requested by a *dānapati*, a single sūtra reading is permitted.[12]

[S2:12] {2:485}

堂のうちにて、はな、たかくかみ、つばき、たかくはくべからず。こえた
かく、わらふべからず。道業の、いまだ通達せぬことを、かなしむべし。
光陰の、ひそかに行道のいのちをうばふことを、をしむべし。おのづから
少水のうほのこころあらん。

Do not blow your nose loudly or cough up phlegm loudly in the hall.
Do not laugh loudly. We should lament the fact that the work of the way
is not yet penetrated. We should regret the fact that the years and months
are imperceptibly robbing us of the life in which to practice the way. We
feel like "fish in dwindling water."[13]

[S2:13]

一堂の衆、あやおりものを、きるべからず、かみ・ぬのなどを、きるべ
し。むかしより、みちをあきらめし人、みなかくのごとし。

The assembly in the hall should not wear patterned textiles. Wear paper or plant fiber fabrics. Since ancient times, those who have clarified
the way have all done so.

[S2:14]

さけにえいて、堂中へいるべからず。わすれてあやまらんは、禮拜・懺悔
すべし。又、さけを、とりいるべからず、にらぎのか、して、堂中へいる
べからず。

11　**counting beads** (*juzu* 數珠): I.e., the rosary used in counting recitations.

12　***dānapati*** (*danna* 檀那): I.e., a lay donor.

13　**"fish in dwindling water"** (*shōsui no uo* 少水のうほ): Japanese version of a well-
known simile for the evanescence of life, found in a verse in the *Faju jing* 法句經
(T.210.4:559a26-27); it is quoted in *Chanyuan qinggui* 禪苑清規 at ZZ.111:886a3-4:

> 是日已過、命亦隨減。如少水魚、斯有何樂。
>
> This day has passed,
> And our lives reduced accordingly.
> Like fish in dwindling water,
> What joy is there in this?

56 DŌGEN'S *SHŌBŌGENZŌ* VOLUME VII

Do not enter the hall drunk. Those who inadvertently make this mistake should make prostrations and repentance. Also, do not bring in wine, and do not enter the hall smelling of leeks and scallions.[14]

[S2:15]

いさかひせんものは、二人ともに、下寮すべし。みづからが道業をさまたぐるのみにあらず、他人をもさまたぐるゆえに。いさかはんをみて制せざらんものも、おなじくとがあるべし。

Quarrelers should both be dismissed to quarters; for they interfere not only with their own work of the way but that of others as well.[15] Those who witness quarrels without preventing them are equally at fault.

[S2:16]

堂中のおしへにかかはらざらんは、諸人、おなじこころにて擯出すべし。をかしと、をなじこころにあらんは、とが、あるべし。

Those who disregard the teaching in the hall should be expelled, with the consent of all. The one in violation and those in sympathy with it are both at fault.[16]

[S2:17] {2:486}

僧・俗を堂内にまねきて、衆を起動すべからず。きんぺんにても、賓客と、ものいひ、こえたかくすべからず。ことさら修練を自稱して、供養をむさぼることなかれ。ひさしく參學のこころざしあらんか、あながちに巡禮のこころあらんは、いるべし。そのときも、かならず堂主にふるべし。

Do not disturb the assembly by inviting monastics or laity into the hall. Do not raise your voice when speaking with a guest in the vicinity of the hall. Do not deliberately praise your own training out of desire for offerings. One who has long aspired to study and is determined to perform the circuit of prostrations should be admitted.[17] At such time, the hall chief should be informed.

---

14 **smelling of leeks and scallions** (*niragi no ka, shite* にらぎのか、して): A tentative translation, based on the reading suggested at *Shōbōgenzō monge* 正法眼藏聞解, SCZ.1:316; taking *niragi* as 韮葱 ("leeks and scallions") and *kashite* as 香して ("smelling"). Vinaya texts prohibit the consumption by monks of leeks, scallions, garlic, and other vegetables in the onion family, which were believed to stimulate libido.

15 **dismissed to quarters** (*aryō* 下寮; also read *geryō*): Or, perhaps, "dismissed from quarters," presumably, a reference to the monks' common quarters (*shuryō* 衆寮).

16 **The one in violation** (*okashi* をかし): A tentative translation, taking *okashi* as 犯し ("violation"); often taken rather to mean "amusing" — hence, "those who find it amusing."

17 **the circuit of prostrations** (*junrei* 順禮): I.e., the ritual of entry into the saṃgha hall.

S2. Procedures for the Hall of Gathered Clouds *Jūundō shiki* 重雲堂式

[S2:18]

坐禪は、僧堂のごとくにすべし。朝參暮請、いささかもおこたることなかれ。

Seated meditation should be done as in the saṃgha hall. Never neglect morning consultation or evening solicitation.[18]

[S2:19]

齋粥のとき、鉢盂の具足を地におとさん人は、叢林の式によりて、罸油あるべし。

Those who drop their *pātra* bowl utensils on the floor during meals should be charged the oil penalty, according to the rules of the monastic grove.[19]

[S2:20]

おほよそ佛祖の制誡をば、あながちにまぶるべし。叢林の清規は、ほねにも銘ずべし、こころにも銘ずべし。

In general, the rules and regulations of the buddhas and ancestors must be strictly observed. We should engrave the rules of purity of the monastic grove on our bones, engrave them on our minds.

[S2:21]

一生安穩にして、辦道無爲にあらんと、ねがふべし。

We should pray that our lives are peaceful and tranquil, and our pursuit of the way effortless.[20]

[S2:22]

以前の數條は、古佛の身心なり、うやまひ、したがふべし。

The above articles are the body and mind of the old buddhas. We should honor and follow them.

---

18 **morning consultation or evening solicitation** (*chōsan boshō* 朝參暮請): The rituals of morning and evening instruction in the master's quarters.

19 **the oil penalty** (*batsuyu* 罸油): I.e., offerings of oil before the icon in the hall; in the saṃgha hall, typically the statue of the "Sacred Monk" Mañjuśrī.

20 **our pursuit of the way effortless** (*bendō mui* 辦道無爲): An unusual phrase, not occurring elsewhere in the *Shōbōgenzō*; the expression *mui* 無爲 may have the sense either of "non-action" or of "unconditioned."

[Kōfukuji MS:]

延應元年己亥四月二十五日

Twenty-fifth day, fourth month of the junior earth year of the pig, the first year of En'ō [29 May 1239]

堂主宗信

Hall Chief Sōshin[21]

[Honzan edition:][22]

延應元年己亥四月二十五日、觀音導利興聖護國寺開闢沙門道元示
觀音導利興聖護國寺重雲堂式、終

Twenty-fifth day, fourth month of the junior earth year of the pig, the first year of En'ō [29 May 1239], presented by the Śramaṇa Dōgen, founder of the Kannon Dōri Kōshō Gokoku Monastery. Here ends the "Procedures for the Hall of Gathered Clouds of Kannon Dōri Kōshō Gokoku Monastery."

爾の時の堂主宗信、この文をうつして、のちにつたふるなり、ゆえに近代流布の本のおはりに、堂主宗信の四字をのするものあり。しかあれども、撰者にあらざること、しるべきなり。

Sōshin, the hall chief at the time, copied this document and passed it down. For this reason, the texts in circulation in recent times have at the end the four glyphs "Hall Chief Sōshin." Nevertheless, we should know that he is not the author.

21　**Hall Chief Sōshin** (*dōshū Sōshin* 堂主宗信): Thought to be the person to whom the text was addressed by Dōgen.

22　This colophon reflects that on the text published in the ninety-five-chapter *Shōbō-genzō* compiled by Handō Kōzen 版橈晃全 (1625–1693).

TREASURY OF THE TRUE DHARMA EYE

SUPPLEMENTARY CHAPTER 3

The *Lotus* Turns the *Lotus*
Hokke ten Hokke

法華轉法華

The *Lotus* Turns the *Lotus*

Hokke ten Hokke

Introduction

This work represents number 12 in the sixty-chapter *Shōbōgenzō* and appears in the ninety-five-chapter Honzan edition as number 17. The text bears an unusual set of colophons, recording that it was composed at Kōshōji, during the summer retreat of 1241, and presented to a monk named Edatsu 慧達 in celebration of his second tonsure. Nothing more is known of this monk, but it was in the spring of this year that Dōgen's community at Kōshōji accepted a number of followers of the so-called Daruma school; and, judging from the pronunciation of his name, it is possible that Edatsu was a colleague of the Daruma school converts Ejō 懷奘 and Ekan 懷鑑.

The title theme of the essay represents Dōgen's interpretation of a verse by the Sixth Ancestor, Huineng 慧能, on the recitation of the *Lotus Sūtra*: "If your mind is deluded, the *Lotus* turns you; if your mind is awakened, you turn the *Lotus*." After an introduction that treats the Zen tradition as the historical embodiment of the sūtra teachings, Dōgen translates the account of Huineng's teaching on the *Lotus* and then proceeds in the remainder of his essay to explore what it means to turn and be turned by the *Lotus*.

Unlike most of the *Shōbōgenzō* texts, the discussion here is remarkably free from reference to the literature of the Chan masters; rather, it is almost wholly given over to elaborate play with the words and lines of the sūtra itself — a character that amply displays the degree to which its author, the former Tendai monk, remained steeped in the text of this scripture. Such is the pervasiveness of the play that a close translation is often quite bewildering without reference to the Chinese source and has required therefore an inordinate amount of annotation.

正法眼藏別輯三

Treasury of the True Dharma Eye
Supplementary Chapter 3

法華轉法華

The *Lotus* Turns the *Lotus*

(六十卷本系・洞雲寺所収本)
(Sixty-chapter edition, Tōunji text)

{2:487}

興聖寺 某甲説
Taught at Kōshōji

[S3:1]

十方佛土中者、法華の唯有なり。これに十方三世諸佛・阿耨多羅三藐三菩
提衆は、轉法華あり、法華轉あり。これすなはち、本行菩薩道の不退不轉
なり、諸佛智慧甚深無量なり、難解難入の安祥三昧なり。あるひは、これ
文殊師利佛として、大海佛土なる唯佛與佛の如是相あり。あるひは、これ
釋迦牟尼佛として、唯我知是相、十方佛亦然なる出現於此あり。これすな
はち、我及十方佛、乃能知是事と欲令衆生、開示悟入せしむる一時なり。
あるひはこれ普賢なり。不可思議の功德なる法華轉を成就し、深大久遠な
る阿耨多羅三藐三菩提を閻浮提に流布せしむるに、三草二木、大小諸樹を
能生する地なり、能潤するあめなり。法華轉を所不能知に盡行成就なるの
みなり。普賢の流布いまだをはらざるも、靈山の大會きたる。普賢の往來
する、釋尊、これを白毫光相と證す。釋迦の佛會、いまだなかばにあらざ
るに、文殊の惟忖、すみやかに彌勒に授記する法華轉あり。普賢・諸佛・
文殊大會、ともに初・中・後善の法華轉を、知見波羅蜜なるべし。

   "*Within the buddha lands of the ten directions*" means the *Lotus* "*only
exists.*"[1] Here, among the buddhas of the ten directions and three times,

---

1 **The *Lotus* Turns the *Lotus*** (*Hokke ten Hokke* 法華轉法華): *Hokke* 法華 ("dharma
blossom") is a common abbreviation of *Hokke kyō* 法華經 (*Dharma Blossom Sūtra*),
itself an abbreviated reference to the *Miaofa lianhua jing* 妙法蓮華經 (*Sūtra of the Lotus
Blossom of the Wondrous Dharma*; S. *Saddharma-puṇḍarīka-sūtra*). To "turn" (*ten* 轉) a
sūtra means to read or recite the sūtra.

   "Within the buddha lands of the ten directions" means the *Lotus* "only exists"
(*jippō butsudo chū sha, hokke no yui u nari* 十方佛土中者、法華の唯有なり): This
odd sentence could also be read, "'Within the buddha lands of the ten directions' is the
'only existence' of the Lotus." As he will do throughout this chapter, Dōgen is playing
here with a line from the *Saddharma-puṇḍarīka-sūtra* (*Miaofa lianhua jing* 妙法蓮華
經, T.262.9:8a17):

62 DŌGEN'S *SHŌBŌGENZŌ* VOLUME VII

the multitude of *anuttara-samyak-saṃbodhi*, there is "turning the *Lotus*," and there is "the *Lotus* turning."[2] This is precisely not regressing from the "*original practice of the bodhisattva path*,"; it is the "*wisdom of the buddhas, extremely profound and incalculable*"; it is "the serene" "samādhi," "hard to understand and hard to enter."[3]

十方佛土中、唯有一乘法。

Within the buddha lands of the ten directions,
There only exists the dharma of the one vehicle.

2 **multitude of *anuttara-samyak-saṃbodhi*** (*anokutara sanmyaku san bodai shu* 阿耨多羅三藐三菩提衆): Subject to two possible readings: (1) "the multitude of [buddhas, who have attained] *anuttara-samyak-saṃbodhi*"; (2) "the multitude of [bodhisattvas, who aspire to] *anuttara-samyak-saṃbodhi*." If the second reading, Dōgen may have had in mind here (and in the following sentence) a line in the description of the audience for the preaching of the *Lotus Sūtra* (*Miaofa lianhua jing* 妙法蓮華經, T.262.9:2a2-3):

菩薩摩訶薩八萬人、皆於阿耨多羅三藐三菩提不退轉。

There were *bodhisattva-mahāsattvas* numbering eighty thousand, all of whom were irreversible in [their progress toward] *anuttara-samyak-saṃbodhi*.

there is "turning the *Lotus*," and there is "the *Lotus* turning" (*ten Hokke ari, Hokke ten ari* 轉法華あり、法華轉あり): Dōgen here alludes to the words of the Sixth Ancestor, Huineng 慧能, that he will quote below, section 4:

心迷法華轉、心悟轉法華。

If your mind is deluded, the *Lotus* turns you;
If your mind is awakened, you turn the *Lotus*.

3 **This is precisely not regressing from the "original practice of the bodhisattva path"** (*kore sunawachi, hongyō bosatsu dō no futai futen nari* これすなはち、本行菩薩道の不退不轉なり): The antecedent of "this" (*kore* これ) here is unclear; perhaps is the activity of "turning the *Lotus*" and "the *Lotus* turning." "The original practice of the bodhisattva path" (*hon gyō bosatsu dō* 本行菩薩道) are the words of Buddha Śākyamuni in the *Lotus Sūtra* (*Miaofa lianhua jing* 妙法蓮華經, T.262.9:4222-23):

諸善男子、我本行菩薩道所成壽命、今猶未盡復倍上數。

Good sons, the lifespan attained by my original practice of the bodhisattva path is even now still not exhausted; it is twice the above [incalculably great] number.

The expression *futai futen* 不退不轉 ("not regressing") is a variant of the term *futaiten* 不退轉 (S. *avaivartika*, etc.), used in reference to the bodhisattva's attainment of "irreversibility" on the path to buddhahood.

"wisdom of the buddhas, extremely profound and incalculable" (*shobutsu chie jinjin muryō* 諸佛智慧甚深無量): This and the following clause are playing with the opening words of Chapter 2 of the *Lotus Sūtra* (*Miaofa lianhua jing* 妙法蓮華經, T.262.9:5bb25-26):

爾時世尊從三昧安詳而起。告舍利弗、諸佛智慧甚深無量。其智慧門難解難入。

At this time, the World-Honored One arose serenely from his samādhi and addressed Śāriputra, "The wisdom of the buddhas is extremely profound and incalculable; the gates of their wisdom are hard to understand and hard to enter."

S3. The *Lotus* Turns the *Lotus* *Hokke ten Hokke* 法華轉法華   63

As Buddha Mañjuśrī, it has "such marks" of "*only buddhas with buddhas*" that are the buddha land of the great ocean; or, as Buddha Śākyamuni, it has the *appearing in this* that is "*I alone know its marks, as do the buddhas of the ten directions.*"[4] This is precisely the "one time" in which he "*wishes to cause living beings to open, show, awaken, and enter*" [the knowledge of] "*I and the buddhas of the ten directions can know these matters.*"[5]

---

4 **The Buddha Mañjuśrī** (*Monjushiri butsu* 文殊師利佛): An unusual designation, not occurring elsewhere in the *Shōbōgenzō*, for the Bodhisattva Mañjuśrī; given the reference here to the (equally unusual) "buddha land of the great ocean" (*daikai butsudo* 大海佛土), likely an allusion to a passage in Chapter 12 of the *Lotus Sūtra* (*Miaofa lianhua jing* 妙法蓮華經, T.262.9:35a22-24):

> 爾時文殊師利、坐千葉蓮華大如車輪、俱來菩薩亦坐寶蓮華、從於大海娑竭羅龍宮自然踊出。
>
> At that time, Mañjuśrī, seated on a thousand-petaled lotus as large as a carriage wheel, accompanied by bodhisattvas also seated on jeweled lotuses, spontaneously emerged from the dragon palace of Sāgara in the great ocean.

"such marks" of "only buddhas with buddhas" (*yui butsu yo butsu no nyoze sō* 唯佛與佛の如是相): The awkward English seeks to convey Dōgen's play with a passage in the *Lotus Sūtra*; see Supplementary Notes, s.v. "Only buddhas with buddhas can exhaustively investigate the real marks of the dharmas."

the appearing in this that is "I alone know its marks, as do the buddhas of the ten directions" (*yui ga chi ze sō, jippō butsu yaku nen naru shutsugen o shi* 唯我知是相、十方佛亦然なる出現於此): The curious Chinese phrase "appearing in this" (*shutsugen o shi* 出現於此), which will recur below, is probably to be understood as "appearing in this world." Further play with two other passages of the *Lotus Sūtra*:

1) *Miaofa lianhua jing* 妙法蓮華經, T.262.9:7a21-22:

> 諸佛世尊唯以一大事因緣故出現於世。
>
> The buddhas, the world-honored ones, appear in the world for the reason of one great matter alone.

2) *Miaofa lianhua jing* 妙法蓮華經, T.262.9:6a18-20:

> 又告舍利弗、無漏不思議、甚深微妙法、我今已具得、唯我知是相、十方佛亦然。
>
> Again, [the Buddha] addressed Śāriputra,
> "The undefiled, inconceivable,
> Extremely profound and subtle dharma
> That I have attained —
> I alone know its marks,
> As do the buddhas of the ten directions."

5 **"one time"** (*ichiji* 一時): Likely a reference to the occasion of the preaching of the *Lotus Sūtra*, from its opening line (*Miaofa lianhua jing* 妙法蓮華經, T.262.9:1c19):

> 如是我聞、一時佛住王舍城耆闍崛山中。
>
> Thus have I heard, at one time the Buddha was staying at Rājagṛha, on Mount Gṛdhrakūṭa.

"wishes to cause living beings to open, show, awaken, and enter" (*yoku ryō shujō, kai ji go nyū seshimuru* 欲令衆生、開示悟入せしむる): Alluding to the "one great matter"

64 DŌGEN'S *SHŌBŌGENZŌ* VOLUME VII

Or it is Samantabhadra.[6] His achieving the turning of the *Lotus* that is his "inconceivable merit" and his "disseminating throughout Jambudvīpa" the "*anuttara-samyak-saṃbodhi*" that is "profound" and "long ago," are the "ground" that "grows" and the "rain" that "moistens" the three herbs and the two trees, the "trees large and small."[7] "While incapable

---

for which buddhas appear in the world; see Supplementary Notes, s.v. "Buddhas, the world-honored ones, appear in the world for the reason of one great matter alone."

"I and the buddhas of the ten directions can know these matters" (*ga gyū jippō butsu, nai nō chi ze ji* 我及十方佛、乃能知是事): Quoting the *Lotus Sūtra* at *Miaofa lianhua jing* 妙法蓮華經, T.262.9:5c21-24:

> 於無量億劫、行此諸道已。道場得成果、我已悉知見。如是大果報、種種性相義。我及十方佛、乃能知是事。

> For incalculable *koṭis* of kalpas,
> Having practiced these ways.
> At the place of awakening, attaining the fruit,
> I knew everything completely.
> Such great effects and recompense,
> The manifold meanings of natures and marks —
> I and the buddhas of the ten directions
> Can know these matters.

6 **Samantabhadra** (*Fugen* 普賢): The bodhisattva who vows (in Chapter 28) to protect the *Lotus Sūtra* (*Miaofa lianhua jing* 妙法蓮華經, T.262.9:61c14-20):

> 世尊。我今以神通力故守護是經。於如來滅後。閻浮提內廣令流布使不斷絕。爾時釋迦牟尼佛讚言。善哉善哉。普賢。汝能護助是經。令多所衆生安樂利益。汝已成就不可思議功德深大慈悲。從久遠來發阿耨多羅三藐三菩提意。而能作是神通之願守護是經。

> "World-Honored One, now, with my spiritual powers, I shall protect this sūtra. After the extinction of the Tathāgata, I shall disseminate it widely throughout Jambudvīpa and not let it disappear."
> At that time, Buddha Śākyamuni praised him, saying, "Excellent. Excellent. Samantabhadra, in protecting this sūtra, you will cause joy and benefit to many living beings. You have achieved inconceivable merit and profound great compassion. Long ago, you brought forth the aspiration for *anuttara-samyak-saṃbodhi* and made this spiritual vow to protect this sūtra."

7 **three herbs and the two trees, the "trees large and small"** (*sansō niboku, daishō shoju* 三草二木、大小諸樹): Allusion to a passage in Chapter 5 of the *Lotus Sūtra* on the one teaching that nurtures the three vehicles of *śrāvaka*, *pratyeka-buddha*, and bodhisattva, both the Great and Small Vehicles (*Miaofa lianhua jing* 妙法蓮華經, T.262.9:19a27-b6):

> 迦葉、譬如三千大千世界、山川谿谷土地所生卉木叢林、及諸藥草種類若干名色各異。密雲彌布遍覆三千大千世界。一時等澍其澤普洽卉木叢林及諸藥草。小根小莖小枝小葉、中根中莖中枝中葉、大根大莖大枝大葉、諸樹大小、隨上中下各有所受。一雲所雨、稱其種性而得生長。華菓敷實。雖一地所生一雨所潤。而諸草木各有差別。迦葉當知。

> Kāśyapa, it is like the grasses, trees, thickets, and forests, as well as the various types of medicinal plants of diverse names and colors, that grow in the mountains, rivers, valleys, and lands of the threefold great chiliocosm. Dense clouds completely cover the threefold great chiliocosm, and at one time it rains everywhere, moistening

S3. The *Lotus* Turns the *Lotus*   *Hokke ten Hokke* 法華轉法華   65

of being known," they are just his "achievement" of the "exhaustive practice" of the turning of the *Lotus*.[8] Though Samantabhadra's dissemination had not yet ended, he came to the great assembly on Vulture Peak.[9] Samantabhadra's arrival was acknowledged by Śākyamuni, the World-Honored One, with light from his white tuft of hair.[10]

equally the grasses, trees, thickets, and forests, as well as the medicinal plants. Those with small roots, small stems, small branches, and small leaves; those with medium roots, medium stems, medium branches, and medium leaves; those with large roots, large stems, large branches, and large leaves — the trees great and small receive it according to whether they are tall, medium, or low. From the rain of a single cloud, they grow in keeping with the nature of their seeds, and their blossoms open and fruit ripens. Although grown on a single ground and moistened by a single rain, the grasses and trees are different.

See Supplementary Notes, s.v. "Dharma rain," "Roots, stalks, branches, and leaves, flowers and fruit, lustrous and colored," and "Three vehicles."

8 **"While incapable of being known"** (*sho funō chi ni* 所不能知に): A phrase seeming to function as an adverb modifying "achievement of the exhaustive practice" (*jingyō jōju* 盡行成就). Dōgen is again alluding here to the opening lines of Chapter 2 of the *Lotus Sūtra* (*Miaofa lianhua jing* 妙法蓮華經, T.262.9:5b25-c1):

爾時世尊從三昧安7詳而起。告舍利弗。諸佛智慧甚深無量。其智慧門難解難入。一切聲聞辟支佛所不能知。所以者何。佛曾親近百千萬億無數諸佛。盡行諸佛無量道法。勇猛精進名稱普聞。成就甚深未曾有法。隨宜所説意趣難解。

At this time, the World-Honored One arose serenely from his samādhi and addressed Śāriputra, "The wisdom of the buddhas is extremely profound and incalculable; the gates of their wisdom are hard to understand and hard to enter. It is not something capable of being known by any *śrāvaka* or *pratyeka-buddha*. Why is this? The buddhas have been close to innumerable hundreds of thousands of myriads of *koṭis* of buddhas; they have exhaustively practiced incalculable dharmas of the way of the buddhas, with courage and vigor, for which they are universally renowned. They have achieved the extremely profound, unprecedented dharma, and their intentions in according their explanations of it to what is appropriate are hard to understand."

9 **he came to the great assembly on Vulture Peak** (*Ryōzen no daie kitaru* 靈山の大會きたる): Reference to the opening of Chapter 28 of the *Lotus Sūtra*, in which the Bodhisattva Samantabhadra arrives at Vulture Peak (*Ryōzen* 靈山), where the sūtra is being preached (*Miaofa lianhua jing* 妙法蓮華經, T.262.9:61a11-13):

到娑婆世界耆闍崛山中、頭面禮釋迦牟尼佛、右繞七匝白佛言。

Arriving at Mount Gṛdhrakūṭa in the Sahā world, he bowed to Buddha Śākyamuni, circled him seven times to the right, and addressed the Buddha, saying . . . .

10 **light from his white tuft of hair** (*byakugō kōmyō* 白毫光明): The "white tuft" (*byakugō* 白毫) refers to the circle of hair between the eyebrows (S. *ūrṇā*), one of the thirty-two marks of a great being. The English here follows Kawamura, where other texts read *byakugō kōsō* 白毫光相 ("radiant mark of white tuft"[?]), an unusual expression, perhaps corrupted from the common *byakugōsō kō* 白毫相光 ("light from his white tuft mark"). In either case, Dōgen may be recalling here the opening lines of Chapter 24 of the *Lotus Sūtra* (*Miaofa lianhua jing* 妙法蓮華經, T.262.9:55a23-24):

爾時釋迦牟尼佛、放大人相肉髻光明、及放眉間白毫相光、遍照東方百八萬億那由他恆河沙等諸佛世界 . . . . 釋迦牟尼佛白毫光明遍照其國。

At that time, Buddha Śākyamuni, emitting light from his topknot, the mark of a great

66 DŌGEN'S *SHŌBŌGENZŌ* VOLUME VII

While Śākyamuni's buddha assembly was not yet half over, Mañjuśrī "presumes" that there will be a turning of the *Lotus* that quickly confers a prediction on Maitreya.[11] Samantabhadra, the buddhas, Mañjuśrī, and the great assembly — all are the *pāramitā* of knowledge and insight regarding the turning of the *Lotus*, good in the beginning, middle, and end.[12]

[S3:2] {2:488}

このゆえに、唯以一乗、爲一大事として出現せるなり。この出現、すなはち一大事なるがゆえに、唯佛與佛、乃能究盡、諸法實相とあるなり。その法、かならず一佛乗にして、唯佛さだめて唯佛に究盡せしむるなり。諸佛・七佛、おのおの佛佛に究盡せしめ、釋迦牟尼佛に成就せしむるなり。

Therefore, they have "appeared" to represent the "*one great matter*" "*only with the one vehicle.*"[13] Since this "appearance" is itself "the one

---

being, and light from the white tuft mark between his eyebrows, illuminated all the buddha worlds in the eastern quarter equal to the sands of a hundred eight myriads of *koṭis* of *nayutas* of Ganges Rivers. . . . The light from the white tuft of hair of Buddha Śākyamuni illuminated that entire realm.

11 **While Śākyamuni's buddha assembly was not yet half over** (*Shaka no butsue, imada nakaba ni arazaru ni* 釋迦の佛會、いまだなかばにあらざるに): Mañjuśrī's prediction of Maitreya's buddhahood occurs in the very first chapter of the *Lotus Sūtra* (*Miaofa lianhua jing* 妙法蓮華經, T.262.9:5b12):

其後當作佛、號名曰彌勒。

Thereafter, he will become a buddha,
With the name Maitreya.

Mañjuśrī "presumes" (*Monju no ison* 文殊の惟忖): Likely recalling Mañjuśrī's presumption, in Chapter 1, that Buddha Śākyamuni was about to preach the *Lotus Sūtra*; see Supplementary Notes, s.v. "Dharma rain."

12 *pāramitā* **of knowledge and insight regarding the turning of the *Lotus*** (*hokke ten o chiken haramitsu* 法華轉を知見波羅蜜): An odd turn of phrase, likely suggested by a sentence in Chapter 2 of the *Lotus Sūtra* (*Miaofa lianhua jing* 妙法蓮華經, T.262.9:5c3-4):

如來方便知見波羅蜜、皆已具足。

The tathāgatas are fully endowed with the *pāramitās* of skillful means, and knowledge and insight.

good in the beginning, middle, and end (*sho chū go zen* 初・中・後善): Variation on a common description of the buddha dharma, found in the *Lotus Sūtra* and many other scriptures; see Supplementary Notes, s.v. "Good in the beginning, middle, and end."

13 **they have "appeared" to represent the "one great matter"** (*i ichidaiji toshite shutsugen seru nari* 爲一大事として出現せるなり): The translation takes the unexpressed grammatical subject to be the members of the Lotus assembly mentioned at the end of section 1, but it might also be understood as Buddha Śākyamuni (or buddhas more generally). This clause reflects the sūtra at *Miaofa lianhua jing* 妙法蓮華經, T.262.9:7a21-22:

諸佛世尊唯以一大事因緣故出現於世。

S3. The *Lotus* Turns the *Lotus* *Hokke ten Hokke* 法華轉法華 67

great matter," it is said, "*only buddhas with buddhas can exhaustively investigate the real marks of the dharmas.*"[14] Those dharmas, being invariably "the one buddha vehicle," "only buddhas" are definitely "exhaustively investigated" by "only buddhas." The buddhas, the seven buddhas, are "exhaustively investigated" by buddha after buddha and achieved in Buddha Śākyamuni.

[S3:3]

西天竺・東震旦にいたる、十方佛土中なり。三十三祖大鑑禪師にいたるも、すなはち究盡にてある唯佛一乘法なり。唯以のさだめて一大事なる、一佛乘なり。いま出現於世なり、出現於此なり。青原の佛風、いまにつたはれ、南嶽の法門、よに開演する、みな如來如實知見なり。まことに、唯佛與佛の究盡なり、嫡佛、佛嫡の開示悟入なり、と法華轉すべし。これを妙法蓮華經ともなづく、教菩薩法なり。これを諸法となづけきたれるゆえに、法華を國土として、靈山も、虚空もあり、大海もあり、大地もあり。これはすなはち實相なり、如是なり、法住法位なり、一大事因縁なり。佛之知見なり、世相常住なり、如實なり、如來壽量なり、甚深無量なり、諸行無常なり。法華三昧なり、釋迦牟尼佛なり、轉法華なり、法華轉なり、正法眼藏涅槃妙心なり、現身度生なり。授記作佛なる保任あり、住持あり。

From Sindhu in the West to Cīnasthāna in the East is "within the buddha lands of the ten directions"; down to the Thirty-third Ancestor, Chan Master Dajian, is also the *dharma of the one vehicle of "only buddhas,"* "exhaustively investigated."[15] "Only with" is definitely "the one buddha vehicle" that is "the one great matter."[16] Now, it is "*appearing in the*

The buddhas, the world-honored ones, appear in the world for the reason of one great matter alone.

"only with the one vehicle" (*yui i ichijō* 唯以一乘): From the concluding verse of Chapter 2 of the *Lotus Sūtra* (*Miaofa lianhua jing* 妙法蓮華經, T.262.9:10b5-6, here and below, substituting *yui* 唯 for the Sūtra's *tan* 但):

普告諸大衆、但以一乘道、教化諸菩薩、無聲聞弟子。

I widely proclaim to the great assemblies,
Only with the path of the one vehicle,
I instruct the bodhisattvas;
I have no *śrāvaka* disciples.

14 **"only buddhas with buddhas can exhaustively investigate the real marks of the dharmas"** (*yui butsu yo butsu, nai nō gūjin, shohō jissō* 唯佛與佛、乃能究盡、諸法實相): See above, Note 4.

15 **down to the Thirty-third Ancestor, Chan Master Dajian** (*sanjūsan so Daikan zenji ni itaru* 三十三祖大鑑禪師にいたる): I.e., the lineage of thirty-three ancestors, from the First Ancestor, Mahākāśyapa, down to the famous Sixth Ancestor, Huineng 慧能. See Supplementary Notes, s.v. "Buddhas and ancestors." "Chan Master Dajian" 大鑑禪師 is Huineng's posthumous honorific title.

16 **"Only with"** (*yui i* 唯以): Dōgen here creates a novel nominative, borrowed presumably from the phrase "only with the one vehicle" (*yui i ichijō* 唯以一乘), quoted in the previous section.

68 DŌGEN'S *SHŌBŌGENZŌ* VOLUME VII

world"; it is *appearing in this*.[17] The buddha style of Qingyuan transmitted now, the dharma gate of Nanyue proclaimed in the world — they are both "*the Tathāgata views as they really are*."[18] Truly, the *Lotus* must turn as "*only buddhas with buddhas*" are "*exhaustively investigating*," and successor buddhas and buddha successors are "*opening, showing, awakening, and entering*."[19] This is also called the "*Sūtra of the Lotus Blossom of the Wondrous Dharma*"; it is the "*dharma taught to bodhisattvas*."[20] Because this has been called "the dharmas," taking the *Lotus* as their land, there are Vulture Peak and empty space; there is the great ocean; there is the whole earth.[21]

---

17 **"appearing in the world"** (*shutsugen o se* 出現於世); **appearing in this** (*shutsugen o shi* 出現於此): See above, Note 4.

18   **buddha style of Qingyuan** (*Seigen no butsufū* 青原の佛風); **dharma gate of Nanyue** *(Nangaku no hōmon* 南嶽の法門): I.e., respectively, the Caodong 曹洞 tradition descended from Qingyuan Xingsi 青原行思 (d. 740), and the Linji 臨濟 tradition from Nanyue Huairang 南嶽懷讓 (677–744).

"the Tathāgata views as they really are" (*nyorai nyojitsu chiken* 如來如實知見): From *Miaofa lianhua jing* 妙法蓮華經, T.262.9:42c13:

如來如實知見三界之相。

The Tathāgata views the marks of the three realms as they really are.

19   **successor buddhas and buddha successors** (*chakubutsu, butsuchaku* 嫡佛、佛嫡): I.e., the members of the lineage of ancestors.

20   **This is also called the "*Sūtra of the Lotus Blossom of the Wondrous Dharma*";** **it is the "dharma taught to bodhisattvas"** (*kore o Myōhō renge kyō to mo nazuku, kyō bosatsu hō nari* これを妙法蓮華經ともなづく、教菩薩法なり): Recalling Mañjuśrī's conjecture that the Buddha was about to teach the *Lotus Sūtra* (*Miaofa lianhua jing* 妙法蓮華經, T.262.9:4b17-18):

是故惟忖、今日如來當説大乘經、名妙法蓮華、教菩薩法、佛所護念。

Therefore, I conjecture that today the Tathāgata will preach a sūtra of the Great Vehicle, called the *Lotus Blossom of the Wondrous Dharma*, a dharma taught to bodhisattvas, which the buddhas bear in mind.

21 **Because this has been called "the dharmas"** (*kore o shohō to nazukekitareru yue ni* これを諸法となづけきたれるゆえに): Likely a reference to the famous passage in which Śākyamuni explains the difficulty of his teaching (*Miaofa lianhua jing* 妙法蓮華經, T.262.9:7a17-21):

舍利弗。諸佛隨宜説法意趣難解。所以者何。我以無數方便種種因緣譬喩言辭演説諸法。是法非思量分別之所能解。唯有諸佛乃能知之。

Śāriputra, the intention of the buddhas' appropriate preaching of the dharma is hard to understand. Why? I expound the dharmas by innumerable expedients and various means, parables, and expressions. This dharma is not something that can be understood by reason and discrimination; only the buddhas can know it.

taking the *Lotus* as their land, there are Vulture Peak and empty space; there is the great ocean; there is the whole earth (*hokke o kokudo toshite, Ryōzen mo, kokū mo ari, daikai mo ari, daichi mo ari* 法華を國土として、靈山も、虚空もあり、大海もあり、大地もあり): Given the context, probably not simply that the sūtra content covers these

S3. The *Lotus* Turns the *Lotus* *Hokke ten Hokke* 法華轉法華 69

This is the "real marks"; it is "such"; it is the "*dharmas abide in their dharma positions*"; it is the "*reason of one great matter.*"[22] It is the "*knowledge and insight of a buddha*"; it is "*the marks of the world ever abiding*"; it is "*as they really are*"; it is the "*lifespan of the Tathāgata*"; it is "*extremely profound and incalculable.*"[23] It is "compounded things are impermanent"; it is the "*Lotus* samādhi"; it is Buddha Śākyamuni; it is "turning the *Lotus*"; it is "the *Lotus* turning."[24] It is the "*treasury of the true dharma eye, the wondrous mind of nirvāṇa,*" it is "*manifesting a body to deliver living beings.*"[25]

---

places but that its preaching occurs everywhere. Dōgen seems here to have moved the meaning of "the dharmas" (*shohō* 諸法) taught by the buddhas from the "teachings" to all "phenomena."

22 **This is the "real marks"** (*kore wa sunawachi jissō nari* これはすなはち實相なり): See above, Note 4. The antecedent of "this" (*kore* これ) throughout this passage is uncertain; perhaps most likely, the teachings of the ancestral masters of Zen, also called the *Lotus Sūtra*.

"such" (*nyoze* 如是): See above, Note 4.

"dharmas abide in their dharma positions" (*hō jū hōi* 法住法位): The English here renders a traditional reading of a line in the *Lotus Sūtra* much cited by Dōgen. See Supplementary Notes, s.v. "Dharmas abide in their dharma positions."

"reason of one great matter" (*ichi daiji innen* 一大事因縁): See above, Note 4.

23 **"knowledge and insight of a buddha"** (*butsu shi chiken* 佛之知見): See above, Note 5,

"the marks of the world ever abiding" (*sesō jōjū* 世相常住): See above, Note 22.

"as they really are" (*nyo jitsu* 如實): See above, Note 18.

"lifespan of the Tathāgata" (*nyorai juryō* 如來壽量): Title of Chapter 16 of the *Lotus Sūtra* (*Miaofa lianhua jing* 妙法蓮華經, T.262.9:42a29), in which Śākyamuni reveals the extraordinary length of his lifespan.

"extremely profound and incalculable" (*jinjin muryō* 甚深無量): See above, Note 8.

24 **"compounded things are impermanent"** (*shogyō mujō* 諸行無常): An extremely common phrase, found throughout the Buddhist literature (though not in the *Lotus Sūtra*).

"*Lotus* samādhi" (*hokke zanmai* 法華三昧): A concentration mentioned in Chapter 24 of the *Lotus Sūtra* (*Miaofa lianhua jing* 妙法蓮華經, T.262.9:55a27, 56c1), the name of which was adopted for a meditation ritual in the Tiantai school.

25 **"treasury of the true dharma eye, the wondrous mind of nirvāṇa"** (*shōbōgenzō nehan myōshin* 正法眼藏涅槃妙心): Reference to the words of Buddha Śākyamuni describing what he was transmitting on Vulture Peak to the First Ancestor, Mahākāśyapa; the essence of the Buddhist teaching, handed down through the lineage of the buddhas and ancestors. See Supplementary Notes, s.v. "Treasury of the true dharma eye."

"manifesting a body to deliver living beings" (*gen shin do shō* 現身度生): Likely an allusion to the thirty-three manifestations of the Bodhisattva Avalokiteśvara taught in Chapter 25 of the *Lotus Sūtra*, the description of which (at *Miaofa lianhua jing* 妙法蓮華經, T.262.9:57a23ff) begins,

70 DŌGEN'S *SHŌBŌGENZŌ* VOLUME VII

It maintains, it sustains, the "*bestowal of the prediction of becoming a buddha.*"[26]

* * * * *

[S3:4] {2:489}

大唐國廣南東路、韶州曹溪山寳林寺大鑑禪師の會に、法達といふ僧、まゐれりき。みづから稱す、われ法華經を讀誦することすでに三千部なり。祖いはく、たとひ萬部におよぶとも、經をえざらんは、とがをしるにもおよばざらん。法達いはく、學人は愚鈍なり、從來、ただ文字にまかせて誦念す、いかでか宗趣をあきらめん。祖いはく、なんぢこころみに一遍を誦すべし、われ、なんぢがために解説せん。法達、すなはち誦經す。方便品にいたりて、祖いはく、とどまるべし。この經は、もと因縁出世を宗旨とせり、たとひおほくの譬喩をとくも、これよりこゆることなし。何者因縁といふに、唯一大事なり。唯一大事は、即佛知見なり、開示悟入なり。おのづから、これ佛之知見なり、已具知見、彼既是佛なり。なんぢいままさに信すべし、佛知見者、只汝自心なり。かさねてしめす偈にいはく、心迷法華轉、心悟轉法華、誦久不明己、與義作讐家、無念念即正、有念念成邪、有無倶不計、長御白牛車。

To the community of Chan Master Dajian, of the Baolin Monastery, Mount Caoxi, in Shaozhou, Guangnan East Circuit, in the Land of the Great Tang, there came a monk named Fada.[27] He said of himself, "I've recited the *Lotus Sūtra* three thousand times already."

若有國土衆生應以佛身得度者、觀世音菩薩即現佛身而爲説法。

If there are in the land living beings who ought to attain deliverance by a buddha body, the Bodhisattva Avalokiteśvara manifests a buddha body and preaches the dharma to them.

See Supplementary Notes, s.v. "Manifesting a body to preach the dharma."

26 **It maintains, it sustains, the "bestowal of the prediction of becoming a buddha"** (*juki sabutsu naru hōnin ari, jūji ari* 授記作佛なる保任あり、住持あり): A loose rendering of a sentence likely meaning something like, "[The tradition of the buddhas and ancestors] upholds the *Lotus Sūtra*'s promise of buddhahood for all." "Bestowal of the prediction of becoming a buddha" (*juki sabutsu* 授記作佛) refers to Śākyamuni's predictions of buddhahood to his disciples; the phrase occurs at the opening of Chapter 3, in the words of Śāriputra (*Miaofa lianhua jing* 妙法蓮華經, T.262.9:10c2-4), upon learning that he can hope to become a buddha:

我昔從佛聞如是法、見諸菩薩授記作佛、而我等不豫斯事。

In the past, I heard such a dharma from the Buddha and saw the bestowal of predictions of becoming a buddha on the bodhisattvas, but we [disciples] did not participate in this matter.

27 **Chan Master Dajian** (*Daikan zenji* 大鑑禪師): I.e., the Sixth Ancestor, Caoxi Huineng 曹溪慧能. The following account in Japanese is based loosely on the biography of Huineng's follower Fada 法達 (dates unknown) in the *Jingde chuandeng lu* 景德傳燈錄 (T.2076.51:237c21ff). Huineng's Baolin Monastery 寳林寺 at Mt. Caoxi 曹溪山 was located in present-day Guangdong Province.

S3. The *Lotus* Turns the *Lotus*   *Hokke ten Hokke*   法華轉法華   71

The Ancestor said, "Even if you reach ten thousand times, without grasping the sūtra, you won't even know your errors."

Fada said, "Your student is stupid and dull. Up till now, I've simply recited according to the words. How can I clarify the meaning?"

The Ancestor said, "Try reciting it once, and I'll explain it to you."

Fada thereupon recited it. When he had reached the "Skill in Means" Chapter, the Ancestor said:

You may stop. Fundamentally, this sūtra takes as its essential point the *reason for [the Tathāgata's] appearing in the world. Although it gives many parables, they don't go beyond this. What is that reason? It's only the one great matter. "Only the one great matter" is the knowledge and insight of a buddha, is opening, showing, awakening, and entering. This itself is the knowledge and insight of a buddha. One who is endowed with this knowledge and insight is already a buddha.* Now you should believe that the *knowledge and insight of a buddha is just your own mind.* In a gāthā repeating this, he said,

> *If your mind is deluded, the Lotus turns you;*
> *If your mind is awakened, you turn the Lotus.*
> *Long recitation without clarifying oneself,*
> *Turns the meaning into your foe.*
> *The thinking of no-thought is correct;*
> *The thinking with thoughts yields the false.*[28]
> *When not concerned with either one,*
> *We drive forever the white ox cart.*[29]

[S3:5]

法達、すなはち偈をききて、かさねて祖にまうす、經にいはく、諸大聲聞、乃至菩薩、みな盡思度量するに、佛智、はかる事あたはず。いま、凡夫をしてただし、自心をさとらしめんを、すなはち佛之知見となづけん。上根にあらずよりは、疑謗をまぬかれがたし。又、經に三車をとくに、大牛車と白牛車と、いかなる區別かあらん。ねがはくは和尚、ふたたび宣説をたれんことを。祖のいはく、經意はあきらかなり、なんぢおのづから迷背す。諸三乘人の、佛智をはかることあたはざる患は、度量にあるなり。

28　**The thinking of no-thought is correct; the thinking with thoughts yields the false** (*munen nen soku shō, unen nen jō ja* 無念念即正、有念念成邪): Following the traditional reading of these lines (which might otherwise be read, "having no thought after thought is correct; having thought after thought yields the false"). "No-thought" (munen 無念) is a famous doctrine of the Sixth Ancestor.

29　**white ox cart** (*byakugo sha* 白牛車): I.e., the one, buddha vehicle; from the famous parable of the burning house in Chapter 3 of the *Lotus Sūtra*, in which a wealthy man lures his children from his burning house with the prospect of goat, deer, and ox carts outside, representing in the parable the three Buddhist vehicles of *śrāvaka*, *pratyeka-buddha*, and buddha, respectively; once they are safely outside, he gives them great carts pulled by white oxen. See Supplementary Notes, s.v. "Burning house."

たとひかれら盡思共推すとも、うたた懸遠ならん。佛は、本爲凡夫説のみなり、不爲佛説なり。この理を信ずること不肯にして退席すとも、ことにしらず、白牛車に坐しながら、さらに門外にして三車をもとむることを。經文、あきらかになんぢにむかひていふ、無二亦無三と。なんぢいかがさとらざる。三車はこれ假なり、昔時なるがゆえに。一乘はこれ實なり、今時なるがゆえに。ただ、なんぢをして假をば去とし、實をば歸とせしむ。歸實するには、實も名もあらず。しるべし、所有は、みな珍寶なり、ことごとくなんぢに屬す。由汝受用なり。さらに、父想ならず、また子想ならず、また用想なしといへども、これは法華經となづくるなり。劫より劫にいたり、晝より夜にいたるに、手不釋卷なれども、誦念にあらざるときなきなり。

Fada, after hearing the gāthā, again asked the Ancestor,

In the sūtra, it is said that *the great śrāvakas and bodhisattvas*, all *exhausting their thinking and gauging*, cannot measure the buddha's wisdom.[30] Now, if making a common person simply understand his or her own mind is to be called the "*knowledge and insight of a buddha*," one who is not of superior faculties could hardly avoid doubting and disparaging it. Also, in the sūtra, in its explanation of the three vehicles, what is the distinction between the great ox cart and the white ox cart?[31] Please, Reverend, could you explain it again.

The Ancestor said,

The meaning of the sūtra is clear; you yourself are rejecting it in your delusion. The trouble people of the three vehicles have in fathoming the buddha's wisdom lies in their reckoning. Even though they exhaust their thoughts thinking together, they get further away from it. The Buddha *fundamentally teaches only for common people; he doesn't teach for buddhas*. Even those who, lacking consent to faith in this principle, leave their seats, don't realize that they are searching for

---

30 **In the sūtra, it is said** (*kyō ni iwaku* 經にいはく): What follows seems to reflect a verse in Chapter 2 (*Miaofa lianhua jing* 妙法蓮華經, T.262.9:6a2-3):

假使滿世間、皆如舍利弗、盡思共度量、不能測佛智。

Even if the entire world
Were filled with such as Śāriputra,
Who exhausted their thoughts gauging together,
They could not fathom the wisdom of the buddhas.

31 **the great ox cart and the white ox cart** (*dai go sha to byakugo sha to* 大牛車と白牛車と): Since these terms do not in fact occur in the parable of the burning house, the exact implication of Fada's question is uncertain. Presumably, it concerns the famous issue in *Lotus Sūtra* exegesis over whether the ox cart initially offered to the children by the father as a lure is the same as the great carts pulled by white oxen that are actually granted to them once they emerge from the house. Some interpreters made a distinction, favored here by Huineng, between the former, representing the traditional bodhisattva vehicle, and the latter, standing for a "higher" buddha vehicle. See Supplementary Notes, s.v. "Burning house."

S3. The *Lotus* Turns the *Lotus*   *Hokke ten Hokke*   法華轉法華   73

the three carts outside the gate while seated in the white ox cart.[32] The text of the sūtra clearly says to you, *"There are not two nor are there three."*[33] How can you not understand? The three carts are provisional, for they are of the past; the one vehicle is real, for it is of the present.[34] [The sūtra] leads you to leave the provisional and return to the real. After one returns to the real, the real has no name. You should realize that everything you have is a precious treasure, all of it belonging to you. It is up to you to make use of it. Beyond this, it is not any ideas of the father, not any ideas of the children, and, though lacking the use of any ideas, this is called the *"Lotus Sūtra."*[35] From kalpa to kalpa, from day to night, while your hand never lets go of the scrolls, there is no time you are not reciting it.

---

32   **leave their seats** (*taiseki* 退席): Allusion to the five thousand saṃgha members who, out of pride in their own understanding, withdrew from the assembly when the Buddha began to preach the new revelation of the *Lotus Sūtra*. (See *Miaofa lianhua jing* 妙法蓮華經, T.262.9:7a5-11.)

they are searching for the three carts outside the gate (*monge ni shite sansha o moto-muru* 門外にして三車をもとむる): I.e., [though already on the buddha vehicle] they are still like the children who came out of the house in search of the three carts offered by their father.

33   **"There are not two nor are there three"** (*mu ni yaku mu san* 無二亦無三): From the verse at *Miaofa lianhua jing* 妙法蓮華經, T.262.9:8a17-18:

十方佛土中、唯有一乘法。無二亦無三、除佛方便説。

In the buddha lands of the ten directions,
There is only the dharma of the one vehicle.
There are not two nor are there three,
Except in the expedient talk of the buddhas.

34   **they are of the past** (*sekiji naru* 昔時なる): Presumably referring to the fact that, prior to his revelation of the one vehicle, the Buddha had been preaching the "provision-al" (*ke* 假) doctrine that there were three separate vehicles.

35 **Beyond this, it is not any ideas of the father, not any ideas of the children, and, though lacking the use of any ideas** (*sara ni, fu sō narazu, mata shi sō narazu, mata yō sō nashi to iedomo* さらに、父想ならず、また子想ならず、また用想なしといへども): A tentative translation of an odd sentence; especially problematic is the phrase *yō sō nashi* (rendered here "lacking the use of any ideas"), by which Dōgen has translated the Chinese *wuyong xiang* 無用想 ("useless ideas"). Indeed, Dōgen's Japanese in this and the following sentence is more obscure than the Chinese original (at *Jingde chuandeng lu* 景德傳燈錄, T.2076.51:238b11-13):

更不作父想。亦不作子想。亦無用想。是名持法華經。從劫至劫手不釋卷。從晝至夜無不念時也。

Not having further ideas about the father, or ideas about the children, or any useless ideas — this is called keeping the *Lotus Sūtra*. From kalpa to kalpa, your hand never lets go of the scrolls; from day to night, there is no time you are not reciting it.

74 DŌGEN'S *SHŌBŌGENZŌ* VOLUME VII

[S3:6] {2:490}

法達、すでに啓發をかうぶりて、踊躍歡喜して、偈、呈し讚していはく、
經誦三千部、曹溪一句亡、未明出世旨、寧歇累生狂、羊・鹿・牛權設、
初・中・後善揚、誰知火宅内、元是法中王。

> Fada, having received this revelation and dancing for joy, presented a gāthā in praise, saying,[36]

>> *The sūtra recited three thousand times —*
>> *With Caoxi's one line, all forgotten.*
>> *Without understanding the meaning of his advent,*
>> *How can we end the madness of lifetimes?*
>> *Goat, deer, and ox, posited as provisional;*
>> *Beginning, middle, and end, proclaimed as good.*
>> *Who knew that within the burning house,*
>> *Was originally the king of the dharma?*

[S3:7] {2:491}

この偈を呈するに、祖いはく、なんぢ、いまよりは念經僧となづけつべ
し。

> When he presented this gāthā, the Ancestor said, "Henceforth, you'll surely be called a monk who thinks on the sūtra."[37]

[S3:8]

法達禪師の、曹溪に參ぜし因縁、かくのごとく、これより、法華轉と轉法
華との法華は、開演するなり。それよりさきは、きかず。まことに佛之知
見をあきらめんことは、かならず正法眼藏ならん、佛祖なるべし。いたづ
らに沙石をかぞふる文字の學者は、しるべきにあらずといふこと、いまこ
の法達の從來にても、見るべし。法華の正宗をあきらめんことは、祖師の
開示を、唯一大事因縁と究盡すべし、餘乘にとぶらはんとすることなか
れ。いま法華轉の實相・實性・實體・實力・實因・實果の如是なる、祖師
より以前には、震旦國にいまだきかざるところ、いまだあらざるところな
り。

Such is the episode of Chan Master Fada's study under Caoxi. Ever
since, the *Lotus* of "the *Lotus* turning" and "turning the *Lotus*" has been
expounded; prior to that, it was not heard.[38] Truly, the clarification of
"*the knowledge and insight of a buddha*" is invariably "the treasury of

---

36 **Fada, having received this revelation** (*Hōtatsu, sude ni keihatsu o kōburite* 法
達、すでに啓發をかうぶりて): Continuing to relate the account in Fada's biography at
Jingde chuandeng lu 景德傳燈錄, T.2076.51:238b13-18).

37 **"you'll surely be called a monk who thinks on the sūtra"** (*nenkin sō to nazuketsu
beshi* 念經僧となづけつべし): In the context, clearly a compliment, though the expression may also refer to the monk who merely reads the sūtras.

38 **Ever since, the *Lotus* of "the *Lotus* turning" and "turning the *Lotus*" has been
expounded** (*kore yori, Hokke ten to ten Hokke to no Hokke wa, kaien suru nari* これよ
り、法華轉と轉法華との法華は、開演するなり): I.e., ever since Huineng introduced

S3. The *Lotus* Turns the *Lotus*　*Hokke ten Hokke*　法華轉法華　　75

the true dharma eye," is the buddhas and ancestors. The fact that the scholars of letters who vainly count sand and pebbles cannot know it can be seen in Fada's past. To clarify the true import of the *Lotus* we should exhaustively investigate the instruction of the Ancestral Master as "*only the reason of the one great matter;*" do not try to make inquiries of other vehicles. That the "real marks," real "natures," real "substance," real "power," real "causes," and real "effects" of the present "*Lotus* turning" are "such" was unheard of, was nonexistent, in the Land of Cīnastāna before the Ancestral Master.[39]

[S3:9]

いはゆる法華轉といふは、心迷なり。心迷は、すなはち法華轉なり。しかあればすなはち、心迷は法華に轉ぜらるるなり。その宗趣は、心迷たとひ萬象なりとも、如是相は法華に轉ぜらるるなり。この轉ぜらるる、よろこぶべきにあらず、まつべきにあらず、うるにあらず、きたるにあらず、しかあれども、法華轉はすなはち無二亦無三なり。唯有一佛乘にてあれば、如是相の法華にてあれば、能轉・所轉といふとも、一佛乘なり、一大事なり、唯以の赤心片片なるのみなり。

"The *Lotus* turning" is "the mind is deluded"; "the mind deluded" is itself "the *Lotus* turning."[40] Thus, "the mind is deluded" is being turned by the *Lotus*. The meaning of this is that, though "the mind is deluded" takes myriad forms, its "such marks" are being turned by the *Lotus*. This "being turned" is not to be welcomed, not to be anticipated, not to be got, not coming; yet "the *Lotus* turning" is precisely "*there are not two nor are there three.*"[41] Because it is "*there is only the one buddha vehicle,*" because it is the *Lotus* of "such marks," whether it is "turning" or "being turned," it is "the one buddha vehicle," "the one great matter"; it is just *the bare mind in pieces* of "only with."[42]

---

the expressions, Chan masters have discussed the *Lotus Sūtra* in terms of "the *Lotus* turning" and "turning the *Lotus*."

39　**That the "real marks," real "natures," real "substance," real "power," real "causes," and real "effects" of the present "*Lotus* turning" are "such"** (*ima hokke ten no jissō jisshō jittai jitsuriki jitsuin jikka no nyoze naru* いま法華轉の實相・實性・實體・實力・實因・實果の如是なる): A play with the famous sūtra passage on the ten "suchnesses" (*nyoze* 如是); see above, Note 4.

Land of Cīnastāna (*Shintan koku* 震旦國): Transliterating a Sanskrit name for China ("Land of the Qin").

40　**"The *Lotus* turning" is "the mind is deluded"** (*iwayuru hokke ten to iu wa shin mei nari* いはゆる法華轉といふは心迷なり): Here, Dōgen begins his extended commentary on the first line of the Sixth Ancestor's verse in section 4, above.

41　**"the *Lotus* turning" is precisely "there are not two nor are there three"** (*hokke ten wa sunawachi mu ni yaku mu san nari* 法華轉はすなはち無二亦無三なり): From the sūtra verse on the one vehicle; see above, Note 33.

42　**Because it is "there is only the one buddha vehicle"** (*yui u ichi butsu jō nite*

76 DŌGEN'S *SHŌBŌGENZŌ* VOLUME VII

[S3:10]

しかあれば、心迷をうらむることなかれ、汝等所行、是菩薩道なり、本行
菩薩道の奉覲於諸佛なり、開・示・悟・入、みな各々の法華轉なり。火宅
に心迷あり、當門に心迷あり、門外に心迷あり、門前に心迷あり、門内に
心迷あり。心迷に門内・門外、乃至當門・火宅等を現成せるがゆえに、白
牛車のうへにも開示悟入あるべし。この車上の莊校として、入を存せんと
き、露地を所入とや期せん、火宅を所出とや認せん、當門は、經歴のとこ
ろなるとのみ究盡すべきか。まさにしるべし、くるまのなかに、火宅を開
示悟入せしむる轉もあり、露地に、火宅を開示悟入せしむる轉もあり、當
門の全門に、開示悟入を轉ずるあり、普門の一門に、開示悟入を轉ずるあ
り。開・示・悟・入の各各に、普門を開示悟入する轉あり、門内に、開示
悟入を轉ずるあり、門外に、開示悟入するあり、火宅に、露地を開示悟入
するあり。

Thus, do not resent "the mind is deluded." It is "*what you are practicing is the bodhisattva path*"; it is having "*audiences with the buddhas*"
of the "*original practice of the bodhisattva path*."[43] "*Opening, showing,*

areba 唯有一佛乗にてあれば): From the sūtra verse at the conclusion of Chapter 7 of
the *Lotus Sūtra*; see Supplementary Notes, s.v. "Three vehicles."

it is just the bare mind in pieces of "only with" (*yui i no sekishin henpen naru nomi
nari* 唯以の赤心片片なるのみなり): Perhaps meaning something like, "the authentic
operation of the mind." An awkward attempt to retain Dōgen's play again with the adverb *yui i* 唯以 ("only with") in the sūtra line "only with the path of the one vehicle"
(see above, Notes 13 and 16). "The bare mind in pieces" (*sekishin henpen* 赤心片片) is a
common expression in Chan texts; see Supplementary Notes, s.v. "Bare mind in pieces."

43　**"what you are practicing is the bodhisattva path"** (*nyo tō shogyō, ze bosatsu
dō* 汝等所行、是菩薩道): Quoting a verse from Chapter 5 of the *Lotus Sūtra* (*Miaofa
lianhua jing* 妙法蓮華經, T.262.9:20b22-24):

今爲汝等、説最實事。諸聲聞衆、皆非滅度。汝等所行、是菩薩道。漸漸修學、
悉當成佛。

Now, for your sakes,
I shall teach the supreme truth:
There are no *śrāvakas*
Delivered to extinction.
What you are practicing
Is the bodhisattva path.
If you keep gradually practicing it,
You will all attain buddhahood.

"audiences with the buddhas" of the "original practice of the bodhisattva path"
(*hon gyō bosatsu dō no bugon o shobutsu* 本行菩薩道の奉覲於諸佛): See above, Note 3.
Perhaps variation on a line in a verse in Chapter 8 of the *Lotus Sūtra* predicting the buddhahood of the disciple Kauṇḍinya (*Miaofa lianhua jing* 妙法蓮華經, T.262.9:28c13-17:

其國土清淨、菩薩皆勇猛、咸昇妙樓閣、遊諸十方國。以無上供具、奉獻於諸
佛。

His land will be pure,
The bodhisattvas, all courageous;
They will all climb wondrous towers
And travel to lands in the ten directions.

S3. The *Lotus* Turns the *Lotus*   *Hokke ten Hokke* 法華轉法華   77

awakening, and entering" are all instances of "the *Lotus* turning." There is "the mind is deluded" in the burning house; there is "the mind is deluded" at the gate; there is "the mind is deluded" outside the gate; there is "the mind is deluded" in front of the gate; there is "the mind is deluded" inside the gate.[44] Because "inside the gate," "outside the gate," and so on, including "at the gate" and "the burning house," appear in "the mind is deluded," there must be "*opening, showing, awakening, and entering*" even on the white ox cart. When we think of "entering" as the "adornment" of this cart, should we anticipate the "open ground" as the place we enter?[45] Should we recognize the "burning house" as the place we exit? Should we exhaustively investigate "at the gate" only as the place we pass through?

We should realize that, within the cart, there is a turning that makes the "burning house" "*open, show, awaken, and enter*"; and on the "open

---

With unsurpassed offerings,
They will have audiences with the buddhas.

44   **there is "the mind is deluded" outside the gate** (*monge ni shin mei ari* 門外に心 迷あり): Presumably, "outside the gate" (*monge* 門外) refers to the children's position once they have exited the gate of the burning house; however, in the sūtra, the term occurs only in the father's false promise of the three carts (*Miaofa lianhua jing* 妙法蓮華經, T.262.9:12c9-10):

羊車鹿車牛車今在門外。

Now, outside the gate, there is a goat cart, a deer cart, and an ox cart.

See Supplementary Notes, s.v. "Burning house."

45   **When we think of "entering" as the "adornment" of this cart** (*kono shajō no shōkyō to shite, nyū o zon sen toki* この車上の莊校として、入を存せんとき): I.e., when we consider the cart in terms of the Buddha's intention to enable us to "enter the way of the buddha's knowledge and insight." The term *shōkyō* 莊校 ("adornment") here recalls the sūtra's description of the great ox carts provided for the children (e.g., at *Miaofa lianhua jing* 妙法蓮華經, T.262.9:12c18-19):

其車高廣衆寶莊校、周匝欄楯四面懸鈴。

These carts were high and wide, adorned with jewels and surrounded by railings with bells suspended on the four sides.

See Supplementary Notes, s.v. "Burning house."

should we anticipate the "open ground" as the place we enter? (*roji o shonyū to ya ki sen* 露地を所入とや期せん): I.e., is escape from the burning house of saṃsāra equivalent to gaining the cart? The term *rochi* 露地 ("open ground") derives from the sūtra's account of the children's escape from the house (*Miaofa lianhua jing* 妙法蓮華經, T.262.9:12c13-15):

是時長者。見諸子等安隱得出。皆於四衢道中露地而坐。無復障礙。其心泰然歡 喜踊躍。

At that time, the wealthy man, seeing his children safely out and seated out of harm's way on open ground at a crossroad, was calmed and rejoiced.

See Supplementary Notes, s.v. "Burning house."

78 DŌGEN'S *SHŌBŌGENZŌ* VOLUME VII

ground" there is a turning that makes the burning house "*open, show, awaken, and enter.*" There is "at the gate" turning "*opening, showing, awakening, and entering*" into the whole gate; there is the "universal gate" turning "*opening, showing, awakening, and entering*" into the "one gate."[46] There is "*opening,*" "*showing,*" "*awakening,*" and "*entering*" each turning the "universal gate" into "*opening,*" "*showing,*" "*awakening,*" and "*entering.*" There is turning "*opening,*" "*showing,*" "*awakening,*" and "*entering*" "inside the gate"; there is "*opening, showing, awakening, and entering*" "outside the gate."[47] There is "*opening, showing, awakening, and entering*" the "open ground" in the burning house.

[S3:11] {2:492}

このゆえに、火宅も不會なり、露地も不識なり。輪轉三界を、たれか
くるまと一乘せん。開示悟入を、たれか門なりと出入せん。火宅より
くるまをもとむれば、いくばくの輪轉ぞ、露地より火宅をのぞめば、
そくばくの深遠のみなり。露地に靈山を安穩せりとや究盡せん、靈山
に露地の平坦なるとや修行せん。衆生所遊樂を我淨土不毀と常在せる
をも、審細に本行すべきなり。

Therefore, the "burning house" is not understood, and the "open ground" is not known. Who would ride the cycles of the three realms on the one vehicle as a cart?[48] Who would exit and enter "*opening, showing,*

---

46 **There is "at the gate" turning "opening, showing, awakening, and entering" into the whole gate** (*tōmon no zenmon ni, kai ji go nyū o tenzuru ari* 當門の全門に、開示悟入を轉ずるあり): Perhaps meaning something like, "the particular gate through which the children escape the burning house can be read as the entire teaching ('the whole gate') for which the buddha appeared in the world."

there is the "universal gate" turning "opening, showing, awakening, and entering" into the "one gate" (*fumon no ichimon ni, kai ji go nyū o tenzuru ari* 普門の一門に、開示悟入を轉ずるあり): The term *fumon* 普門 ("universal gate") likely alludes to the *Lotus Sūtra*'s chapter on the Bodhisattva Avalokiteśvara, entitled "The Universal Gateway" (Fumon bon 普門品). The "one gate" (*ichimon* 一問) here refers to the single doorway of the rich father's house through which the children escape (at *Miaofa lianhua jing* 妙法蓮華經, T.262.9:12b15):

其家廣大、唯有一門。

His house was vast but had only one gate.

See Supplementary Notes, s.v. "Burning house."

47 **there is "opening, showing, awakening, and entering" "outside the gate"** (*monge ni, kai ji go nyū suru ari* 門外に、開示悟入するあり): Some texts read here *kai ji go nyū o ten zuru* 開示悟入を轉ずる ("turning 'opening, showing, awakening, and entering'").

48 **Who would ride the cycles of the three realms on the one vehicle as a cart?** (*rinden sangai o, tare ka kuruma to ichijō sen* 輪轉三界を、たれかくるまと一乘せん): "The cycles of the three realms" (*rinden sangai* 輪轉三界) refers to repeated births in the three realms of saṃsāra; see Supplementary Notes, s.v. "Three realms." The predicate *ichijō sen* 一乘せん plays with "the one vehicle" (*ichijō* 一乘) as a verb.

S3. The *Lotus* Turns the *Lotus* *Hokke ten Hokke* 法華轉法華 79

awakening, and entering" as a gate? When we seek the cart from the burning house, how many cycles will there be? When we gaze upon the burning house from the "open ground," how remote will it be? Should we exhaustively investigate how Vulture Peak has "remained secure" on the "open ground"?[49] Should we practice how the "open ground" is level on Vulture Peak? And we should "originally practice" in detail how "*where living beings disport themselves*" has "always remained" as "*my pure land, indestructible.*"[50]

---

49 **Vulture Peak has "remained secure" on the "open ground"** (*roji ni Ryōzen o annon seri* 露地に靈山を安穩せり): Reflecting the verse at *Miaofa lianhua jing* 妙法蓮華經, T.262.9:43c5-7; see following note. For the motif of "open ground" (*rochi* 露地), see Supplementary Notes, s.v. "Burning house."

50 **And we should "originally practice" in detail how "where living beings disport themselves" has "always remained" as "my pure land, indestructible"** (*shujō sho yūraku o ga jōdo fuki to jōzai seru o mo, shinsai ni hongyō su beki nari* 衆生所遊樂を我淨土不毀と常在せるをも、審細に本行すべきなり): Probably meaning something like, "we should carefully study the Buddha's claim that this world is his indestructible pure land." The sentence combines a series of expressions from the *Lotus Sūtra*. "Originally practice" (*hongyō* 本行): See above, Note 3. "Where living beings disport themselves" (*shujō sho yūraku* 衆生所遊樂): This phrase and the remainder of the sentence derive from the verse conclusion to Chapter 16 of the sūtra, in which the Buddha explains that, despite his apparent *parinirvāṇa*, he continues to dwell in this world, a lovely buddha land for those who can see it as such (*Miaofa lianhua jing* 妙法蓮華經, T.262.9:43c4-13):

> 於阿僧祇劫、常在靈鷲山、及餘諸住處。衆生見劫盡、大火所燒時、我此土安隱。天人常充滿、園林諸堂閣、種種寶莊嚴、寶樹多花菓、衆生所遊樂、諸天擊天鼓、常作衆伎樂、曼陀羅花、散佛及大衆。我淨土不毀、而衆見燒盡、憂怖諸苦惱、如是悉充滿。

For *asaṃkheya-kalpas*,
I always remained on Vulture Peak,
As well as other places.
At the end of the kalpa, when beings see
Everything consumed by the great fire,
This land of mine remains secure.
Always full of devas and humans,
Its gardens and palaces
Adorned with jewels,
Its jeweled trees filled with flowers and fruit.
Where living beings disport themselves,
And the devas beat heavenly drums,
Always making all sorts of music,
And *mandārava* blossoms
Fall on the Buddha and his great assembly.
My pure land is indestructible,
Though beings see it as destroyed in flames
And everywhere filled with
Anxiety and suffering.

80　DŌGEN'S *SHŌBŌGENZŌ* VOLUME VII

[S3:12]

一心欲見佛は、みづからなりとや参究する、他なりとや参究する。分身と成道せしときあり、全身と成道せしときあり。倶出靈鷲山は、身命を自惜せざるによりてなり。常住此説法なる開示悟入あり、方便現涅槃なる開示悟入あり。而不見の雖近なる、たれか一心の會・不會を信ぜざらん。天人常充滿のところは、すなはち釋迦牟尼佛・毘盧遮那の國土、常寂光土なり。おのづから四土に具するわれら、すなはち如一の佛土に居するなり。微塵をみるとき、法界をみざるにあらず、法界を證するに、微塵を證せざるにあらず。諸佛の、法界を證するに、われらを證にあらざらしむるにあらず。その初・中・後善なり。

"*Wishing single-mindedly to see the Buddha*" — is this to be investigated as oneself, or is it to be investigated as another?[51] There are times when the way is attained as a "separate body"; there are times when the way is attained as the "whole body."[52] "*Appearing together on Vulture Peak*" depends on "not begrudging their bodies and lives."[53] There is "*opening, showing, awakening, and entering*" that is "*I always abide*

51　**"Wishing single-mindedly to see the Buddha"** (*isshin yoku kenbutsu* 一心欲見佛): Quoting a line of verse at the conclusion to Chapter 16 of the *Lotus Sūtra* (*Miaofa lianhua jing* 妙法蓮華經, T.262.9:43b22-24), in which Śākyamuni promises to appear to the faithful:

> 衆生既信伏、質直意柔軟、一心欲見佛、不自惜身命、時我及衆僧、倶出靈鷲山。
> When living beings are submissive in faith,
> When they are upright and pliant,
> Wishing single-mindedly to see the Buddha,
> Not begrudging their bodies and lives,
> Then will I and my saṃgha
> Appear together on Vulture Peak.

is this to be investigated as oneself (*mizukara nari to ya sankyū suru* みづからなりとや参究する): It is unclear whether this should be taken as "is it oneself that wishes to see?" or "is it oneself that one wishes to see?" (or both).

52　**"separate body"** (*bunshin* 分身); **"whole body"** (*zenshin* 全身): The sentence would seem to be raising the question of which sort of buddha body one wishes to see. Both these terms reflect their several occurrences in the *Lotus Sūtra*. For example, at *Miaofa lianhua jing* 妙法蓮華經, T.262.9:32c15-16):

> 我滅度後、欲供養我全身者、應起一大塔。
> [The Buddha Prabhūtaratna said,] "After my extinction, those wishing to make offerings to my whole body should erect a great stūpa."

And later, in the same passage (*Miaofa lianhua jing* 妙法蓮華經, T.262.9:32c28-29):

> 世尊、我等亦願欲見世尊分身諸佛、禮拜供養。
> [Mahāpratibhāna addressed the Buddha, saying] "World-Honored One, we also wish to see the buddhas that are the separate bodies of the World-Honored One, to pay obeisance and make offerings to them."

53　**"Appearing together on Vulture Peak"** (*kushutsu Ryōjusen* 倶出靈鷲山): Quoting again the verse cited just above in "wishing single-mindedly to see the Buddha" (*Miaofa lianhua jing* 妙法蓮華經, T.262.9:43b23).

S3. The *Lotus* Turns the *Lotus*   *Hokke ten Hokke*   法華轉法華   81

here preaching the dharma."[54] There is "*opening, showing, awakening, and entering*" that is "*by skillful device I show my nirvāṇa.*"[55] "*Not to see me*" is "*though I am near*": who would not believe that this is the understanding or not understanding of the "single-minded."[56]

The place "*always full of devas and humans*" is precisely the land of Buddha Śākyamuni and Vairocana, the land of eternal serene light.[57] We

---

54 **"I always abide here preaching the dharma"** (*jō jū shi seppō* 常住此説法): Here and in the next two sentences, Dōgen is incorporating earlier lines from the same verse at the end of Chapter 16 (*Miaofa lianhua jing* 妙法蓮華經, T.262.9:43b16-17):

> 爲度衆生故、方便現涅槃。而實不滅度、常住此説法。我常住於此、以諸神通力、令顛倒衆生、雖近而不見。
>
> For the sake of living beings,
> By skillful device I show my nirvāṇa;
> But, in fact, I do not enter extinction
> And always abide here preaching the dharma.
> I always abide here,
> But by means of my spiritual powers,
> I cause the deluded living beings
> Not to see me, though I am near.

55 **"by skillful device I show my nirvāṇa"** (*hōben gen nehan* 方便現涅槃): Quoting another line in the verse cited in the previous note here (*Miaofa lianhua jing* 妙法蓮華經, T.262.9:43b16).

56 **"Not to see me" is "though I am near"** (*ni fuken no sui gon naru* 而不見の雖近なる): A tentative translation of a problematic sentence. Dōgen is playing here with the final line in the passage cited just above in the note "I always abide here preaching the dharma" (*Miaofa lianhua jing* 妙法蓮華經, T.262.9:43b19). "Single-minded" (*isshin* 一心) here likely refers to those appearing just above who "wish single-mindedly to see the Buddha."

57   **The place "always full of devas and humans"** (*ten nin jō jūman no tokoro* 天人常充滿のところ): From the verse passage cited above, Note 50 (*Miaofa lianhua jing* 妙法蓮華經, T.262.9:43c7):

> 我此土安隱、天人常充滿。
>
> This land of mine remains secure,
> Always full of devas and humans.

land of eternal serene light (*jō jakkō do* 常寂光土): As Dōgen himself comments in his next sentence, one of the four lands (*shido* 四土) discussed especially in the Tiantai literature (e.g., in the *Fo shuo guan wuliang shou jing shu* 佛説觀無量壽經疏, by Zhiyi 智顗 [538-597], T.1750.37:188b16ff):

> 四種淨土、謂凡聖同居土、方便有餘土、實報無障礙土、常寂光土也。
>
> The four types of pure land are [1] the land where common people and sages live together, [2] the land of expedience, with remainder, [3] the land of real recompense, without obstacles, and [4] the land of eternal serene light.

The same text (T.1750.37:188c4-6) defines the fourth land as follows:

> 常寂光者、常即法身、寂即解脱、光即般若。是三點不縱橫並別。名祕密藏、諸佛如來所遊居處、眞常究竟極極爲淨土。
>
> "Eternal serene light": "eternal" is the dharma body; "serene" is liberation; "light" is

82 DŌGEN'S *SHŌBŌGENZŌ* VOLUME VII

who are naturally possessed of the four lands reside in the buddha land that is "as one."[58] When we see an infinitesimal dust mote, it is not that we are not seeing the dharma realm; when we verify the dharma realm, it is not that we fail to verify the infinitesimal dust mote. When the buddhas verify the dharma realm, it is not that they fail to include us in the verification. Their beginning, middle, and end are good.[59]

[S3:13] {2:493}

しかあれば、いまも證の如是相なり、驚・疑・怖・畏も、如是にあらざるなし。ただこれ佛之知見をもて微塵をみると、微塵に坐するとの、ことなるのみなり。法界に坐するとき、廣にあらず、微塵に坐するとき、せばきにあらざるゆえは、保任にあらざれば、坐すべからず、保任するには、廣・狹に驚疑なきなり。これ法華の體・力を究盡せるによりてなり。

Thus, the present is also "such marks" of the verification; and "alarm, doubt, and fear" are also no other than "such."[60] It is just that, in the "*the knowledge and insight of a buddha*," seeing the infinitesimal dust mote and sitting in the infinitesimal dust mote are different. When we sit in the dharma realm, it is not vast; when we sit in the infinitesimal dust mote, it is not minute. Therefore, we cannot sit when we do not entrust ourselves to it; when we do entrust ourselves to it, there is no alarm or doubts about

---

wisdom. These three are not horizontal or vertical, together or separate. It is called the secret treasury. It is the place inhabited by the buddhas, the tathāgatas; a pure land of the extreme of the ultimate, truly eternal.

58 **the buddha land that is "as one"** (*nyoitsu no butsudo* 如一の佛土): Or "one and the same buddha land." The expression likely reflects the sūtra at *Miaofa lianhua jing* 妙法蓮華經, T.262.9:52a12-13:

于時十方世界通達無礙、如一佛土。

At that time, the worlds in the ten directions penetrated each other without obstruction, as if one buddha land.

59 **Their beginning, middle, and end are good** (*sono sho chū go zen nari* その初・中・後善なり): Usually used in reference to a buddha's teaching (see, e.g., above, Note 12); but here, perhaps, the antecedent of "their" (*sono* その) is the set of Dōgen's own three sentences just above.

60 **the present is also "such marks" of the verification** (*ima mo shō no nyoze sō nari* いまも證の如是相なり): Perhaps meaning something like, "our present state is included in such verification [by the buddha]." For "such marks" (*nyoze sō* 如是相), see above, Note 4.

"alarm, doubt, and fear" (*kyōgi fui* 驚・疑・怖・畏): From a passage in Chapter 10 of the *Lotus Sūtra* (*Miaofa lianhua jing* 妙法蓮華經, T.262.9:31c19-21):

若有菩薩、聞是法華經驚疑怖畏、當知是爲新發意菩薩。若聲聞人、聞是經驚疑怖畏、當知是爲增上慢者。

If there are bodhisattvas who are alarmed, doubtful, and fearful upon hearing this sūtra, know that they are bodhisattvas who have only newly brought forth the aspiration [for buddhahood]. If there are *śrāvakas* who are alarmed, doubtful, and fearful upon hearing this sūtra, know that they are the arrogant ones.

S3. The *Lotus* Turns the *Lotus*　*Hokke ten Hokke*　法華轉法華　83

vast or minute. This is based on our having exhaustively investigated the "substance and power" of the *Lotus*.[61]

[S3:14]

しかあれば、われらがいまの相・性、この法界に本行すとやせん、微塵に本行すとやせん。驚疑なし、怖畏なし、ただ法華轉の本行なる、深遠・長遠なるのみなり。この微塵をみるに、法界をみると有作有量にあらざるなり。有量有作も、法華量をならひ、法華作をならふべし。開示悟入をきかんには、欲令衆生ときくべし。いはゆる、開佛知見の法華轉なる、示佛知見にならふべし、悟佛知見の法華轉なる、入佛知見にならふべし、示佛知見の法華轉なる、悟佛知見にならふべし。かくのごとく、開・示・悟・入の法華轉、おのおの究盡のみちあるべし。

So, do we take our present "marks and natures" as "originally practicing" in this dharma realm, or do we take them as "originally practicing" in an infinitesimal dust mote? Without "alarm or doubt," without "fear," it is just that the "original practice" that is the "*Lotus turning*" is so deep and long. This seeing the infinitesimal dust mote and seeing the dharma realm, are not construction or measurement; with measurement and construction as well, we should study the measurement of the *Lotus*, the construction of the *Lotus*.[62]

In hearing "*opening, showing, awakening, and entering*," we should hear them as "*wishing to cause living beings*."[63] That is, "*opening the knowledge and insight of a buddha*" as the "*Lotus* turning," we should study in "*showing the knowledge and insight of a buddha*." "*Awakening to the knowledge and insight of a buddha*" as the "*Lotus* turning," we should study in "*entering the knowledge and insight of a buddha.*" "*Showing the knowledge and insight of a buddha*" as the "*Lotus* turn-

---

61　**"substance and power" of the *Lotus*** (*hokke no tai riki* 法華の體力): Two of the ten "suchnesses" (*nyoze* 如是); see above, Note 4.

62　**This seeing the infinitesimal dust mote and seeing the dharma realm** (*kono mijin o miru ni, hokkai o miru to* この微塵をみるに、法界をみると): Following those texts that read here the less problematic *kono mijin o miru to* この微塵をみると.

construction or measurement (*usa uryō* 有作有量): Adopting the common practice of reading these terms here as referring to the mental state of "seeing." Taken as referring to the objects of the seeing, they might be rendered "conditioned or measured" — i.e., the distinction between the mote of dust and the dharma realm is not a matter of whether or not they are conditioned or limited.

63　**In hearing "opening, showing, awakening, and entering"** (*kai ji go nyū o kikan ni wa* 開示悟入をきかんには): Dōgen returns here to the sūtra passage (*Miaofa lianhua jing* 妙法蓮華經, T.262.9:7a22-27) cited above, Note 5.

we should hear them as "wishing to cause living beings" (*yoku ryō shujō to kiku beshi* 欲令衆生ときくべし): Borrowing the causative phrase repeated for each of the four verbs in the same sūtra passage; perhaps meaning that we should regard the four verbs here as diverse expressions of the Buddha's wish to guide beings.

84 DŌGEN'S *SHŌBŌGENZŌ* VOLUME VII

ing," we should study in "*awakening to the knowledge and insight of a buddha.*" In this way, each of the "*Lotus* turnings" of "*opening, showing, awakening, and entering*" has a path of exhaustive investigation.

[S3:15] {2:494}

おほよそ、この諸佛如來の知見波羅蜜は、廣大深遠なる法華轉なり。授記は、すなはち自己の開佛知見なり、他のさづくるにあらざる法華轉なり。これすなはち、心迷法華轉なり。

In sum, this "*pāramitā of knowledge and insight*" of the buddhas, the tathāgatas, is the "*Lotus* turning" that is "*vast and deep.*"[64] The "prediction" is precisely one's own "*opening of the knowledge and insight of a buddha*"; it is "the *Lotus* turning" not conferred by another. This, then, is "*if your mind is deluded, the Lotus turns you.*"

[S3:16]

心悟轉法華といふは、法華を轉ずるといふなり。いはゆる、法華の、われらを轉ずるちから究盡するときに、かへりてみづからを轉ずる如是力を現成するなり。この現成は、轉法華なり。從來の轉、いまもさらにやむことなしといへども、おのづからかへりて法華を轉ずるなり。驢事、いまだをはらざれども、馬事到來すべし。出現於此の唯以一大事因緣あり。地涌千界の衆、ひさしき法華の大聖尊なりといへども、みづからに轉ぜられて地涌し、他に轉ぜられて地涌す。地涌のみを轉法華すべからず、虚空涌をも轉法華すべし。地・空のみにあらず、法華涌とも佛知すべし。

"*If your mind is awakened, you turn the Lotus*" means turning the *Lotus*.[65] That is, when we exhaustively investigate the power of the *Lotus* to turn us, we realize on the other hand "such power" to turn ourselves.[66] This realization is "turning the *Lotus*." While the previous turning does not stop even now, on the other hand, now we turn the *Lotus*. "The donkey business isn't over, but the horse business will have arrived."[67] We

---

64 **this "*pāramitā* of knowledge and insight" of the buddhas, the tathāgatas, is the "*Lotus* turning" that is "vast and deep"** (*kono shobutsu nyorai no chiken haramitsu wa, kōdai jin'on naru hokke ten nari* この諸佛如來の知見波羅蜜は、廣大深遠なる法華轉なり): Reflecting the passage in the *Lotus Sūtra* (*Miaofa lianhua jing* 妙法蓮華經, T.262.9:5c4-5) immediately following that cited in Note 12, above:

舍利弗、如來知見廣大深遠。

Śāriputra, the knowledge and insight of the tathāgatas is vast and deep.

65 **"If your mind is awakened, you turn the *Lotus*"** (*shin go ten Hokke* 心悟轉法華): Here, Dōgen begins his comments on the second line of the Sixth Ancestor's verse quoted in section 4 above.

66 **"such power" to turn ourselves** (*mizukara o tenzuru nyoze riki* みづからを轉ずる如是力): The awkward "such power" (*nyoze riki* 如是力) here is borrowed from the famous list of ten "suchnesses" (*nyoze* 如是) at *Miaofa lianhua jing* 妙法蓮華經, T.262.9:5c10-13; see above, Note 4.

67 **"The donkey business isn't over, but the horse business will have arrived"** (*roji, imada owarazaredomo, baji tōrai su beshi* 驢事、いまだをはらざれども、馬事到來

S3. The *Lotus* Turns the *Lotus* *Hokke ten Hokke* 法華轉法華   85

have "*the reason of the one great matter alone*" for "*appearing here.*"[68]

Although those in the assembly that "sprang from the earth" in the thousand realms were equally great sages of the *Lotus*, they "earth-spring," turned by themselves, and "earth-spring," turned by another.[69] We should not turn the *Lotus* only of "earth-springing": we should also turn the *Lotus* of "empty-space-springing." And not just earth and sky: we should also have the buddha knowledge of "*Lotus*-springing."[70]

すべし): I.e., "turning" and "being turned" will overlap. Dōgen's Japanese version of a Chinese saying with a sense something like the English "one damned thing after another." The saying, attributed to Lingyun Zhiqun 靈雲志勤 (dates unknown), appears in several Chan sources (see, e.g., *Jingde chuandeng lu* 景德傳燈錄, T.2076.51:285b12-13) and Dōgen's *shinji Shōbōgenzō* 眞字正法眼藏 (DZZ.5:206, case 156):

師問、如何是佛法大意。雲云、驢事未去、馬事到來。

The Master [Changqing Huileng (854-932)] asked, "What is the great meaning of the buddha dharma?"

Yun said, "The donkey business isn't gone yet, and the horse business has already arrived."

68   We have "the reason of the one great matter alone" for "appearing here" (*shutsugen o shi no yui i ichi daiji innen ari* 出現於此の唯以一大事因緣あり): I.e., we are now, like the buddhas, preachers of the *Lotus Sūtra* doctrine of the one vehicle. Again, reflecting the sūtra at *Miaofa lianhua jing* 妙法蓮華經, T.262.9:7a21-22:

諸佛世尊唯以一大事因緣故出現於世。

Buddhas, the world-honored ones, appear in the world for the reason of one great matter alone.

See Supplementary Notes.

69   assembly that "sprang from the earth" in the thousand realms (*chiyū sengai no shu* 地涌千界の衆): Reference to the famous scene, in Chapter 15 of the *Lotus Sūtra*, in which a multitude of bodhisattva disciples of Buddha Śākyamuni emerge from the earth and hover in the sky (*Miaofa lianhua jing* 妙法蓮華經, T.262.9:41a6-8):

其佛侍者、各各見是菩薩大衆、於三千大千世界四方、從地踊出住於虛空。

Every one of the attendants of these buddhas saw this great assembly of bodhisattvas that sprang out from the earth and hovered in empty space in the four directions of the trichiliocosm.

great sages (*dai shōson* 大聖尊): A term (typically rendering S. *mahārṣi*) normally used in reference to buddhas, here applied to Śākyamuni's bodhisattva disciples.

they "earth-spring" (*chiyū shi* 地涌し): Dōgen has invented a verb "to earth-spring" from the sūtra's phrase "sprang out from the earth" (*jūchi yōshutsu* 從地踊出). Similarly, *mutatis mutandis*, the following "empty-space springing" and "*Lotus*-springing."

70   we should also have the buddha knowledge of "*Lotus*-springing" (*hokke yū tomo butchi su beshi* 法華涌とも佛知すべし): "Have the buddha knowledge" renders Dōgen's neologistic predicate *butchi su* 佛智す ("to buddha-know"), presumably derived from the sūtra's recurrent "knowledge and insight of a buddha" (*butsu chiken* 佛知見).

86 DŌGEN'S *SHŌBŌGENZŌ* VOLUME VII

[S3:17]

おほよそ法華の時は、かならず父少而子老なり。子の子にあらざるにはあらず、父の父にあらざるにはあらず、まさに、子は老なり、父は少なり、とならふべし。世の不信にならうて、おどろくことなかれ、世の不信なるは、法華の時なり。これをもって一時佛住を轉法華すべし。開示悟入に轉ぜられて地涌し、佛之知見に轉ぜられて地涌す、この轉法華のとき、法華の心悟あるなり、心悟の法華あるなり。あるいは下方といふ、すなはち空中なり。この下、この空、すなはち轉法華なり、すなはち佛壽量なり。佛壽と法華と法界と一心とは、下とも現成し、空とも現成すると、轉法華すべし。かるがゆえに、下方空といふは、すなはち轉法華の現成なり。おほよそこのとき、法華を轉じて、三草ならしむることあり、法華を轉じて、二木ならしむることもあり。有覺とまつべきにあらず、無覺とあやしむべきにあらず。自轉して發菩提なるとき、すなはち南方なり。この成道、もとより南方に集會する靈山なり、靈山かならず轉法華なり。虚空に集會する十方佛土あり、これ轉法華の分身なり。すでに十方佛土と轉法華す、一微塵のいるべきところなし。色即是空の轉法華あり、若退若出にあらず。空即是色の轉法華あり、無有生死なるべし。在世といふべきにあらず、滅度のみにあらんや。われに親友なるは、われもかれに親友なり。親友の禮勤、わするべからざるゆえに、髻珠をもあたふ、衣珠をもあたふる時節、よくよく究盡すべし。佛前に寶塔ある轉法華あり、高五百由旬なり。塔中に佛坐する轉法華あり、量二百五十由旬なり。從地涌出、住在空中の轉法華あり、心も礙罣なし、色も罣礙なし。從空涌出、住在地中の轉法華あり、まなこにもさへらる、身にもさへらる。塔中に靈山あり、靈山に寶塔あり。寶塔は虚空に寶塔し、虚空は寶塔を虚空す。塔中の古佛は、坐を靈山のほとけにならべ、靈山のほとけは、證を塔中のほとけに證す。靈山のほとけ、塔中へ證入するには、すなはち靈山の依・正ながら、轉法華入するなり。塔中のほとけ、靈山に涌出するには、古佛土ながら、久滅度ながら、涌出するなり。涌出も轉入も、凡夫二乘にならはざれ、轉法華を學すべし。久滅度は、佛上にそなはれる證莊嚴なり。塔中と佛前と、寶塔と虚空と、靈山にあらず、法界にあらず、半段にあらず、全界にあらず、是法位のみにかかはれず、非思量なるのみなり。

Generally speaking, at the time of the *Lotus*, invariably "*the father is young while the children are old*."[71] It is not that the children are not the

---

71 **"the father is young while the children are old"** (*fu shō ni shi rō* 父少而子老): A reference to the apparent miracle in the *Lotus Sūtra* that the great assembly of bodhisattvas that sprang from the earth to bear witness to the sūtra could have been trained by Buddha Śākyamuni during the short span of his human lifetime as a buddha. In a verse at the conclusion to Chapter 15 (*Miaofa lianhua jing* 妙法蓮華經, T.262.9:42a11-14), the Bodhisattva Maitreya expresses his doubts through a simile:

譬如少壯人、年始二十五、示人百歲子、髮白而面皺、是等我所生、子亦説是父。父少而子老、擧世所不信。

It is as if a young man,
His years barely twenty-five,
Says of people of a hundred years,
Their hair white, their faces wrinkled,
"These are my offspring,"
And the children also say, "This is our father."

S3. The *Lotus* Turns the *Lotus*　*Hokke ten Hokke*　法華轉法華　87

children, nor that the father is not the father. We should just understand that the children are old and the father young. Do not imitate "the disbelief of the world" and be shocked.[72] That the world does not believe is the time of the *Lotus*.[73] With this, we should turn the *Lotus* of "*at one time, the Buddha was staying.*"[74] Turned by "*opening, showing, awakening, and entering,*" we "earth-spring"; turned by the "*knowledge and insight of a buddha,*" we "earth-spring." At the time of this turning the *Lotus*, we have "the mind is awakened" of the *Lotus*; we have the *Lotus* of "the mind is awakened."

Again, "beneath" means "in space."[75] This "beneath" and this "space" are turning the *Lotus,* are the "lifespan of the Buddha." We should turn the *Lotus* so that the buddha's lifespan, and the *Lotus*, and the dharma realm, and the single-minded appear beneath and appear in space.[76] Therefore, the "space beneath" means the appearance of turning the *Lotus*. At this time, more generally, in turning the *Lotus,* we make it into "the three herbs"; in turning the *Lotus*, we make it into "the two trees."[77]

The father is young while the children are old:
No one in the whole world would believe it.

72　**"disbelief of the world"** (*yo no fushin* 世の不信): Allusion to the line in Maitreya's verse (*Miaofa lianhua jing* 妙法蓮華經, T.262.9:42a14):

舉世所不信。

No one in the whole world would believe it.

73　**That the world does not believe is the time of the *Lotus*** (*yo no fushin naru wa, hokke no ji nari* 世の不信なるは、法華の時なり): Perhaps to be understood as saying that, even at the time the *Lotus Sūtra* was preached, people did not believe in it. Alternatively, it could be read as a reflection of the sūtra's repeated claims to be a beacon of dharma in dark times of disbelief.

74　**we should turn the *Lotus* of "at one time, the Buddha was staying"** (*ichiji butsu jū o ten Hokke su beshi* 一時佛住を轉法華すべし): Perhaps meaning that we should turn the *Lotus* as it was originally taught by Buddha Śākyamuni on Vulture Peak; from the opening line of the sūtra (*Miaofa lianhua jing* 妙法蓮華經, T.262.9:1c19-20):

如是我聞。一時佛住王舍城耆闍崛山中、與大比丘衆萬二千人俱。

Thus have I heard. At one time, the Buddha was staying on Mount Gṛdhrakūṭa, at Rājagṛha, together with a great bhikṣu assembly of twelve thousand.

75　**"beneath" means "in space"** (*gehō to iu, sunawachi kūchū nari* 下方といふ、すなはち空中なり): Reference to a line of verse in Chapter 15 of the *Lotus Sūtra*, in which the Buddha describes the subterranean dwelling place of his bodhisattva disciples who sprang from the earth (*Miaofa lianhua jing* 妙法蓮華經, T.262.9:41b20):

在娑婆世界、下方空中住。

They dwell in space beneath
The Sahā world.

76　**the single-minded** (*isshin* 一心): Taken here as a reference to those "wishing single-mindedly to see the Buddha" (q.v., above, Note 51).

77　**we make it into "the three herbs"** (*sansō narashimuru koto ari* 三草ならしむる

88 DŌGEN'S *SHŌBŌGENZŌ* VOLUME VII

We need not anticipate having awakening; we need not be doubtful of lacking awakening.[78]

The time when we turn ourselves and bring forth bodhi, that is "the south."[79] This attaining the way is originally the Vulture Peak that assembles in the south; it is the Vulture Peak always turning the *Lotus*.[80] There are buddha lands in the ten directions that assemble in empty space; they are "separate bodies" that turn the *Lotus*. Since they turn the *Lotus* as the buddha lands in the ten directions, there is nowhere that a single infinitesimal dust mote can enter.

There is turning the *Lotus* of "*form is itself emptiness*"; it is not "*whether withdrawing or emerging*."[81] There is turning the Lotus of

ことあり); **we make it into "the two trees"** (*nimoku narashimuru koto mo ari* 二木ならしむることもあり): Perhaps meaning something like, "we make it [i.e., the dharma] applicable to followers of the three vehicles"; see above, Note 7.

78 **We need not anticipate having awakening** (*ukaku to matsu beki ni arazu* 有覺とまつべきにあらず): It is unclear whether "awakening" in this and the following phrase refers to the spiritual state of the one turning the *Lotus* or the "three herbs" and "two trees" for whom the *Lotus* is being turned.

79 **"the south"** (*nanpō* 南方): Likely a reference to the Stainless (S. *vimalā*) world in the south where the daughter of the dragon king attained buddhahood, as recounted in Chapter 12 of the *Lotus Sūtra* (*Miaofa lianhua jing* 妙法蓮華經, T.262.9:35c16-19):

当時衆會皆見龍女、忽然之間變成男子、具菩薩行、即往南方無垢世界、坐寶蓮華成等正覺、三十二相八十種好、普爲十方一切衆生演説妙法。

At that time, the assembly saw the dragon daughter suddenly become a male, equip herself with the practices of the bodhisattva, go to the Stainless world in the south, sit upon a jeweled lotus, attain perfect awakening, with the thirty-two marks and eighty auspicious signs, and universally expound the wondrous dharma for the sake of all living beings in the ten directions.

80 **This attaining the way is originally the Vulture Peak that assembles in the south** (*kono jōdō, motoyori nanpō ni shūe suru Ryōzen nari* この成道、もとより南方に集會する靈山なり): Some readers take this odd claim to mean something like, "this attaining the way originally [takes place on] Vulture Peak, where [the audience] assembles in the south." The translation here assumes that Dōgen is personifying Vulture Peak and the following "buddha lands of the ten directions" as themselves turners of, and assembled audience for, the *Lotus Sūtra*.

81 **"form is itself emptiness"** (*shiki soku ze kū* 色即是空): This and the line in the following sentence, "emptiness is itself form" (*kū soku ze shiki* 空即是色), are best known from the *Heart Sūtra*: see Supplementary Notes, s.v. "Form is itself emptiness; emptiness is itself form."

"whether withdrawing or emerging" (*nyaku tai nyaku shutsu* 若退若出): This phrase and the expressions in the following two sentences, "there is no birth or death" (*mu u shōji* 無有生死), "existence in the world" (*zaise* 在世), and "extinction" (*metsudo* 滅度) are drawn from a passage in Chapter 16 of the *Lotus Sūtra* (*Miaofa lianhua jing* 妙法蓮華經, T.262.9:42c13-15):

如來、如實知見三界之相。無有生死、若退若出。亦無在世及滅度者。非實非虚

S3. The *Lotus* Turns the *Lotus* *Hokke ten Hokke* 法華轉法華   89

"*emptiness is itself form*"; it is "*there is no birth or death.*" We cannot call it "existence in the world"; could it be only "extinction"? His being a friend of mine is my being a friend of his.[82] Because we should not forget the etiquette of friendship, we should exhaustively investigate well the occasion when "the jewel in the topknot" is given, when "the jewel in the robe" is given.[83]

There is a turning of the *Lotus* in which the "jeweled stupa" is "before the Buddha"; it is "five hundred yojanas in height."[84] There is a turning of the *Lotus* of the buddha seated inside the stupa; it is "two hundred fifty yojanas" in size.[85] There is a turning of the *Lotus* of "*springing forth from the earth and hovering in space*": the mind has no obstruction; form

---

非如非異。不如三界見於三界。

The Tathāgata views the marks of the three realms as they really are: there is no birth or death, whether withdrawing or emerging; there is also no existence in the world or extinction; they are neither true nor false, neither the same nor different. He does not view the three realms as [those in] the three realms view them.

82 **His being a friend of mine is my being a friend of his** (*ware ni shinyū naru wa, ware mo kare ni shinyū nari* われに親友なるは、われもかれに親友なり): The implication here is unclear. Some would take the pronoun *kare* かれ as referring to the Buddha; but elsewhere (in his "Shōbōgenzō zazen shin" 正法眼藏坐禪箴), Dōgen uses this same expression to exemplify the logical interdependence of two terms, and it may be that here too he is simply personifying the mutual entailment of the phrases "form is emptiness" and "emptiness is form."

83 **"jewel in the topknot"** (*keiju* 髻珠); **"jewel in the robe"** (*eju* 衣珠): Allusion to two parables in the *Lotus Sūtra*. The former term refers to the jewel in a king's topknot, which marks his royal status and, therefore, cannot casually be given away; it is used in Chapter 14 of the sūtra as a metaphor for the teachings of the *Lotus*. The latter term alludes to the parable, in Chapter 8, in which the hitherto unrecognized truth that the Buddha's followers can themselves become buddhas is likened to a gem sewn by a friend into the robe of a sleeping pauper. See Supplementary Notes, s.v. "Jewel in the topknot," and "Jewel in the robe."

84 **the "jeweled stupa" is "before the Buddha"** (*butsu zen ni hōtō aru* 佛前に寶塔ある): Allusion to the opening lines of Chapter 11 of the *Lotus Sūtra* (*Miaofa lianhua jing* 妙法蓮華經, T.262.9:32b16-18):

爾時佛前有七寶塔、高五百由旬、縱廣二百五十由旬。從地踊出住在空中。

At that time, there was before the buddha a seven-jeweled stūpa, five hundred yojanas in height and two hundred fifty yojanas in breadth. It sprang from the earth and hovered in space.

"five hundred yojanas in height" (*kō gohyaku yujun* 高五百由旬): The yojana (*yujun* 由旬) is a measure of distance, varying greatly depending on the source, ranging from roughly 4.5 miles to twice that number (thus, yielding a stupa 2250-4500 miles in height, extending far into the earth's exosphere).

85 **the buddha seated inside the stūpa** (*tōchū ni butsuza suru* 塔中に佛坐する): Reference to Buddha Prabhūtaratna (*Tahō butsu* 多寶佛), who vowed that after his nirvāṇa, his stūpa would appear wherever the *Lotus Sūtra* was preached. (*Miaofa lianhua jing* 妙法蓮華經, T.262.9:32c8ff.)

90   DŌGEN'S *SHŌBŌGENZŌ* VOLUME VII

has no obstruction. There is *springing forth from space and hovering in the earth*: it is obstructed by the eye; it is obstructed by the body.[86]

There is Vulture Peak inside the stūpa; there is a jeweled stūpa inside Vulture Peak. The jeweled stūpa makes a jeweled stūpa in empty space; empty space makes empty space of the jeweled stūpa.[87] The old buddha inside the stūpa shares his seat with the buddha of Vulture Peak; the buddha of Vulture Peak verifies his verification with the buddha inside the stūpa.[88] When the buddha of Vulture Peak enters verification inside the stūpa, even while being the secondary and primary recompense of Vulture Peak, he enters the turning of the *Lotus*.[89] When the buddha inside

---

86   **springing forth from space and hovering in the earth** (*jū kū yu shutsu, jū zai chichū* 從空涌出、住在地中): Dōgen's play with the preceding sūtra line. If we take "earth" and "space" (or "sky") as metaphors, we might read the sūtra's line as representing "form is emptiness," and Dōgen's reversal as "emptiness is form"; in the former, the turning of the Lotus is unobstructed by "mind" and "form"; in the latter, it is defined by "eye" and "body."

obstructed by the eye (*manako ni mo saeraru* まなこにもさへらる): Dōgen regularly uses the pattern "obstructed by X" in the sense "defined by X," "identified with X." The expression "obstructed by the eye" occurs elsewhere in his writing, probably inspired by a saying of Fayan Wenyi 法眼文益 (885-958) that Dōgen records in his *shinji Shōbōgenzō* 眞字正法眼藏 (DZZ.5:186, case 111); see Supplementary Notes, s.v. "Obstructed by the eye."

87   **The jeweled stūpa makes a jeweled stūpa in empty space; empty space makes empty space of the jeweled stūpa** (*hōtō wa kokū ni hōtō shi, kokū wa hōtō o kokū su* 實塔は虚空に實塔し、虚空は實塔を虚空す): Dōgen here invents the verbs *hōtō shi* 實塔 し and *kokū su* 虚空す; hence, more literally, "the jeweled stūpa jewel-stūpas in empty space; empty space empty-spaces the jeweled stūpa."

88   **The old buddha inside the stūpa shares his seat with the buddha of Vulture Peak** (*tōchū no kobutsu wa, za o Ryōzen no hotoke ni narabe* 塔中の古佛は、座を靈山のほとけにならべ): Reference to the famous scene in which Buddha Śākyamuni joins Buddha Prabhūtaratna inside the latter's stūpa (*Miaofa lianhua jing* 妙法蓮華經, T.262.9:33c5-8):

> 爾時多寶佛、於寶塔中分半座、與釋迦牟尼佛、而作是言、釋迦牟尼佛、可就此座。即時釋迦牟尼佛、入其塔中坐其半座、結加趺坐。

> At that time, Buddha Prabhūtaratna shared half his seat within the jeweled stūpa with Buddha Śākyamuni, saying, "Buddha Śākyamuni, you may have this seat." Thereupon, Buddha Śākyamuni entered that stūpa and sat cross-legged on half the seat.

the buddha of Vulture Peak verifies his verification with the buddha inside the stūpa (*Ryōzen no hotoke wa, shō o tōchū no hotoke ni shōsu* 靈山のほとけは、證を塔中のほとけに證す): Or, perhaps, "verifies verification in the buddha inside the stūpa."

89   **even while being the secondary and primary recompense of Vulture Peak** (*Ryōzen no e shō nagara* 靈山の依・正ながら): I.e., even while remaining himself as the buddha of Vulture Peak. "Secondary and primary recompense" (*eshō* 依正) is a standard Buddhist term for the results of past karma reflected respectively in the circumstances into which one is born and the mental and physical makeup of the person; see Supplementary Notes, s.v. "Secondary and primary recompense."

S3. The *Lotus* Turns the *Lotus*   *Hokke ten Hokke*   法華轉法華

the stūpa springs out at Vulture Peak, even while from an ancient buddha land, even while long extinct, he springs out.[90] "Springing out" and "entering the turning" are not to be learned from common people or the two vehicles; we should study the turning of the *Lotus*. "Long extinct" is an adornment of verification belonging to a buddha land. "Inside the stūpa" and "before the buddha," "the jeweled stūpa" and "empty space" — they are not Vulture Peak; they are not the dharma realm; they are not half of it; they are not the whole realm. They have nothing to do merely with their "dharma position"; they are merely "nonthinking."[91]

[S3:18] {2:496}

或現佛身、而爲説法、或現此身、而爲説法なる轉法華あり。或現提婆
達多なる轉法華あり、或現退亦佳矣なる轉法華あり。合掌瞻仰待、か
ならず六十小劫と、はかる事なかれ。一心待の量をつづめて、しばら
くいく無量劫といふとも、なほこれ不能測佛智なり。待なる一心、い
く佛智の量とかせん。この轉法華は、本行菩薩道のみなりと認ずるこ
となかれ。法華一坐のところ、今日、如來説大乘と轉法華なる功德な
り。法華のいまし法華なる、不覺不知なれども、不識不會なり。しか
あれば、五百塵點は、しばらく一毛許の轉法華なり、赤心片片の佛壽
の、開演せらるるなり。

There is turning the *Lotus* in which one "*manifests a buddha body and preaches the dharma to them,*" or one *manifests this body and preaches the dharma to them.*[92] There is turning the *Lotus* in which one manifests

---

90   **even while from an ancient buddha land, even while long extinct** (*kobutsu do nagara, ku metsudo nagara* 古佛土ながら、久滅度ながら): After the description of Buddha Prabhūtaratna in Chapter 11; e.g., at *Miaofa lianhua jing* 妙法蓮華經, T.262.9:33c17-18:

> 聖主世尊、雖久滅度、在寶塔中、尚爲法來。
> The Sage, the World-Honored One,
> Although long extinct,
> In his jeweled stūpa,
> Has come for the dharma.

91   **their "dharma position"** (*ze hōi* 是法位): See above, Note 22.

they are merely "nonthinking" (*hi shiryō naru nomi nari* 非思量なるのみなり): Readers familiar with Dōgen will immediately recall his famous discussion of "thinking" (*shiryō* 思量), "not thinking" (*fu shiryō* 不思量), and "nonthinking" (*hi shiryō* 非思量), in his "Shōbōgenzō zazen shin" 正法眼藏坐禪箴 (see Supplementary Notes, s.v. "Yaoshan's not thinking"); but in this context, he may well be reflecting the well-known lines in the *Lotus Sūtra* (*Miaofa lianhua jing* 妙法蓮華經, T.262.9:7a20-21), in which the negative *hi* 非 does not in fact govern "thinking" (*shiryō* 思量):

> 是法非思量分別之所能解。唯有諸佛乃能知之。
> This dharma is not something that can be understood by thinking and discrimination. Only the buddhas can know it.

92   **"manifests a buddha body and preaches the dharma to them"** (*waku gen busshin ni i seppō* 或現佛身而爲説法): Quoting the *Lotus Sūtra*, Chapter 25, on the first

92 DŌGEN'S *SHŌBŌGENZŌ* VOLUME VII

Devadatta; there is turning the *Lotus* in which one manifests [those who] "it *is well that they withdraw*."[93]

Do not reckon the "*waiting in adoration, with palms together*" as necessarily "sixty minor kalpas."[94] Even if we were for now to abbreviate

---

of the thirty-three manifestations of the Bodhisattva Avalokiteśvara (Kanzeon bosatsu 觀世音菩薩) (*Miaofa lianhua jing* 妙法蓮華經, T.262.9:57a23-24):

若有國土衆生應以佛身得度者、觀世音菩薩、即現佛身而爲説法。

If there are in the land living beings who ought to attain deliverance by a buddha body, the Bodhisattva Avalokiteśvara manifests a buddha body and preaches the dharma to them.

See Supplementary Notes, s.v. "Manifesting a body to preach the dharma."

one manifests this body and preaches the dharma to them (*waku gen shi shin ni i seppō* 或現此身而爲説法): This and the following two parallel clauses represent Dōgen's variations on the sūtra passage.

93   **one manifests Devadatta** (*waku gen Daibadatta* 或現提婆達多): The Buddha's evil cousin Devadatta is described in Chapter 12 of the *Lotus Sūtra* as having previously been a seer who taught the sūtra to a king who was Śākyamuni in a previous life (*Miaofa lianhua jing* 妙法蓮華經, T.262.9:34c3-4):

時有仙人來白王言、我有大乘、名妙法華經。若不違我當爲宣説。

At that time, there was a seer who came and said to the king, "I have the Great Vehicle, called the *Lotus Sūtra of the Wondrous Dharma*. If you do not disobey me, I shall expound it for you."

one manifests [those who] "it is well that they withdraw" (*waku gen tai yaku kei i* 或現退亦佳矣): I.e., one among those five thousand followers who withdrew from the assembly when the Buddha announced that he would deliver the new revelation of the *Lotus Sūtra*. Upon their departure, the Buddha said to Śāriputra (*Miaofa lianhua jing* 妙法蓮華經, T.262.9:7a12-13):

我今此衆無復枝葉、純有貞實。舍利弗、如是增上慢人、退亦佳矣。

Now, this assembly of mine has no more branches or leaves but purely firm fruit. Śāriputra, it is well that arrogant ones such as these withdraw.

94   **"waiting in adoration, with palms together"** (*gasshō sengō tai* 合掌瞻仰待): From the verse in Chapter 2 of the *Lotus Sūtra*, in which Śāriputra entreats the Buddha to preach (*Miaofa lianhua jing* 妙法蓮華經, T.262.9:6c1-2):

佛口所生子、合掌瞻仰待。願出微妙音、時爲如實説。

The sons born of the Buddha's mouth,
Wait in adoration, with palms together.
We beseech you to use your subtle voice,
Now to speak for us the truth.

"sixty minor kalpas" (*rokujū shōkō* 六十小劫): From the verse in Chapter 1 of the *Lotus Sūtra*, in which Mañjuśrī recalls the time, in the far distant past, that Buddha Candrasūryapradīpa taught the sūtra (*Miaofa lianhua jing* 妙法蓮華經, T.262.9:5a5-6):

説是法華經、滿六十小劫、不起於此座。

He taught this *Lotus Sūtra*
For fully sixty minor kalpas,
Without rising from his seat.

S3. The *Lotus* Turns the *Lotus* *Hokke ten Hokke* 法華轉法華   93

the amount of "single-minded waiting" to some number of innumerable kalpas, we would still be "*unable to fathom the wisdom of the buddhas.*"[95] What amount of the Buddha's wisdom shall we take as the "single mind" that is "waiting"?

Do not consider this turning of the *Lotus* merely as the "*original practice of the bodhisattva path*": where there is a *Lotus* assembly, it is the merit that is turning the *Lotus* as "*today, the Tathāgata will preach the Great Vehicle.*"[96] That the *Lotus* is the *Lotus* right now, though we "do not perceive and do not know," is not known and not understood.[97] Thus, five hundred "bits of ink" are but one hair's worth of turning the *Lotus*; they are the Buddha's lifespan of *the "bare mind in pieces"* being expounded.[98]

---

95   **"single-minded waiting"** (*isshin tai* 一心待): From the verse in Chapter 1 of the *Lotus Sūtra*, in which Mañjuśrī predicts that the Buddha is about to preach the sūtra; see Supplementary Notes, s.v. "Dharma rain."

"unable to fathom the wisdom of the buddhas" (*funō shiki butchi* 不能測佛智): See above, Note 30.

96   **it is the merit that is turning the *Lotus* as "today, the Tathāgata will preach the Great Vehicle"** (*konnichi, nyorai setsu daijō to ten Hokke naru kudoku nari* 今日、如來説大乘と轉法華なる功德なり): I.e., [our turning of the Lotus] is equivalent to the Tathāgata's preaching, as predicted by Mañjuśrī in Chapter 1 of the sūtra (*Miaofa lianhua jing* 妙法蓮華經, T.262.9:4b17-18):

今日如來當説大乘經、名妙法蓮華教菩薩法佛所護念。

Today, the Tathāgata will preach a sūtra of the Great Vehicle called the *Lotus of the Wondrous Dharma*, a dharma taught to bodhisattvas and born in mind by the buddhas.

97   **though we "do not perceive and do not know," is not known and not understood** (*fukaku fuchi naredomo, fushiki fue nari* 不覺不知なれども、不識不會なり): For "not known and not understood" (*fushiki fue* 不識不會), see above, section 11. "Do not perceive, do not know" (*fukaku fuchi* 不覺不知) likely reflects the human condition described in Chapter 3 of the *Lotus Sūtra*, in which we are likened to the children playing in the burning house (*Miaofa lianhua jing* 妙法蓮華經, T.262.9:13a23-25):

如是等種種諸苦、衆生沒在其中、歡喜遊戲。不覺不知不驚不怖、亦不生厭、不求解脱。

Livings beings, although sunk in a multitude of such sorrows, rejoice and play; they do not perceive it, do not know it, are not alarmed, are not afraid; unrepulsed, they do not seek liberation.

See Supplementary Notes, s.v. "Burning house."

98   **five hundred "bits of ink" are but one hair's worth of turning the *Lotus*** (*gohyaku jinten wa, shibaraku ichimōko no ten Hokke nari* 五百塵點は、しばらく一毛許の轉法華なり): A "hair" (*mō* 毛) is a minute measure of length, equal to one-tenth of a *rin* 厘. "Bits of ink" (*jinten* 塵點) suggests an incalculable length of time, reflecting a passage in Chapter 7 of the *Lotus Sūtra* (*Miaofa lianhua jing* 妙法蓮華經, T.262.9:22b7-17) describing the time that has passed since the *parinirvāṇa* of Buddha Mahābhijñānābhibū:

如人以力磨、三千大千土、盡此諸地種、皆悉以爲墨。過於千國土、乃下一塵

[S3:19]

おほよそ震旦にこの經つたはれ、轉法華してよりこのかた數百歳、あるひは疏釋をつくるともがら、ままにしげし。又、この經によりて、上人の法をうるもあれども、いま、われらが高祖曹溪古佛のごとく、法華轉の宗旨をえたるなし、轉法華の宗旨、つかふあらず。いま、これをきき、いま、これにあふ、古佛の古佛にあふにあへり、古佛土にあらざらんや。よろこぶべし、劫より劫にいたるも法華なり、晝より夜にいたるも法華なり、法華これ從劫至劫なるがゆえに、法華これ乃晝乃夜なるがゆえに。たとひ自身心を強弱すとも、さらにこれ法華なり。あらゆる如是は珍寶なり、光明なり、道場なり、廣大深遠なり、深大久遠なり、心迷法華轉なり、心悟轉法華なる、實にこれ法華轉法華なり。

In sum, over the several hundred years since this sūtra was transmitted to Cīnasthāna and the *Lotus* was turned, those who produced commentaries have been many. Moreover, some have attained the dharma of a superior person on the basis of this sūtra.[99] Yet none got the essential point of "the *Lotus* turning" or used the essential point of "turning the *Lotus*," as did our Eminent Ancestor, the Old Buddha of Caoxi, here. Hearing it now, encountering it now, we have encountered an old buddha encountering an old buddha; is it not an old buddha land?[100]

We should rejoice: from kalpa to kalpa is the *Lotus*; from day to night is the *Lotus*; for the *Lotus* is "*from kalpa to kalpa*"; for the *Lotus* is

---

點。如是展轉點、盡此諸塵墨。如是諸國土、點與不點等、復盡末爲塵、一塵爲一劫、此諸微塵數、其劫復過是、彼佛滅度來、如是無量劫。

Suppose a man, with all his might, ground
The earth of the trichiliocosm,
And exhausting the various kinds of earth,
Made them all into powdered ink.
Then, passing a thousand lands,
He dropped a single bit of powder.
And, in this way, continued dropping the bits,
Till he had exhausted all of the ink.
If all these lands —
Both where he dropped and where he did not —
Were again completely turned to dust,
And each grain were one kalpa,
The number of these infinitesimal dust motes
Would be surpassed by the kalpas
Since that buddha entered extinction.
Such are the innumerable kalpas.

"bare mind in pieces" (*sekishin henpen* 赤心片片): See above, Note 42.

99　**dharma of a superior person** (*shōnin no hō* 上人の法): I.e., the status of a respected cleric.

100　**an old buddha encountering an old buddha** (*kobutsu no kobutsu ni au* 古佛の古佛にあふ): The exact sense is uncertain; perhaps to be understood as Huineng encountering Śākyamuni. See Supplementary Notes, s.v. "Old buddha."

S3. The *Lotus* Turns the *Lotus* *Hokke ten Hokke* 法華轉法華 95

"from day to night."[101] Though one's own body and mind grows strong or weak, this too is the *Lotus*. All its suchness is a "precious treasure," is the "ray of light," is the "place of awakening," is "vast and deep," is "profound" and "long ago," is *"if your mind is deluded, the Lotus turns you,"* is *"if your mind is awakened, you turn the Lotus"* — truly this is the *Lotus* turning the *Lotus*.[102]

---

101 **for the *Lotus* is "from kalpa to kalpa"; for the *Lotus* is "from day to night"** (*hokke kore jū gō shi gō naru ga yue ni, hokke kore nai chū nai ya naru ga yue ni* 法華これ從劫至劫なるがゆえに、法華これ乃晝乃夜なるがゆえに): Recalling the Sixth Ancestor's words to Fada (see above, Note 35):

從劫至劫手不釋卷。從晝至夜無不念時也。

From kalpa to kalpa, your hand never lets go of the scrolls; from day to night, there's no time you're not reciting it.

102 **"precious treasure"** (*chinbō* 珍寶): Perhaps recalling the Sixth Ancestor's words (quoted above, section 5): "Everything you have is a precious treasure" (*shou wa mina chinbō nari* 所有はみな珍寶なり); and likely reflecting the *Lotus Sūtra*'s description of the great ox cart given to the rich man's children (*Miaofa lianhua jing* 妙法蓮華經, T.262.9:13a2-3):

是長者等與諸子珍寶大車。

The wealthy man equally gave the children a great cart decorated with precious treasures.

"ray of light" (*kōmyō* 光明): Likely a reference to the light emitted from the forehead of the Buddha as a sign that he would preach the *Lotus Sūtra*; see above, Note 10.

"place of awakening" (*dōjō* 道場): I.e., the place of a buddha's awakening. Dōgen may here be recalling the verse, in Chapter 1 of the sūtra, in which Maitreya asks about the meaning of the ray of light emitted by the Buddha (*Miaofa lianhua jing* 妙法蓮華經, T.262.9:3c6-7):

何所饒益、演斯光明。佛坐道場、所得妙法、爲欲説此。

What is the benefit
Of his spreading this light?
When the Buddha sat at the place of awakening,
The wondrous dharma that he attained —
Does he wish to preach it to us?

"vast and deep" (*kōdai jin'on* 廣大深遠): See above, section 15.

"profound" and "long ago" *(jindai ku'on* 深大久遠): This phrase, which also occurs above, section 1, may reflect the Buddha's praise of the Bodhisattva Samantabhadra, in Chapter 28 of the sūtra; see above, Note 6.

[S3:20] {2:497}

心迷法華轉、心悟轉法華、究盡能如是、法華轉法華。

> *If your mind is deluded, the Lotus turns you;*
> *If your mind is awakened, you turn the Lotus;*
> *When exhaustive investigation can be such,*
> *The Lotus turns the Lotus.*

[S3:21]

かくのことく供養、恭敬、尊重、讚歎する、法華是法華なるべし。

To *offer, revere, honor, and praise* like this is *the Lotus being the Lotus.*[103]

正法眼藏法華轉法華第十二
Treasury of the True Dharma Eye
The Lotus Turns the Lotus
Number 12

[Tōunji MS:]

仁治二年辛丑夏安居日、これをかきて慧達禪人にさづく。これ出家修道を感喜するなり。ただ鬢髮をそる、なほ好事なり。かみをそり、又かみをそる、これ眞出家兒なり。今日の出家は、從來の轉法華の如是力の如是果報なり。いまの法華、かならず法華の法華果あらん。釋迦の法華にあらず、諸佛の法華にあらず、法華の法華なり。ひごろの轉法華は、如是相も不覺不知、かかれり。しかも、いまの法華、さらに不識不會にあらはる。昔時も出息入息なり、今時も出息入息なり。これを妙難思の法華と保任すべし。

On a day of the summer retreat in the junior metal year of the ox, the second year of Ninji [1241], I wrote this and gave it to the Zen person Etatsu, to celebrate his leaving home to practice the way.[104] Just shaving one's head is already auspicious; to shave one's head and shave it again — this is a true home-leaving child.[105] Today's leaving home

---

103 **offer, revere, honor, and praise** (*kuyō, kugyō, sonjū, santan* 供養、恭敬、尊重、讚歎): A fixed phrase typically used in the *Lotus Sūtra* to describe the worship of a buddha.

104 **day of the summer retreat** (*ge ango no hi* 夏安居日): Dates of the summer retreat vary; a common practice put it from the fifteenth of the fourth lunar month through the fifteenth of the seventh month; in 1241, this would have corresponded to 27 May through 23 August.

Zen person Etatsu (*Etatsu zennin* 慧達禪人): Otherwise unknown; from the pronunciation of his name, possibly, a colleague of Ejō 懷奘 and Ekan 懷鑑, members of the so-called Daruma school who converted to Dōgen's community.

105 **a true home-leaving child** (*shin shukke ji* 眞出家兒): A fixed expression, found

S3. The *Lotus* Turns the *Lotus*　Hokke ten Hokke　法華轉法華　　97

is "such effects" of "such power" of his previous turning the *Lotus*.[106] With the present *Lotus*, the *Lotus* will inevitably bear *Lotus* fruit. It is not the *Lotus* of Śākyamuni; it is not the *Lotus* of the buddhas: it is the *Lotus* of the *Lotus*. In our usual turning of the *Lotus*, "such marks" were governed by our "not perceiving and not knowing"; but the present *Lotus* appears anew as "not known and not understood."[107] In the past, we exhaled and inhaled; now, we exhale and inhale. We should maintain this as the *Lotus, "wondrous and hard to comprehend."*[108]

開山觀音導利興聖寶林寺、入宋傳法沙門御名記。在御判

Written by the founder of Kannon Dōri Kōshō Hōrin Monastery (his name), the śramaṇa who entered the Song and transmitted the dharma. (His seal)[109]

[Myōshōji MS:][110]

仁治辛丑仲夏中三日、書寫之于首座寮。懷奘

Copied in the Head Seat's Quarters, third day of mid-summer, the junior metal year of the ox, in Ninji [13 June 1241]. Ejō[111]

---

especially in Chan texts, for a renunciant. That Etatsu shaved his head a second time suggests he may have been a monk who renewed his ordination under Dōgen when he underwent a conversion, or "change of robes" (*kōe* 更衣).

106　**"such effects" of "such power"** (*nyoze riki no nyoze kahō* 如是力の如是果報): From the *Lotus Sūtra*'s list of ten "suchnesses" (*jū nyoze* 十如是) (see above, Note 4); similarly, the "such marks" *(nyoze sō* 如是相) occurring just below in this section.

107　**"not perceiving and not knowing"** (*fukaku fuchi* 不覺不知); **"not known and not understood"** (*fushiki fue* 不識不會): See, above, Note 97.

108　**"wondrous and hard to comprehend"** (*myō nanshi* 妙難思): From Chapter 2 of the *Lotus Sūtra* (*Miaofa lianhua jing* 妙法蓮華經, T.262.9:6c19):

　　我法妙難思

　　My dharma is wondrous and hard to comprehend.

109　Copyist unknown. "His name" and "his seal" refer to Dōgen.

110　The Myōshoji MS 妙昌寺本 of the sixty-chapter *Shōbōgenzō* was completed in 1751; its colophon attributed to Ejō 懷奘 is unknown in earlier manuscript witnesses.

111　**mid-summer** (*chūka* 仲夏): I.e., the fifth lunar month.

TREASURY OF THE TRUE DHARMA EYE
SUPPLEMENTARY CHAPTER 4

The Mind Cannot Be Got
Shin fukatoku
心不可得

The Mind Cannot Be Got

Shin fukatoku

INTRODUCTION

This work is preserved in the twenty-eight-text *Himitsu Shōbōgenzō* collection, where it occurs as number 3 of the first fascicle; it is included in the ninety-five-chapter Honzan edition as number 19. The chapter is often referred to as "Go Shin fukatoku" 後心不可得 (the "Latter Mind Cannot be Got"), to distinguish it from another chapter of the same title (translated above in Volume I), appearing as number 18 in the Honzan edition, number 8 in the seventy-five-chapter *Shōbōgenzō*, and number 4 of fascicle 1 in the *Himitsu* collection. It bears a colophon similar to that of the seventy-five-chapter Shōbōgenzō text, identifying it as a work written at Dōgen's Kōshōji, during the summer retreat of 1241.

The text is clearly divided into two parts, of roughly equal length. The first deals with the title theme, the famous story of an old woman selling cakes who bests the monk Deshan 德山, a learned scholar of the *Diamond Sūtra*. This part corresponds, often quite closely, to the text of the "Shin fukatoku" chapter of the seventy-five-chapter *Shōbōgenzō*. The second part of our essay treats the well-known story of Chan Master Huizhong's 慧忠 test of the mind-reading powers of an Indian monk. This story is the focus of the "Tashin tsū" 他心通, a work of 1245 occurring as number 73 in the seventy-five-chapter *Shōbōgenzō* and number 80 in the Honzan edition. Here again, the correspondence in content and language is often quite close. It is now generally assumed that the present text represents an early draft of a work from 1241 that was subsequently divided into two separate essays, perhaps around 1245, when the "Tashin tsū" chapter is dated.

The notes to the translation below will be limited to material specific to this text and its relationship to chapters 8 and 73 of the seventy-five-chapter *Shōbōgenzō*, where more complete annotation can be found.

正法眼藏別輯四

Treasury of the True Dharma Eye
Supplementary Chapter 4

心不可得

The Mind Cannot Be Got

(草案本系・「秘密正法眼藏」初冊所收)
(Draft version, in the first volume of the *Himitsu Shōbōgenzō*)

{2:498}

観音導利興聖寶林寺
Kannon Dōri Kōshō Hōrin Monastery

[S4:1]

心不可得者、諸佛なり。みづから阿耨多羅三藐三菩提と保任し來れり。

"*The mind cannot be got*" is the buddhas. They have themselves maintained it as *anuttara-samyak-saṃbodhi*.

[S4:2]

金剛經云、過去心不可得、現在心不可得、未來心不可得。

It is said in the Diamond Sūtra, "The past mind cannot be got; the present mind cannot be got; the future mind cannot be got."[1]

[S4:3]

これすなはち、諸佛なる心不可得の保任の現成せる、三界心不可得なり、諸法心不可得なり、と保任し來れるなり。これをあきらむる保任は、諸佛にならはざれば、證取せず、諸祖にならはざれば、正傳せざるなり。ならふ、と云は、丈六身にならひ、一莖草にならふなり。諸祖にならふ、と云は、皮肉骨髓にならひ、破顔微笑にならふなり。この宗旨は、正法眼藏あきらかに正傳しきたりて、佛佛祖祖の心印、まさに直指なること、嫡嫡單傳せるにとぶらひならふに、かならずその骨髓面目つたはれ、身體髮膚うくるなり。佛道をならはず、祖室にいらざらんは、見聞せず、會取せず。問取の法におよばず、道取の分、夢にもいまだみざるところなり。

This has expressed how they have maintained "*the mind cannot be got*" that is the buddhas; they have been maintaining it as *the three realms*

---

1   ***Diamond Sūtra*** (*Kongō kyō* 金剛經): This quotation represents section 1 in the seventy-five-chapter *Shōbōgenzō* text of the "Shin fukatoku" chapter.

are *"the mind cannot be got,"* as *the dharmas are "the mind cannot be got."* The maintaining of it that makes this clear cannot be verified if not learned from the buddhas, cannot be directly transmitted if not learned from the ancestors. "To learn" means to learn from "the sixteen-foot body," to learn from "a single blade of grass."[2] "To learn from the ancestors" means to learn from their skin, flesh, bones, and marrow, to learn from *breaking into a smile.*[3] The essential point of this is that, when we inquire of and learn from those who clearly have directly transmitted the treasury of the true dharma eye, who have uniquely transmitted through successor after successor the fact that the mind seal of buddha after buddha and ancestor after ancestor is directly pointed at, invariably, their bones and marrow, face and eyes are passed down to us, and we receive their body, hair, and skin. Those who do not learn the way of the buddhas, who do not enter the chambers of the ancestors, do not see or hear it, do not understand it; the way to ask about it is beyond them, and the status to speak of it, they have never even dreamt of.[4]

[S4:4] {2:499}

徳山の、そのかみ不丈夫なりしとき、金剛經に長ぜりき。ときの人、これを周金剛王と稱しき。八百餘家のなかに王なり。ことに、青龍疏をよくせるのみにあらず、さらに十二擔の書籍を釋集せり、齊肩の講者あることなし。ちなみに、南方に無上道の嫡嫡相承せるありと聞て、書をたづさへて山川をわたりゆく。龍潭にいたらんとするみちの左に歇息するに、婆子來り逢ふ。徳山問、汝はこれなに人ぞ。婆子云く、我は、もちひ、うる老婆也。徳山云、我がために、もちひを賣るべし。婆子云、和尚、かうてなにかせん。徳山の云、もちを買うて、點心にすべし。婆子云く、和尚の、そこばくたづさへてあるは、これなにものぞ。徳山云く、汝聞かずや、我是周金剛王なり、金剛經に長ぜり、通達せずといふところなし、このたづさへてあるは、金剛經の解釋也。これをききて、婆子云く、老婆に一問あり、和尚、これをゆるすやいなや。徳山云く、ゆるす、汝が心ろにまかせ

---

2 **"To learn" means to learn from "the sixteen-foot body," to learn from "a single blade of grass"** (*narau, to iu wa, jōroku shin ni narai, ikkyō sō ni narau nari* ならふ、と云は、丈六身にならひ、一莖草にならふふなり): Some versions of our text read here *shobutsu ni narau to iu wa* 諸佛にならふと云は ("'To learn from the buddhas' means . . ."). For the association of the "sixteen-foot body" with "one blade of grass," see Supplementary Notes, s.v. "One blade of grass."

3 **skin, flesh, bones, and marrow** (*hi niku kotsu zui* 皮肉骨髓); **breaking into a smile** (*hagan mishō* 破顔微笑): Allusions respectively to the story of Bodhidharma's transmission to the second Chinese ancestor, Huike 慧可, and to the story of Śākyamuni's transmission to the first Indian ancestor, Mahākāśyapa. See Supplementary Notes, s.v. "Skin, flesh, bones, and marrow" and "Break into a smile."

4 **Those who do not learn the way of the buddhas, who do not enter the chambers of the ancestors** (*butsudō o narawazu, soshitsu ni irazaran* 佛道をならはず、祖室にいらざらん): I.e., those outside of Dōgen's tradition of the buddhas and ancestors; a point reiterated in the seventy-five-chapter *Shōbōgenzō* text of the "Shin fukatoku," section 2.

S4. The Mind Cannot Be Got *Shin fukatoku* 心不可得

て問べし。云、我、かつて金剛經をきくに云く、過去心も不可得、現在心不可得、未來心不可得、いま、もちひをしていづれの心をか點ぜんとする、和尚、若道得ならんには、もちひ、うるべし、和尚、もし道不得ならんには、もちひをうるべからず。德山、ときに茫然として、祇對すべきことをえざりき。婆子、すなはち拂袖して出ぬ、つひにもちひ餅を德山にうらず。

Deshan, at a time when he was not much of a man, excelled at the *Diamond Sūtra*.[5] People at the time called him "Zhou, King of the *Diamond*." He was king among over eight hundred scholars. Not only was he particularly versed in the *Qinglong Commentary*, but he also compiled twelve piculs of books. He was without peer as a lecturer.

Once, upon hearing that in the south the unsurpassed way had been inherited by successor after successor, he packed his books and crossed mountains and rivers. As he paused for a rest to the left of the road he was taking to Longtan, an old woman came along.[6]

Deshan asked, "Who are you?"

The old woman said, "I'm an old woman selling cakes."

Deshan said, "Sell me a cake."

The old woman said, "Why is the Reverend buying a cake?"

Deshan said, "I'm buying the cake for a refreshment."

The old woman said, "What is that load the Reverend is carrying?"

Deshan said, "Haven't you heard? I'm Zhou, King of the *Diamond*. I'm an expert on the *Diamond Sūtra*. There's nothing [in it] I haven't penetrated. What I'm carrying here are interpretations of the *Diamond Sūtra*."

Hearing this, the old woman said, "This old woman has a question. Does the Reverend grant it?"

Deshan said, "Granted. Feel free to ask."

The old woman said, "I once heard it said in the *Diamond Sūtra*, 'The past mind cannot be got; the present mind cannot be got; the future mind cannot be got.' Now which mind will you refresh with the cake? If the Reverend can answer, I'll sell you the cake; if the Reverend can't answer, I won't sell you the cake."

---

5   **Deshan** (*Tokusan* 德山): The retelling of the Deshan story in this section of our text corresponds to sections 3-6 of the seventy-five-chapter *Shōbōgenzō* text of the "Shin fukatoku."

not much of a man (*fujōbu* 不丈夫): From the common Chinese usage of *zhangfu* 丈夫 for the manly male.

6   **Longtan** (*Ryūtan* 龍潭): A reference to Longtan Chongxin 龍潭崇信 (dates unknown; a disciple of Tianhuang Daowu 天皇道悟 [748-807], in the lineage of Qingyuan 青原) with whom Deshan would subsequently study.

104 DŌGEN'S *SHŌBŌGENZŌ* VOLUME VII

Deshan was at a loss and could think of nothing to reply. The old woman thereupon shook out her sleeves and left. She never sold Deshan the cake.

[S4:5]

うらむべし、數百軸の釋主、數十年の講者、わづかに弊婆の一問をうるに、すみやかに負處におちぬること。師承あると師承なきと、正師の室にとぶらふと正師の室に入らざると、はるかにことなるによりてかくのごとし。不可得の言をききては、彼此ともにおなじく、うることあるべからず、とのみ解せり、さらに活路なし。又、うべからず、といふは、もとよりそなはれるゆゑに云ふ、なんどおもふ人もあり。これを、いかにもあたらぬことなり。德山、このときはじめて、えにかける餅、うゑをやむるにあたはず、としり、又、佛道修行には、必ずその人に逢べきとおもひしりき。又、いたづらに經書にのみかかはれるが、まことのちからをうべからざることをも、おもひしりき。つひに、龍潭に參じて、師資のみち見成せりしより、まさにその人なりき。いまは、雲門・法眼の高祖なるのみにあらず、人中・天上の導師なり。

What a pity.[7] A commentator of several hundred rolls, a lecturer of several tens of years, gets but a single question from a tired, worn-out old woman and is immediately defeated. This happens because of the great difference between those who have succession from a master and those who lack succession from a master, those who have visited the rooms of a true master and those who have not entered the rooms of a true master. Hearing the words "cannot be got," they understand only that this and that are all equally impossible to get, and they have no way out. Again, there are people who think that [the sūtra] says "cannot be got" because we possess it from the start; this does not get it at all. At this time, Deshan first recognized that "a painted cake can't satisfy hunger"; and he understood that, to practice the way of the buddhas, we have to encounter "that person"; and he understood that one fruitlessly engaged only with books cannot develop real strength.[8] Eventually, he studied with Longtan and, after realizing the way of master and disciple, was truly "that person." Now, he is not only the eminent ancestor of Yunmen and Fayan but a guide to humans and devas.[9]

---

7 **What a pity** (*uramu beshi* うらむべし): This section parallels material in sections 7-8 of the seventy-five-chapter *Shōbōgenzō* text of the "Shin fukatoku."

8 **"that person"** (*sono hito* その人): I.e., a true master.

9 **the eminent ancestor of Yunmen and Fayan** (*Unmon Hōgen no kōso* 雲門・法眼の高祖): I.e., an ancestor in the lineage leading to the Yunmen 雲門 and Fayan 法眼 houses of Chan. This line has no parallel in the seventy-five-chapter *Shōbōgenzō* text.

S4. The Mind Cannot Be Got *Shin fukatoku* 心不可得 105

[S4:6] {2:500}

この因縁をおもふに、徳山、むかし、あきらめざることは、いまみゆる處なり。婆子、いま、徳山を杜口せしむればとても、實に、その人にてあらんことも、さだめがたし。しばらく心不可得のことばをききて、心あるべきにあらず、とばかりおもひて、かくのごとくとふにてあるらん、とおぼゆ。徳山の、丈夫にてありしかば、かんがふるちからもありなまし。かんがふることあらば、婆子がその人にてありけるときもきこゆべかりしかども、徳山の、徳山にてあらざりしときにてあれば、婆子がそのひとなることも、いまだしられず、みえざるなり。

When we think about this episode, we can see here that at that time Deshan had not clarified [the dharma].[10] Although here the old woman may have shut Deshan's mouth, it is still difficult to decide that she was really "that person." It seems likely that she asks as she does because, merely having heard the words "the mind cannot be got," she thinks simply that there must be no mind. Had Deshan been a man, he would have had the strength to judge her; and, had he judged her, we would have heard when the old woman was "that person." But, since this was a time when Deshan was not yet Deshan, whether the old woman was "that person" is still not known, still cannot be seen.

[S4:7] {2:501}

又、いま婆子を疑著すること、ゆえなきにあらず。徳山道不得ならんに、などか徳山にむかうて云はざる、和尚、いま道不得なり、さらに老婆に問べし、老婆、かへりて和尚のためにいふべし、と。このとき、徳山の問をえて、徳山にむかひていふことありせば、老婆がまことにてあるちからも、あらはれぬべし。

Again, we are not without reasons to doubt the old woman here.[11] When Deshan was unable to say anything, why did she not say to him, "Since the Reverend is unable to say anything, ask this old woman, and the old woman will answer for the Reverend"? At this time, having got Deshan's question, if she had something to say to Deshan, the old woman's real strength would have appeared.

---

10 **When we think about this episode** (*kono innen o omou ni* この因縁をおもふに): This section parallels material in section 8 of the seventy-five-chapter *Shōbōgenzō* text of the "Shin fukatoku."

11 **we are not without reasons to doubt the old woman here** (*ima bashi o gijaku suru koto, yue naki ni arazu* いま婆子を疑著すること、ゆえなきにあらず): This section parallels material in section 9 of the seventy-five-chapter *Shōbōgenzō* text of the "Shin fukatoku."

106 DŌGEN'S *SHŌBŌGENZŌ* VOLUME VII

[S4:8]

かくのごとくの古人の骨髄も面目も、古佛の光明も現瑞も、同参の功夫あ
りて、德山をも婆子をも、不可得をも可得をも、餅をも心をも、把定にわ
づらはざるのみにあらず、放行にもわづらはざるなり。

With the concentrated effort that studies together with the bones and marrow, face and eyes of the ancients, with the radiance and auspicious signs of the old buddhas, one has no trouble, not only getting hold of, but also letting go of Deshan, of the old woman, of "cannot be got," of "can be got," of the "cake," and of the "mind."[12]

[S4:9]

いはゆる、佛心はこれ三世なり。心と三世と、あひへだたること毫釐にあ
らずと雖も、あひはなれ、あひさる事を論ずるには、則ち十萬八千よりも
あまれる深遠なり。いかにあらんか是過去心、と云ば、かれにむかひて云
ふべし、是不可得、と。如何にあらんかこれ現在心、と云ば、かれにむか
ひていふべし、是不可得、と。如何にあらんか是未來心、と云はば、かれ
に向ていふべし、是不可得、と。

That is, the buddha mind is itself the three times. Although the mind and the three times are not separated by a hair's breadth, when we discuss their separation, their departure from each other, it is a profound distance, exceeding one hundred eight thousand. If we are asked, "What is the 'past mind'?" we should answer, "It is 'cannot be got.'" If we are asked, "What is the 'present mind'?" we should answer, "It is 'cannot be got.'" If we are asked, "What is the 'future mind'?" we should answer, "It is 'cannot be got.'"

[S4:10]

云はくのこころは、心をしばらく、不可得となづくる心あり、とは云は
ず、しばらく、不可得なり、と云ふ。心うべからず、とはいはず、ひとへ
に、不可得、と云ふ。心うべし、とはいはず、ひとへに、不可得、と云ふ
なり。又、如何なるか過去心不可得、といわば、生死去來、と云べし。如
何なるか現在心不可得、と云はば、生死去來、といふべし。如何なるか未
來心不可得、と云はば、生死去來、と云ふべし。をほよそ、牆壁瓦礫にて
在る佛心在り、三世諸佛、共に是を不可得にてありと證す。佛心にて在る
牆壁瓦礫のみ在り、諸佛、三世に是を不可得なりと證す。況や、山河大地
にてある不可得の、自にて在るあり、草木風水なる不可得の、則ち心なる
在り、又、應無所住、而生其心の、不可得なるあり、又、十方諸佛の、一
代の代にて八萬法門をとく。不可得の心、其れかくのごとし。

---

12 **the radiance and auspicious signs of the old buddhas** (*kobutsu no kōmyō mo genzui mo* 古佛の光明も現瑞も): I.e., the nimbus surrounding the body of a buddha and the miraculous portents of his actions. The Honzan version of our text reads here *gentan* 現端 ("beauty"[?]; perhaps from *jigen tanshō* 示現端正 ["to display beauty"]). This and the following two sections have no parallel in the seventy-five-chapter *Shōbōgenzō* text of the "Shin fukatoku," which concludes with Dōgen's suggestions on how the conversation between Deshan and the old woman could be improved.

The point of this is that we are not saying of the mind that there is a mind that, for now, we call "cannot be got"; we are saying, for now, it is "cannot be got."[13] We are not saying that we cannot get the mind; we are saying solely, "it cannot be got." We are not saying that we can get the mind; we are saying solely, "it cannot be got." Again, if we are asked, "What is 'the past mind cannot be got'?" we should say, "birth and death, coming and going." If asked, "What is 'the present mind cannot be got'?" we should say, "birth and death, coming and going." If asked, "What is 'the future mind cannot be got'?" we should say, "birth and death, coming and going."

In general, there is a buddha mind that is "fences, walls, tiles, and pebbles"; the buddhas of the three times all verify this as "it cannot be got."[14] There are only the fences, walls, tiles, and pebbles that are the buddha mind; in the three times, the buddhas verify them as "it cannot be got." Not to mention that there is [the case in which] the "it cannot be got" that is the "mountains, rivers, and the whole earth" exists in itself; there [the case in which] the "it cannot be got" that is "grasses, trees, wind, and water" is the mind.[15] Or, again, there is [the case in which] "*one should produce a thought that does not abide anywhere*" is "it cannot be got."[16] Again, the mind of "it cannot be got" with which the buddhas of the ten directions, in each age, preach the eighty thousand dharma gates is like this.

* * * * *

13 **we are not saying of the mind that there is a mind that, for now, we call "cannot be got"** (*shin o shibaraku, fukatoku to nazukuru shin ari, to wa iwazu* 心をしばらく、不可得となづくる心あり、とは云はず): Presumably, meaning something like, "it is not that 'cannot be got' is an attribute of the mind."

14 **a buddha mind that is "fences, walls, tiles, and pebbles"** (*shō heki ga ryaku nite aru busshin ari* 牆壁瓦礫にて在る佛心在り): Allusion to a well-known saying in Chan texts first attributed to Nanyang Huizhong 南陽慧忠 (d. 775). See Supplementary Notes, s.v. "Fences, walls, tiles, and pebbles."

15 **there is [the case in which] the "it cannot be got" that is the "mountains, rivers, and the whole earth" exists in itself** (*senga daichi nite aru fukatoku no, onozukara nite aru ari* 山河大地にてある不可得の、自にて在るあり): A tentative rendering of an odd locution. "Mountains, rivers, and the whole earth" (*senga daichi* 山河大地) is a fixed expression occurring often in Chan texts; here, perhaps, reflecting a conversation between Weishan Lingyou 潙山靈祐 (771-853) and his disciple Yangshan Huiji 仰山慧寂 (803-887) recorded in Dōgen's *shinji Shōbōgenzō* 眞字正法眼藏 (DZZ.5:212, case 168); see Supplementary Notes, s.v. "Sun, moon, and stars."

16 **"one should produce a thought that does not abide anywhere"** (*ō mushojū, ni shō go shin* 應無所住、而生其心): From the famous line in the *Diamond Sūtra* (*Jingang bore boluomi jing* 金剛般若波羅蜜經, T.235.8:749c22-23), on hearing which it is said the future Sixth Ancestor, Huineng 慧能, was awakened.

108 DŌGEN'S *SHŌBŌGENZŌ* VOLUME VII

[S4:11] {2:502}

又、大證國師のとき、大耳三藏、はるかに西天より到京せり。他心通をえ
たりと講ず。唐の肅宗皇帝、ちなみに國師に命じて試驗せしむるに、三藏
わづかに國師をみて、速に禮拜して右にたつ。國師つひに問、なんぢ、他
心通を得りやいなや。三藏まうす、不敢、と。國師の云、汝云ふべし、老
僧、今いづれの處にか在る。三藏まうす、和尚、是一國の師也、なんぞ西
川に行て競渡のふねをみる。國師やや久くして再問す、なんぢ云べし、老
僧、今何處にか在る。三藏まうす、和尚は一國の師也、なんぞ天津橋の上
に行て、獼猴を弄するをみる。國師又問、汝云べし、老僧、今何處にか在
る。三藏、やや久く在れ共、しることなし、みるところなし。國師、ちな
みに叱して云、この野狐精、汝が他心通、何の處にかある。三藏、又祇對
なし。

Again, at the time of the National Teacher Dazheng, the Tripiṭaka Master Daer arrived in the capital from distant Sindh in the West.[17] He claimed to have attained the knowledge of other minds. The Tang Emperor Suzong thus ordered the National Teacher to test him. As soon as the Tripiṭaka Master saw the National Teacher, he quickly paid obeisance and stood off to the right.

After a while, the National Teacher asked him, "You have the knowledge of other minds, do you?"

The Tripiṭaka Master said, "I wouldn't presume."

The National Teacher said, "Tell me, where's this old monk right now?"

The Tripiṭaka Master said, "The Reverend is the teacher to a nation. Why has he gone off to Xichuan to watch the boat races?"

The National Teacher after a while asked again, "Tell me, where's this old monk right now?"

The Tripiṭaka Master said, "The Reverend is the teacher to a nation. Why has he gone onto the Tianjin bridge to watch the monkeys play?"

The National Teacher asked once more, "Tell me, where's this old monk right now?"

The Tripiṭaka Master was silent for a while but did not know, did not see anything.

The National Teacher then rebuked him, saying, "This fox spirit! Where's his knowledge of other minds?"

The Tripiṭaka Master had no response.

---

17 **the National Teacher Dazheng** (*Daishō kokushi* 大證國師): Dōgen begins here his discussion of material found in the "Shōbōgenzō tashin tsū" 正法眼藏他心通. His Japanese retelling of the encounter between Huizhong and Daer here corresponds to the Chinese version in section 1 of that text. His comments in the following two sections, however, while consistent with his treatment there, have no exact parallel.

S4. The Mind Cannot Be Got *Shin fukatoku* 心不可得

[S4:12]

かくのごとくの事と、しらざればあし、きかざればあやしみぬべし。佛祖と三藏とひとしかるべからず、天地懸隔なり。佛祖は、佛法をあきらめてあり、三藏は、いまだあきらめず。まことにそれ三藏は、在俗も三藏なることあり。たとへば文華にところをえたらんがごとし。然あれば、ひろく竺漢の言音をあきらめてあるのみにあらず、他心通をも修得せりと云へども、佛道の身心におきては、ゆめにもいまだみざるゆえに、佛祖の位に證せる國師にまみゆるには、すなはち勘破せらるるなり。いはゆる佛道に心をならふには、萬法即ち心なり、三界唯心なり。唯心これ唯心なるべし、是佛即心なるべし。たとひ自なりとも、たとひ他なりとも、佛道の心をあやまらざるべし。いたづらに西川に流落すべからず、天津橋におもひわたるべからず。佛道の身心を保任すべくは、佛道の智通を學習すべし。

If we did not know of such a matter, it would be bad; if we had not heard of it, we would have been suspicious. The buddhas and ancestors and the tripiṭaka masters cannot be equal; the gap is as great as heaven and earth. The buddhas and ancestors have clarified the buddha dharma; the tripiṭaka masters have not clarified it. Indeed, with tripiṭaka masters, there are cases where laymen are tripiṭaka masters, as when one has attained a place in literary culture. Thus, while he may not only have widely understood the languages of Sindh and Han but also cultivated the knowledge of other minds, because he has never seen even in his dreams the body and mind of the way of the buddhas, when he meets with the National Teacher, who has verified the status of the buddhas and ancestors, he is immediately seen through.

When we study the mind in the way of the buddhas, it is, the myriad dharmas are the mind; it is, the three realms are only mind.[18] It should be, only mind is only mind; it should be, this buddha is this mind itself.[19] Whether it is one's own or another's, we should not be mistaken about the mind in the way of the buddhas. It does not vainly drift off to Xichuan; it does not wander over the Tianjin bridge. To maintain the body and mind of the way of the buddhas, we should study the spiritual knowledge of the way of the buddhas.[20]

18　**the myriad dharmas are the mind** (*manbō sunawachi shin nari* 萬法即ち心なり): Japanese rendering of the phrase *wanfa jixin* 萬法即心, occurring in Chan texts (see, e.g., *Zongjing lu* 宗鏡錄, T.2016.48:603c25).

the three realms are only mind (*sangai yui shin* 三界唯心): A very common expression found throughout Chan literature as well as other Chinese texts of the Mahāyāna; see Supplementary Notes, s.v. "The three realms are only mind."

19　**this buddha is this mind itself** (*ze butsu soku shin* 是佛即心): Playing with the well-known expression "this mind itself is the buddha" (*soku shin ze butsu* 即心是佛); see Supplementary Notes.

20　**spiritual knowledge of the way of the buddhas** (*butsudō no chitsū* 佛道の智通): Probably meaning "paranormal knowledge as it is properly understood in the way of

110 DŌGEN'S *SHŌBŌGENZŌ* VOLUME VII

[S4:13] {2:503}

いはゆる佛道には、盡地みな心なり、起滅にあらたまらず。盡法みな心
なり、盡心を智通とも學すべし。三藏すでにこれをみず、野狐の精のみ
なり。然あれば、已然兩度も、いまだ國師の心をみず、國師の心に通ずる
ことなし。いたづらなる西川と天津と、競渡・猢猻とのみにたはむるる野
狐子なり、いかにしてか國師を見ん。又、國師の在處をみるべからざる道
理、あきらけし。老僧今いづれの處にかある、と三たび問に、このことば
をきかず。若しきくことあらば、たづぬべし、きかざれば蹉過するなり。
三藏、若し佛法をならふことありせば、國師のことばをきかまし、國師の
身心をみることあらまし。ひごろ佛法をならはざるが故に、人中・天上の
導師にうまれあふといへども、いたづらにすぎぬるなり、あはれむべし、
かなしむべし。おほよそ三藏の學者、いかでか佛祖の行履におよばん、國
師の邊際をしらん。況や、西天の論師および竺乾三藏、たえて國師の行履
をしるべからず。三藏のしらんことは、天帝もしるべし、論師もしるべ
し。論師・天帝しらんこと、補處の智力、およばざらんや。十聖三賢も、
およばざらんや。國師の身心は、天帝もしるべからず、補處もいまだあき
らめざる也。身心を佛家に論ずること、かくのごとし。しるべし、信ずべ
し。我が大師釋尊の法、いまだ二乘・外道等の野狐の精には、おなじから
ざるなり。

That is, in the way of the buddhas, all the earth is mind; it does not change in arising and ceasing. All the dharmas are mind; we should also study all the mind as the spiritual powers.[21] Since the Tripiṭaka Master does not see this, he is just the spirit of a fox. Thus, in the previous two times as well, he never sees the mind of the National Teacher, he does not know the mind of the National Teacher. He is a fox cub just idly playing around at Xichuan and Tianjin, boat races and monkeys. How could he see the National Teacher? Again, the reason that he cannot see the whereabouts of the National Teacher is obvious. Asked three times "where's this old monk right now?" he does not hear these words. If he heard them, he could have inquired about them; since he did not hear them, he missed them. Had he learned the buddha dharma, the Tripiṭaka Master would have heard the words of the National Teacher, would have seen the body and mind of the National Teacher. Because he did not regularly learn the buddha dharma, though he may have been born to meet a guide of humans and devas, he idly passes it by.[22] How pathetic. How sad.

---

the buddhas." The term *chitsū* 知通 ("spiritual knowledge"), occurring here and in the following section, is not found elsewhere in the *Shōbōgenzō*; it is synonymous with *jinzū* 神通 ("spiritual powers"; S. *abhijñā*). See Supplementary Notes, s.v. "Spiritual powers."

21 **all the mind** (*jinshin* 盡心): In parallel with "all the earth"; or, perhaps, "all minds," in parallel with "all dharmas." In common parlance, the term *jinshin* 盡心 means "to exhaust the mind" in wholehearted effort.

22 **though he may have been born to meet a guide of humans and devas** (*ninchū tenjō no dōshi ni umareau to iedomo* 人中・天上の導師にうまれあふといへども): I.e., though he had the opportunity to encounter Huizhong, of whom tradition held that he

S4. The Mind Cannot Be Got *Shin fukatoku* 心不可得　　　111

In general, how could scholars of the tripiṭaka reach the conduct of the buddhas and ancestors or know the whereabouts of the National Teacher? It goes without saying that the treatise masters of Sindh in the West and the Indian tripiṭaka masters could know nothing of the conduct of the National Teacher. What the tripiṭaka master knows is known as well by the Deva Lord, is known as well by the treatise master.[23] What the treatise master or the Deva Lord knows — how could it not be equaled by the knowledge power of the heir apparent?[24] How could it not be equaled by the ten sages and three worthies?[25] The body and mind of the National Teacher cannot be known even by the Deva Lord and is still not clarified even by the heir apparent. This is how body and mind are discussed in the house of the buddhas. We should know it; we should believe it. The dharma of our great master Śākya, the World-Honored One, has never been the same as the fox spirits of the two vehicles and other paths.

[S4:14] {2:504}
然あるに、この一段の因縁、ふるくより諸代の尊宿おのおの參究するに、その話、のこれり。

Now, from long ago, venerables over the generations have investigated this episode, and their talk on it remains.

[S4:15]
僧ありて趙州にとふ、三藏、なにとしてか第三度に國師の所在をみざる。趙州云、國師在三藏鼻孔上、所以不見。又僧ありて玄沙問、既在鼻孔上、爲甚不見。玄沙云、只爲太近。海會端云、國師若在三藏鼻孔上、有什麼難。又、玄沙、三藏を徴して云く、汝道、前兩度還見麼。雪竇顯云、敗也、敗也。又、僧ありて仰山に間、第三度、なにとしてか、三藏ややひさしくあれど國師の所在をみざる。仰山云、前兩度是渉境心、後入自受用三昧、所以不見。

A monk asked Zhaozhou, "Why did the Tripiṭaka Master not see the whereabouts of the National Teacher the third time?"[26]

---

was teacher, on earth, to the emperors of China and, in the heavens, to Indra, king of the gods.

23　**Deva Lord** (*Tentai* 天帝): I.e., Indra, king of the gods.

24　**heir apparent** (*fusho* 補處): I.e., a bodhisattva destined to become the next buddha.

25　**ten sages and three worthies** (*jisshō sanken* 十聖三賢): Also read *jisshō sangen*. Reference to those on the path of the bodhisattva: the ten stages, or "grounds" (*chi* 地; S. *bhūmi*), of the "sage," or "noble" (*shō* 聖; S. *ārya*), ones — i.e., those on the advanced levels of the path — and the three types of "wise," or "worthy" (*ken* 賢; S. *bhadra*) ones — i.e., those on the level just preceding the *ārya*.

26　**A monk asked Zhaozhou** (*sō mon Jōshū* 僧問趙州): This section (throughout which Dōgen switches back and forth between Chinese quotation and Japanese translation) corresponds to the Chinese text in section 2 of the "Shōbōgenzō tashin tsū."

112 DŌGEN'S *SHŌBŌGENZŌ* VOLUME VII

Zhaozhou said, "The National Teacher was on the Tripiṭaka Master's nose; that's why he didn't see him."

Again, a monk asked Xuansha, *"Since he was on his nose, why didn't he see him?"*

Xuansha said, "Because he was too close."

Duan of Haihui said, "If the National Teacher was on the Tripiṭaka Master's nose, why would it be hard?"[27]

Again, Xuansha summoned the Tripiṭaka Master, saying, *"Tell me, did you in fact see him the first two times?"*

Chan Master Mingjue Zhongxian of Xuedou said, "Defeated! Defeated!"

Again, a monk asked Yangshan, "On the third time, although he was silent for a while, why didn't the Tripiṭaka Master see the National Teacher's whereabouts?"

Yangshan said, "The first two times were the mind that plays across objects. After that, he entered the samādhi of personal enjoyment; that's why he didn't see him."

[S4:16] {2:505}

この五位尊宿、そのともに諦當なれども、國師の行履は蹉過せり。いはゆる、第三度しらず、とのみ論じて、前兩度は知れり、とゆるすに似たり。是即ち古先の蹉過する處なり、晩進のしるべきなり。

These five venerables may all be on the mark, but they have missed the conduct of the National Teacher: they discuss only the fact that he did not know the third time and seem to accept that he knew the first two times.[28] This is a place our old forebears missed, and latecomers should recognize it.

[S4:17]

興聖、今、五位の尊宿を疑著すること、兩般あり。一には云、國師の、三藏を試驗する意趣をしらず。二には云、國師の身心をしらず。しばらく國師、三藏を試驗する意趣を不知と云ふは、第一番に國師云く、汝道老僧即今在什麼處、と問こころは、三藏、若佛法をしれりや、いまだしらずや、と試問するとき、三藏、もし佛法を聞ことあらば、老僧今在甚麼處、ときくことばを、佛法にならふべきなり。佛法にならふ、と云ふは、國師の、

---

27 **Duan of Haihui** (*Kaie Tan* 海會端): Our version here is missing some text; the original, given in full in the "Shōbōgenzō tashin tsū" and also below, section 27, has:

> 國師若在三藏鼻孔上、有什麼難見、殊不知國師在三藏眼睛裏。

> If the National Teacher was on the Tripiṭaka Master's nose, why would it be hard to see him? He's completely unaware that the National Teacher was in the Tripiṭaka Master's eye.

28 **These five venerables** (*kono goi sonshuku* この五位尊宿): This section corresponds to material in section 3 of the "Shōbōgenzō tashin tsū."

S4. The Mind Cannot Be Got *Shin fukatoku* 心不可得

老僧今いづれの處にかある、と云ふは、這邊にあるか、那邊にあるか、無上菩提にあるか、般若波羅蜜にあるか、空にかかれるか、地にたてるか、草菴にあるか、實所にあるか、と問なり。三藏、この心を不知、いたづらに凡夫二乘等の見解をたてまつる。國師かさねて問、汝道老僧即今在什麼處。ここに三藏、更にいたづらのことばをたてまつる。國師かさねてとふ、汝道老僧即今在甚麼處。ときに三藏、ややひさしくあれども、ものいはず、ここち茫然なり。ちなみに國師、即三藏を叱して云、這野狐精、他心通在甚麼處。かくいふに、三藏、なほ云ふことなし。

Kōshō's doubts about the five venerables here are of two sorts: first, they do not know the National Teacher's basic intention in testing the Tripiṭaka Master; second, they do not know the body and mind of the National Teacher.[29]

Now, for a start, when I say that they are ignorant of the National Teacher's basic intention in testing the Tripiṭaka Master, I mean this: that the National Teacher's thought in saying the first time, "*Tell me, where's this old monk right now?*" is to test whether the Tripiṭaka Master knew the buddha dharma or not.

When asked this, if the Tripiṭaka Master had heard the buddha dharma, the words asking, "where's this old monk right now?" he should have learned from the buddha dharma.[30] To "learn from the buddha dharma," means that the National Teacher's asking, "Where's this old monk right now?" is "Am I here?" "Am I there?" "Am I in unsurpassed bodhi?" "Am I in *mahā-prajñā-pāramitā*?" "Am I suspended in space?" "Am I standing on the earth?" "Am I in a thatched hut?" "Am I at the treasure trove?"[31]

The Tripiṭaka Master, not recognizing this thought, worthlessly offers the views of common people and the two vehicles. The National Teacher asks him again, "*Tell me, where's this old monk right now?*" Here, the Tripiṭaka Master again offers worthless words. The National Teacher asks yet again, "*Tell me, where's this old monk right now?*" At this point, the Tripiṭaka Master, though silent for a while, says nothing and feels at a loss. Whereupon the National Teacher rebukes the Tripiṭaka

---

29 **Kōshō** 興聖: Dōgen uses the custom of referring to himself in the third person by the name of his monastery, Kōshōji 興聖寺. This section loosely corresponds to sections 4-6 in the "Shōbōgenzō tashin tsū."

30 **he should have learned from the buddha dharma** (*buppō ni narau beki nari* 佛法にならふべきなり): Perhaps meaning, "he should have understood in terms of the buddha dharma."

31 **treasure trove** (*hōsho* 寶所): The metaphor of the treasure trove as the true goal of Buddhism comes from a famous parable in the *Lotus Sūtra*, in which the buddha is depicted as a caravan leader, taking people to a treasure (*Miaofa lianhua jing* 妙法蓮華經, T.262.9:25c26ff).

114　　　　DŌGEN'S *SHŌBŌGENZŌ* VOLUME VII

Master, saying *"This fox spirit! Where's his knowledge of other minds?"*
Thus spoken to, the Tripiṭaka Master had nothing to say.

[S4:18]
つらつらこの因縁をおもふに、古先ともにおもはくは、今國師の、三藏を
叱すること、前兩度は國師の所在をしるといへども、第三度、しらざるが
ゆえに叱するなりと。然かにはあらず。おほよそ三藏の、野狐精のみにし
て、佛法は夢也未見在なることを、叱するなり。前兩度はしれり、第三度
はしらざる、とは云ぬなり。叱するは、惣じて三藏を叱するなり。國師の
こころは、まづ佛法を、他心通と云ことありやいなや、ともおもふ。又た
とひ他心通と云とも、他も、佛道にならふ他を擧すべし、心も、佛道にな
らふ心を擧すべし、通も、佛道にならふ通を擧すべきに、今三藏いふとこ
ろは、かつて佛道にならふ處にあらず、いかでか佛法といはん、と國師は
おもふなり。試驗す、と云ふは、たとひ第三度云ふ處ありとも、前三度の
如くあらば、佛法の道理にあらず、國師の本意にあらず、されば叱すべき
なり。三度問著するは、三藏もし國師のことばを聞くたびやあると、かね
て問著するなり。

Fully thinking through this episode, our old forebears have all thought
that, the National Teacher's rebuking the Tripiṭaka Master here was
because, though he may have known the whereabouts of the National
Teacher the first two times, the third time he did not know. This is not
so. He rebuked him for being nothing but a fox spirit that had never seen
the buddha dharma even in its dreams. He did not say that he knew the
first two times and did not know the third time. The rebuke was a general
rebuke of the Tripiṭaka Master.

The National Teacher's thought was, first of all, to consider whether
there is such a thing as speaking of the buddha dharma as "knowing other minds." Then, even if spoken of as "knowing other minds," for "other," we should take up the other learned in the way of the buddhas; for
"minds," we should take up the mind learned in the way of the buddhas;
and for "knowing," we should take up the knowing learned in the way of
the buddhas. Yet, the National Teacher thought, what the Tripiṭaka Master is saying here is nothing ever learned in the way of the buddhas; how
could we call it the buddha dharma? In his testing him, even if he had
had something to say the third time, had it been like the first two times,
it would not have been the truth of the buddha dharma, would not have
been the basic intention of the National Teacher, and therefore would
have been criticized.[32] Asking him three times was repeatedly asking the
Tripiṭaka Master whether he had heard the National Teacher's words.

32　**had it been like the first two times** (*zen sando no gotoku araba* 前三度の如くあ
らば): Reading *zen ryōdo* 前兩度 ("the first two times") for the problematic *zen sando*
("the first three times"). This section corresponds to sections 7-8 in the "Shōbōgenzō
tashin tsū."

S4. The Mind Cannot Be Got *Shin fukatoku* 心不可得   115

[S4:19] {2:506}

二に、國師の身心をしらず、と云は、いはゆる國師の身心は、三藏のしる
べきにあらず、通ずべきにあらず。十聖三賢およばず、補處・等覺のあき
らむるにあらず、凡夫三藏いかでかしらんと。

Secondly, to say that they do not know the body and mind of the National Teacher is to say that the body and mind of the National Teacher are not something the Tripiṭaka Master could know, not something he could read.[33] The ten sages and three worthies cannot reach it; the heir apparent and virtually awakened do not clarify it — how could a commoner tripiṭaka master know it?

[S4:20]

この道理、あきらかに決定すべし。國師の身心は、三藏もしるべし、およ
ぶべし、と擬するは、おのれ、すでに國師の身心をしらざるによりてな
り。他心通をえんともがら、國師をしるべしと云はば、二乗、更に國師を
しるべきか、しかあるべからず、二乗人は、たえて國師の邊際におよぶべ
からざるなり。今、大乗經をよむ二乗人おほし、かれらも、國師の身心を
しるべからず、又、佛法の身心、夢にも見るべからざるなり、たとひ大乗
經を讀誦するに似たれども、またくかれは小乗人也、とあきらかにしるべ
し。おほよそ國師の身心は、神通修證をうるともがらの、しるべきにあら
ざるなり。國師の身心は、國師猶はかりがたからん。故如何。行履ひさし
く作佛を圖せず、ゆえに佛眼も覷不見なり。去就、はるかに窠窟を脱落せ
り、籠羅の拘牽すべきにあらざるなり。

Clearly, we should be firmly convinced of this principle.[34] Those who suppose that the body and mind of the National Teacher could be known, could be reached by, the Tripiṭaka Master do so because they themselves clearly do not know the body and mind of the National Teacher. If we say that those who have got the knowledge of other minds could know the National Teacher, could those of the two vehicles then know the National Teacher? This could not be. Those of the two vehicles could never reach the borders of the National Teacher. Now, there are many people of the two vehicles that read the scriptures of the Great Vehicle; they too cannot know the body and mind of the National Teacher, nor can they see even in their dreams the body and mind of the buddha dharma. We should clearly recognize that, while they seem to read and recite the scriptures of the Great Vehicle, they are wholly people of the Small Vehicle. In sum, the body and mind of the National Teacher cannot be known by those who attain the practice and verification of the spiritual

---

33 **Secondly** (*ni ni* 二に): This section corresponds to the first part of section 9 of the "Shōbōgenzō tashin tsū."

34 **Clearly, we should be firmly convinced of this principle** (*kono dōri, akiraka ni ketsujō su beshi* この道理、あきらかに決定すべし): This section parallels material in section 9 of the "Shōbōgenzō tashin tsū."

116 DŌGEN'S *SHŌBŌGENZŌ* VOLUME VII

powers. The body and mind of the National Teacher might be difficult even for the National Teacher to gauge. Why? For long, his conduct has not figured to make a buddha; hence, even the buddha eye cannot see it. In going and staying, he has cast off the nest; he cannot be constrained by nets and cages.

[S4:21] {2:507}

いま五位尊宿、ともに勘破すべし。

Now we need to see through each of our five venerables.[35]

[S4:22]

趙州云、國師は三藏の鼻孔上にある、ゆえに見ず。この話、なにとかいふ。本をあきらめずして末を云ふには、かくの如くのあやまりあり。國師、いかにしてか三藏の鼻孔の上にあらん、三藏、いまだ鼻孔なし。又、國師と三藏、あひみるたよりあるに似れども、相近みちなし。明眼は、まさに辨看すべし。

Zhaozhou said, "The National Teacher was on the Tripiṭaka Master's nose; that's why he didn't see him."[36] What is this saying? When we talk about the branches without clarifying the root, we get this sort of mistake. How could the National Teacher be on the Tripiṭaka Master's nose? The Tripiṭaka Master does not yet have a nose. Again, while it may seem as if there is a basis for the National Teacher and the Tripiṭaka Master to see one another, there is no way for them to approach one another. Clear eyes should discern this.

[S4:23]

玄沙云く、只爲太近。まことに太近は、さもあらばあれ、あたりにはあたらず。いかなるをか太近といふ、なにをか太近と擧する。玄沙いまだ太近をしらず、太近を參ぜず、佛法におきては遠之遠矣。

Xuansha said, "*Because he was too close.*"[37] To be sure, "too close" may be as it may; but, as for hitting it, this does not hit it. What is he calling "too close"? What does he bring up as "too close"? Xuansha has not understood "too close," has not studied "too close"; in terms of the buddha dharma, he is the farthest of the far.

[S4:24]

仰山云、前兩度渉境心、後入自受用三昧、所以不見。これ、小釋迦のほまれ西天にたかくひらくと雖も、この不是なきにあらず。相見のところは必ず渉境なり、と云はば、佛祖相見の處なきがごとし、授記作佛の功德、な

---

35 **Now we need to see through each of our five venerables** (*ima goi sonshuku, tomo ni kanpa su beshi* いま五位尊宿、ともに勘破すべし): Paralleling section 16 of the "Shōbōgenzō tashin tsū."

36 **Zhaozhou** (*Jōshū* 趙州): Paralleling section 17 in the "Shōbōgenzō tashin tsū."

37 **Xuansha** (*Gensha* 玄沙): Paralleling section 18 in the "Shōbōgenzō tashin tsū."

S4. The Mind Cannot Be Got *Shin fukatoku* 心不可得 　　117

らはざるに似たり。前兩度は、實に三藏よく國師の所在をしれり、とい
ふ、國師の一毛の功德をしらずといふべし。

Yangshan said, "The first two times were 'the mind that plays across objects.'[38] *After that, he entered 'the samādhi of personal enjoyment'; that's why he didn't see him."* Even if he has a towering reputation in Sindh in the West as a little Śākyamuni, he is not without wrong here. If we say that, where there is seeing each other it is always "playing across objects," then it would seem there is nowhere that the buddhas and ancestors see each other; it is as if he had never learned of the virtue of granting a prediction of becoming a buddha.[39] To say that the first two times the Tripiṭaka Master really knew the whereabouts of the National Teacher, we must say is not to know the virtue of a single hair of the National Teacher.

[S4:25] {2:508}
玄沙の徴に云く、前兩度還見麼。この還見麼の一句、いふべきを云ふに似
たりといへども、見如不見と云はんとす。ゆえに是にあらず。

Xuansha summoned him, saying, *"Did you in fact see him the first two times?"*[40] Although these words, "Did you in fact see him?" sound as if they are saying what needs to be said, it seeks to say that *his seeing is like not seeing.* Hence, it is not right.

[S4:26]
これをききて、雪竇明覺禪師云く、敗也、敗也。これ玄沙の道を道とする
とき、しか云ふべし。道にあらずとせんとき、しかいふべからず。

Hearing this, Chan Master Mingjue of Mount Xuedou said, "Defeated! Defeated!" When we take Xuansha's saying as saying something, we should say this; when we take it as not saying anything, we should not say it.[41]

[S4:27]
海會端云く、國師もし在三藏鼻孔上、有什麼難見。殊不知、國師在三藏眼
睛裏。是又、第三度を論ずるなり。前兩度もみざることを、呵すべきを呵
せず、いかんが國師の鼻孔上にあり、眼睛裏にありともしらん。

38　**Yangshan** (*Kyōzan* 仰山): Paralleling section 19 in the "Shōbōgenzō tashin tsū."

39　**granting a prediction of becoming a buddha** (*juki sabutsu* 授記作佛): Presumably, Dōgen's point here is that, if knowledge of another's mind is limited to the ordinary mind that "plays across objects," the buddhas would be unable to predict (as they are held to do) the future buddhahood of the advanced adept.

40　**Xuansha** (*Gensha* 玄沙): Corresponding to section 21 in the "Shōbōgenzō tashin tsū."

41　**When we take Xuansha's saying as saying something** (*Gensha no dō o dō to suru toki* 玄沙の道を道とするとき): Corresponding to section 22 in the "Shōbōgenzō tashin tsū."

118   DŌGEN'S *SHŌBŌGENZŌ* VOLUME VII

Duan of Haihui said, "If the National Teacher was *on the Tripiṭaka Master's nose, why would it be hard to see him?*[42] *He's completely unaware that the National Teacher was in the Tripiṭaka Master's eye.*" This also discusses the third time. It does not scoff, as it should scoff, at the fact that he also fails to see him the first two times. How can he know either that the National Teacher is on his nose or is in his eye?

[S4:28]

五位尊宿、何れも國師の功德にくらし、佛法の辦道、ちからなきに似たり。しるべし、國師は即ち一代の佛なり、佛正法眼藏あきらかに正傳せり。小乘の三藏・論師等、さらに國師の邊際をしらざる、その證、これなり。他心通といふこと、小乘のいふが如きは、他念通といひぬべし。小乘三藏の他心通のちから、國師の一毛端をも、半毛端をも、しるべしとおもへるは、あやまりなり。小乘の三藏、すべて國師の功德の有所在、みるべからずと、一向ならふべきなり。たとひ、もし國師、さきの兩度は所在をしるるといへども、第三度にしらざらんは、三分に兩分の能あらん、叱すべきあらず。たとひ叱すとも、全分虧闕にあらず。これを叱せん、たれか國師を信ぜん。意趣は、三藏すべていまだ佛法の身心あらざることを、叱せしなり。五位尊宿、すべて國師の行李をしらざるによりて、かくのごとくの不是あり。

The five venerables are all ignorant of the virtues of the National Teacher and appear to lack the power of pursuing the way of the buddha dharma.[43] We should realize that the National Teacher was a buddha for his age, who directly transmitted the treasury of the true dharma eye of the Buddha. The proof that the tripiṭaka masters, the treatise masters, and the like, of the Small Vehicle can never know the borders of the National Teacher is this. Knowledge of other minds of the sort described by the Small Vehicle should be called knowledge of others' thoughts. It is a mistake to think that the power of the knowledge of other minds of a tripiṭaka master of the Small Vehicle might know even the tip of a single hair, or of half a hair, of the National Teacher. We should learn solely that a tripiṭaka master of the Small Vehicle cannot see anything of the whereabouts of the National Teacher. If he could know the whereabouts of the National Teacher the first two times, but failed to know the third time, he would have had the ability to get two out of three; he should not have been rebuked. Or, even if rebuked, it would not be as completely deficient. Had he rebuked him for this, who would trust the National Teacher? His intention was to rebuke the Tripiṭaka Master entirely for lacking the body and mind of the buddha dharma. Because none of the five venerables understood the conduct of the National Teacher, they had errors like this.

---

42 **Duan of Haihui** (*Kaie Tan* 海會端): Corresponding to the first part of section 23 of the "Shōbōgenzō tashin tsū."

43 **The five venerables** (*goi sonshuku* 五位尊宿): This section corresponds to material in sections 24-25 of the "Shōbōgenzō tashin tsū."

S4. The Mind Cannot Be Got *Shin fukatoku* 心不可得　119

[S4:29] {2:509}

このゆえに、いま佛道の心不可得をきかしむるなり。この一法を通ずるこ
とえざらんともがら、自餘の法を通ぜりといはんこと信じがたしといへど
も、古先もかくの如く將錯就錯ありとしるべし。

Therefore, we tell of "mind cannot be got" in the way of the buddhas. It is hard to believe that those who cannot penetrate this one dharma have penetrated other dharmas; yet even our old forebears have *made mistakes of mistakes* like this.[44]

[S4:30]

あるとき、僧ありて國師に問、いかにあらぬかこれ古佛心。國師いはく、
牆壁瓦礫。これも、心不可得なり。

Once, the National Teacher was asked by a monk, "What is the old buddha mind?"[45] The National Teacher said, "Fences, walls, tiles, and pebbles."

This is also "*the mind cannot be got.*"

[S4:31]

あるとき、僧ありて國師に問、いかにあらんかこれ諸佛常住心。國師いは
く、幸遇老僧參内。これも、不可得の心を參究するなり。

Once, the National Teacher was asked by a monk, "What is the constantly abiding mind of the buddhas?"[46] The National Teacher said, "*Fortunately, you've encountered this old monk's palace visit.*"

This is also studying the mind that "cannot be got."

[S4:32]

天帝釋、あるとき國師に問、いかにしてか有爲を解脱せん。國師の云く、
天子、修道して有爲を解脱すべし。天帝釋、かさねて問、いかならんか是
道。國師云く、造次心、これ道。天帝釋云く、いかならんかこれ造次心。
國師、ゆびをもつてさして云く、這箇是般若臺、那箇是眞珠網。天帝釋、
禮拜す。

44　**made mistakes of mistakes** (*shōshaku jushaku* 將錯就錯): A fixed expression occurring several times in the *Shōbōgenzō*; often understood in the sense, "to recognize a mistake for what it is," but here more likely simply something like "to make mistake after mistake"; see Supplementary Notes, s.v. "Make a mistake of a mistake."

45　**"What is the old buddha mind?"** (*ika ni aranu ka kore kobutsushin* いかにあらぬかこれ古佛心): A well-known dialogue (see, e.g., *Jingde chuandeng lu* 景德傳燈錄, T.2076.51:438a9), appearing several times in Dōgen's writings (although not in the "Shōbōgenzō tashin tsū").

46　**"What is the constantly abiding mind of the buddhas?"** (*ika ni aran ka kore shobutsu jōjū shin* いかにあらんかこれ諸佛常住心): The source of this dialogue is unknown (and the significance of Huizhong's response is unclear). Again, not a dialogue appearing in the "Shōbōgenzō tashin tsū."

The National Teacher was once asked by Deva Lord Śakra, "How is one liberated from the conditioned?"[47]

The National Teacher said, "Deva, by practicing the way, one is liberated from the conditioned."

Deva Lord Śakra asked again, "What is the way?"

The National Teacher said, "One's fleeting mind is the way."

Deva Lord Śakra said, "What is the fleeting mind?"

The National Teacher pointed and said, "*This is the altar of prajñā; that is the net of pearls.*"

Deva Lord Śakra bowed.

[S4:33]

おほよそ佛道に身心を談ずること、佛佛祖祖の會におほし。ともにこれを參學せんことは、凡夫・賢聖の念慮・知覺にあらず。心不可得を參究すべし。

In sum, in the way of the buddhas, talk of body and mind is common in the communities of buddha after buddha and ancestor after ancestor. To study any of them is not the thinking or perception of the common people or the worthies and sages. We should investigate "*the mind cannot be got.*"

正法眼藏心不可得
Treasury of the True Dharma Eye
The Mind Cannot Be Got[48]

仁治二年辛丑夏安居日、書于興聖寶林寺
Written at Kōshō Hōrin Monastery; a day of the summer retreat, in the junior metal year of the ox, the second year of Ninji [1241][49]

---

47 **Deva Lord Śakra** (*Ten Taishaku* 天帝釋): I.e., the god Indra, in whose heaven it is said Huizhong preached. The source of this dialogue, absent in the "Shōbōgenzō tashin tsū," is unknown.

48 The "Shin fukatoku" of the seventy-five-chapter *Shōbōgenzō* adds here "Number 8" (*daihachi* 第八).

49 This date represents a correction, found in the Honzan edition, of the era name Hōji 寶治 given in the *Himitsu Shōbōgenzō* MS colophon; the second year of Hōji would have been 1248, the senior earth year of the monkey (*boshin* 戊申), long after Dōgen had left Kōshōji. Dates of the summer retreat vary; a common practice put it from the fifteenth of the fourth lunar month through the fifteenth of the seventh lunar month; in 1241, the equivalent of 27 May through 23 August.

TREASURY OF THE TRUE DHARMA EYE

SUPPLEMENTARY CHAPTER 5

The Four Attractions of the Bodhisattva
Bodaisatta shishōbō

菩提薩埵四攝法

The Four Attractions of the Bodhisattva

Bodaisatta shishōbō

INTRODUCTION

This short work was preserved as number 28 in the sixty-chapter *Shōbō-genzō* and included in the ninety-five-chapter Honzan edition as number 45. The Tōunji 洞雲寺 manuscript version translated here lacks a colophon for this chapter; the eighteenth-century Myōshōji 妙昌寺 manuscript ascribes it to the late spring of 1243, shortly before its author was to abandon his Kōshōji near the capital and withdraw to the province of Echizen.

As its title indicates, the text deals with the traditional set of four practices through which the bodhisattva attracts converts to Buddhism. The treatment of this theme is noteworthy for its use of examples from Chinese literature, and for its lack of reference to the Chinese Chan literature or use of Chan locutions of the sort we see in Dōgen's other *Shōbōgenzō* texts from the early 1240s; in this, the work seems closer to the style and themes of the twelve-chapter *Shōbōgenzō*.

正法眼藏別輯五
Treasury of the True Dharma Eye
Supplementary Chapter 5

菩提薩埵四攝法
The Four Attractions of the Bodhisattva

(六十卷本系・洞雲寺所収本)
(Sixty-Chapter Compilation, Tōunji text)

[S5:1] {2:510}

一者、布施。二者、愛語。三者、利行。四者、同事。

First is giving, second is kind speech, third is beneficial acts, fourth is cooperation.[1]

[S5:2]

その布施といふは、不貪なり。不貪といふは、むさぼらざるなり。むさぼらずといふは、よのなかにいふ、へつらはざるなり。たとひ四洲を統領すれども、正道の教化をほどこすには、かならず不貪なるのみなり。たとへば、すつるたからを、しらぬ人にほどこさんがごとし。遠山の華を、如來に供じ、前生のたからを、衆生にほどこさん、法におきても、物におきても、面面に布施に相應する功德を本具せり。我物にあらざれども、布施をさへざる道理あり。そのもののかろきをきらはず、その功の實なるべきなり。道を道にまかするとき、得道す。得道のときは、道、かならず道にまかせられゆくなり。財の、たからにまかせらるるとき、財、かならず布施となるなり。自を自にほどこし、他を他にほどこすなり。この布施の因緣力、とほく天上・人間までも通じ、證果の賢・聖までも通ずるなり。そのゆえは、布施の、能受となりて、すでに緣をむすぶがゆえに。

"Giving" means "not craving." "Not craving" means "not being greedy." "Not being greedy" means, in worldly terms, "not currying fa-

---

1 **giving** (*fuse* 布施): The first in the standard list of the "four things that attract" (*shi shōbō* 四攝法; S. *catvāri-saṃgraha-vastūni*): giving (*fuse* 布施; S. *dāna*), kind words (*aigo* 愛語; S. *priyavacana*), beneficial acts (*rigyō* 利行; S. *arthakṛtya*), and cooperation (*dōji* 同事; S. *samānārtha*). In the "Shōbōgenzō ippyakuhachi hōmyōmon" 正法眼藏一百八法明門, Dōgen quotes the *Abhiniṣkramaṇa-sūtra* (*Fo benxing ji jing* 佛本行集經, T.190.3:682a16-17):

四攝法是法明門。攝受一切衆生。得菩提已、施一切衆生法故。

The four things that attract are a gateway to the illumination of the dharma, for one gathers in all living beings and, after attaining bodhi, offers the dharma to all living beings.

vor." Even if one rules the four continents, in offering the teaching of the true way, one is necessarily simply not craving. It is like offering discarded jewels to a stranger. In offering the flowers of a distant mountain to a tathāgata or offering treasures from a previous life to a living being, whether it is the dharma or an object, each is originally endowed with the merit accompanying giving. There is a principle that, even if they are not one's own objects, this does not obstruct giving. Without despising the fact that the object is trivial, [we should recognize] that its merit is real. When we leave the way to the way, we gain the way; when we gain the way, the way invariably continues to be left to the way. When possessions are left to possessions, the possessions invariably become giving. It is offering the self to the self; offering the other to the other. The causal efficacy of this giving penetrates even to the distant heavens and human realms, penetrates even to the worthies and sages who have verified the fruit. The reason for this is that the giving, becoming experience, has formed a bond with them.[2]

[S5:3] {2:511}
ほとけののたまはく、布施する人の、衆會のなかにきたるときは、まづその人を、諸人、のぞみみる。

The Buddha said, "When the person who gives enters the assembly, the people immediately look to that person.[3]

[S5:4]
しるべし、ひそかにそのこころの通ずるなり、と。しかあればすなはち、一句・一偈の法をも布施すべし、此生他生の善種となる。一錢・一草の財をも布施すべし、此世多世の善根をきざす。法もたからなるべし、財も法なるべし。願樂によるべきなり。

"We should understand that the person's mind imperceptibly penetrates."[4]

---

2 **The reason for this is that the giving, becoming experience, has formed a bond with them** (*sono yue wa, fuse no, nōju to narite, sude ni en o musubu ga yue ni* そのゆえは、布施の、能受となりて、すでに縁をむすぶがゆえに): A tentative translation, taking *nōju* 能受 here to refer to the "experience" of those to whom the "causal efficacy" (*innen riki* 因縁力) has penetrated. The term might well be rendered "recipient" (as it is below, section 5), though it is unclear how that would work in this context.

3 **The Buddha said** (*Hotoke no notamawaku* ほとけののたまはく): The Buddha's words, given here in Japanese, appear to extend to the final quotation marker *to* と, at the end of the first sentence of the following section. The source is uncertain, though commonly said to reflect a line in the *Ekottarāgama* (*Zengyi ahan jing* 増一阿含經, T.125.2:681a4-5):

檀越施主、衆人敬仰見者歡悦。
The chief donor is admired by the people and looked upon with joy.

4 **"We should understand that the person's mind imperceptibly penetrates"** (*shi-*

S5. The Four Attractions of the Bodhisattva *Bodaisatta shishōbō* 菩提薩埵四攝法 125

Thus, we should give even one line or one gāthā of dharma; it will form good seeds for this life and other lives. We should give one coin or one blade of grass of possessions; it will portend good roots in this world and many worlds. The dharma should be one's wealth, and one's wealth should be the dharma; it depends on one's expectations.

[S5:5]

まことにすなはち、ひげをほどこしては、もののこころをととのへ、いさごを供じては、王位をうるなり。ただかれが報謝をむさぼらず、みづからがちからをわかつなり。舟をおき、橋をわたすも、布施の檀度なり。もしよく布施を學するときは、受身・捨身ともにこれ布施なり、治生産業もとより布施にあらざる事なし。はなを風にまかせ、鳥をときにまかするも、布施の功業なるべし。阿育大王の半菴羅果、よく數百の僧に供養せし、廣大の供養なりと證明する道理、よくよく能受の人も學すべし。身力をはげますのみにあらず、便宜をすごささざるべし。まことに、みづからに布施の功徳の本具なるゆえに、いまのみづからは、えたるなり。

Truly, therefore, offering a beard fixes someone's heart; offering sand gets one the rank of king.[5] Without desiring the other's gratitude, one simply shares one's own strengths. Providing a boat and building a

---

ru beshi, hisoka ni sono kokoro no tsūzuru nari, to しるべし、ひそかにそのこころの通ずるなり、と): Apparently, a continuation of the Buddha's words quoted in section 3, presumably, as an explanation of why the people look to the donor.

5 **offering a beard** (*hige o hodokoshite* ひげをほどこして): Likely an allusion to the story of the Tang Emperor Taizong's 太宗 (r. 626-649) contributing the hair of his beard to a medicine to cure General Li Ji 李勣 (594-669) (see, e.g., *Hanyuan xinshu* 翰苑新書, KR.3k0038.100.9a):

勣既忠力、帝謂可托大事。嘗暴疾。醫曰、用須灰可治。帝乃自翦須以和藥。及愈、入謝、頓首流血。帝曰、吾爲社稷計、何謝爲。

Ji served with complete loyalty, the Emperor entrusting him with great matters. Once, he suddenly became ill. The doctor said, "He can be healed with ashes."
The Emperor thereupon cut his own beard and mixed it into the medicine. [Ji] then recovered and offered thanks, kowtowing till he bled.
The Emperor said, "I was thinking of the country. Why thank me?"

offering sand gets one the rank of king (*isago o kūjite* いさごを供じて): Allusion to the story of a prior life of King Aśoka, when, as a boy, he offered sand to Buddha Śākyamuni; see, e.g., *Ayuwang jing* 阿育王經 (T.2043.50:131c9ff). Once, when the Buddha was traveling, he came upon two boys playing in the sand. One of them put some sand in the Buddha's begging bowl. The Buddha accepted it, smiled, and emitted a multi-colored light from his body that reached throughout the three-thousandfold world and then returned. When Ānanda questioned the Buddha, he replied (T.2043.50:132a26-b2.):

阿難、汝見小兒以手捧沙置鉢中不。阿難白佛、唯然已見。世尊又言、此兒者我入涅槃百年後、當生波吒利弗多城王名阿育。爲四分轉輪王信樂正法。當廣供養舍利起八萬四千塔饒益多人。

"Ānanda, did you see the boy offer sand to the bowl?"
Ānanda said to the Buddha, "Just so, I saw it."
The World-Honored One continued, "One hundred years after my entrance into nirvāṇa, this boy will be born as a king of Pāṭaliputra named Aśoka. He will become

126 DŌGEN'S *SHŌBŌGENZŌ* VOLUME VII

bridge are also the *dāna-pāramitā* of giving.[6] When we study giving well, receiving a body and discarding a body are both giving; earning a living and working are fundamentally nothing other than giving. Leaving flowers to the wind, leaving birds to the time must also be meritorious acts of giving.[7] The Great King Aśoka made an offering of half an *āmalaka* to several hundred monks; the principle demonstrating that it was a vast offering should be carefully studied as well by the recipients.[8] Not only should we exert our physical strength, but we should not miss opportunities. Truly, it is because we are originally endowed with the merit of giving that we have attained ourselves now.

[S5:6]

ほとけののたまはく、於其自身、尚可受用、何況能與父母妻子。

The Buddha said, "*They can even enjoy it themselves, how much more give it to their father or mother, wife or child.*"[9]

---

a wheel-turning king of the four quarters, having faith in the true dharma. He will make offerings widely to the *śarīra*, erect 84,000 stūpas, and benefit many people."

6 **Providing a boat and building a bridge** (*fune o oki, hashi o watasu* 舟をおき、橋をわたす): The fourth and fifth of the seven good deeds leading to birth in the heaven of Brahmā according to the *Zhudefutian jing* 諸德福田經 (T.683.16:777b2ff). The others are, first, constructing Buddhist buildings; second, providing shade trees; third, providing medicines; sixth, digging wells; seventh, providing latrines. The fourth and fifth are given (at T.683.16:777b5-6) as:

四者、作牢堅船濟度人民。五者、安設橋梁過度羸弱。

Fourth, constructing sturdy boats to take the people across the water. Fifth, setting up bridges for the frail to cross.

7 **Leaving flowers to the wind, leaving birds to the time** (*hana o kaze ni makase, tori o toki ni makasuru* はなを風にまかせ、鳥をときにまかする): I.e., letting nature take its course: letting the wind carry away the spring blossoms; letting the cocks crow in the morning.

8 **The Great King Aśoka** (*Aiku daiō* 阿育大王): Reference to the story that, at the end of his life, King Aśoka had nothing left to give the saṃgha but the piece of fruit in his hand. (The fruit in question, given here as *anraka* 菴羅果, is regularly taken as the mango [S. *āmra*]; Sanskrit *āmalaka* is the emblic, or Indian gooseberry.) According to the version of the story in the *Ayuwang jing* 阿育王經 (T.2043.50:148b16-20), addressing his ministers in attendance, the king said,

唯此一事汝應當作。此半阿摩勒菓送與鷄寺、宣我語曰、阿育王禮衆僧足。昔領一切閻浮提地、今者唯有半阿摩勒菓。是我最後所行布施。願僧受之。此物雖小以施衆僧福德廣大。

There is but one thing you should do for me. Send this half *āmalaka* to Kurkuṭārāma and report my words: "King Aśoka prostrates himself at the feet of the saṃgha. In the past, he ruled all the territory of Jambudvīpa; now he has only half an *āmalaka*. This is my final donation. I beg the saṃgha to receive it. The thing is small, but the merit of giving it to the saṃgha is vast."

9 **The Buddha said** (*hotoke no tamawaku* ほとけののたまはく): The source is uncertain, but it appears that the quotation as given here may be playing with a line of scrip-

S5. The Four Attractions of the Bodhisattva *Bodaisatta shishōbō* 菩提薩埵四攝法 127

[S5:7] {2:512}

しかあればしりぬ、みづからもちいるも、布施の一分なり、父母・妻子に
あたふるも、布施なるべし。もし、よく布施に一塵を捨せんときは、みづ
からが所作なりといふとも、しづかに隨喜すべきなり。諸佛のひとつの功
德を、すでに正傳しつくれるゆえに。菩薩の一法を、はじめて修行するが
ゆえに。

Thus, we know that using it oneself is a part of giving; offering it to
father or mother, wife or child is giving. When we relinquish one parti-
cle of dust in giving, we should quietly rejoice, though we have done it
ourselves. For we have already directly transmitted and produced one of
the merits of the buddhas; for we are practicing for the first time one of
the dharmas of the bodhisattva.

[S5:8]

轉じがたきは衆生のこころなり、一財をきざして衆生の心地を轉じはじむ
るより、得道にいたるまでも轉ぜんとおもふなり。そのはじめ、かならず
布施をもてすべきなり。かるがゆえに、六波羅蜜のはじめに、檀波羅蜜あ
るなり。心の大小は、はかるべからず、物の大小も、はかるべからず。さ
れども、心轉物のときあり、物轉心の布施あるなり。

Hard to change are the minds of living beings. One seeks to change
them, from beginning to change the mind ground, with one possession
as a start, until they reach gaining the way. At this beginning, we should
always use giving. Therefore, at the beginning of the six *pāramitās* is the
dāna-pāramitā. We should not measure the size of the mind; we should
not measure the size of the object. Still, there are times when the mind
changes the object; there is giving in which the object changes the mind.

* * * * *

[S5:9]

愛語、といふは、衆生をみるに、まづ慈愛の心をおこし、顧愛の言語をほ
どこすなり。おほよそ、暴惡の言語なきなり。世俗には、安否をとふ禮儀
あり、佛道には、珍重のことばあり、不審の孝行あり。慈念衆生、猶如

---

ture. The reading of the first clause, "can even enjoy" (*shō ka juyū* 尚可受用), is attested
in several MS witnesses; but the Tōunji text, on which this edition is based, has "do not
even enjoy " (*shō fu juyū* 尚不受用), a reading that mirrors a passage in the *Bhaiṣajya-
guru-pūrva-praṇidhāna-sūtra* (*Yaoshi benyuan jing* 藥師本願經, T.450.14:405c11-19),
in which the Buddha criticizes the stingy who do not share their wealth:

> 積集資財。於其自身尚不受用。何況能與父母妻子奴婢作使及來乞者。彼諸有情
> 從此命終。生餓鬼界或傍生趣。

> They pile up wealth, which they do not even enjoy themselves, much less give to
> father or mother, wife or child, servant or envoy, or the beggar who approaches them.
> When these sentient beings end their lives, they are born in the realm of hungry
> ghosts or the animal destiny.

128 DŌGEN'S *SHŌBŌGENZŌ* VOLUME VII

赤子おもひをたくはへて言語するは、愛語なり。徳あるは、ほむべし、
徳なきは、あはれむべし。愛語をこのむよりは、やうやく愛語を増長する
なり。しかあれば、ひごろしられず、みえざる愛語も、現前するなり。現
在の身命の存せらんあひだ、このむで愛語すべし、世世生生にも、不退轉
ならん。怨敵を降伏し、君子を和睦ならしむること、愛語を根本とするな
り。むかひて愛語をきくは、おもてをよろこばしめ、こころをたのしく
す。むかはずして愛語をきくは、肝に銘じ、魂に銘ず。しるべし、愛語
は、愛心よりおこる、愛心は、慈心を種子とせり。愛語、よく回天のちか
らあることを、學すべきなり、ただ、能を賞するのみにあらず。

"Kind speech" means that, when we see a living being, we first of all
give rise to a mind of compassion and offer caring words. In general, it
means having no rough or bad words. In the secular world, we have the
etiquette of asking if another is well or not; in the way of the buddhas,
there are the words "take care of yourself," and the filial act of "how
are you?"[10] Speaking with the feeling, "*she thinks compassionately on
living beings, as if they were her babies,*" is kind speech.[11]

Those with virtue are to be praised; those without virtue are to be pitied. From a fondness for kind speech, kind speech is gradually extended.
Thus, the kind speech that we ordinarily do not recognize and do not
notice appears. While our present life exists, we should be fond of using
kind speech; in age after age and life after life, we shall not regress from
it. Kind speech is fundamental to overcoming enemies and creating har-
mony among the virtuous. To hear kind speech directly makes the face
happy and the heart joyful; to hear of kind speech indirectly inscribes
it on one's being, inscribes it on one's spirit. We should know that kind
speech arises from a kind heart, and a kind heart represents the seed of a
compassionate heart. We should study that kind speech has the power to
reverse the heavens; it is not merely praising ability.[12]

* * * * *

[S5:10] {2:513}
利行、といふは、貴賤の衆生におきて、利益の善巧をめぐらすなり。たと
へば、遠近の前途をまぼりて、利他の方便をいとなむ。窮龜をあはれみ、
病雀をやしなふべし。窮龜をみ、病雀をみしとき、かれが報謝をもとめ
ず、ただひとへに、利行にもよほさるるなり。

---

10   **"take care of yourself"** (*chinchō* 珍重); **"how are you?"** (*fushin* 不審): Salutations
used among Buddhist clerics: the former is a farewell; the latter, a greeting.

11   **"she thinks compassionately on living beings, as if they were her babies"** (*jinen
shujō, yū nyo shakushi* 慈念衆生、猶如赤子): The words of Mañjuśrī in the *Lotus Sūtra*
(*Miaofa lianhua jing* 妙法蓮華經, T.262.9:35b19-20), as a description of the eight-year-
old daughter of the nāga king Sāgara.

12   **reverse the heavens** (*kaiten* 回天): I.e., reverse a bad situation.

S5. The Four Attractions of the Bodhisattva *Bodaisatta shishōbō* 菩提薩埵四攝法 129

"Beneficial acts" means using skillful means to benefit living beings, both high and low; for example, looking to the near and distant future, we carry out expedient acts to benefit others. We should take pity on the distressed tortoise and take care of the sick sparrow.[13] When they saw the distressed tortoise and saw the sick sparrow, without seeking their gratitude, they simply carried out beneficial acts.

[S5:11]
愚人おもはくは、利他をさきとせば、自が利、はぶかれぬべし、と。しかには、あらざるなり。利行は、一法なり、あまねく自他を利するなり。むかしの人、ひとたび沐浴するに、みたびかみをゆひ、ひとたび飡食するに、みたび、はきいだしは、ひとへに他を利せしこころなり。ひとのくにの民なれば、をしへざらんとにはあらざりき。

Foolish people think that, if they give priority to benefiting others, their own benefit will be excluded. This is not the case. Beneficial acts are a single dharma, widely benefiting self and other. The person long ago who bound his hair three times in one bath and spat out his food three times in one meal had in mind only the benefit of others; it was not that he would teach them because they were subjects of another's land.[14]

[S5:12]
しかあれば、怨親、ひとしく利すべし、自他おなじく利するなり。もし、このこころをうれば、草木・風水にも、利行の、おのれづから不退不轉なる道理、まさに利行せらるるなり。ひとへに愚をすくはんと、いとなむなり。

13　**distressed tortoise** (*kyūki* 窮龜): Allusion to the story, found in the *Jinshu* 晉書 and included in the Tang anthology *Mengqiu* 蒙求 (Kong Yu fang gui 孔愉放龜, KR.3k0010.002.68a-b), of Kong Yu 孔愉 of the Jin dynasty, governor of Yubu 餘不, who once released a tortoise from captivity; as the tortoise swam away it turned its head to the left to look back at him. Thereafter, when the tortoise depicted on the governor's seal was cast, the head seemed to be turned to the left. This and the following reference to the sick sparrow also appear together in the "Shōbōgenzō gyōji" 正法眼藏行持 (2).

sick sparrow (*byōjaku* 病雀): Allusion to the story, also found in the *Mengqiu* 蒙求 (Yang Bao huang qui 楊寶黃雀, KR.3k0010.001.121a-b), of Yang Bao 楊寶 of the Later Han dynasty, who as a boy saved a baby sparrow; he was subsequently visited by an emissary of the Queen Mother of the West (Xiwangmu 西王母), who gave him four rings symbolizing the four generations of his descendants who would hold the three highest government offices.

14　**The person long ago** (*mukashi no hito* むかしの人): Reference to another story anthologized in the *Mengqiu* 蒙求 (Zhou Gong wo fa 周公握髮, KR.3k0010.002.10a-b), the saying attributed to the Duke of Zhou in the *Shiji* 史記 (Lu Zhou Gong shijia 魯周公世家, KR.2a0001.400.126a), as advice to his son, recently appointed governor of Lu 魯, that, in order to keep wise men in the land, he would leave his bath ("bind his hair") three times and interrupt his meal ("spit out his food") three times to receive them. The reference to "subjects of another's land" (*hito no kuni no tami* ひとのくにの民) likely reflects the status of Lu as a vassal state of Zhou.

130 DŌGEN'S *SHŌBŌGENZŌ* VOLUME VII

Thus, we should benefit friend and enemy equally; we benefit self and other alike. If we attain this mind, the principle that beneficial acts naturally do not regress will be beneficially practiced even by the grasses and trees, winds and waters. We single-mindedly endeavor to save the foolish.

* * * * *

[S5:13]

同事、といふは、不違なり。自にも不違なり、他にも不違なり。たとへば、人間の如來は、人間に同ぜるがごとし。人界に同ずるをもてしりぬ、同餘界なるべし。同事をしるとき、自他一如なり。かの琴・詩・酒は、人を、ともとし、天を、ともとし、神を、ともとす。人は、琴・詩・酒をともとす、琴・詩・酒は、琴・詩・酒をともとし、人は、人をともとし、天は、天をともとし、神は、神をともとすることわりあり。これ、同事の習學なり。

"Cooperation" means "not differing"; it is not differing from self, not differing from others.[15] For example, it is like the human tathāgata identifying with humans: given that he identifies with the human realm, we know he must identify with other realms. When we understand cooperation, self and other are one. Those "lute, poetry, and wine" make friends with people, make friends with devas, make friends with the gods.[16] There is a principle that people make friends with the lute, poetry, and wine; the lute, poetry, and wine make friends with the lute, poetry, and wine; people make friends with people; devas make friends with devas; gods make friends with gods. This is the study of "cooperation."

[S5:14] {2:514}

たとへば、事といふは、儀なり、威なり、態なり。他をして自に同ぜしめて、のちに自をして他に同ぜしむる道理あるべし。自・他は、ときにしたがうて無窮なり。

"Thing," for example, means conduct, means deportment, means attitude.[17] There is a principle that one lets the other identify with the self, and then subsequently lets the self identify with the other. According to the time, self and other are limitless.

---

15 **"Cooperation" means "not differing"** (*dōji, to iu wa, fui nari* 同事、といふは、不違なり): The translation obscures Dōgen's interpretation here and below. The term for "cooperation" is more literally "the same thing" (*dōji* 同事); hence, it suggests "not differing" (*fui* 不違) from others, as exemplified by the tathāgata's being "the same as" (*dōzeru* 同ぜる) those in the realms where he appears.

16 **lute, poetry, and wine** (*kin shi shu* 琴・詩・酒): I.e., the famous "three friends" (*sanyou* 三友) of the Tang poet Bai Juyi 白居易 (772-846).

17 **"Thing"** (*ji* 事): Dōgen is here giving examples of the "things" intended by the term *dōji* 同事 ("the same thing").

S5. The Four Attractions of the Bodhisattva *Bodaisatta shishōbō* 菩提薩埵四攝法 131

[S5:15]

管子云、海不辭水、故能成其大。山不辭土、故能成其高。明主不厭人、故能成其衆。

In the Guanzi, it is said,[18]

The ocean does not reject water; therefore, it is able to achieve its size. The mountain does not reject earth; therefore, it is able to achieve its height. The wise ruler does not depise people; therefore, he is able to achieve his following.

[S5:16]

しるべし、海の、水を辭せざるは、同事なり。さらにしるべし、水の、海を辭せざる德も、具足せるなり。このゆえに、よく水あつまりて海となり、土かさなりて山となるなり。ひそかにしりぬ、海は、海を辭せざるがゆえに、海をなし、おほきなることをなす。山は、山を辭せざるがゆえに、山をなし、たかきことをなすなり。明主は、人をいとはざるがゆえに、その衆をなす。衆とは、國なり。いはゆる明主とは、帝王をいふなるべし。帝王は、人をいとはざるなり、人をいとはずといへども、賞・罰なきにあらず、賞・罰ありといへども、人をいとふことなし。

We should know that the ocean's not rejecting water is cooperation. Further, we should know that water is also endowed with the virtue of not rejecting the ocean. Therefore, water accumulates and becomes the ocean; earth piles up and becomes the mountain. We personally know that, because the ocean does not reject the ocean, it becomes the ocean and becomes big; because the mountain does not reject the mountain, it becomes the mountain and becomes tall. Because he does not despise people, the wise ruler forms his following. "His following" means the country; "the wise ruler" is the emperor. The emperor does not despise people. He does not despise people, but this does not mean there is no reward and punishment; there is reward and punishment, but this does not mean he despises people.

[S5:17] {2:515}

むかし、すなほなりしときは、國に賞・罰なかりき。かのときの賞・罰は、いまと、ひとしからざればなり。いまも、賞をまたずして道をもとむる人もあるべきなり、愚夫の思慮の、およぶべきにあらず。明主は、あきらかなるがゆえに、人をいとはず。人、かならず國をなし、明主をもとむるこころあれども、明主の明主たる道理をことごとくしる事まれなるゆえに、明主にいとはれずとのみよろこぶといへども、わが、明主をいとはざるとしらず。このゆえに、明主にも、暗人にも、同事の道理あるがゆえに、同事は、薩埵の行願なり。ただまさに、やはらかなる容顔をもて、一切にむかふべし。

---

18   *Guanzi* (*Kanshi* 管子): Quoting a line at *Guanzi* 管子, Xingshi jie 形勢解, KR.3c0001.020.7a.

132 DŌGEN'S *SHŌBŌGENZŌ* VOLUME VII

Long ago, when people were obedient, countries had no reward and punishment; for the reward and punishment of that time was not the same as now. Even now, there are people who seek the way without expecting rewards, something beyond the thoughts of fools. Because the wise ruler is wise, he does not despise people. Although people invariably wish to form a country and seek out a wise ruler, it is rare that they fully understand the principle that makes a wise ruler a wise ruler; therefore, they rejoice simply that they are not despised by the wise ruler but do not realize that they themselves do not despise the ruler. Therefore, because the principle of cooperation is possessed by both the wise ruler and the ignorant people, cooperation is the practice and vow of the bodhisattva. We should simply face everyone with a gentle countenance.

[S5:18]
この四攝、おのおの四攝を具足せるがゆえに、十六攝なるべし。

Because each of these four attractions is endowed with the four attractions, it is sixteen attractions.

正法眼藏菩提薩埵四攝法第二十八
Treasury of the True Dharma Eye
The Four Attractions of the Bodhisattva
Number 28

[Myōshōji MS:]
仁治癸卯端午日記録
Recorded on the day of the initial horse, the junior water year of the rabbit, in Ninji [24 May 1243][19]

[Honzan edition:]
仁治癸卯端午日記録、入宋傳法沙門道元記
Recorded on the day of the initial horse, the junior water year of the rabbit, in Ninji [24 May 1243], recorded by the Śramaṇa Dōgen, who entered the Song and transmitted the dharma

---

19 The Tōunji 洞雲寺MS lacks a colophon for this chapter; this colophon is first found in the Myōshoji MS 妙昌寺本 of the sixty-chapter *Shōbōgenzō* completed in 1751.
initial horse (*tango* 端午): I.e., the fifth day of the fifth lunar month.

TREASURY OF THE TRUE DHARMA EYE

SUPPLEMENTARY CHAPTER 6

Instructions for the Administration Cloister
Ji kuin mon
示庫院文

Instructions for the Administration Cloister

Ji kuin mon

INTRODUCTION

In medieval times, this work was never included in any *Shōbōgenzō* manuscript tradition; rather, it survived only in the *Kenzei ki* 建撕記, the hagiography of Dōgen compiled in 1452 by Kenzei 建撕 (1415–1474), fourteenth abbot of Eiheiji. It was first included in the *Shōbōgenzō* by Manzan Dōhaku 卍山道白 (1636–1714), in his 1686 *Shōbōgenzō* compilation in eighty-nine chapters; and, thereafter, was published in the 1815 Honzan edition as number 81 (or 82 in the Iwanami and Shūmuchō versions). Kenzei's version was in Chinese, followed by a note stating that it represents a summary of Dōgen's Japanese original. Unfortunately, that original is not extant; and the Japanese text in the Honzan edition, on which this translation is based, represents a *yomikudashi* 訓み下し, or Japanese reading, of Kenzei's Chinese.

Rather like the *Jū undō shiki* 重雲堂式, another text first added to the *Shōbōgenzō* by Manzan, the *Ji kuin mon* is purely a work of instruction on monastic practice, without the sort of commentary typical of the *Shōbōgenzō* texts; thus, in terms of content, if not in style, it belongs with Dōgen's other, more formal, writings on monastic regulations. Unlike the *Jū undō shiki*, which dates from its author's early career, this text is clearly identified as a work of his later years, composed in the early autumn of 1246, when Dōgen was concerned with establishing the rules of a proper Zen monastery at his newly founded Eiheiji.

The administrative cloister (*kuin* 庫院) in medieval Chinese Chan and Japanese Zen monasteries was the hall housing the kitchen, storerooms, and administrative offices of the institution. As here, the name was also used in reference simply to the kitchen.

正法眼藏別輯六
Treasury of the True Dharma Eye
Supplementary Chapter 6

示庫院文

Instructions for the Administration Cloister

(本山版正法眼藏所収)

(In the Honzan *Shōbōgenzō*)

[S6:1] {2:516}

寛元四年八月六日、示衆云、齋僧之法、以敬爲宗。

Sixth day, eighth month, fourth year of Kangen, instructing the assembly: "In the manner of offering meals to the saṃgha, reverence is essential."[1]

[S6:2]

はるかに、西天竺の法を正傳し、ちかくは、震旦國の法を正傳するに、如來滅度ののち、あるいは諸天の天供を、佛ならびに僧に奉獻し、あるいは國王の王膳を、佛ならびに僧に供養したてまつりき。そのほか、長者・居士のいへよりたてまつり、毘闍・首陀のいへよりたてまつるもありき。かくのごとくの供養、ともに敬重するところ、ねんごろなり。よく天上・人間のなかに、極重の敬禮をもちい、至極の尊言をして、うやまひたてまつりて、飯饌等の供養のそなへを、造作するなり、深意あり。いま、遠方の深山なりとも、寺院の香積局、その禮儀・言語、したしく正傳すべきなり。これ、天上・人間の、佛法を習學するなり。

In the correct transmission of the dharma in distant Sindhu in the West and the correct transmission of the dharma in the nearby Land of Cīnasthāna, after the passing of the Tathāgata, the devas have presented celestial offerings to the buddhas and saṃgha members, and the kings have made offerings of royal fare to the buddhas and saṃgha members. In addition, they have been made by the wealthy and the laity, and by the vaiśya and the śūdra. All such offerings are sincere in their reverence. In

---

1 **Sixth day, eighth month, fourth year of Kangen** (*Kangen shinen hachigatsu rokunichi* 寛元四年八月六日): Corresponding to 17 September 1246 in the Gregorian calendar.

"In the manner of offering meals to the saṃgha, reverence is essential" (*saisō shi hō, i kyō i shū* 齋僧之法、以敬爲宗): Quoting the opening line of the section on feeding the saṃgha in the *Chanyuan qinggue* 禪苑清規, by Changlu Zongze 長蘆宗賾 (d. 1107?) (ZZ.111:930a16).

136　　　DŌGEN'S *SHŌBŌGENZŌ* VOLUME VII

the heavens above and among humans, they create preparations of offerings of food and the like, paying homage by showing the utmost respect and using the most honorific language. There is profound significance in this. Now, although it is deep in the mountains of a remote quarter, the Office of Aromatic Provisions of our monastery should correctly transmit this ceremony and language.[2] This is studying the buddha dharma in the heavens above and among humans.

[S6:3] {2:517}

いはゆる粥をば、御粥、とまをすべし、朝粥、ともまをすべし、粥、とまをすべからず。齋をば、御齋、とまをすべし、齋時、ともまをすべし、齋、とまをすべからず。よね、しろめまいらせよ、とまをすべし、よね、つけ、といふべからず。よね、あらひまゐらするをば、淨米しまゐらせよ、とまをすべし、よね、かせ、とまをすべからず。

For instance, we should refer to gruel as the "esteemed gruel" or the "morning gruel"; we should not call it "gruel." We should refer to the midday meal as the "esteemed midday meal" or the "midday mealtime"; we should not call it "midday meal."[3] We should say, "Would you whiten the rice"; we should not say, "polish the rice." Referring to washing rice, we should say, "Would you clean the rice"; we should not say, "Rinse the rice."

[S6:4]

御菜の御料のなにもの、えりまいらせよ、とまをすべし、菜えれ、とまをすべからず。御汁のもの、し、まいらせよ、とまをすべし、汁、によ、とまをすべからず。御羹、しまいらせよ、とまをすべし、羹せよ、とまをすべからず。御齋・御粥は、むませさせたまひたる、とまをすべし。齋・粥いれたてまつらん調度、みなかくのごとく、うやまふべし。不敬は、かへりて映過をまねく、功徳をうること、なきなり。

We should say, "Would you select an esteemed ingredient for the esteemed vegetable"; we should not say, "Pick a vegetable." We should say, "Would you prepare the esteemed soup"; we should not say, "Heat the soup." We should say, "Would you prepare the esteemed broth"; we should not say, "Make the broth." We should say, "The esteemed midday meal — or the esteemed gruel — has been well prepared." All utensils in

---

2　**the Office of Aromatic Provisions** (*kōjaku kyoku* 香積局): I.e., the monastic kitchen.

3　**"esteemed gruel"** (*okayu* 御粥); **"esteemed midday meal"** (*otoki* 御齋): Terms attaching the respectful prefix *o* 御 (also read *on* or *go*), an untranslatable use, here and below infelicitously rendered by "esteemed" simply to indicate the distinction from the unadorned noun. "Gruel" (*shuku* or *kayu* 粥) is used both for porridge in general and for the monastery morning meal in particular; "midday meal" (*sai* or *toki* 齋) refers to the monastery meal taken before noon (as well as Buddhist meals more generally).

S6. Instructions for the Administration Cloister *Ji kuin mon* 示庫院文 137

which the midday meal or gruel is to be placed should be shown respect in this way. Lack of respect invites disaster and never gains merit.[4]

[S6:5]

齋・粥をととのへまいらするとき、人の息にて、米・菜、およびいづれの
ものをも、ふくべからず。たとひ、かわきたるものなりとも、綴袖に觸す
ることなかれ。頭・顔に觸たる手を、いまだあらはずして、齋・粥の器お
よび齋・粥に、手、ふるることなかれ。よねをえりまいらするより、乃
至、飯羹につくりまいらする經營のあひだ、身のかゆきところかきては、
かならずその手をあらふべし。齋・粥ととのへまいらするところにては、
佛經の文および祖師の語を、諷誦すべし。世間の語、雜穢の話、いふべか
らず。おほよそ米・菜・鹽・醬等のいろいろのもの、まします、とまをす
べし。米あり、菜あり、とまをすべからず。齋・粥のあらんところをすぎ
んには、僧・行者は問訊したてまつるべし。零菜・零米等ありとも、齋・
粥ののち使用すべし。齋・粥、をはらざらんほど、をかすべからず。齋・
粥、ととのへまゐらする調度、ねんごろに護惜すべし、他事にもちいるべ
からず。在家よりきたれらんともがらの、いまだ手をきよめざらんには、
手をふれさすべからず。在家よりきたれらん菜果等、いまだきよめずば、
洒水して行香し行火してのちに、三寶・衆僧にたてまつるべし。現在大宋
國の諸山・諸寺には、もし在家より饅頭・乳餅・蒸餅等きたらんは、かさ
ねてむしまいらせて、衆僧にたてまつる。これ、きよむるなり。いまだむ
さざれば、たてまつらざるなり。

When preparing the midday meal or gruel, we should not breathe on the rice, vegetables, or any other dishes. Do not touch even dried goods with the sleeve. If you have touched your head or face, do not touch the midday meal or gruel, or the utensils for them, until you have washed your hands. We should always wash our hands if we have scratched an itch at any time during the meal preparation, from selecting the rice through cooking the rice and broth. Where the midday meal and gruel are prepared, we should recite passages from the sūtras of the buddhas or the words of the ancestral masters; we should not engage in worldly talk or idle chatter. In general, we should use [the verb] *mashimasu* in reference to the rice, vegetables, salt, sauce, and so on; we should not say [using the more informal predicate], "there's rice" or "there are vegetables."[5] When passing the place where the midday meal or gruel is,

---

4   **invites disaster** (*ōka o maneku* 殃過をまねく): Japanese version of an expression best known in Chan and Zen literature from the line in the *Zhengdao ge* 證道歌 (T.2014.48:396a27-28):

豁達空撥因果、莽莽蕩蕩招殃禍。
A wide-open void, dismissing cause and effect;
An endless vastness, inviting disaster.

5   **we should use [the verb]** *mashimasu* (*mashimasu, to mōsu beshi* まします、とま をすべし): The verb *masu* ます is a polite substitute for *ari* ("to exist"), the predicate in the following phrases here: "there's rice," "there are vegetables."

monks and postulants should make a bow.[6] Spilled vegetables, spilled rice, and the like, should be used after the midday meal or gruel; so long as the midday meal or gruel has not finished, we should not intrude.[7] We should maintain and care for the utensils used in preparation of the midday meal and gruel, and should not use them for other purposes. They should not be touched by those coming from lay households until they have washed their hands. Fruits, vegetables, and the like, coming from lay households, if they are not yet purified, should be offered to the three treasures and the monks after they have been washed, incensed, and cooked. At present, at the various mountains and other monasteries in the Land of the Great Song, when dumplings, milk cakes, steamed cakes, and the like, come from lay households, they are re-steamed and presented to the monks.[8] This is to purify them. If they have not been steamed, they are not presented.

[S6:6] {2:518}
これ、おほかるなかに、すこしばかりなり。この大旨をえて、庫院香積、これを行すべし。萬事、非儀なることなかれ。

These are but a few [items] among many. The Administration Cloister and Aromatic Provisions should grasp the main points and apply them. In the myriad matters, do not be improper.

[Honzan edition:]

右條條、佛祖之命脈、衲僧之眼睛也。外道未知、天魔不堪、唯有佛子、乃能傳之。庫院之知事、明察莫失焉。

開闢沙門、道元示

The above articles constitute the very lifeblood of the buddhas and ancestors, the very eye of the patch-robed monk. The other paths do not know them; the deva-māras could not manage them; only the descendants of the buddhas can transmit them. The kitchen stewards should clearly note them and never omit them.

Presented by the founding Śramaṇa Dōgen,[9]

---

6 **monks and postulants should make a bow** (*sō anja wa monjin shitatematsuru beshi* 僧・行者は問訊したてまつるべし): "Make a bow" here renders *monjin* 問訊 (literally, "make inquiries"), the Buddhist standing bow, with palms together, used in greeting, acknowledgement, reverence, etc.

7 **we should not intrude** (*okasu bekarazu* をかすべからず): Presumably, the point here is that we should not interrupt the meal service by dealing with spilled food.

8 **various mountains** (*shozan* 諸山): Also read *shosan*. A term for the major Buddhist monasteries.

9 This colophon is found in the earliest extant copy of the *Ji kuin mon*, the 1552 Zuichō 瑞長 MS of the *Kenzei ki* 建撕記, where it is followed by this note, presumably by the

S6. Instructions for the Administration Cloister *Ji kuin mon* 示庫院文 139

[S6:7]

永平寺　今告知事。自今已後、若過午後檀那供飯、留待翌日。如其麵餅菓子、諸般粥等、雖晩猶行、乃佛祖會下藥石也。況大宋國之內、有道之勝躅也。如來曾許雪山僧之裹腹衣、當山亦許雪時之藥石矣。

Eiheiji hereby informs the stewards:[10]

Hereafter, if a dānapati offers rice after noon has passed, it is kept until the following day. With noodles, cakes, fruit, various gruels, and the like, proceed to serve, even in the evening; for they are medicinals in the communities of the buddhas and ancestors.[11] *Indeed, there is excellent precedent among those on the path in the Land of the Great Song. The Tathāgata permitted an undergarment for monks in the Snowy Mountains; and this mountain likewise permits medicinals during the snowy season.*[12]

開闢永平沙門、希玄
Kigen, Śramaṇa founder of Eihei[13]

---

author, Keizei 建撕 (reproduced at DZZ.2:652):

此正本ハ假名也、今以眞字書寫之肝要也、此正本筆者靈梅院開基壇那勝義也、此人ハ三世壇那ノ二男、四世壇那兄也、屋敷ノ名字從此始ル也。

The original manuscript is in Japanese script (*kana*). I have summarized its key points in Chinese script (*shinji*). The original manuscript was copied by Katsuyoshi, founding patron of Reibai'in [at Eiheiji]. He was the second son of [Eiheiji's] third-generation patron [Shigemichi 重通] and the older brother of its fourth-generation patron [Tomomichi 朝通]. Their domestic names began with these [numerical designations].

10　This appended note and its colophon, appearing in the Honzan edition, is not found in the *Kenzei ki* 建撕記. Rather, it reproduces a text known as the *Eiheiji koku chiji mon* 永平寺告知事文 (DZZ.7:284), preserved in a MS owned by Myōōji 妙應寺, in Gifu Prefecture.

Eiheiji 永平寺: Presumably, Dōgen here refers to himself by the name of his monastery.

11　**medicinals in the communities of the buddhas and ancestors** (*busso e ge yakuseki* 佛祖會下藥石): I.e., food consumed after the noon meal in Chan monasteries. Dōgen uses the common euphemism *yakuseki* 藥石 ("medicine and stone" [acupuncture needles]) for such food.

12　**Snowy Mountains** (*Sessen* 雪山): I.e., the Himalayas.

13　**Kigen** 希玄: I.e., Dōgen.

TREASURY OF THE TRUE DHARMA EYE

SUPPLEMENTARY CHAPTER 7

Only Buddhas with Buddhas
Yui butsu yo butsu

唯佛與佛

Only Buddhas with Buddhas

Yui butsu yo butsu

INTRODUCTION

This relatively short work is not included in either the seventy-five or sixty-chapter compilations of the *Shōbōgenzō*; rather, it was found among the texts of the *Himitsu Shōbōgenzō* collection, as number 6 of fascicle 3. The colophon identifies it as "Treasury of the True Dharma Eye, Number 38," though the source and significance of this number are unclear. It was included in the Honzan edition as number 91.

The title of the work comes from the famous passage in the *Lotus Sūtra*, in which Buddha Śākyamuni warns that "only buddhas with buddhas can exhaustively investigate the real marks of the dharmas" — i.e., only the fully awakened buddhas know what things are really like. The theme of the buddhas' awakening is introduced in the first sections of the text, and the claim that only buddhas know what is on the mind of buddhas reappears in the final sections. In between, Dōgen explores several Zen sayings on "the whole earth" as the body of a buddha and our own true body.

正法眼藏別輯七

Treasury of the True Dharma Eye
Supplementary Chapter 7

唯佛與佛

Only Buddhas with Buddhas

(秘密正法眼藏後冊所収)

(*Himitsu Shōbōgenzō,* last volume)

[S7:1] {2:519}

佛法は、人の知るべきにはあらず。この故に昔しより、凡夫として佛法を
悟るなし、二乘として佛法をきはむるなし、獨り佛にさとらるる故に、唯
佛與佛、乃能究盡、と云ふ。

The buddha dharma is not to be known by humans. Therefore, from long
ago, the common people have not awakened to the buddha dharma, and
those of the two vehicles have not mastered the buddha dharma; since
buddhas alone awaken to it, it is said, "*only buddhas with buddhas can
exhaustively investigate it.*"[1]

[S7:2]

其れをきはめ悟る時、われながらも、かねてより、悟るとはかくこそあら
め、とおもはるる事はなきなり。縦ひおぼゆれども、そのおぼゆるにたが
はぬ悟にてなきなり。悟りも、おぼえしが如にてもなし。かくあれば、兼
て思ふ、そのように、たつべきにあらず。悟りぬる折りは、いかにありけ
る、故に悟りたりとおぼえぬなり。是にてかへりしるべし、悟りより先
に、兔角おもひけるは、悟りの用にあらぬと。さきのさまざまおもふ、お
もひのやうにあらざりけるは、おもひの、まことにあしくて、其のちから
の、なきにてはなし。こしかたのおもひも、さながら悟りにて有けるを、

---

1   **from long ago** (*mukashi yori* 昔しより): It is also possible to read this phrase as
governing the final verb: "from long ago, it has been said . . . ."

two vehicles (*nijō* 二乘): I.e., the non-Mahāyāna Buddhists of the *śrāvaka-yāna* (*shōmon
jō* 聲聞乘) and *pratyeka-buddha-yāna* (*engaku jō* 緣覺乘); a common term of dismissal
in Dōgen's writings.

"only buddhas with buddhas can exhaustively investigate it" (*yui butsu yo butsu,
nai nō gūjin* 唯佛與佛、乃能究盡): From a line in Kumārajīva's translation of the *Lotus
Sūtra*; see Supplementary Notes, s.v. "Only buddhas with buddhas can exhaustively investigate the real marks of the dharmas." The rather clumsy "only buddhas with buddhas"
(or "only a buddha and a buddha") renders Kumārajīva's four-glyph Chinese phrase for
what in his Sanskrit text was probably simply *tathāgata eva* ("only a tathāgata").

144 DŌGEN'S *SHŌBŌGENZŌ* VOLUME VII

其をりは、さかさまにせんとしける故に、ちからのなきとは、おもひも、いひもするなり。えうにあらずとおぼゆる事は、しるべき處、必ずあり。いはゆる、ちひさくはならじ、と恐れける。若、悟りよりさきのおもひをちからとして、悟りのいでこんは、たのもしからぬ悟りにてありぬべし。悟りよりさきにちからとせず、はるかに越えて來れる故に、悟りとは、ひとすぢに、さとりのちからにのみたすけらる。まどひはなきものぞ、とも知べし、さとりはなき事ぞ、とも知るべし。

When we completely awaken to it, there is nothing that we ourselves had previously thought awakening to be like. We may think about it, but it is not an awakening like what we think about it. Awakening is not as we thought; hence, thinking about it in advance is not helpful. When we have awakened, we do not know what it was that caused us to be awakened. We should reflect on this: having thought of this and that prior to awakening is of no use for awakening. That it was not as our various earlier thoughts had imagined is not because our thoughts were actually wrong and lacked force. Our previous thoughts were themselves awakening; but, at that time, because we were taking them as the opposite, we thought, and we said, that they had no force. In thinking that they are of no use, there is always something we should recognize: we were afraid that they could not get smaller.[2] An awakening that came about on the strength of our thoughts before awakening would be an unreliable awakening. Because we did not give them force prior to awakening and have far transcended them, our awakening is solely assisted only by the force of awakening itself. We should realize that there is no such thing as delusion; we should realize that there is no such thing as awakening.

[S7:3] {2:520}

無上菩提の人にて有をり、是を佛と云ふ。佛の無上菩提にてあるとき、是を無上菩提と云ふ。この道に有時の面目、しらざらんはおろかなりぬべし。いはゆる其の面目は、不染汚なり。不染汚とは、趣向なく、取舍なからんと、しひていとなみ、趣向にあらざらん處、つくろひするにはあらずなり。いかにも趣向せられず、取舍せられぬ不染汚の有なり。たとへば、人にあふに、面目のいかやうなると、おぼえぬ。はなにも、月にも、今ひとつの光・色おもひかさねず。はるは、ただはるながらの心、あきも又、あきながらの美・悪にて、のがるべきにあらぬを、われにあらざらんとするには、われなるにても、おもひしるべし。このはる・あきのこえ、われならんとするにも、われにあらざるにても、かへりみるべし。われにつもれるにてもなし、今も我に有おもひにてもなきなり。其心は、今の四大五蘊、各われと我とすべきにてもあらず、たれ、とたどるべからず。然れば、花・月のもよほす心のいろ、又、我とすべきにあらぬを、われとおもふ。われにあらぬを、われとおもひ、さもあらばあれ、そむくべきかたの

---

2 **we were afraid that they could not get smaller** (*chiisaku wa naraji, to osorekeru* ちひさくはならじ、と恐れける): Tentatively taking this to mean that we disparaged our thoughts as unawakened.

S7. Only Buddhas with Buddhas *Yui butsu yo butsu* 唯佛與佛   145

色も、おもむくべきかたの、そめられぬべきもなしとてらす時、おのづから、道に有る行履もかくれざりける、本來の面目なり。

When unsurpassed bodhi is a person, we call it "buddha"; when a buddha is unsurpassed bodhi, we call it "unsurpassed bodhi." Failing to recognize the face when one is on this path is stupid. "The face" here is "not defiled."[3] "Not defiled" does not mean intentionally acting so as to have no direction or to have no picking and choosing, or to keep on with what is not our direction. In fact, there is a "not defiled" that is without direction, without picking and choosing. For example, when we meet someone, we do not think about what kind of face it is; with a flower, with the moon, we do not imagine another brightness or color. We should recognize that when, though we cannot escape the fact that spring simply has the heart of spring, and autumn also is just the beauty and ugliness of autumn, we try to be other than ourselves, we are ourselves. We should also reflect that, when we try to make the voices of this spring and autumn ourselves, they are not ourselves. They have not accumulated in us; they are not thoughts in us just now. The point here is that we cannot take any of the present four elements or five aggregates as any self of ourselves or seek it out in another.[4] The colors of the mind moved by the flower or the moon, which therefore should also not be ourselves, we think of as ourselves. Let thinking of what is not ourselves as ourselves be as it may, when we illumine the fact that both the colors to be rejected and those to be approached were never stained, [the fact] that the conduct naturally on the way has never been hidden is our original face.[5]

---

3   **"The face" here is "not defiled"** (*iwayuru sono menmoku wa, fuzenna nari* いはゆる其の面目は、不染汚なり): Perhaps recalling the conversation, alluded to throughout the *Shōbōgenzō*, between the Sixth Ancestor and his disciple Nanyue Huairang 南嶽懷讓 (677-744), to the effect that buddhas and ancestors are "not defiled" (*fuzenna* 不染汚) by Buddhist practice and verification. (See Dōgen's *shinji Shōbōgenzō* 眞字正法眼藏, DZZ.5:178, case 101.)

4   **four elements or five aggregates** (*shidai goun* 四大五蘊): Standard Buddhist technical terms for the physical and mental constituents of the world; see Supplementary Notes, s.v. "Four elements and five aggregates." Here, as elsewhere, Dōgen seems to be using these terms to refer to what we might call the psychophysical organism, much as he uses the expression "body and mind" (*shinjin* 身心).

5   **[the fact] that the conduct naturally on the way has never been hidden is our original face** (*onozukara, dō ni aru anri mo kakurezarikeru, honrai no menmoku nari* おのづから、道に有る行履もかくれざりける、本來の面目なり): Following Kawamura's punctuation after *kakurezarikeru* かくれざりける; the sentence could be read without it, yielding something like, "The conduct that is naturally on the way is our original face, never hidden." On either reading, the argument of this difficult sentence would seem to be that, while we may mistake the objects of the mind as ourselves, once we realize that these objects are undefiled, we recognize that our life with them has always been the Buddhist practice of our true nature.

146 DŌGEN'S *SHŌBŌGENZŌ* VOLUME VII

[S7:4] {2:521}

ふるき人の云、盡大地、これ自己の法身、にて有れ共、法身にさへられざ
るべし。もし法身にさへられぬるには、いささか、身を轉ぜんとするにも
かなはず。出身の道あるべし、いかなるか是諸人の出身の道、と。若、こ
の出身のみちをいはざるらんものは、法身のいのちも、たちまちにたえ
て、ながく苦海にしづみぬべし。如是とはんに、いかにといはんか、法身
をもいけ、苦海にもしづまざるべきと。このとき云べし、盡大地、自己の
法身なりと。もしこの道理にてあらん、盡大地自己の法身、と云ふをりは
いはれぬ。又、いはれざらんとき、ふつといはぬとやこころうべき。いは
ぬ、いはぬ古佛のいへること有、死のなかにいけること有、いけるなかに
死せること有。死せるがつねに死せるあり、いけるがつねにいけるあり。
是、人の、しひてしかあらしむるにあらず、法の、かくのごとくなるな
り。

A person of old has said,[6]

All the whole earth is one's own dharma body; nevertheless, we are not
obstructed by the dharma body. If we were obstructed by the dharma
body, we could not turn our bodies at all. There should be a way out of
the body. What is your way out of the body? Those who cannot speak
of this way out of the body, with the life of the dharma body immediately coming to an end, will be forever sunk in the sea of suffering.[7]

When asked in this way, what should we say to keep alive the dharma
body and not sink into the sea of suffering? At this time, we should say,
"All the whole earth is one's own dharma body." If this is the truth, when
we say, "All the whole earth is one's own dharma body," we have said
it.[8] Again, when we cannot speak, we should set our minds not to speak
at all. The old buddha who "doesn't say, doesn't say" has a saying that,
in death there is being alive; in being alive there is being dead.[9] Being

---

6   **A person of old** (*furuki hito* ふるき人): A Japanese passage that, like the quotation
in section 10, below, seems to be based very loosely on a saying by the Song-dynasty
Chan Master Yaoshan Liyu 藥山利昱 (dates unknown; disciple of Liangshan Yuanguan
梁山緣觀); see Supplementary Notes. s.v. "Iron bull."

7   **"Those who cannot speak of this way out of the body"** (*moshi, kono shusshin no
michi o iwazaran mono* 若、この出身のみちをいはざるらんもの): Though it follows
the word *to* と that marks the end of the quotation, in fact, this sentence continues Dōgen's Japanese version of Liyu's words (as seen in the note above). Oddly, a second quotation marker occurs at the end of the subsequent sentence, which is not found in Liyu's
saying and almost certainly represents the beginning of Dōgen's comment on the saying.

8   **we have said it** (*iwarenu* いはれぬ): Presumably, meaning, "[if what we say is true,]
we have spoken of the way out of the body."

9   **The old buddha who "doesn't say, doesn't say"** (*iwanu, iwanu kobutsu* いは
ぬ、いはぬ古佛): Presumably, a reference to Daowu Yuanzhi 道吾圓智 (769-835), who,
when asked at a funeral whether what was in the coffin was alive or dead, refused to say;
but the saying attributed to him here does not, in fact, seem to be his words. Rather, it
appears to be Dōgen's interpretation of why he "doesn't say," perhaps inspired by the
verse comment on the Daowu story by Yuanwu Keqin 圜悟克勤 (1063–1135), cited in

S7. Only Buddhas with Buddhas *Yui butsu yo butsu* 唯佛與佛 147

dead is always being dead; being alive is always being alive. This is the way the dharma is, without anyone intentionally bringing it about.

[S7:5]

然かあれば、法輪の轉ずるをりも、如是の光り有、こえあり、現身度生に
も、しかありとしるべし。是を、無生の知見、とは云。現身度生とは、度
生現身にて有りけるなり。度にむかひて現をたどらず、現をみるに度をあ
やしむことなかるべし。是度に、佛法はきはめつくせりと、心うべし、と
くべし、證すべし。現にも身にも、度のごとくにありけると、聞くなり、
とくなり。是も、現身度生の、しかあらしめけるとなり。この旨を證しけ
るにぞ、得道のあしたより、涅槃のゆふべにいたるまで、一字をもとかざ
りけるとも、とかることばの、自在なりける。

Thus, we should know that, when the wheel of dharma turns, he has a radiance, he has a voice, such as this; and, when he manifests a body and delivers living beings, it is like this.[10] This is called "the knowledge of non-arising."[11] "Manifesting a body and delivering living beings" means it was "delivering living beings and manifesting a body."[12] We do

---

"Shōbōgenzō zenki" 正法眼藏全機. For the story and Yuanwu's verse, see Supplementary Notes s.v. "Manifestation of the full function."

10 **when the wheel of dharma turns** (*hōrin no tenzuru ori* 法輪の轉ずるをり): The unexpressed agent is taken here as "Buddha Śākyamuni." The antecedent of "such as this" (*kaku no gotoku* 如是) and "like this" (*shika ari* しかあり) is unclear; the most likely interpretation of the sentence would seem to be that the Buddha's teachings ("radiance" [*hikari* 光り], "voice" [*koe* こえ]) are like the saying of "the old buddha who 'doesn't say, doesn't say.'"

11 **This is called "the knowledge of non-arising"** (*kore o, mushō no chiken, to wa iu* 是を、無生の知見、とは云): "Non-arising" (*mushō* 無生) most often refers to the emptiness (*kū* 空; S. *śūnyatā*) of dharmas (i.e., that they do not really occur); but here Dōgen is quite likely playing on the glyph *shō* 生 in the sense "being alive" (*ikeru* 生ける), as in the old buddha's saying above, "in death there is being alive" (*shi no naka ni ikeru koto ari* 死のなかにいけること有).

12 **"Manifesting a body and delivering living beings" means it was "delivering living beings and manifesting a body"** (*genshin doshō to wa, doshō genshin nite arikeru nari* 現身度生とは、度生現身にて有りけるなり): The implication of the chiasmus here is subject to interpretation; often taken to mean that the deliverance of beings was (or caused) the manifestation of the body. The use of the past tense here (*nite arikeru* にて有りける) and below suggests that Dōgen has in mind the historical advent of Buddha Śākyamuni.

Though not identical, the language of "manifestation" and "deliverance" here is reminiscent of that used in the famous description in the *Lotus Sūtra* of the thirty-three manifestations of the Bodhisattva Avalokiteśvara, which begins (at *Miaofa lianhua jing* 妙法蓮華經, T.262.9:57a23-24):

若有國土衆生應以佛身得度者、觀世音菩薩即現佛身而爲説法。

If there are in the land living beings who ought to attain deliverance by a buddha body, the Bodhisattva Avalokiteśvara manifests a buddha body and preaches the dharma to them.

not seek the "manifesting" while facing the "delivering"; we should not doubt the "delivering" while seeing the "manifesting."[13] We should understand, should preach, and should verify that the buddha dharma was ultimately completed in this "delivering"; it is hearing and preaching that, in "manifesting" and in "a body," it was the same as "delivering." This too was brought about by his "manifesting a body and delivering living beings." In having verified this point, from the morning of his gaining the way to the evening of his nirvāṇa, even if he never preached a single word, the words he preached were masterful.

[S7:6] {2:522}

古佛云、盡大地是眞實人體なり、盡大地是解脱門也、盡大地是毘盧一隻の
まなこなり、盡大地是自己法身なり。

An old buddha has said, "All the whole earth is the true human body; all the whole earth is the gate of liberation; all the whole earth is the single eye of Vairocana; all the whole earth is one's own dharma body."[14]

[S7:7]

いはゆるこころは、眞實とは、まことの身、となり。盡大地を、われらが
かりにあらざりけるまことしき身にてありける、とはしるべし。ひごろ
は、なにとしてかしらざりける、と問人あらば、盡大地是眞實人體といひ
つることを我にかへせ、と云べし。又、盡大地眞實人體とは、かくのごと

See Supplementary Notes, s.v. "Manifesting a body to preach the dharma."

13 **We do not seek the "manifesting" while facing the "delivering"** (*do ni mukaite gen o tadorazu* 度にむかひて現をたどらず): I.e., once we have the one, we already have the other; the following clause expresses the same point in reverse.

14 **An old buddha** (*kobutsu* 古佛): Words akin to one or another of these sayings, given here in mixed Chinese and Japanese, can be found in the records of various Chan masters; but a source for the four together in this form seems extant only in a lecture by Chan Master Renwang Qin of Xishu 西蜀仁王欽禪師, in a passage that also contains the verse by Xingjiao Hongshou (944-1022) quoted below, section 15 (*Jiatai pudeng lu* 嘉泰普燈錄, ZZ.137:342b17-343a1):

要見一切諸法不離本心。大地虚空非心外法。所以撲落非他物、縱横不是塵。山河及大地、全露法王身。方明山河及大地、全露法王身。方明盡大地是眞實人體。大地是解脱門。盡大地是毘盧一隻眼。盡大地是自己法身。恁麼見得。心外無法

You must see that all the dharmas are not apart from the original mind; the whole earth and empty space are not dharmas outside the mind. Therefore,
Scattered, but not another thing;
Their dimensions, not a mote of dust.
The mountains, rivers, and the whole earth
Fully expose the body of the Dharma King.
Only then will you clarify that all the whole earth is the true human body; the whole earth is the gate of liberation; all the whole earth is the single eye of Vairocana; all the whole earth is one's own dharma body. When you can see like this, there is no dharma outside the mind.

S7. Only Buddhas with Buddhas *Yui butsu yo butsu* 唯佛與佛 149

く知共云べし。又、盡大地これ解脱門とは、いかにもまつはれ、かかふる
ことなきに、なづくるなり。盡大地、のことばは、ときにも、としにも、
心にも、ことばにも、したしくして、ひまなく親密なり。かぎりなく、ほ
とりなきを、盡大地、と云べきなり。この解脱門にいらんことをもとめ、
いでんことをもとめんに、又うべからざるなり。なにとして如是なる。
發問をかへり見るべし。あらぬ處を尋ねばやとおもはんにも、かなふべか
らざるものなり。又、盡大地は、是毘盧のひとつのまなこなり、とは、佛
は、ひとつのまなこといへる、かならずしも人のまなこのやうにあらんず
る、とはおもはざれ。人にも目こそは二もあれ、まなこを云ときは、人
眼、とばかりいひて、二とも三ともいはぬなり。教をまなぶものの、佛
眼、といひ、法眼、といひ、天眼、などといふも、めにてあり、とはなら
はぬなり。目のやうにあらんとしれるをば、はかなきといふ。今は、ただ
佛けの眼こひとつにて、盡大地ありける、ときくべし。千眼もあれ、萬の
まなこもあれ、まづしばらく盡大地が、そのなかのひとつにてあるとな
り。かくおほかるなかに、ひとつぞ、と云も、とがなし。又、佛にはただ
まなこはひとつのみあり、としるもあやまらず。まなこは、さまざまある
べきぞかし、三あるもあり、千眼あるもあり、八萬四千ありと云事もあれ
ば、まなこの、かくの如くなりとききて、耳をおどろかさざるべし。又、
盡大地はみづから法身なり、ときくべし。みづからをしらん事をもとむる
は、いけるもののさだまれる心なり。然れ共、まことのみづからをば、み
るものまれなり、ひとり佛のみ、これをしれり。其外の外道等は、いたづ
らにあらぬをのみ、われとおもふなり。佛の云ふみづからは、則ち盡大地
にてあるなり。然ば、みづから知も知ぬも、皆ともにおのれにあらず盡大
地はなし。この時のことば、かのときの人に、ゆづるべし。

The meaning of this is that the "true" is the real "body." We should recognize "all the whole earth" as, not our provisional, but our real body. If
someone asks, "Why did I not know this before?" we should say, "Give
me back my saying that 'all the whole earth is the true human body.'"[15]
Or we should say, "We know like this that 'all the whole earth is the true
human body.'"

Again, "all the whole earth is the gate of liberation" designates having
nothing at all to be entangled or burdened with. The words "all the whole
earth" are closely, inseparably intimate with the time, the year, the mind,
the words. We should call the limitless, the borderless, "all the whole
earth." When we seek to enter or to exit this "gate of liberation," we cannot do it. Why is this so? We should reflect on this question. We may think
to seek out some non-existing place, but this is something impossible.

Again, "all the whole earth is the single eye of Vairocana" says that the
Buddha has one eye, but do not think that it is necessarily like a human
eye. In humans, there are two eyes; so, in speaking of the eye, we just
say "the human eye," without speaking of two or three. Those who study

---

15 **"Give me back my saying"** (*iitsuru koto o ware ni kaese* いひつることを我にか
へせ): Japanese rendering of a Chinese linguistic pattern that appears elsewhere in the
Shōbōgenzō: *kan ga . . . rai* 還我…來 ("give me back. . .").

150
DŌGEN'S *SHŌBŌGENZŌ* VOLUME VII

the teachings speak of the "buddha eye," the "dharma eye," the "deva eye," and the like; but they do not learn that these are eyes.[16] Those who understand them as being like eyes are called "unreliable." Here, we should just hear that "all the whole earth" existed as the one eye of the Buddha.[17] There may be a thousand eyes or ten thousand eyes; but first of all, for now, "the whole earth" is one among them. There is no error in saying that it is one among so many; nor are we mistaken in understanding that the Buddha has but a single eye. There should be various kinds of eyes: there are cases of three; there are cases of a thousand eyes; there are cases of eighty-four thousand; so, the ear should not be surprised to hear that the eye is like this.[18]

Again, we should hear that "all the whole earth is one's own dharma body." Seeking to know oneself is the fixed intention of living beings. Yet, those who see their true self are rare; only a buddha knows it. Others, on other paths, think in vain of only what does not exist as their self. The self of which the buddhas speak is "all the whole earth." Thus, for everyone, whether they know or do not know themselves, there is no "all the whole great earth" that is not their own. The words of this time, we should defer to people of that time.

[S7:8] {2:523}

昔し僧有て古德に問、百千萬境、一時に來らん時、いかがすべき。古德云く、莫管他。

Long ago, there was a monk who asked an old worthy, "When a hundred thousand myriad objects all come at once, what should we do?"[19]

---

16 **speak of the "buddha eye," the "dharma eye," the "deva eye," and the like** (*butsugen, to ii, hōgen, to ii, tengen, nado to iu* 佛眼、といひ、法眼、といひ、天眼、などといふ): Reference, no doubt, to the standard list of the "five eyes" (*gogen* 五眼); see Supplementary Notes, s.v. "Eye."

17 **"all the whole earth" existed as the one eye of the Buddha** (*hotoke no manako hitotsu nite, jin daichi arikeru* 佛けの眼こひとつにて、盡大地ありける): Taking *nite* にて as *ni arite* にありて: "The eye of the Buddha being one, there was 'the whole earth.'" The past tense here may represent a reference back to the quotation.

18 **there are cases of three; there are cases of a thousand eyes; there are cases of eighty-four thousand** (*mitsu aru mo ari, sengen aru mo ari, hachiman yonsen ari to iu koto mo areba* 三あるもあり、千眼あるもあり、八萬四千ありと云事もあれば): "Three eyes" (*sangen* 三眼) may refer to the first three of the five eyes (q.v.) or, again, to the convention of the third, wisdom eye between the eyebrows. The most familiar instance of a "thousand eyes" is the thousand-armed, thousand-eyed Avalokiteśvara (*senju sengen Kannon* 千手千眼觀音). "Eighty-four thousand eyes" (*hachiman yonsen gen* 八萬四千眼) does not seem to be a common expression and probably represents here simply the use of this stock Buddhist number for "a multitude."

19 **there was a monk** (*sō arite* 僧有て): Dōgen's Japanese version of this exchange seems to be combining two Chinese sources:

S7. Only Buddhas with Buddhas *Yui butsu yo butsu* 唯佛與佛　　151

The old worthy said, "Don't deal with them."

[S7:9]

云心は、來ん事はさもあらば有れ、兎も角もうごかすべからず、となり。
是、すみやかなる佛法にてあり、境にてはなし。このことばをば、炳誡と
は心うべからず、諦實にて有り、と心得べし。いかにも管ずるかとすれ
ば、管ぜられざりけるなり。

What this means is that, let their "coming" be as it may, in any case
we should not move them.[20] They are the pure buddha dharma, not "objects."[21] We should not take these words as a clear warning; we should
take them as the truth: however much we try to deal with them, they
cannot be dealt with.[22]

---

1) *Jingde chuandeng lu* 景德傳燈錄 (T.2076.51:294c13-15):

鎮州寶壽沼和尚僧問、萬境來侵時如何。師曰、莫管他。僧禮拜。師曰、不要
動著。動即打折汝腰。

Reverend Zhao, Baoshou of Zhenzhou, was asked by a monk, "How about when the
ten thousand objects assail you?"
The Master said, "Don't deal with them."
The monk bowed. The Master said, "Don't move. If you move, you'll break your
back."

2) *Liandeng huiyao* 聯燈會要 (ZZ.136:544a17-18; see also *Tanzhou Weishan Lingyu
chanshi yulu* 潭州潙山靈祐禪師語錄, T.1989.47:579c26-28):

仰山問、百千萬境一時來作麼生。師云。青不是黃、長不是短。諸法各住自位、
非干我事。仰山乃作禮。

Yangshan [Huiji] asked, "When a hundred thousand myriad objects all come at once,
what should we do?"
The Master said, "Green is not yellow; long is not short. Each of the dharmas abides
in its own position and is none of my business."
Yang made a bow.

20 **we should not move them** (*ugokasu bekarazu* うごかすべからず): Perhaps based
on Baoshou's telling the monk, "Don't move" (*buyao dongje* 不要動著) — though one
would then expect an intransitive form. The object of the verb here is unexpressed; presumably, the "objects" that are "coming" at us.

21 **They are the pure buddha dharma, not "objects"** (*kore, sumiyaka naru buppō nite
ari, kyō nite wa nashi* 是、すみやかなる佛法にてあり、境にてはなし): Or, perhaps,
"they are pure buddha dharmas" — i.e., what is coming at us are sacred phenomena (or
truths), not merely the objects of our senses.

22 **We should not take these words as a clear warning** (*kono kotoba o ba, heikai to wa
kokoro u bekarazu* このことばをば、炳誡とは心うべからず): I.e., the sentence, "don't
deal with them," is not to be understood as an imperative.

152 DŌGEN'S *SHŌBŌGENZŌ* VOLUME VII

[S7:10] {2:524}

ふるき佛の云く、山河大地と諸人と同くむまれ、三世の諸佛と諸人と同く
行ひ來れり。

An old buddha said, "Mountains, rivers, and the whole earth are born together with all of you; the buddhas of the three times have been practicing together with all of you."[23]

[S7:11]

然あればすなはち、一人むまるるをりに、山河大地をみるに、この一人が
むまれざりつるさきよりありける山河大地のうへに、いまひとへかさねて
むまれいづるとみえず。しかあればとても、又ふるきことばのむなしかる
べきにはあらず。いかにか心うべき。心えられずとて、さしおくべきには
あらねば、かならずこころうべし、とふべし。すでにとけることばにてあ
れば、きくべし、ききては、また心うべきなり。

This being the case, when a person is born, when we look at the mountains, rivers, and whole earth, we do not see that anything has been added on top of the mountains, rivers, and the whole earth that were there before the person was born.[24] Still, the words of old are not empty. How should we understand them? Since we should not ignore them just because we have not understood them, we should definitely understand them, definitely ask about them. Since they are clearly the words of a buddha, we should listen to them and, having listened, should understand them.

[S7:12]

是を心えんやうは、このむまるる一人がかたより、この生をたづぬるに、
この生と云ことは、いかにあることと、はじめ・をはり、明めける人はた
れぞ。終も始じめも知ざれ共、うまれきたれり。夫れ、ただ山河大地の
きはもしらざれ共、ここをばみる、この處をばふみありくがごとし。生
のごとくにあらぬ山河大地よりと、うらむるおもひなかれ。山河大地をひ
としき我生なりといへりけりと、あきらむべし。又、三世諸佛は、すでに
おこなひて、道をも、なり、悟りも、をはれり。この、佛と我とひとし、
とは、又いかにか心うべき。まづしばらく佛の行をこころうべし。佛の行
は、盡大地とおなじくおこなひ、盡衆生、ともにおこなふ。もし盡一切に
あらぬは、いまだ佛の行にてはなし。

---

23 **An old buddha** (*furuki hotoke* ふるき佛): Seeming to reflect the opening lines of the lecture by Yaoshan Liyu 藥山利昱 suggested by the quotation in section 4, above (q.v.) (*Tiansheng guangdeng lu* 天聖廣燈録, ZZ.135:837b3-4):

山河大地日月星辰與諸上座同生。三世諸佛與諸上座同參。

Mountains, rivers, and the whole earth, the sun, moon, and the stars, are born together with you senior seats; the buddhas of the three times study together with you senior seats.

24 **This being the case** (*shika areba sunawachi* 然あればすなはち): Presumably, meaning that, if mountains, rivers, and the whole earth are born together with people, we would expect some change in them when a person is born, but we do not see that.

S7. Only Buddhas with Buddhas *Yui butsu yo butsu* 唯佛與佛 153

The way to understand them is [to ask], when we inquire about this birth from the side of the person who was born, who is the person who has clarified the beginning and end of what this birth is? Although we do not understand the end or the beginning, we have been born. It is like the fact that, although we do not know the boundaries of the mountains, rivers, and whole earth, we see here and walk about in this place. Do not resent the mountains, rivers, and the whole earth for not being like birth; we should clarify the mountains, rivers, and the whole earth as they are said to be equivalent to our birth.[25]

Again, "the buddhas of the three times" having practiced, have already attained the way and completed awakening. How, then, are we to understand this [saying that] the buddhas are the same as us? First of all, we should understand the practice of a buddha. The practice of a buddha is carried out together with all the whole earth, together with all living beings. If it is not all of everything, it is not the practice of a buddha.

[S7:13] {2:525}
然かあれば、心をおこすより、さとりをうるにいたるまで、かならず盡大地と盡衆生と、さとりも、おこなひもするなり。これにいかにかうたがふおもひもあるべきに、しられぬおもひもまじるにたたをあきらめんとて、如是のこえのきこゆるも、人のよう、とはあやしまざるべし。是は、心うる、をしへにては、三世の諸佛のこころをもおこし、おこなふは、かならず、われらが身心をばもらさぬことわりの有なり、としるべし。

Thus, from bringing forth the mind [of bodhi] until attaining awakening, both the awakening and the practice invariably take place with all the whole earth and all living beings. Should we have doubts about this, in seeking to clarify what seems to mix in what we cannot know, we should not be suspicious like [ordinary] people when we hear a voice such as this. As the teaching to be understood, we should know that there is a principle that the bringing forth of the mind and the practice of the buddhas of the three times never exclude our body and mind.

[S7:14]
これをうたがひおもふは、すでに三世の諸佛をそしるなり。しづかにかへりみれば、我らが身心は、まことに三世の諸佛とおなじくおこなひける道理あり、發心しける道理もありぬべくみゆるなり。この身心のさき・のちを、かへりみ、てらせば、尋ぬべき人の、我にあらず、人にあらざらんには、なにをとどこほる處としてか、三世には、へだたれりとおもはん。このおもひども、しかしながらあれにあらず。なにとてかは、又、三世の諸佛の本心の處行道のときをば、さへんとはすべき。しばらく道は、知・不知にはあらぬとはなづくべし。

---

25 **Do not resent the mountains, rivers, and the whole earth for not being like birth** (*shō no gotoku ni aranu senga daichi yori to, uramuru omoi nakare* 生のごとくにあらぬ山河大地よりと、うらむるおもひなかれ): Reading *yo to* よと for *yori to* よりと.

154   DŌGEN'S *SHŌBŌGENZŌ* VOLUME VII

To doubt this is surely to slander the buddhas of the three times. When we quietly reflect, we can see that in fact there must be a truth that our bodies and minds have been practicing with, a truth that we brought forth the mind [of bodhi] with, the buddhas of the three times. When we reflect and illumine the before and after of our bodies and minds, since the person we should be looking for is neither ourselves nor another, where do we think they are stuck, such that they are separated from the three times? These thoughts are by no means of ourselves.[26] Why, furthermore, should we obstruct the time of the practice of the way of the original mind of the buddhas of the three times? For now, let us just call it "the way is neither knowing nor not knowing."[27]

[S7:15]

ふるき人の云く、撲落も他物にあらず、縦横、これ論にあらず。山河およ
び大地、すなはち全露法王身なり。

An ancient said,[28]

Scattered, but not another thing;
Their dimensions beyond discussion.
The mountains, rivers, and the whole earth
Fully expose the body of the Dharma King.

---

26 **These thoughts are by no means of ourselves** (*kono omoidomo, shikashi nagara are ni arazu* このおもひども、しかしながらあれにあらず): Reading *ware* われ for *are* あ れ. Perhaps the sense here is that the thoughts that suppose we are separated from the buddhas of the three times are not thoughts about ourselves "before and after our bodies and minds."

27 **"the way is neither knowing nor not knowing"** (*dō wa, chi fuchi ni wa aranu* 道は、知不知にはあらぬ): Likely reflecting the words of Nanquan Puyuan 南泉普 願 (748-835) to Zhaozhou Congshen 趙州從諗 (778-897) recorded in Dōgen's *shinji Shōbōgenzō* 眞字正法眼藏 (DZZ.5:134, case 19); see Supplementary Notes, s.v. "Ordinary mind is the way."

28 **An ancient** (*furuki hito* ふるき人): Japanese rendering of a verse appearing in several Chinese texts, including the *Jiatai pudeng lu* 嘉泰普燈錄 passage (at ZZ.137:342b16-17) that seems to have provided Dōgen's quotation in section 6, above. Most often cited as a source are the opening lines of the *Linjian lu* 林間錄, by Juefan Huihong 覺範慧洪 (1071-1128):

杭州興教小壽禪師、初隨天台韶國師。普請、聞墮薪而悟。作偈曰、撲落非他 物、縦横不是塵。山河及大地、全露法王身。

Chan Master Hongshou [reading *hong* 洪 for *xiao* 小], Xingjiao of Kangzhou, initially followed the National Teacher Shao of Tiantai. At communal labor, upon hearing a faggot of firewood fall, he was awakened and composed a gāthā:

Scattered, but not another thing;
Their dimensions, not a mote of dust.
The mountains, rivers, and the whole earth
Fully expose the body of the Dharma King.

S7. Only Buddhas with Buddhas *Yui butsu yo butsu* 唯佛與佛　　155

[S7:16]

いまの人も、昔の人のいへるが如く、ならふべし。すでに法王の身にて
あり、しかれば、撲落もことなるものにはあらざりけると、心うる法王
ありける。このこころは、山の、地にあるが如し、地の、山をのせてある
ににたり。心うるに、心えざりつるをりのきたりて、心うる、さまたげ
ず。又、心うるが、心えざりつるをやぶることもなくして、しかも心うる
と、心えぬとの、はるのころ、あきのこえあり。それをも心えざりつる
は、聲、おほきにしてときける、その聲、耳にいらず、耳、こえのなかに
あそびありきける。心うるは、こえ、すでに耳に入りて三昧あらはるをり
にてあるべし。この心うるは、ちひさく、心えぬは、おほきにてありける
とも思はざるべし。わたくしにおもひえたる事にはあらねば、法王の、如
是なりけるとしるべし。法王のみとは、まなこも、身のごとくにあり、心
も、みと、ひとしかるべし。心と、みと、一毫の隔てなく、全露にてある
べし。光明にも説法も、かみに云が如くに、法王身にてあり、と心うるな
り。

People today also should learn according to what was said by a person
of the past. Since they are "the body of the Dharma King," there was
a Dharma King who understood that "though scattered, they were not
another thing." The meaning of this is like the mountains being on the
earth, like the earth supporting the mountains.[29] When we understand,
the time when we did not understand does not come back to interfere
with our understanding. Also, understanding does not destroy not understanding; rather, understanding and not understanding have the colors of
spring and the sounds of autumn.[30] Our failure to understand this too is
because, while it was said in a loud voice, that voice did not enter our
ears; our ears were wandering about within the voice. Understanding
should be when, the voice having entered our ears, samādhi appears. We
should not think that this understanding is small, while not understanding was large: we should recognize that, because it is not something we

---

29　**like the mountains being on the earth, like the earth supporting the mountains**
(*yama no, chi ni aru ga gotoshi, chi no, yama o nosete aru ni nitari* 山の、地にあるが如
し、地の、山をのせてあるにによたり): Perhaps meaning that the "scattered" phenome-
na are to the Buddha's "body" as the mountains are to the earth. The image may reflect
a saying of the eighth-century figure Panshan Baoji 盤山寶積 (dates unknown) invoked
in the "Shōbōgenzō sanjūshichi hon bodai bunpō" 正法眼藏三十七品菩提分法; found at
Jingde chuandeng lu 景德傳燈錄, T.2076.51:253b20-21:

> 似地擎山不知山之孤峻。如石含玉不知玉之無瑕。

> It is like the earth that bears the mountain not knowing the mountain is steep, like the
> stone that contains the gem not knowing the gem is flawless.

30　**understanding and not understanding have the colors of spring and the sounds
of autumn** (*kokoro uru to, kokoro enu to no, haru no koro, aki no koe ari* 心うると、
心えぬとの、はるのころ、あきのこえあり): Reading *iro* いろ for *koro* ころ; the Hon-
zan edition reads *kokoro* こころ. Whatever the reading, the sense is probably that both
understanding and not understanding are equally valuable phases of the spiritual life.

156　DŌGEN'S *SHŌBŌGENZŌ* VOLUME VII

could think up, the Dharma King was like this.[31] "The body of the Dharma King" means that his eye is also like his body; his mind must also be the same as his body. His mind and his body must be "fully exposed," without a hair's breadth of separation. We understand that, in his radiance as well, his preaching the dharma is also the body of the Dharma King as it is discussed above.[32]

[S7:17] {2:526}

昔しより自いへること有り、いはゆる、うをにあらざれば、うをのこころを知ず、とりにあらざれば、鳥のあとを尋づねがたし。このことわりをも、よく知れる人まれなり。人の、うをの心をしらぬと、人の、うをの心をしらぬとのみおもへるは、あしくしれり。これを知るやうは、魚と魚とは、かならずあひたがひに其の心を知るなり。人のやうにしらぬことはなくて、龍門をさかのぼらんとおもふにも、ともにしられ、同く心をひとつにするなり。九浙をしのぐ心もかよひ、しらるなり。これを、うをにあらぬは、しることなし。

From long ago, there has been a saying that, if you are not a fish, you do not know the mind of the fish; if you are not a bird, you cannot follow the traces of the bird.[33] The people who know the reasoning in this are rare. Those who have thought only that humans do not know the mind of the fish and that humans do not know the mind of the fish have misunderstood: the way to understand this is that fish invariably know each other's minds; they do not fail to understand as humans do.[34] Even

---

31　**We should not think that this understanding is small, while not understanding was large** (*kono kokoro uru wa, chiisaku, kokoro enu wa, ooki nite arikeru to mo omowazaru beshi* この心うるは、ちひさく、心えぬは、おほきにてありけるとも思はざるべし): Perhaps meaning that we should not overemphasize the significance of our earlier misunderstanding of the body of the Dharma King: that body was like this quite apart from our misunderstanding of it.

32　**in his radiance as well, his preaching the dharma is also the body of the Dharma King as it is discussed above** (*kōmyō ni mo seppō mo, kami ni iu ga gotoku ni, hōō shin nite ari* 光明にも説法も、かみに云が如くに、法王身にてあり): The Honzan text has here *kōmyō ni mo seppō ni mo* 光明にも説法も, which suggests a reading, "In his radiance and in his preaching the dharma, it is also the body of the Dharma King as it is discussed above." "Radiance" (*kōmyō* 光明) can refer both to the physical aureola said to emanate from a buddha's body and to a buddha's wisdom that illumines the world.

33　**From long ago, there has been a saying** (*mukashi yori mizukara ieru koto ari* 昔より自いへること有り): The odd *mizukara* 自 (*onozukara*?) here, though apparently found across witnesses, looks suspiciously like a copyist's *kanbun* duplication of the preceding *yori* より ("from").

34　**Those who have thought only that humans do not know the mind of the fish and that humans do not know the mind of the fish** (*hito no, uo no kokoro o shiranu to, hito no, uo no kokoro o shiranu to nomi omoeru* 人の、うをの心をしらぬと、人の、うをの心をしらぬとのみおもへる): Some MS witnesses, as well as the Honzan edition, read the oddly repetitive clause following the conjunction as "humans do not know the mind of the bird" (*hito no tori no kokoro o shiranu* 人の鳥の心をしらぬ).

S7. Only Buddhas with Buddhas *Yui butsu yo butsu* 唯佛與佛 157

when they think to go back through the dragon gate, they all know it and are all of one mind about it.[35] The determination to push through the ninefold breaks is shared and known to them; those who are not fish do not know it.[36]

[S7:18] {2:527}

又、鳥の、空を飛ぬるをば、いかにも、ことけだものは、このあしのあと
をしり、このあとをみて尋ることは、夢にもいまだおもひよらず。さあり
と知らねば、おもひよるためしもなし。しかあるを、鳥は、よくちひさき
鳥の、いく百千むらがれすぎにける。これは、おほきなる鳥の、いくつ
ら、みなみにさり、きたに飛けるあとよと、かずかずにみるなり。車の
跡の、路にのこり、馬の跡の、草にみゆるよりも、かくれなし。鳥は鳥の
あとを見る也。

Again, with the flight of birds in the sky, other animals have never imagined, even in their dreams, knowing their tracks or seeing and following their traces. Since they do not know that such a thing exists, they do not try to imagine it. Birds, however, see in many ways the traces of small birds passing in a flock of some hundred thousand, or see that this is the trace of so many large birds that went south or flew north. They are even less hidden than the traces left by a cart on a road or the traces of a horse seen in the grass. Birds see the traces of birds.

[S7:19]

この理は、佛にも有り。佛の、いくよよにおこなひすぎにけるよとおもは
れ、ちひさき佛け、おほきなる佛、かずにもれぬるかずながらしるなり。
佛にあらざるをりは、いかにも知らざる事なり。いかにしられざるぞ、と
云ふ人もありぬべし。佛のまなこにて、其あとをみるべきが故に、佛にあ
らぬは、佛の眼をそなへず。佛の、ものかぞふるかずなり。しらねば、す
べて佛の路のあとをば、たどりぬべし。このあと、若、めにみえば、佛に
てあるやらんと、足のあとをもたくらぶべし。たくらぶる處に、佛のあと
もしられ、佛のあとの長短も、淺深もしられ、我があとの、あきらめらる
ることは、佛のあとをはかるよりうるなり。このあとをうるを、佛法とは
云なるべし。

This principle also holds for the buddhas. They think of how many ages the buddhas have spent in practice and know small buddhas and large buddhas in numbers beyond reckoning. When we are not buddhas, this is something we cannot possibly know. There may be people who

---

35 **the dragon gate** (*ryūmon* 龍門): Or the Yu Gate (*Umon* 禹門), the rapids on the Yellow River at Longmen (in present-day Shansi Province) beyond which the climbing carp is said to change into a dragon.

36 **the ninefold breaks** (*kyūsetsu* 九淅): Taking *kyū* 九 ("nine") as "manifold," "multiple" (as in *kyūen* 九淵; "ninefold abyss"), and reading *setsu* 淅 as *setsu* 折, in reference to the bends (or rapids?) in a river. Some take *setsu* 淅 as a reference to the Zhe River 淅 江. Dōgen uses the term *kyūsetsu* 九折 in a verse recorded in the *Eihei kōroku* 永平廣錄 (DZZ.4:230, no. 70).

ask why we cannot know it. Because those traces must be seen with the eye of a buddha, and those who are not buddhas are not endowed with the eye of a buddha. [The number of buddhas] is a number counted by a buddha. If we do not know it, all should follow the traces on the road taken by the buddhas. If these traces appear, we should compare [our own] footprints to see if they are those of a buddha. Where we compare them, we recognize the traces of a buddha, we know the length and depth of the traces of a buddha; the clarification of our own traces is gained through taking the measure of the traces of a buddha. Gaining these traces should be called the buddha dharma.

正法眼藏第三十八唯佛與佛
Treasury of the True Dharma Eye
Number 38
Only Buddhas with Buddhas

弘安十一年季春晦日、於越州吉田縣志比莊、吉祥山永平寺知賓寮南軒
書寫之。

Copied this under the southern eves of the guest quarters of Eihei Monastery, Mount Kichijō, Shihi Estate, Yoshida District, Esshū; last day of the end of spring, Kōan 11 [1 May 1288]

TREASURY OF THE TRUE DHARMA EYE

SUPPLEMENTARY CHAPTER 8

Birth and Death
Shōji
生死

Birth and Death

Shōji

Introduction

This work, one of the shortest in the *Shōbōgenzō*, represents the second text of fascicle 1 in the twenty-eight-text *Himitsu Shōbōgenzō*; it is included in the Honzan edition as number 92. The work bears only an end title but no colophon; hence, its date and place of composition are unknown. Since the seventeenth century, when Handō Kōzen 版橈晃全 (1625–1693) first included it in his new ninety-five-chapter *Shōbōgenzō*, doubts have been raised regarding its authorship — doubts arising from its lack of colophon, extreme brevity, pedestrian homiletic style, and textual parallels with other medieval Japanese Buddhist sources.

The work begins with the words of two Chan masters, but Dōgen does not go on here to pursue the sort of close reading of the words that we see elsewhere in the *Shōbōgenzō*. Instead, he simply invokes the familiar claim that saṃsāra (i.e., birth and death) is itself nirvāṇa, that it is the very life of the buddha, and that we should therefore neither cling to nor seek to escape from it. Abandoning concern for ourselves, he concludes, we should "throw ourselves into the house of the buddhas," and let the buddhas act through us.

正法眼藏別輯八
Treasury of the True Dharma Eye
Supplementary Chapter 8
生死
Birth and Death

(「秘密正法眼藏」初册所收)
(In the first volume of the *Himitsu Shōbōgenzō*)

[S8:1] {2:528}

生死の中に佛あれば、生死なし。又云く、生死の中に佛なければ、生死に
まどはず。

"Since there's a buddha within birth and death, there's no birth and death." It is also said, "Since there isn't a buddha within birth and death, we aren't deluded by birth and death."

[S8:2]

こころは、夾山・定山といはれし、ふたりの禪師のことばなり。得道の人
のことばなれば、さだめてむなしくまうけじ。

These thoughts were expressed by Jiashan and Dingshan; they are the words of two Chan masters.[1] Since they are the words of those who have gained the way, they were certainly not spoken frivolously.

---

1 **Jiashan and Dingshan** (Kassan Jōzan 夾山定山): I.e., Jiashan Shanhui 夾山善會 (805-881) and Dingshan Shenying 定山神英 (dates unknown). Their sayings appear in an episode recorded in the *Jingde chuandeng lu* 景德傳燈錄 (T.2076.51:254c27-255a4) and other Chan texts. Here is the version found in the *Liandeng huiyao* 聯燈會要, ZZ.136:500a13-b1:

定山與夾山同行、言話次、定山云、生死中無佛、即無生死。夾山云、生死中有佛、即不迷生死。是非不已。二人上山、求決親疏。纔人事罷、夾山舉前話。問云、不知那箇較親。師云、一親一疏。山復問、那箇親。師云、且去明日來。夾山明日又問。師云、親者不問、問者不親。夾山住後云、我當時在大梅失却一隻眼。

Dingshan and Jiashan were walking together and talking. Dingshan said, "Since there's a buddha within birth and death, there's no birth and death." Jiashan said, "Since there isn't a buddha within birth and death, we aren't deluded by birth and death." They kept on arguing.

The two climbed the mountain to seek a decision [from Chan Master Fachang of Mount Damei 大梅山法常禪師] on which was closer to it. As soon as they had greeted him, Jiashan raised the previous conversation and said, "We don't know which is closer."

162 DŌGEN'S *SHŌBŌGENZŌ* VOLUME VII

[S8:3]

生死をはなれんとおもはん人、まさにこのむねをあきらむべし。もし人、生死のほかに、ほとけをもとむれば、ながえをきたにして、越にむかひ、おもてをみなみにして、北斗をみんとするがごとし。いよいよ生死の因をあつめて、さらに解脱のみちをうしなへり。ただ、生死すなはち涅槃、とこころえて、生死としていとふべきもなく、涅槃としてねがふべきもなし。このとき、はじめて生死をはなるる分あり。

Those who would be free from birth and death should clearly understand the meaning of this. If one seeks the buddha apart from birth and death, it is like turning your cart thills north to head for Yue, like facing south to see the Northern Dipper.[2] More and more accumulating the causes of birth and death, one will have completely lost the way to liberation. Just understanding that birth and death is itself nirvāṇa, one should neither despise birth and death nor seek after nirvāṇa. Only then will one be in a position to get free from birth and death.

[S8:4]

生より死にうつる、と心うるは、これ、あやまりなり。生は、ひとときのくらゐにて、すでにさきあり、のちあり。故に、佛法の中には、生すなはち不生、といふ。滅も、ひとときのくらゐにて、又、さきあり、のちあり。これによりて、滅すなはち不滅、といふ。生といふときには、生よりほかにものなく、滅といふとき、滅のほかにものなし。かるがゆえに、生、きたらばただこれ生、滅、來らばこれ滅にむかひて、つかふべしといふことなかれ、ねがふことなかれ。

To think that we move from birth to death is a mistake. Birth is one position in time and clearly has a before and after.[3] Therefore, in the

---

The Master said, "One is close, and one is distant."

Jiashan asked, "Which is closer?"

The Master said, "Go away and come back tomorrow."

The next day, Jiashan asked again. The Master said, "The close one doesn't ask. The one who asks isn't close."

Later, Jiashan said, "At the time, when I was at Damei, I lost an eye."

2 **turning your cart thills north to head for Yue** (*nagae o kita ni shite, Etsu ni mukai* ながえをきたにして、越にむかひ): I.e., to head in the opposite direction from your intended destination ("Yue" 越 here referring to the territory south of China); a Japanese version of the Chinese idiom *bei yuan shi yue* 北轅適楚. Dōgen uses the same simile in his "Bendōwa" 辨道話.

like facing south to see the Northern Dipper (*omote o minami ni shite, hokuto o min to suru ga gotoshi* おもてをみなみにして、北斗をみんとするがごとし): Japanese version of a common saying, *mian nan kan beidou* 面南看北斗, appearing often in Chan texts.

3 **Birth is one position in time** (*shō wa, hitotoki no kurai nite* 生は、ひとときのくらゐにて): In this section, Dōgen shifts from discussion of "birth and death" (*shōji* 生死), used in reference to sentient existence in saṃsāra, to "birth and extinction," or "arising and ceasing" (*shōmetsu* 生滅), used in reference to the occurrence of the dharmas that

S8. Birth and Death *Shōji* 生死

buddha dharma it is said that birth is "unborn." Cessation is also one position in time and also has a before and after. Consequently, it is said that cessation is "unceasing." When we say "birth," there is nothing apart from birth; when we say "cessation," there is nothing apart from cessation. Therefore, when birth comes, when cessation comes, we should face them and make use of them as birth and cessation; do not despise them, do not seek them.[4]

[S8:5] {2:529}

この生死は、即ち佛の御いのちなり。これをいとひすてんとすれば、すなはち佛の御いのちをうしなはんとするなり。これにとどまりて、生死に著すれば、これも、佛のいのちを、うしなふなり、佛のありさまを、とどむるなり。いとふことなく、したふことなき、このとき、はじめて佛のこころにいる。

This birth and death is itself the life of a buddha. When we despise and would abandon it, this is precisely to lose the life of a buddha. When we are mired in it and are attached to birth and death, this is also to lose the life of a buddha, to restrict the buddha's state. Without despising it, without yearning for it — only at this time do we enter into the mind of the buddha.

[S8:6]

ただし、心を以て、はかることなかれ、ことばをもって、いふことなかれ。ただ、わが身をも心をもはなちわすれて、佛のいへになげいれて、佛のかたよりおこなはれて、これにしたがひもてゆくとき、ちからをもいれず、こころをもつひやさずして、生死をはなれ、佛となる。たれの人か、こころにとどこほるべき。

However, do not calculate with your mind; do not talk about it with your words. When we just cast aside and forget about our own body and mind, throwing ourselves into the house of the buddhas, letting the buddhas act and according with them, then without exerting ourselves, without expending our minds, we are free from birth and death and become a buddha. Who would remain stuck in the mind?

---

make up phenomenal existence. The argument here seems to be that the arising and the ceasing of these dharmas occupy (or represent) discrete positions in the flow of time (and therefore do not themselves arise and cease). See Supplementary Notes, s.v. "Dharmas abide in their dharma positions."

4 **Therefore, when birth comes** (*karu ga yue ni, shō, kitaraba* かるがゆえに、生、きたらば): A tentative translation of an awkward sentence; the English follows the common practice of amending the phrase *tsukau beshi to iu koto nakare* つかふべしといふことなかれ (which might be read something like "do not say we should use") to *tsukau beshi itou koto nakare* つかふべしいとふことなかれ ("we should use; do not despise").

164 DŌGEN'S *SHŌBŌGENZŌ* VOLUME VII

[S8:7]
佛となるに、いとやすきみちあり。もろもろの惡をつくらず、生死に著す
るこころなく、一切衆生のためにあはれみふかくして、上をうやまひ、下
をあはれみ、よろづをいとふこころなく、ねがふ心なくて、心におもふこ
となく、うれふることなき、これを佛となづく。又ほかに、たづぬること
なかれ。

There is a very easy way to become a buddha. Not to do any evil, not
to have a mind that clings to birth and death, to have profound compassion for all living beings, with respect for those above us and pity for
those beneath us, not to despise or to yearn for anything, without worry,
without distress — this is called buddhahood. Do not seek it elsewhere.

正法眼藏生死
Treasury of the True Dharma Eye
Birth and Death

TREASURY OF THE TRUE DHARMA EYE
SUPPLEMENTARY CHAPTER 9

The Way of the Buddhas
Butsudō
佛道
(*Dōshin* 道心)

The Way of the Buddhas

Butsudō

INTRODUCTION

This short, undated work is preserved in the *Himitsu Shōbōgenzō* collection in twenty-eight texts, where it occurs as number 7 of fascicle 1. The same text was included in the Honzan edition as number 93, under the new title "Dōshin" 道心 ("Mind of the Way"), to distinguish it from the "Butsudō" text of the seventy-five-chapter *Shōbōgenzō* compilation. The content of the latter work is completely different from our text here.

Our text is striking, not only for its extreme brevity, but for the simplicity both of its language and its message. It represents a very basic guide to Buddhist devotional practice, with none of the linguistic and intellectual challenges characteristic of Zen literature and of Dōgen's more arcane writing. The guide recommends five practices: cultivation of the aspiration for awakening; recitation of the three refuges, sponsorship of the making of buddha images, copying of the *Lotus Sūtra*, and practice of seated meditation. Only the last of these would distingish this kind of Buddhism from that recommended for lay householders in other vernacular Buddhist homilies of Dōgen's day. The fact that the practitioner is enjoined here to wear the monastic *kāṣāya* during meditation suggests that at least this practice was intended for the professional religious.

正法眼藏別輯九
Treasury of the True Dharma Eye
Supplementary Chapter 9

佛道

The Way of the Buddhas

(「秘密正法眼藏」初冊所收)
(In the first volume of the *Himitsu Shōbōgenzō*)

[S9:1] {2:530}
佛道をもとむるには、まづ道心をさきとすべし。道心のありやう、しれる
人、まれなり。あきらかにしれらん人に，問うべし。

In seeking the way of the buddhas, we should give first priority to the
mind of the way.[1] Those who know the nature of the mind of the way are
rare; we should ask those who have clearly understood it.

[S9:2]
よの人は、道心ありといへども、まことには、道心なき人あり。まことに
道心ありて、人にしられざる人あり。かくのごとく、あり・なし、しるが
たし。おほかた、おろかに、あしき人のことばを信ぜず、きかざるなり。
また、わがこころを、さきとせざれ、佛のとかせたまひたるのりを、さき
とすべし。よくよく道心あるべきやうを、よる・ひるつねにこころにかけ
て、この世にいかでかまことの菩提あらまし、と、ねがひ、いのるべし。

Among people of the world, there are those who are said to have the
mind of the way who in fact lack the mind of the way. There are those
who in fact have the mind of the way but are unrecognized by people.
Thus, it is hard to tell who has it and who does not. As a general rule,
we do not believe, do not listen to, the words of foolish or bad people.
Also, we do not put forward our own thoughts but put forward the law
preached by the Buddha. Constantly concerned, day and night, with the
state of the mind of the way, we should wish and pray that somehow
there will be true bodhi in this world.

---

1 **mind of the way** (*dōshin* 道心): Equivalent to the more common *bodai shin* 菩提心
("thought of bodhi"; S. *bodhi-citta*), from the use of *dō* 道 as a translation of *bodhi*. See
Supplementary Notes, s.v. "Bring forth the mind."

[S9:3]

世のすえには、まことある道心者、おほかたなし。しかあれども、しばらく心を無常にかけて、世のはかなく、人のいのちのあやふきこと、わすれざるべし。われは、世のはかなきことをおもふと、しらざるべし。あひかまへて、法をおもくして、わが身、我がいのちをかろくすべし。法のためには、身もいのちも、をしまざるべし。

At the end of the age, there are not many with a true mind of the way.[2] Still, paying attention to impermanence, we should not forget that the world is fleeting and human life precarious. [Yet] we should not be aware that we are thinking that the world is fleeting. We should always take the dharma seriously and our own bodies, our own lives, lightly. We should not begrudge our bodies or our lives for the sake of the dharma.

[S9:4] {2:531}

つぎには、ふかく佛・法・僧三寶を、うやまひたてまつるべし。生をかへ、身をかへても、三寶を供養し、うやまひたてまつらんことを、ねがふべし。ねてもさめても、三寶の功德を、おもひたてまつるべし、ねてもさめても、三寶を、となへたてまつるべし。たとひこの生をすてて、いまだ後の生にむまれざらんそのあひだ、中有と云ふことあり。そのいのち七日なる、そのあひだも、つねにこえもやまず、三寶を、となへたてまつらんと、おもふべし。七日をへぬれば、中有にて死して、また中有の身をうけて、七日あり。いかにひさしといへども、七ヶ日をばすぎず。このとき、なにごとを見、きくも、さはりなきこと、天眼のごとし。かからんとき、心をはげまして三寶をとなへたてまつり、

南無歸依佛、南無歸依法、南無歸依僧

と、となへたてまつらんこと、わすれず、ひまなく、となへたてまつるべし。

Next, we should deeply revere the three treasures of buddha, dharma, and saṃgha. We should wish to make offerings to and revere the three treasures even as we change our births and change our bodies. Whether sleeping or waking, we should think on the virtues of the three treasures; whether sleeping or waking, we should recite the three treasures. In the interval after we have abandoned this life but have yet to be born into the next life, there is what is called the "intermediate state." During that life of seven days as well, we should think to recite the three treasures without ceasing. After seven days, we die in the intermediate state and again receive a body in the intermediate state for seven days — for seven days at the longest. At this time, we see and hear everything without obstruction, like the deva eye. At such time, we should push ourselves to recite the three treasures, reciting without forgetting, without pausing,

---

2 **end of the age** (*yo no sue* 世のすえ): I.e., the age of the final dharma (*mappō* 末法), when the Buddha's teaching is in decline.

S9. The Way of the Buddhas *Butsudō* 佛道   169

I take refuge in the Buddha, I take refuge in the dharma, I take refuge in the saṃgha.

[S9:5]

すでに中有をすぎて、父母のほとりにちかづかんときも、あひかまへてあひかまへて、正知ありて託胎せん。處胎藏にありても、三寶を、となへたてまつるべし。むまれおちんときも、となへたてまつらんこと、おこたらざらん。六根にへて、三寶を、くやうしたてまつり、となへたてまつり、歸依したてまつらんと、ふかくねがふべし。

After we have passed the intermediate state and are drawing near our parents, we should enter the womb making repeated efforts to maintain right knowledge.[3] In the womb as well, we should recite the three treasures. And at the time of birth as well, we do not neglect our recitation. And as we develop the six faculties, we should wish to make offerings to, recite, and take refuge in the three treasures.[4]

[S9:6] {2:532}

また、この生のをはるときは、二つの眼、たちまちにくらくなるべし。そのときを、すでに生のをはりとしりて、はげみて、南無歸依佛、ととなへたてまつるべし。このとき、十方の諸仏、あはれみをたれさせたまふ縁ありて、悪趣におもむくべきつみも轉じて、天上にむまれ、佛前にうまれて、ほとけををがみたてまつり、佛のとかせたまふのりを、きくなり。

Again, when this life is ending, our eyes will suddenly go dark. At this time, knowing that our life is ending, we should strive to recite "*I take refuge in the buddha.*" At this time, we form a connection in which the buddhas of the ten directions take pity on us, and the sins that would lead us to the evil destinies are transformed; born in a heaven, born in the presence of a buddha, we bow down to the buddha and hear the law preached by the buddha.[5]

---

3 **drawing near our parents** (*bumo no hotori ni chikazukan* 父母のほとりにちかづかん): I.e., approaching conception in the next life, when the gandharva (the intermediate being) finds those who will be its parents.

4 **as we develop the six faculties** (*rokkon o hete* 六根をへて): I.e., as the fetus develops into a fully formed sentient being.

5 **born in a heaven, born in the presence of a buddha** (*tenjō ni mumare, butsuzen ni umarete* 天上にむまれ、佛前にうまれて): The relationship between these two phrases is probably disjunctive: buddhas do not typically inhabit the heavens but, rather, establish their own buddha "fields" (S. *kṣetra*). Conspicuous by its absence here is any reference to the practice, increasingly popular in Dōgen's day, of deathbed prayer directed at birth in the Western Pure Land of Buddha Amitābha.

170 DŌGEN'S *SHŌBŌGENZŌ* VOLUME VII

[S9:7]

眼の前に、やみのきたらんよりのちは、たゆまずはげみて、三歸依、とな
へたてまつること、中有までも、後生までも、おこたるべからず。かくの
ごとくして、生生世世をつくして、となへたてまつるべし。佛果菩提にい
たらんまでも、おこたらざるべし。これ、諸佛菩薩の、おこなはせたまふ
みちなり。これを、深く法りをさとる、とも云ふ、佛道の、身にそなは
る、とも云ふなり。更に、ことおもひをまじへざらん、とねがふべし。

After the darkness falls before our eyes, ceaselessly encouraging ourselves, we should not neglect to recite the three refuges, until the intermediate existence, until the next life. In this way, throughout life after
life, in age after age, we should recite it. We should not neglect it until
we reach the buddha fruit of bodhi. This is the way practiced by the buddhas and bodhisattvas. It is called profound awakening to the law; it is
called the embodiment of the way of the buddhas. We should hope not to
mix it together with any other thoughts.

[S9:8]

又、一生のうちに、佛をつくりたてまつらんと、いとなむべし。つくりた
てまつりては、三種の供養、したてまつるべし。三種とは、草座・石蜜
漿・燃燈なり。これを、くやうしたてまつるべし。

Again, we should work to produce a buddha during this life.[6] Having
produced it, we should make three kinds of offerings to it.[7] The three
kinds are the grass seat, sugar syrup, and lamps. We should offer these.

[S9:9]

又、この生のうちに、法華經、つくりたてまつるべし。かきもし、摺寫
も、したてまつりて、たもちたてまつるべし。つねには、いただき、禮
拜したてまつり、華・香・みあかし・飲食・衣服も、まいらすべし。つね
に、いただきをきよくして、いただきまいらすべし。

Again, we should produce a *Lotus Sūtra* during this life. We should
write, copy, and retain it. We should always place it on our head and pay
obeisance to it, offering it flowers, incense, lamps, food and drink, and
robes. We should always receive it in purity.[8]

---

6   **produce a buddha** (*butsu o tsukuritatematsuran* 佛をつくりたてまつらん): I.e.,
construct (or sponsor construction of) an image of a buddha.

7   **three kinds of offerings** (*sanshu no kuyō* 三種の供養): A set of offerings found,
e.g., in the *Dazhidu lun* 大智度論 (T.1509.25:83b18).

8   **We should always receive it in purity** (*tsune ni, itadaki o kiyoku shite, itadaki
mairasu beshi* つねに、いただきをきよくして、いただきまいらすべし): Some read
itadaki いただき here as the concrete act of "receiving on the head" and take "receiving
with purity" (*itadaki o kiyoku shite* いただきをきよくして) to mean "having cleansed
the head."

S9. The Way of the Buddhas *Butsudō* 佛道

[S9:10] {2:533}

又、つねに、けさをかけて、坐禪すべし。袈裟は、第三生に得道する先蹤
あり。すでに、三世の諸佛の衣なり、功德、はかるべからず。坐禪は、三
界の法にあらず、佛祖の法なり。

Again, we should always don the *kāṣāya* and engage in seated meditation. There is precedent that the *kāṣāya* [enables the wearer to] gain the
way in the third lifetime.[9] Since it is the robe of the buddhas of the three
times, its virtues cannot be measured. Seated meditation is not the dharma of the three realms; it is the dharma of the buddhas and ancestors.

正法眼藏佛道
Treasury of the True Dharma Eye
The Way of the Buddhas

9　**There is precedent that the *kāṣāya* [enables the wearer to] gain the way in the
third lifetime** (*kesa wa, daisan shō ni tokudō suru senshō ari* 袈裟は、第三生に得道
する先蹤あり): Likely a reference to the tale of the Bhikṣuṇī Utpalavarṇā, who became
an arhat in three lifetimes after she put on the Buddhist robe as a joke. Dōgen quotes
this story (from *Dazhidu lun* 大智度論, T.1509.25:161a27-b17) in his "Shōbōgenzō kesa
kudoku" 正法眼藏袈裟功德 and "Shukke kudoku" 出家功德.

Variant Texts
of the *Shōbōgenzō*

Introduction to the Variant Texts

of the *Shōbōgenzō*

The seven works in this section represent drafts of chapters the edited versions of which are found elsewhere in the various compilations of the *Shōbōgenzō*. We know that, throughout his career, Dōgen was in the habit of revising his work, a practice revealed in comparisons of the texts in the sixty-chapter *Shōbōgenzō* with those of the more polished seventy-five-chapter compilation; the drafts in the present section preserve important additional evidence regarding the evolution of Dōgen's thinking, teaching, and writing style. The sources of these seven works are of three types:

A. Drafts preserved in the sixty-chapter *Shōbōgenzō*:
   V4. "Washing the Face," *Senmen* 洗面: number 50 in the sixty-chapter *Shōbōgenzō*; revised as number 50 in the seventy-five-chapter compilation.
   V5. "Extensive Study," *Henzan* 遍參: number 37 in the sixty-chapter *Shōbōgenzō*; revised as number 57 in the seventy-five-chapter compilation.
   V7. "Karma of the Three Times," *Sanji gō* 三時業: number 6 in the sixty-chapter *Shōbōgenzō*; revised as number 8 in the twelve-chapter compilation.

B. Draft preserved in the twenty-eight-text *Himitsu Shōbōgenzō* collection:
   V3. "Beyond the Buddha," *Butsu kōjō ji* 佛向上事: number 1 of fascicle 1 in the *Himitsu* collection; revised as number 26 in the seventy-five-chapter *Shōbōgenzō*.

C. Drafts preserved in individual manuscripts:
   V1. "Talk on Pursuing the Way," *Bendōwa* 辨道話: the Shōbōji 正法寺 manuscript; revised as number 1 in the Honzan edition (i.e., the Gentō 玄透 print, translated here as Supplementary Text 1).
   V2. "The Inheritance Certificate," *Shisho* 嗣書: the Kōjakuji 香積寺 manuscript; revised as number 39 in the seventy-five-chapter *Shōbōgenzō*.
   V6. "Great Awakening," *Daigo* 大悟: the Shinpukuji 真福寺 manuscript; revised as number 10 in the seventy-five-chapter *Shōbōgenzō*.

Treasury of the True Dharma Eye
Variant Text 1

Talk on Pursuing the Way
Bendōwa
辨道話

Talk on Pursuing the Way

Bendōwa

Introduction

This text is a variant version of the "Bendōwa," usually thought to represent an earlier draft of the Honzan text (the 1788 woodblock print by Gentō Sokuchū 玄透即中, translated above as Supplementary Text 1). It is preserved in a manuscript, discovered in the late 1930s, copied in 1515 by Juun Ryōchin 壽雲良椿, abbot of Shōbōji 正法寺, from a 1332 manuscript copied by the monk Shikoku 旨國 of Yōkōji 永光寺. A colophon gives the same date of composition (12 September 1231) as the Gentō text but mistakenly identifies the author as resident at Kannon Dōriin 觀音導利院 (the monastery that Dōgen would open the following year).

In general, this version of the "Bendōwa" is quite similar to the Honzan text, with only occasional interesting variations. The most notable of these is that, while the latter gives a set of eighteen questions and answers, the Shōbōji text includes an additional, nineteenth question and answer (in section 26, below).

The annotation here does not repeat the notes given in the translation of the Gentō text; rather, it is limited to material specific to this version and to noting the relationship of the material in this version to the Gentō text.

正法眼藏拾遺一
Treasury of the True Dharma Eye
Variant Text 1
草案本
Draft Text

辦道話
Talk on Pursuing the Way

(正法寺所藏本)
(Shōbōji collection text)

永平開山元和尚記
Written by Reverend Gen, founder of Eihei[1]

[V1:1] {2:536}

諸佛如來、共に妙法を單傳して、阿耨菩提を證するに、最上無爲の妙術あり。是れ、但だ佛、ほとけに授け柱なる事無は、則ち自受用三昧、其標準なり。此三昧に遊戲するに、端坐參禪を直道とせり。

The buddhas, the tathāgatas, all have a wondrous skill, supreme and unconditioned, for uniquely transmitting the wondrous dharma and verifying *anuttara-bodhi*. That it is bestowed only from buddha to buddha without error is because the samādhi of self-enjoyment is its standard. To disport oneself in this samādhi, studying Zen in upright sitting, is considered the direct path.[2]

---

1 **Written by Reverend Gen, founder of Eihei** (*Eihei kaisan Gen oshō ki* 永平開山元和尚記): I.e., Dōgen, founder of Eiheiji 永平寺. The use of the title *oshō* 和尚 here and the identification of Dōgen as founder of Eiheiji (founded 1246) indicate that this attribution was added by a later copiest. It does not occur in the Gentō text.

2 **direct path** (*jikidō* 直道): The Gentō text reads here the "main gateway" (*shōmon* 正門).

[V1:2]

此の法、人人の分上にゆたかなりと雖も、未修には不顯、不證無得。放てば手に滿り、一・多のきはならむや、語れば口に滿つ、縱横無極。諸佛の、常に此の中に住持たる、各各の方面に知覺を不殘。群生の、長此の中に使用する、各各の知覺に方面不顯。

Although this dharma is abundantly allotted to each person, when we have not practiced it, it does not appear, and when we do not verify it, it is not attained. Let it go, and it fills the hand — how could it be bounded by one or many? Speak of it, and it fills the mouth — vertically and horizontally without limit. The buddhas are always within it, dwelling in and maintaining it, without leaving perception of it in any of its quarters; living beings are continuously within it, making use of it, without its quarters appearing in any of their perceptions.

[V1:3]

今ま教る功夫辨道は、證上に萬法を集、出路に一如を行ずるなり。其の超關脱落のとき、此節目にかかはらむや。

The concentrated effort in pursuit of the way that I teach here gathers the myriad dharmas based on verification and practices their oneness on the path leading out.[3] When we pass beyond those barriers and slough them off, how could we be concerned with these particulars?

* * * * *

[V1:4] {2:537}

道元、發心求法よりこのかた、わが朝の遍方に知識をとぶらひき。因みに建仁の全公にまみえて、九廻霜華すみやかにせし程に、聊か臨濟の宗風を聞き、始て沙を算るが如く、實にあらざる旨を知る。全公は、祖師西和尚の上足として、獨り無上の佛法を正傳せり。印可、但だ此の室にあり。函丈に獨歩せる、敢て餘輩の及ぶべきにあらず。予、重て大宋國に趣て、知識を兩浙に訪ひ、家風を五門に聽く。終に大白峰の淨和尚に參じて、一生の大事、此こに終ぬ。其より後、大宋紹定の初、本郷に趣きし、則ち弘法教生をもひとせり、尚ほ重担を肩におけるが如し。然るに、弘通の心を放下せむ激揚の時を待つ故に、暫く雲遊萍寄なり、先哲の風を聽えんとす。何ぞ只し自ら名利に不拘、道念を先きとせん眞實の參學有んか、徒づらに邪師に纏わされて、妄りに正解をおほひ、虛く自狂に酔て、久しく迷郷に沈まん。何によりてか般若の妙種を長じ、得道の正緣を得ん。貧道は今、雲遊萍寄を事とすれば、何れの山川をかとぶらはん。是を憐む故に、まのあたり大宋國にして禪林の風規を見聞し、知識の玄旨を裏持せしを記して、參學閑道の人に殘し、佛家の正法を知らしめんとす。是、眞訣ならん。

---

3 **gathers the myriad dharmas** (*manbō o atsume* 萬法を集): The Gentō text reads "brings the myriad dharmas into existence" (*manbō o arashime* 萬法をあらしめ).

V1. Talk on Pursuing the Way *Bendōwa* 辨道話   179

From the time that Dōgen brought forth the mind [of bodhi] and sought the dharma, I inquired of wise friends throughout our kingdom.[4] Thus, I met the Honorable Zen of Kennin; and, as nine rounds of frost and flowers swiftly passed, I heard something of the lineage style of Linji and first knew that those who count grains of sand are not genuine.[5] The Honorable Zen, the foremost disciple of the Ancestral Master Reverend Sai, alone received the direct transmission of the unsurpassed buddha dharma. The seal of approval only exists in this room; he walked alone in the abbot's quarters; none of the others could compare.[6]

Thereafter, journeying to the Land of the Great Song, I called on wise friends in the Two Zhes and heard of the house styles at the five gates. Finally, I went to study under Reverend Jing of Taibai Peak, and here the great matter of my entire life was resolved.

Thereafter, at the beginning of Shaoding in the Great Song, I returned to my native land, with the intention of spreading the dharma and saving beings. It was just as if I had shouldered a heavy burden. Nevertheless, I put aside my thoughts of propagation and, in order to wait for a time when I could fully devote myself to it, *I drifted like a cloud and floated like a water plant*, seeking to convey the style of the former wise men.

Still, there could occasionally be a few genuine students, unconcerned with fame or profit and giving priority to thoughts of the way. Led astray in vain by false teachers, rashly obscuring the correct understanding and worthlessly drunk on their own delusions, they may sink into the land of delusion. How could they nurture the wondrous seed of prajñā and gain the right circumstances for gaining the way? If this humble wayfarer is now "*drifting like a cloud and floating like a water plant*," what mountains and rivers will they visit? Out of pity for them, recording what I personally experienced of the customs and rules of the Chan groves and what I received of the dark import of the wise friends while I was in the Land of the Great Song, I leave them for those who would study and

---

4   **From the time that Dōgen brought forth the mind [of bodhi] and sought the dharma** (*Dōgen, hosshin guhō yori kono kata* 道元、發心求法よりこのかた): Dōgen speaks of himself in the third person. This section corresponds to sections 4-6 in the Gentō text.

5   **first knew that those who count grains of sand are not genuine** (*hajimete isago o kazouru ga gotoku, makoto ni arazaru mune o shiru* 始て沙を算るが如く、實にあらざる旨を知る): A criticism of scholastic Buddhists who merely study the details of doctrine; see Supplementary Notes, s.v. "Counting sand." This line does not occur in the Gentō text.

6   **The seal of approval only exists in this room; he walked alone in the abbot's quarters** (*inka, tada kono shitsu ni ari. kanjō ni dokuho seru* 印可、但だ此の室にあり。函丈に獨歩せる): This line does not occur in the Gentō text.

180 DŌGEN'S *SHŌBŌGENZŌ* VOLUME VII

master the way, that they may know the true dharma of the house of the buddhas. This is the true arcanum.

[V1:]

大師釋尊、靈山會上にして、法を迦葉につけ、祖祖正傳して、菩提達磨尊
者に至る。尊者、自ら神丹國に趣て、法を慧可大師につけき。是れ東地の
佛法の初祖なり。如是單傳してより、六祖大鑑禪師に至る。此の時、正
に眞實の佛法、唐家に流演して、節目にかかはらぬ旨、顯れき。時に六
祖に二位の神足あり、南嶽の懷讓と、青原の行思となり。共に佛印を傳持
して、同く人天の導師なり。其の二派の流通するに、好く五門開けたり。
所謂、法眼宗・潙仰宗・雲門宗・臨濟宗・曹洞宗也。見在大宋には、臨濟
宗・曹洞宗のみ天下普し。五家異れども、唯だ一佛心印也。大宋國も、後
漢より以來、教法流傳して一天にしけりと雖も、雌雄未だ定めざりき。祖
師西來の後、直に葛藤の根源を截斷して、純一の佛法おこなはる。華夷、
其の慶を蒙れり、我國にも、又しかあらん事を喜ばざらんや。

Great Master Śākya, the Honored One, at an assembly on Vulture Peak, entrusted the dharma to Kāśyapa.[7] Directly transmitted by ancestor after ancestor, it reached Venerable Bodhidharma. The Venerable himself traveled to the Land of Cīnasthāna and entrusted the dharma to Great Master Huike. This was the First Ancestor of the buddha dharma in the Land of the East.[8] In this way, having been uniquely transmitted, [the buddha dharma] reached the Sixth Ancestor, Chan Master Dajian. At this time, truly, the genuine buddha dharma spread throughout the Tang, and its message, uninvolved in particulars, became apparent. At the time, the Sixth Ancestor had two superior disciples: Huairang of Nanyue and Xingsi of Qingyuan. Both received transmission of the buddha seal and were equally the guides of humans and devas. As their two factions spread, five gates were opened: the Fayan lineage, Weiyang lineage, Yunmen lineage, Linji lineage, and Caodong lineage. At present in the Great Song, only the Linji lineage and Caodong lineage are widespread throughout the land.[9] Although the five houses differ, they are but one buddha mind seal.

---

7 **Great Master Śākya, the Honored One** (*daishi Shakuson* 大師釋尊): This section corresponds to sections 7-8 in the Gentō text.

8 **This was the First Ancestor of the buddha dharma in the Land of the East** (*kore Tōchi no buppō no shoso nari* 是れ東地の佛法の初祖なり): The reference is to Bodhidharma. The Gentō text reads here, "This was the start of the transmission of the buddha dharma in the Land of he East" (*kore Tōchi no buppō denrai no hajime nari* これ東地の佛法傳來のはじめなり).

9 **only the Linji lineage and Caodong lineage are widespread throughout the land** (*Rinzai shū Sōtō shū nomi tenka amaneshi* 臨濟宗・曹洞宗のみ天下普し): The Gentō text reads here, "the Linji lineage alone is widespread throughout the land" (*Rinzai shū nomi tenka ni amaneshi* 臨濟宗のみ天下にあまねし).

V1. Talk on Pursuing the Way *Bendōwa* 辨道話 181

Even in the Land of the Great Song, although since the Later Han the teachings had spread throughout the realm, their strengths and weaknesses were still undetermined. After the Ancestral Master came from the west, the roots of the tangled vines were immediately severed, and the pure buddha dharma put into practice. This felicity has been enjoyed in the Chinese territories; would it not be a matter of rejoicing were the same to occur in our land as well?[10]

[V1:6] {2:537}

可知、佛法を住持せし諸祖ならびに諸佛、共に自受用三昧に端坐するを以て開悟の直道とせり。西天東地、悟をえし人、此の清規に隨へり。此れ師資、正しく妙術を正傳し、眞訣を稟持せしによりて、佛印のあとある、其如是。

We should know that the ancestors, along with the buddhas, who maintained the buddha dharma have all regarded upright sitting in the samādhi of self-enjoyment as the direct path to the opening of awakening. From Sindh in the West to the Land of the East, those who have attained awakening have followed these rules of purity.[11] It is because the masters and disciples correctly transmitted directly the wondrous skill that the traces of the buddha seal are like this.

[V1:7]

宗門の正規に云く、單傳正直の佛法は、最上の中に最上なり。參見知識の初めより、更に燒香・禮拜・念佛・修懺・看經を不用、唯だ專ら打坐して身心脱落する事を得よ。

In the correct rules of our school it is said, "the uniquely transmitted, true and direct buddha dharma is supreme among the supreme. From the start of your consultation with a wise friend, without further need of burning incense, making bows, recollecting the buddha, practicing repentance or reading sūtras, just single-mindedly sit and attain the sloughing off of body and mind."

[V1:8]

若し人、一時も、三業に佛印を持し、三昧に端坐する時、遍法界皆な佛身と現じ、盡虚空盡く悟になる。故に、諸佛如來をして、本地の法樂を益し、覺道の莊嚴を新たにす。及び十方世界・三途六道の群類、皆な共に一時に身心明淨にして、大解脱を證し、本來の面目現前する時、諸法皆な正覺を證會し、萬物ともに佛身を使用して、速に證會の邊際を一超して、覺樹王に端坐し、一時に無等等の大法輪を轉じ、究竟無爲の深般若を開演す。

---

10 **Chinese territories** (*kai* 華夷): More literally, "the Chinese and barbarians," but here more likely a reference to the territory of the Song state.

11 **rules of purity** (*shingi* 清規): A term usually used for monastic codes; here, probably something like "norm of practice." The Gentō text, section 9, reads here "style" (*fū* 風).

182 DŌGEN'S *SHŌBŌGENZŌ* VOLUME VII

If someone, even once, keeps the buddha seal in the three modes of karma and sits upright in samādhi, at that time, everything throughout the dharma realms appears as the buddha body and everywhere in all empty space becomes awakening.[12] Therefore, for the buddhas, the tathāgatas, it increases the bliss of the dharma of their original ground and renews the adornments of their awakening to the way. And beings throughout the dharma realms in the ten directions, in the three roads and six paths, being bright and pure in body and mind, all together simultaneously verify the great liberation and manifest their original face. At that time, the dharmas, all realizing right awakening, and the myriad things, all using the buddha body, quickly transcending the boundaries of realization, sit upright at the king tree of awakening, simultaneously turn the great dharma wheel, equal to the unequalled, and proclaim the profound prajñā, ultimate and unconditioned.

[VI:9] {2:539}

是れこの等正覺、更にかへりて親くあひ冥資する道かよふ故に、此の坐禪人、確爾として身心脱落し、從來の雜穢の知見思量を截斷して、天眞の佛位に證會し、遍く微塵際そこばくの諸佛如來の道場ごとに、佛事を助發し、博く佛向上の機にかうぶらしめて、好く佛向上の法を激揚す。此時、十方法界の土地・草木・墻壁・瓦礫、皆な佛事を行ずるを以て、其の起す所の風水の利益に預る輩ら、甚妙不可思議の佛化を受用する故に、深き迷を掃蕩し、近き悟を獲得して、小節に不拘。

Because these perfectly awakened ones then return and follow the path of intimately providing mutual dark assistance, the person of seated meditation, definitely having body and mind sloughed off and severing previous confused and defiled knowledge and thinking, realizes the natural buddha dharma and, at every practice place of the buddhas, the tathāgatas, numerous as infinitesimal dust motes, furthers the buddha work and, widely providing for listeners beyond the buddha, vigorously promotes the dharma beyond the buddha.[13] At this time, by all the lands, grasses and trees, fences and walls, tiles and pebbles of dharma realms in the ten directions practicing the buddha work, all those enjoying the benefits of wind and water thereby produced, because they enjoy the extremely wondrous inconceivable buddha conversion, deeply removing delusion and intimately attaining awakening, have no concern for trifles.[14]

---

12 **appears as the buddha body** (*busshin to genji* 佛身と現じ): The Gentō text, section 11, reads here, "becomes the buddha seal" (*butsu'in to nari* 佛印となり).

13 **these perfectly awakened ones** (*kono tōshōgaku* この等正覺): I.e., the awakened beings described in the preceding section. This section corresponds to the first half of section 12 in the Gentō text.

14 **because they enjoy** (*juyū suru yue ni* 受用する故に): The Gentō text has for this

V1. Talk on Pursuing the Way *Bendōwa* 辨道話

[V1:10]

此の水火を受用する類、皆本證の佛化を周旋する故に、彼等と共に住し同語する者、盡く相互に無窮の佛德具て、展轉廣作して、無盡、無間斷、不可思議、不可商量の佛法を、遍法界の内外に流通する者なり。雖然、此の各各の當人の知覺、昆雜せず、汚染せられぬ事は、靜中の無造作にして、直證なるを以てなり。若し迷人の思へるが如く、修證を兩段に有らしめば、各各相ひ覺知すべきなり。もし覺知に交るは、證則にあらず、覺知の、迷情にかかはらざる故なり。又、心・境共に静中の静入・悟出有れども、自受用の軌則なるを以て、一塵を不動、一相を壞らず、廣大の佛事、甚深微妙の佛化を成す。此の化道の及ぶ所の草木・土地、共に大光明を放て、深妙法を説くこと、辨ときなし。草木・牆壁は、能く凡聖・含靈の爲に宣揚し、凡聖・含靈は、草木・牆壁の爲に演暢す。自覺・覺他の境界、元とより證相を具へて欠けたる事なく、證則行れて懈たる時き無らしむ。

Because the ones who receive and use this water and fire all circulate the buddha conversion of original verification, those who dwell and speak with them are ones who, endowed together with inexhaustible buddha virtues, gradually expanding their work, disseminate the inexhaustible, ceaseless, inconceivable, inestimable buddha dharma throughout the interior and exterior of the dharma realms.[15] The reason that, nevertheless, all these do not confuse, do not defile, the perception of that person is that it is a direct verification, unconstructed in stillness. If, as is thought by deluded people, practice and verification were located on two levels, each would perceive the other; but, [for them] to be mixed into [that] perception would not meet the standard of verification, for [that] awareness has nothing to do with deluded feelings.

Moreover, although, in the stillness, both mind and object enter verification and exit awakening, since it is governed by self-enjoyment, without disturbing a single dust mote, without destroying a single aspect, one engages in the vast buddha work, the extremely profound and subtle buddha conversion. All the grasses and trees and the lands reached by this guidance emit a great radiance, and their preaching of the profound, wondrous dharma is without ever discriminating.[16] The grasses and trees, fences and walls, proclaim it to commoners, sages, and all the

---

clause, "darkly assisted by the extremely wondrous inconceivable buddha conversion, manifest an intimate awakening" (*jinmyō fukashigi no bukke ni myōshi serarete, chikaki satori o arawasu* 甚妙不可思議の佛化に冥資せられて、ちかきさとりをあらはす).

15   **the ones who receive and use this water and fire** (*kono sui ka o juyū suru tagui* 此の水火を受用する類): The first half of this section corresponds to the second half of section 12 in the Gentō text.

16   **is without ever discriminating** (*wakimaeru toki nashi* 辨ときなし): A tentative translation; the sense of *wakimaeru* 辨 here is uncertain. This half of the section corresponds to section 13 of the Gentō text, which reads here, "is without end" (*kiwamaru toki nashi* きはまるときなし).

184 DŌGEN'S *SHŌBŌGENZŌ* VOLUME VII

animate; the commoners, sages, and all the animate in turn proclaim it to the grasses and trees, fences and walls. The realm of self-awakening and awakening others is endowed from the start with the marks of verification, with nothing lacking, and carries out the standard of verification, leaving no time for negligence.

[V1:11] {2:540}

爰を以て、僅に一時の坐禪なりとも、諸法と相冥し、諸事を圓に通ずるを以て、無盡法界の中に、去・來・現に、常恒の佛化道事を作すなり。彼彼共に一等の同修なり、同證なり。但だ坐上の修のみにあらず、空を打て響を作こと、撞の前後に妙聲綿綿たるなり。此のきはのみならんや、百頭皆本面目顯れ、本修おこなはれて、計り量るべきにあらず。可知、縱へ十方無量恒河沙數の諸佛、共に力を励し、佛智慧を以て、一人坐禪の功德を計り窮せんに、敢てほとりを得ん事難し。

Accordingly, even if it is the seated meditation of merely one time, because it is imperceptibly one with the dharmas and perfectly penetrates the times, it carries out the constant work of the way of buddha conversion within inexhaustible dharma realms in the past, present, and future. For each and every one, it is equally the same practice, the same verification. It is not just practice while seated: striking the sky and making an echo has a wondrous sound that continues on and on both before and after the strike. How could it be just this time? The hundred heads, all endowed with the original practice by their original faces, are not to be calculated or measured. We should know that, even if the buddhas of the ten directions, numerous as the incalculable sands of the Ganges, using their powers together and by their buddha wisdom, were to calculate and fully know the merit of the seated meditation of a single person, they still would not be able to get to the end of it.

* * * * *

[V1:12]

今此の坐禪の功德、廣大なる事、聞き終りぬ。

Now, we have heard how vast and great are the merits of this seated meditation.[17]

[V1:13]

おろかなる人疑て、佛法におほくの門あり、何を以てか偏へに坐禪を勸むるや。 示曰、是佛法の正門なるを以てなり。

---

17 **Now** (*ima* 今): Here begins the question and answer portion of the text, corresponding to section 15 of the Gentō version.

V1. Talk on Pursuing the Way *Bendōwa* 辨道話　　185

Foolish people will doubt this, saying, "The buddha dharma has many gates; why do you only recommend seated meditation?"[18]

Answer: Because it is the main gate to the buddha dharma.

[V1:14]

問曰、何を以てか、獨り正門とする。示曰、大師釋尊、まさしく得道の妙術を正傳し、七佛共に傳はって、坐禪より得道せり。此の故に、正門なる事相ひ傳へ知るなり。しかのみにあらず、西天東地の諸祖、みな坐禪より得道せるなり。故に、正門を人天に勸むるなり。

Question: Why do you take it alone as the main gate?

Answer: Definitely, the Great Master, Śākya, the Honored One, directly transmitted this wondrous skill for gaining the way, and the seven buddhas all transmitted it and gained the way by seated meditation. Therefore, they have handed down and known the fact that it is the main gate. Not only that, but the ancestors of Sindh in the West and the Land of the East all gained the way from seated meditation. Therefore, I teach the main gate to humans and devas.

[V1:15]

問曰、或は如來の妙術を正傳し給はば、祖師のあとを尋るに依ん、凡慮の及にあらず。然れども、讀經・念佛は、自ら悟りの因緣となりぬべし。但だむなしく坐して成らん、何によりてか悟を得る便りとならん。示曰、汝ぢ今、諸佛の三昧、無上大法を、空く坐して成す所ろなし、と思はん、是を大乘を謗ずる罪とす。迷のいと深き、大江の中に居ながら、水なし、と言んが如し。既に辱く、諸佛、自受用三昧に安坐せり、是廣大の功德を作にあらずや。可憐、眼未開、心猶ほ醉に有る事を。

Question: Directly to transmit the wondrous technique of the tathāgatas, or to follow in the tracks of the ancestral masters, is certainly beyond the thought of the common person.[19] However, reading the sūtras or recollecting the buddhas can themselves be the causes of awakening. How can sitting idly without doing anything be the basis for attaining awakening?

Answer: To think, as you do here, that the samādhi of the buddhas, their unsurpassed great dharma, is "sitting idly without doing anything" — this constitutes the offense of blaspheming the Greater Vehicle. It is very deep delusion, like saying there is no water while being in a great river. Fortunately, the buddhas surely sat peacefully in the samādhi of self-enjoyment. Was this not creating vast merit? How pitiful you are, that your eyes are still not open, and your mind is still intoxicated.

18　**Foolish people** (*orokanaru hito* おろかなる人): This section corresponds to sections 16 and 17 in the Gentō text.

19　**Question** (*tōte iwaku* 問曰): The question and answer in this section correspond respectively to sections 19 and 20 in the Gentō text.

DŌGEN'S *SHŌBŌGENZŌ* VOLUME VII

[V1:16] {2:541}

凡そ諸佛の境界は、不可思議也、心識の及ぶべきにあらず、況不信劣智の
知る事を得んや。只正信の大機のみ、能く入る事を得るなり。不信の人
は、縱ひ、をしふるとも、可受あらず。靈山になほ退亦佳矣の類ひあり。
只心に正信起らば、參學し、修行すべし。迷疑のこらば、止むべし、訓に
不足、昔より法水の澤ひ無き事を可悲。

In sum, the realm of the buddhas is inconceivable; it is beyond the
reach of mind or consciousness, much less can it be known by those of
no faith and deficient wisdom. Only one of great capacity for true faith
can enter it; the person without faith cannot accept it even when taught
about it. Even on Vulture Peak, there was the type [of which it was said,]
"*it is just as well that they withdraw.*" If true faith arises in the mind,
we should study and practice; if delusion and doubt remain, we should
stop and regret the fact that we are deficient in instruction and lack the
moistening of the dharma water from long ago.

[V1:17]

亦、讀經・念佛等の、勤めてうる所の功德を、汝、計り知るや。只是れ舌
を動し、音をあぐれば、佛事功德と思へる、いとはかなし。讀經・念佛を
勸むる事は、是によりて、下根劣智の輩らをして、無作三昧を心地に發得
せしめんが爲なり。徒に春の田の蝦のごとく、無隙聲をあげても、終に無
益とにはあらず。此れ等の人は、佛法にはうたた遠く、彌よ遥なり。佛智
を得ること、必しも有心・無心のちからにあらぬなり。

Furthermore, can you gauge the merit derived from working at reading sūtras, recollecting the buddha, and the like?[20] To think that merely moving the tongue and raising the voice is the merit of the buddha
work is pure vanity. Reading the sūtras and recollecting the buddhas are
recommended in order to cause those of inferior faculties and deficient
wisdom to produce the non-intentional samādhi in the mind ground; it
is not so that, like the frog in the spring paddy field, we ceaselessly raise
our voices in vain, without benefit in the end.[21] These people are getting
further away from the buddha dharma, ever more distant. Gaining the
wisdom of the buddhas is not necessarily on the strength of having mind
or not having mind.[22]

---

20 **Furthermore** (*mata* 亦): This and the following section loosely parallel section 22
of the Gentō version, with considerable variation.

21 **non-intentional samādhi** (*musa zanmai* 無作三昧): Typically taken as a synonym
of the "wishless samādhi" (*mugan zanmai* 無願三昧), in which one is free from seeking.
A term not found in the Gentō version or elsewhere in the *Shōbōgenzō*.

22 **Gaining the wisdom of the buddhas is not necessarily on the strength of having
mind or not having mind** (*butchi o eru koto, kanarazushimo ushin mushin no chikara
ni aranu nari* 佛智を得ること、必しも有心・無心のちからにあらぬなり): This sen-
tence has no parallel in the Gentō text, and its point here is not clear. The pair "mind"

V1. Talk on Pursuing the Way *Bendōwa* 辨道話

[V1:18]

亦、經の教を開く事は、如來、頓・漸の修行を誨るをや。明に知りて、教の如く修行すれば、必ず證を取らしめんとなり、徒らに思量念度を費して、菩提を得る功德に擬せんとにはあらず。愚に千萬誦の口業を頻りにして、佛道に至らんとするは、猶ほ是れ轅を北にして、越に向はんと思はんが如し。又、圓穴に方木を擬するににたり。佛教に、縱へ妙旨有りとも、執見の眼の前には、顯れ難し。必ず宗師に玄旨を稟て修行し、開悟するなり。

Again, opening the books of scripture is so that, clearly knowing what the Tathāgata teaches on the gradual and sudden practices, when we practice in accordance with these teachings, we invariably gain verification of them; it is not so that, wasting our thinking and calculating, we try in vain to assess their merit for attaining bodhi. Trying to reach the way of the buddhas by foolishly repeating the verbal acts of a thousand or ten thousand recitations is like facing your cart thills to the north and thinking to head to Yue. Again, it is the same as trying to put a square peg in a round hole. Even though there is a wondrous import in the teaching of the buddhas, it is hard for it to appear to the eye of those attached to their views.[23] Invariably, by receiving the dark import from a master in the lineage and then practicing, we open awakening.

[V1:19] {2:542}

漢土にも、昔、師によらず、自解する者、ままに有りき。皆な邪見に堕き。然れども、彼國には明師宗匠あれば、邪見を救ふ方便をめぐらす。我國には無し、いかがせん。三四百歳の前後に、佛教、わが國に傳はれりと云へども、明眼宗師なし、明文の學者、尚ほ稀なり。縱へ藥なれども、服する方にくらければ、曾毒をなす事深し。佛教の甘露、汝服せば、毒と成るべし。

On Han soil as well, from ancient times, there were sometimes those who had their own understandings, without relying on a master.[24] They all fell into false views. Still, in that land, since there were wise masters and lineage teachers, they thought up means to save those with false views. In our land, there are none. What shall we do? While the teachings of the buddhas were transmitted to our land roughly three or four

---

(*ushin* 有心) and "no-mind" (*mushin* 無心) may refer here to "intentional" and "non-intentional," as suggested by the aforementioned "non-intentional samādhi" (*musa zanmai* 無作三昧).

23 Even though there is a wondrous import in the teaching of the buddhas (*bukkyō ni tatoe myōshi aritomo* 佛教に縱へ妙旨有りとも): This and the following sentence have no parallel in the Gentō text, which instead ends its section 22 with a criticism of those "deluded by fame and profit" (*fukaku myōri ni madowasaruru yakara* ふかく名利にまどはさるるやから).

24 On Han soil as well (*Kando ni mo* 漢土にも): This section lacks a parallel in the Gentō text.

188　DŌGEN'S *SHŌBŌGENZŌ* VOLUME VII

hundred years ago, there are no lineage teachers with clear eyes, and even scholars clear on the texts are rare.[25] Even if it is medicine, when one is ignorant of how to take it, it is likely to become poison. If one medicates oneself with the ambrosia of the teaching of the buddhas, it will become poison.

[V1:20]

當知、七佛の妙法は、得道明心の宗匠に、契會の參學、順て正傳すれば、的旨顯れて稟持するなり、文字習學の法師の、知り及ぶべきにあらず。然れば即、此の疑迷を掃持して、正師の訓へに隨て、得道因由を知るべし。

We should know that the exact import of the wondrous dharma of the seven buddhas appears and is instilled when students who have matched their understanding follow and receive direct transmission from lineage teachers who have gained the way and clarified their minds. This is not something that the dharma masters who study words and letters can know. Thus, sweeping away this doubt and delusion, and following the instructions of a true master, we should know the causes of gaining the way.[26]

[V1:21]

問曰、今我朝に傳はれる所の法華宗・華嚴教、共に大乘の究竟なり。況眞言宗は、毘盧遮那、金剛薩埵に傳て、師資みだらず。其の談ずる旨、即心是佛、是心作佛と云て、多劫の修行をふる事なく、即座に五佛の正覺を唱、佛法の極妙と云べし。然るに、今云所の行、何の勝たる事有れば、彼を措おきて單に此を進むるや。

Question: The Hokke school and Kegon teachings now transmitted to our kingdom are both the ultimate versions of the Great Vehicle. Not to mention the Shingon school, personally transmitted by Tathāgata Vairocana to Vajrasattva, with the line of masters and disciples undisrupted. The gist of what they say is that "*this mind itself is the buddha*," "*this mind itself becomes the buddha*"; they proclaim that, without spending

---

25　**While the teachings of the buddhas were transmitted to our land roughly three or four hundred years ago** (*sanshihyaku sai no zengo ni, bukkyō, waga kuni ni tsutawareri to iedomo* 三四百歳の前後に、佛教、わが國に傳はれりと云へども): It is unclear why Dōgen, writing in the thirteenth century, would have dated the transmission of Buddhism to Japan (traditionally dated in the sixth century) so recently — unless, perhaps, he was thinking only of the establishment of the Tendai 天台 order in which he had studied, which was introduced in the ninth century, and which included the "Buddha Mind" (i.e., Zen) teachings as part of its curriculum.

26　**we should know the causes of gaining the way** (*tokudō inyu o shiru beshi* 得道因由を知るべし): Cf. the Gentō version (section 23) here:

坐禪辦道して諸佛自受用三昧を證得すべし。

We should pursue the way in seated meditation and verify the samādhi of self-enjoyment of the buddhas.

V1. Talk on Pursuing the Way *Bendōwa* 辦道話

189

many kalpas of practice, one has the right awakening of the five buddhas in a single sitting. This must be called the most wondrous expression of the buddha dharma. So, what is so superior in the practice you speak of here that you would set them aside and solely recommend it?

[V1:22] {2:543}

示曰、知べし、佛家には、教の殊・劣を對論する事無く、法の淺・深を不擇。皆是れ小兒の啼を止し楊葉なる故に、只修行の眞僞を咎問すべきなり。若修行の眞道を通ずるが如きは、草花・山水にひかれて佛道に流入するありき、土石沙礫を握りて佛印を稟持する事あり。況廣大の文字は、萬象に餘りて猶ほ豊かなり。轉大法輪、亦一塵に収まれりと云へども、各各晦跡出路有れば、無爲の道に自在なり。然れば、即心即佛のことは、猶是水中の月なり、取らんとわづらひしは癡猿也。即座成道の旨、更に亦鏡の裏の像也、ともなはんとおもへるは、狂兒なり。此の魚の目を握て玉と思事なかれ。荊璞夜光、其の中にあらじ、舌の響にかかはるべからず。今、佛祖單傳の妙道を示すことは、眞實の道人と成しめんと思ふなり。

Answer: We should know that, in the house of the buddhas, we do not debate the superiority or inferiority of the teachings, nor distinguish the dharmas as shallow or deep; for they are all willow leaves to stop the crying of a child.[27] We should just ask whether the practice is genuine or spurious. Of those who penetrate the true path of practice, there were those who drifted onto the way of the buddhas having been drawn to it by grass and flowers, mountains and waters; there are cases of receiving the buddha seal by holding earth and rocks, sand and pebbles. Not to mention that the vast writings are even more abundant than the myriad forms. And, though the turning of the great dharma wheel is contained within a single dust mote, when they each cover their tracks and have a path leading out, they are free on the unconditioned way.[28]

Thus, the matter of "*this mind itself is the buddha*," is just the moon in the water; those worried about getting it are foolish monkeys.[29] The mes-

---

27 **willow leaves to stop the crying of a child** (*shōni no naki o tomeshi yōyō* 小兒の啼を止し楊葉): I.e., merely skillful means, like yellow leaves that can mollify crying children who mistake their color for gold. This phrase does not occur in the parallel section 25 of the Gentō text.

28 **when they each cover their tracks and have a path leading out, they are free on the unconditioned way** (*ono ono kaiseki shutsuro areba, mu'i no michi ni jizai nari* 各各晦跡出路有れば、無爲の道に自在なり): A tentative translation that assumes the referent of "each" (*ono ono* 各各) is the aforementioned "those who penetrate the true path of practice" (*shugyō no shindō o tsūzuru ga gotoki* 修行の眞道を通ずるが如き). This clause has no parallel in the Gentō text, which reads here simply, "Not to mention that the vast writings are even more abundant than the myriad phenomena, and the turning of the great dharma wheel is contained within a single dust mote."

29 **the matter of "this mind itself is the buddha"** (*soku shin soku butsu no koto wa* 即心即佛のことは): Perhaps better to read the final *koto wa* ことは ("the matter") here as

190 DŌGEN'S *SHŌBŌGENZŌ* VOLUME VII

sage of "*attaining the way in this very sitting*" is likewise the reflection in the mirror; those thinking to accompany it are crazy children.[30] Do not clutch this fish eye thinking it is a jewel. There is probably not a night light within the uncut gem of Jing.[31] We should not have anything to do with the sound of wagging tongues. My teaching here of the wondrous way uniquely transmitted by the buddhas and ancestors is intended to make you a true person of the way.

[V1:23]

又、佛法を傳授する事は、必ず證契の人を其の宗師とすべし。文字を算る學者を以て、其の導師とするにたらず、一盲の衆盲を引かんが如し。今の佛祖正傳の門下には、皆得道證契の哲匠を敬て、佛法を住持せしむるが故に、冥陽神道も來り歸依し、證果の羅漢も來て問法するに、各各心地を開明する手を授けずと云ことなし。餘門に未聞所也、只佛弟子は佛法を學はん志を運ぶべし。

Furthermore, in the transmitting of the buddha dharma, we should always take as our teacher a person who has verified and accorded [with the dharma]. It is not enough to take as one's guiding master a scholar who counts words and letters; this would be like the blind leading the blind. In this present tradition directly transmitted by the buddhas and ancestors, all venerate the wise instructors who have gained the way and verified and accorded [with the dharma] and have them maintain the buddha dharma; and, for this reason, when the deities of the dark and bright come to take refuge, and the arhats, who have verified the fruit, come to inquire about the dharma, [the masters] never fail to extend a hand that reveals the mind ground of each. This is something never heard of in other traditions. Disciples of the Buddha should just pursue the intention to study the buddha dharma.

---

kotoba ことば ("the words"), as in the Gentō text.

those worried about getting it are foolish monkeys (*toran to wazuraishi wa chien nari* 取らんとわづらひしは癡猿也): Recalling the popular tale of the monkeys who, upon seeing the reflection of the moon in the water at the bottom of well, fell in while trying to retrieve it. This sentence does not occur in the Gentō text.

30 **those thinking to accompany it are crazy children** (*tomonawan to omoeru wa, kyōji nari* ともなはんとおもへるは、狂兒なり): This clause and the following two sentences do not occur in the Gentō text.

31 **There is probably not a night light within the uncut gem of Jing** (*Keiboku yakō, sono naka ni araji* 荊璞夜光、其の中にあらじ): The "night light" (*yakō* 夜光) is a jewel so bright it lights up the dark; the "uncut gem of Jing" (*Keiboku* 荊璞) refers to the famous jade discovered by Bian He 卞和, of the ancient kingdom of Chu 楚, and presented to King Wen of Zhou 周文王. Dōgen's sentence seems to reflect a line from the *Yilin* 意林 (Fuzi yibai ershi juan 傳子一百二十卷, KR.5g0071.005-23a):

荊璞無夜光之美。

The uncut gem of Jing lacks the beauty of the night light.

V1. Talk on Pursuing the Way *Bendōwa* 辨道話

[V1:24]

亦可知、我等は無上菩提欠けたるに非ず、鎮へに受用すと云へども、承當する事を不得故に、虚知見を起す事を習として、是を物と思によりて、大道、徒らに蹉過す。此の知見によりて、空華増増重なりて、あるいは十二轉輪・二十五有の境界と思ひ、三乗・五乗、有佛・無佛の見、盡事なし。此の知見を習て、佛法修行の正道と思ふべからず。

We should also know that, although from the beginning we have never lacked supreme bodhi and have always been enjoying it, because we are unable to accede to it, we form the habit of mindlessly producing views and think of them as things, thereby pointlessly missing the great way.[32] Based on these views, the sky flowers proliferate: we may think of the turning wheel of the twelve or the realms of the twenty-five forms of existence, or views of the three vehicles or five vehicles, of the existence of buddhas or the nonexistence of buddhas — there is no end to them. Accustomed as we are to these views, we should not think them the correct path of the practice of the buddha dharma.

[V1:25] {2:544}

然るを、今は正しく佛印によりて、萬事を放下し、一向に坐禪する時、迷悟情量の舊窠を出て、凡聖測度の草庵を捨、速に格外に逍遙し、大菩提を受用する者のなり。彼の文字の筌罤に拘者の、肩を雙ぶるに不及。

Now, however, when, based on the buddha seal, we truly cast aside the myriad affairs and single-mindedly sit in meditation, transcending the old den of the feelings of delusion and awakening, abandoning the thatched hut of reckoning the common person and sage, we are one who quickly wanders beyond the norm and enjoys the great bodhi.[33] How could those caught up in the traps and snares of words and letters stand shoulder to shoulder with us?

---

32 **We should also know** (*mata shiru beshi* 亦可知): This and the following section correspond to section 27 in the Gentō text.

think of them as things (*kore o mono to omou* 是を物と思): The Gentō text reads here "chase after them as things" (*kore o mono to ou* これを物とおふ).

33 **abandoning the thatched hut of reckoning the common person and sage** (*bonshō shikitaku no sōan o sutete* 凡聖測度の草庵を捨): I.e., leaving the [mental] hermitage in which we are concerned with the stages of the Buddhist spiritual path. The Gentō text reads here, "without regard for the path of the common person and sage" (*bonshō no michi ni kakawarazu* 凡聖のみちにかかはらず).

192 DŌGEN'S *SHŌBŌGENZŌ* VOLUME VII

[V1:26]

問曰、法華・眞言・華嚴教等は、其の教主勝れたり、樹下の應身にあら
ず、説く所の法も亦すぐれたり。今云所は、釋尊・迦葉に對せり。是應
身の佛け、聲聞に蒙らしむる處、先きの大乘教の宗に及ぶべきにあらず、
如何。示曰、一瞖眼に有れば、空華亂れ墜つ、委く顧るべし。況汝が云處
の顯密の大乘教に、釋迦の外に教主ありと知れる、己れが教主をも未だ知
ざるなり。此外に覓ば、捨父逃逝の初めなるべし。迦葉は偏に聲聞と思へ
る、村人愚なるが、王宮の臣位の列排を定んが如し。佛法の大道を錯るの
みにあらず、教家の旨にも暗し。汝は外道か、天魔か。暫く歸て己が宗師
に語れ、再び來らば汝が爲に説ん、我れ法を惜むべからず。

Question: The teaching authorities for such teachings as the Lotus,
Shingon, and Kegon are superior, not the response body under the tree;
and the dharma that they preached is also superior.[34] What you have said
here concerns Śākya and Kāśyapa; but what this response body buddha
offers to a *śrāvaka* cannot reach the doctrines of the aforementioned
teachings of the Great Vehicle.[35] What about this?

Answer: When there is a single cataract, sky flowers fall in rank confusion; we should give this detailed attention. How much more so when,
in what you say about the exoteric and esoteric Great Vehicle, you recognize that there are teaching authorities other than Śākya but have not
recognized your own teaching authority. If you search outside of that, it
will be the beginning of "*abandoning the father and running away*."[36] To
think of Kāśyapa only as a *śrāvaka* is like deciding that a village idiot
belongs in the ranks of the ministers in the royal palace. You are not only

---

34 **Question** (*tōte iwaku* 問日): the question and answer of this section are not found
in the Gentō text.

**The teaching authorities for such teachings as the Lotus, Shingon, and Kegon are
superior** (*Hokke Shingon Kegon kyō tō wa, sono kyōshu suguretari* 法華・眞言・華嚴
教等は、其の教主勝れたり): At issue here is the question of which of the three buddha
bodies initially reveals the doctrine of the school. The claim, common in the Japanese
Buddhism of Dōgen's day, was that the esoteric teachings of Shingon were taught directly by the ultimate, dharma body (*hosshin* 法身) of the buddha, while the highest of the
exoteric teachings, the *Hokke* and *Kegon*, were taught by glorified, reward bodies (*hōjin*
報身). In contrast, Buddha Śākyamuni, who transmitted the dharma to Mahākāśyapa on
Vulture Peak, was merely the historical, transformation body (*keshin* 化身), or response
body (*ōjin* 應身), that attained awakening, as is said here, "under the [bodhi] tree."

35 **what this response body buddha offers to a *śrāvaka*** (*kono ōjin no hotoke, shōmon
ni kōmurashimuru tokoro* 是應身の佛け、聲聞に蒙らしむる處): Mahākāśyapa was
considered to have followed the *śrāvaka* path and become an arhat under Buddha Śākyamuni; his future as a bodhisattva and eventual buddhahood is predicted in the *Lotus
Sūtra*.

36 **"abandoning the father and running away"** (*shafu tōzei* 捨父逃逝): From the
famous parable of the prodigal son in the *Lotus Sūtra* (*Miaofa lianhua jing* 妙法蓮華經,
T.262.9:16b26).

V1. Talk on Pursuing the Way *Bendōwa* 辦道話 193

mistaken about the great way of the buddha dharma; you are ignorant of the purport of the teaching houses.[37] Are you a follower of an other path? A Deva-māra?[38] For the time being, you should withdraw and speak with your master. If you come back again, I will talk with you; I will not begrudge you the dharma.

[V1:27]

問曰、三學の中に定學あり、六度の中に禪度あり、共に是一切の菩薩、初心より所學、利鈍をわかず修行す。今の坐禪も其の一つ成るべし。何によりてか佛法の嫡意とする、又此の中に佛法を集めたと云や。示曰、如來一大事の正法眼藏無上大法を、禪宗と名くる故に、此の問、來れり。知べし、此の禪宗の號は、神丹以東に起れり、印土には聞かず。初め達磨大師、京兆の嵩山少林寺にして、九年面壁の間だ、道俗未知佛正法、坐禪宗とする婆羅門と名き。後、代代の諸祖、皆常に坐禪を專らとす、故に愚なる俗家は、實を知らずして、ひたたけて坐禪宗と云、今は坐のみを簡要として、只禪宗と云なり、其比諸祖廣語にあきらかなり。六度及び三學の禪定に、並べ云べきにあらず。此相傳嫡意なる事、一代に隱れなし。

Question: Among the three disciplines is the discipline of concentration; within the six perfections is the perfection of meditation.[39] These are both studied by all bodhisattvas from their first thought [of awakening] and practiced without distinction of sharp or dull [faculties]. The seated meditation here must be one of these. Why do you take it as the legitimately inherited intent of the buddha dharma and say that the buddha dharma is consolidated within it?

Answer: This question arises because this unsurpassed great dharma, the treasury of the true dharma eye that is "the one great matter" of the tathāgatas, has been called the "Zen school." We should realize that this name, "Zen school," occurred in Cīnasthāna to the east and was never heard of in India.

In the beginning, while Great Master Dharma spent nine years facing a wall at the Shaolin Monastery on Mount Song in Jingzhao, the clerics and lay people, not yet knowing the true dharma of the buddhas, called him "the brahman who takes seated meditation as the essential point." Thereafter, the ancestors of generation after generation took seated med-

---

37 **teaching houses** (*kyōke* 教家): I.e., the Buddhist traditions, like the Hokke, Shingon, and Kegon, that Zen regards as transmitting only the teachings (*kyō* 教), as opposed to the intention (*i* 意), of the Buddha.

38 **Are you a follower of an other path? A Deva-māra?** (*nanji wa gedō ka, tenma ka* 汝は外道か、天魔か): I.e., are you a member of a non-Buddhist religion or Māra, the Evil One, who seeks to obstruct the buddha dharma; a common combination of pejorative epithets.

39 **Question** (*tōte iwaku* 問曰): This section parallels sections 28-30, and the first sentence of section 31, in the Gentō text.

194 DŌGEN'S *SHŌBŌGENZŌ* VOLUME VII

itation as their main focus; and, therefore, foolish lay people, not knowing the reality of the matter, casually called them the "seated meditation school." Nowadays, just the word "seated" has been omitted, and they just say, "the meditation [or *zen*] school." Its meaning is clear in the extensive records of the ancestors. It is not to be equated with the meditations of the six perfections or three disciplines. The fact that this is the legitimately inherited intent of the transmission has never been hidden for a single generation.

[V1:28] {2:545}

如來、昔靈山會上にして、正法眼藏涅槃妙心無上の大法を以て、只迦葉にのみ付法せし儀式は、現在して上界に有る梵王・釋王等、まのあたり見し者の存せり、疑べきにたらず。又佛法は、必ず三學に不限、六度不限なり。如來、小兒の泣を止るに、無量の手を授け、方便を廻らす。然れども、小兒の泣を止つる後は、一法も有る事なし。只此の、相傳の佛法の全道なる事を可知。漢土に未だ此門の外に、付法の正しき事無きなり。教家に師子尊者に至る迄で付法すとしるせしとも、其より以來、未だ師資相向て稟持せる事不聞。いかでか此門に祖祖正傳して廿八世に及び、自ら洪波を不亂、東土に來り、法を殘し置けるに似たる事有らん。

There are those at present in the higher realms, King Brahmā, King Śakra, and the like, who personally witnessed the ceremony long ago at the assembly on Vulture Peak, in which the Tathāgata bequeathed the unsurpassed great dharma of the treasury of the true dharma eye, the wondrous mind of nirvāṇa, to Venerable Kāśyapa.[40] It is not to be doubted.

Also, the buddha dharma is not limited to the three disciplines, not limited to the six perfections.[41] In order to stop the tears of his little children, the Tathāgata extended his incalculable hands and employed his skillful means; but after he has stopped the tears of the little children, he is without even a single dharma. We should recognize the fact that this is the entire way of the buddha dharma that has been transmitted. On Han soil, apart from this gateway, there has yet to be any correct bequest of the dharma. Although it is said that in the teaching houses the dharma was bequeathed down to Venerable Siṃhabhikṣu, thereafter we have never

40　**There are those at present in the higher realms, King Brahmā, King Śakra, and the like** (*genzai shite jōkai ni aru Bonnō Shakuō tō* 現在して上界に有る梵王・釋王等): A sentence corresponding to the second sentence of section 31 in the Gentō text — though that version mentions only those among the "host of devas" (*tenshu* 天衆) as witness to the ceremony.

41　**Also, the buddha dharma is not limited to the three disciplines** (*mata buppō wa, kanarazu sangaku ni kagirazu* 又佛法は、必ず三學に不限): This sentence and the remainder of the section do not occur in the Gentō text, which ends its section 31 with:

> Those deva hosts forever protect the buddha dharma, and their efforts never flag. We should know that this is the entire way of the buddha dharma; nothing else can compare with it.

V1. Talk on Pursuing the Way *Bendōwa* 辨道話 195

heard that the masters and disciples met and were invested.[42] How could it resemble this gateway, in which the direct transmission of ancestor after ancestor reached down to the twenty-eighth generation, who, unfazed by the waves, personally came to the Land of the East and left the dharma.[43]

[V1:29]
問曰、佛家に、何によりてか四威儀の中に、但坐にのみおほせて、修行を勸め證入を云や。昔より坐時に得道する人有り、又餘儀に開悟せる者の多し。如何。

Question: In saying that it recommends meditation for entering verification, on what basis does the house of the buddhas solely pursue sitting among the four deportments? From ancient times, there have been people who gained the way while sitting but many who opened awakening in the other deportments.[44] What about this?

[V1:30]
示曰、諸佛相ひ續てまさしく修行し證入せる道ち、はかり知るべきにあらず。何によりてか然るぞと知らんと思はば、千佛共に正傳せる故に、と知るべきなり、又この外に、所以を尋ぬ不可。但だ祖師譽て曰、坐禪は即安樂の法門なり。四儀の中に安樂なる故なるべし、金剛座に坐する坐にあらずば不聞。

Answer: The ways by which the buddhas, one after another, practiced and entered verification cannot be calculated. If we want to know on what basis they did so, we should know that it is because the thousand buddhas all directly transmitted it; we should not seek any reason other than this.[45] Still, the ancestral masters praise it, saying, "seated meditation is the dharma gate of ease and joy." The reason must be that, among the four deportments, it is the one of "ease and joy." We do not hear this of sitting that is not the sitting practiced on the vajra seat.[46]

---

42 **in the teaching houses the dharma was bequeathed down to Venerable Siṃhabhikṣu** (*kyōke ni Shishi sonja ni itaru made fuhō su* 教家に師子尊者に至る迄で付法す): A reference to the lineage of Indian ancestors recognized by the Tiantai 天台 school. The *Fu fazang yinyuan zhuan* 付法藏因緣傳 (T.2058) lists 23 (or 24) generations, ending with Siṃhabhikṣu (*Shishi* 獅子; also reconstructed as Ārasiṃha or Siṃha), who is said to have been beheaded without dharma issue by the king of Kaśmīra.

43 **unfazed by the waves, personally came to the Land of the East** (*mizukara kōha o midasazu, Tōdo ni kitari* 自ら洪波を不亂、東土に來り): A tentative translation, taking *kōha o midasazu* 洪波を不亂 as a reference to the twenty-eighth Indian ancestor Bodhidharma's journey to China by sea.

44 **From ancient times** (*mukashi yori* 昔より): This and the final sentence here do not occur in the parallel section 32 of the Gentō text.

45 **thousand buddhas** (*sen butsu* 千佛): I.e., all the buddhas in each kalpa.

46 **We do not hear this of sitting that is not the sitting practiced on the vajra seat** (*kongō za ni zasuru za ni arazuba kikazu* 金剛座に坐する坐にあらずば不聞): The exact

196 DŌGEN'S *SHŌBŌGENZŌ* VOLUME VII

[V1:31] {2:546}

又實を論ぜば、南嶽と大寂と相ひ見て得法咨參せし因緣を可明。一撥兩頭
動の旨有り。坐の外に開悟せしも、皆曾て坐の力有るなり。田を耕さで稻
を得る人未聽、此法の深意を知らんと思はば、修して可知。洪波に不入、
弄潮の方にくらし。

Also, if we are to discuss the reality of the matter, we should clarify
the episode in which Nanyue and Daji met and consulted on attaining the
dharma.[47] There is the point of *one chop and both move*.[48] Even those
who open awaking outside of sitting all have the power of their previous
sitting. We have yet to hear of someone getting rice without cultivating
the paddy. If you want to know the deep meaning of this dharma, practice it and you will know it. If you do not enter the waves, you will not
know how to play in the surf.

[V1:32]

問曰、此の坐禪の行は、未だ佛法を證會せざらん者は、坐禪辨道して其の
證を可待。既に佛正法に明ならん人は、坐禪、なにの待つ所か有らん。示
曰、癡人の前に夢を説かず、山子の手には舟棹を與へがたしと雖ども、更
に訓をたるべし。其れ、修證は一に有らずと思へる、即外道の見なり。佛
法には、修證是一等なり。今も證上の修なるが故に、初心の辨道即本證の
全體也。故に、修行の用心を授くるにも、修の外に證を待つ思ひなかれ、
と教ふ、直指の本證なるが故なるべし。既に修の證なれば、證に極め無

---

sense is uncertain; perhaps meaning that sitting would not be described as "ease and joy"
were it not the posture adopted by the buddhas on the seat of their awakening. This sentence does not occur in section 33 of the Gentō text, which ends with the sentence, "Not
to mention that it is the way of practice of not just one or two buddhas; all the buddhas
and ancestors had this way."

47 **episode in which Nanyue and Daji met and consulted on attaining the dharma**
(*Nangaku to Daijaku to aimamiete tokuhō shisan seshi innen* 南嶽と大寂と相ひ見て
得法咨參せし因緣): Presumably, a reference to the famous episode, appearing often in
the *Shōbōgenzō*, in which Nanyue Huairang 南嶽懷讓 (677-744) teases Mazu Daoyi 馬
祖道一 (709–788) for practicing seated meditation in order to become a buddha. See
Supplementary Notes, s.v. "Nanyue polishes a tile." This section does not occur in the
Gentō text.

48 **one chop and both move** (*ippatsu ryōtō dō* 一撥兩頭動): The point here is not clear.
The phrase would seem to allude to an interesting question posed to the ninth-century
figure Changsha Jingcen 長沙景岑 (dates unknown) (see, e.g., *Liandeng huiyao* 聯燈會
要, ZZ.136:538a13-14):

> 竺尚書問、蚯蚓斬爲兩段、兩頭俱動。未審佛性在阿那箇頭。師曰、莫妄想。
>
> Minister Chu asked, "When you cut a worm in two pieces, both of them move. I
> don't understand, in which one is the buddha nature?"
> The Master said, "Don't have deluded ideas."

If this conversation, which Dōgen discusses in his "Shōbōgenzō busshō" 正法眼藏佛
性, is behind our phrase, the point may be that the buddha nature is present both inside
and outside seated meditation — or, less graciously, a reminder to the interlocutor of
Changsha's response to the minister.

V1. Talk on Pursuing the Way *Bendōwa* 辨道話 197

く、證の修なれば、修に初め無し。爰以て、釋迦如來・達磨尊者、共に證
上の修に受用せられ、迦葉師兄・大鑑高祖、同く證上の修に引轉せらる。
佛法住持のあと、皆以如是。

Question: Regarding this practice of seated meditation, someone who
has yet to verify an understanding of the buddha dharma should get
that verification by pursuing the way in seated meditation; but what can
someone who has already clarified the true dharma of the Buddha expect
from seated meditation?[49]

Answer: "One does not tell dreams in front of a fool"; "one cannot
put an oar in the hands of a woodsman." Nevertheless, I shall give you
further instruction.

Now, to think that practice and verification are not one is a view of
other paths. In the buddha dharma, practice and verification are identical. Even now, because it is practice based on verification, the pursuit of
the way by the beginner is the complete embodiment of original verification. For this reason, in giving cautionary advice on practice as well,
it is taught not to expect verification outside of practice, which must be
because it is the original verification directly pointed at.

Since it is the verification of practice, verification has no limit; since it
is the practice of verification, practice has no beginning. Hence, Tathāgata Śākya and Venerable Dharma both enjoyed practice based on verification; the Senior Disciple Kāśyapa and the Eminent Ancestor Dajian
were similarly pulled along by practice based on verification. The traces
of those who have maintained the buddha dharma are all like this.

[V1:33]
既に證を離れぬ修あり、我等、幸に一分妙修を單傳せる、初心の辨道、即ち
十分の本證を無爲の地にうるなり。知べし、修を離れぬ證を染汚せざらしめ
んが爲に、佛祖頻に修行の寛くすべからざると教ふ。妙修を放下すれば、本
證、満手に餘る、本證を出身すれば、妙修、通身におこなはる。亦、まのあ
たり大宋國にして見しにも、諸方の禪院、皆坐禪堂を構て、一二千僧を、床
を安じ連て、日夜に坐禪を勸めき。其の席主とせる傳佛心印の宗師に、佛法
の大意を問らひしかば、修證の兩段にあらぬ旨をきこえき。

There being a practice already inseparable from verification, and we
fortunately having been uniquely transmitted one share of wondrous
practice, our beginner's pursuit of the way attains a full share of original
verification at the ground of the unconditioned.[50]

---

49 **Question** (*tōte iwaku* 問曰): This section corresponds to sections 35-36 and the first
part of 37 in the Gentō text.

50 **There being a practice already inseparable from verification** (*sude ni shō o
hanarenu shu ari* 既に證を離れぬ修あり): This section corresponds to the last sentence
of section 37 and sections 38 and 39 in the Gentō text.

We should know that, in order to avoid defiling the verification inseparable from practice, the buddhas and ancestors repeatedly teach us not to relax our practice. When we cast aside wondrous practice, original verification overflows our hands; when the body escapes from original verification, wondrous practice occurs in the body throughout.

Moreover, as I personally saw in the Land of the Great Song, Chan cloisters in all quarters had all built halls for seated meditation, where one or two thousand monks lined the platforms engaged in seated meditation day and night. When I asked the teachers who transmit the buddha mind seal who were regarded as seat holders there about the great meaning of the buddha dharma, they taught me the message that practice and verification are not on two different levels.

[V1:34] {2:547}

此故に、門下の參學のみにあらず、求法の高流、佛法の中に眞實を願ん人、初心・後心を擇らばず、凡人・聖人を不論、佛祖の訓により、宗匠の道をおうて、坐禪辨道すべしと勸む。

Therefore, we recommend that, not only students in our tradition, but eminent persons, persons seeking the truth within the buddha dharma, without discriminating between beginner or advanced, without considerations of common person or sage, should pursue the way in seated meditation, following the path of a teacher according to the instructions of the buddhas and ancestors.

[V1:35]

不聞や祖師の日、修證は無きにあらず、汚染する事はえじ。又曰、道を見るもの、道を修す、と。知るべし、得道の中に修行すべし、と云事を。

Have you not heard that the ancestral masters have said, "It's not that it lacks practice and verification, but it can't be defiled by them." And they have said, "One who sees the way practices the way." We should know that this means we should practice within gaining the way.

[V1:36]

問日、我朝の先代に、教を弘めし諸師、共に是入唐傳法せしに、何ぞ此の旨をさしおきて、只教をのみ傳し。示日、昔の人師、此の法を傳へざりし事、昔の人に問ふべし。我は今の人なり。

Question: Why is it that all the masters who spread the teachings in our kingdom in former ages, when they entered the Tang and transmitted the dharma, set aside this message and only transmitted the teachings?[51]

Answer: Why the teachers of humans in the past did not transmit this

---

51 **Question** (*tōte iwaku* 問曰): This section corresponds to sections 42-43 in the Gentō text.

V1. Talk on Pursuing the Way *Bendōwa* 辨道話 199

dharma, you should ask the people of the past.[52] I am a person of the present.

[V1:37]

問曰、彼の上代の師、是法を得せりや。示曰、會せば、通じてん。

Question: Did those masters of antiquity get this dharma?[53]

Answer: If they had understood it, they would have communicated it.

[V1:38]

問曰、あるが云く、生死を歎く事なかれ、生死を出離するに、いと速かなる道あり。所謂、心性の常住なる事わりを知るなり。其の旨たらく、此身體は、既に生有れば必ず滅にうつされゆくとも、心性は敢て滅する事なし。能く生滅に遷されぬ心性、我が身に有る事を知りぬれば、是を本來性とするが故に、身は假りの姿なり、死此生彼、定り無し。心は是常住なり、去・來・現在、かはるべからず。如是しるを、生死を離れたりとは云なり。此の旨を知る者は、從來の生死永く絶えて、此身了る時、性海に入。性海に朝宗する時に、諸佛如來の如く、妙德正に具る。縱へ知ると云へども、前世妄業にひかされたる身體なるが故に、諸聖と等しからず。未だ此の旨を知らざる者は、久生死に廻るべし。然れば即、いそぎて心性の常住なる旨を了知すべし。徒らに閑坐して一生を過さん、何の待つ處か有らん。如是云旨、實に佛祖の道に叶へりや、如何。示曰、今云處の見、全く佛法にあらず、先尼外道が見なり。曰く、彼の外道が見は、我が身の内に一の靈知あり、彼の知、即緣に相ふ處に、よく好惡を辨まえ、是非をわきまふ、痛痒を知り、苦樂を知る、皆彼の靈知の力なり。然るに、彼の靈性は、此の身の滅する時、もぬけて彼こに生るる故に、ここに滅すと見えれども、かしこの生を受くれば、永く滅せずして常住也と云なり。彼の外道の見、如是。然るを、此の見を習て佛法とせん、瓦礫を握て金寶と思はんよりも尚ほ誤れり。癡迷の可恥、喩へるにものなし。大唐國の慧忠國師、深く禁たり。心常相滅の邪見を計して、諸佛の妙法に等うして、生死の本因をまして、生死を離れたりと思はん、おろかなるにあらずや、最も可憐。只是れ外道の邪見なりと知れ、耳に觸るべからず。事やむこと不能、今猶ほ憐を垂て、汝が邪見を救はん。

Question: Some say,

Do not lament birth and death.[54] There is a very quick path to escape from birth and death: it is to know the fact that the nature of the mind

---

52 **Answer** (*shimeshite iwaku* しめしていはく): C.f. the answer given in section 43 of the Gentō text:

しめしていはく、むかしの人師、この法をつたへざりしことは、時節のいまだいたらざりしゆゑなり。

Answer: The fact that the teachers of humans in the past did not transmit this dharma is because the occasion had not yet arrived.

53 **Question** (*tōte iwaku* 問曰): This section corresponds to sections 44-45 in the Gentō text.

54 **Question** (*tōte iwaku* 問曰): This section corresponds to sections 46-47 and the first part of 48 in the Gentō text.

is permanent. The basic doctrine is that, while this body, having been born, inevitably moves on to extinction, the nature of the mind is never extinguished. When we have understood that the nature of the mind that does not move from birth to extinction is within us, insofar as we take it as our original nature, our body is a temporary form, dying here, born there, indefinitely; our mind is permanent, unchanging across past, present, and future. To understand in this way is said to have escaped from birth and death. For those who know this doctrine, the birth and death up till now cease forever, and, when this body ends, they enter the ocean of the nature. When they flow into the ocean of the nature, they are endowed with wondrous virtues, like those of the buddhas, the tathāgatas; though they know [the doctrine], since their bodies are made from the deluded karma of former lives, they are not equivalent to the sages. Those who do not know this doctrine will long revolve in birth and death. Thus, we should just quickly recognize the doctrine that the nature of the mind is permanent. What can one expect from spending one's life idly sitting in vain?

What about such a doctrine? Does it truly conform to the way of the buddhas and ancestors?

Answer: The view you describe here is definitely not the buddha dharma; it is the view of the other path of Śreṇika. The view of that other path holds that, within our body, there is a numinous awareness, and that, upon encountering objects, it distinguishes likes and dislikes, distinguishes right and wrong, feels pains and itches, feels suffering and joy — all these due to the powers of that numinous awareness. Yet, when this body perishes, that numinous awareness withdraws and is born elsewhere; hence, though it appears to perish here, since it receives a birth elsewhere, it is forever unchanging and permanent. Such is the view of that other path.

Still, to study this view and take it as the buddha dharma is more erroneous than grasping tiles and pebbles and thinking them to be gold and jewels. There is nothing to compare with such shameful delusion. The National Teacher Huizhong of the Land of the Great Tang has strictly warned against it. Is it not foolish to treat the false view here that *the mind is permanent while its attributes cease* as equivalent to the wondrous dharma of the buddhas, and to think that one is free from birth and death even while creating the fundamental cause of birth and death? This is most pathetic. We should just recognize this as the false view of other paths and not give ear to it. Yet the matter cannot be helped: I shall still show you pity here and save you from your false view.

V1. Talk on Pursuing the Way *Bendōwa* 辨道話

[V1:39] {2:549}

知るべし、佛法には、本より身心一如にして、性相不二なりと談ずる、西天東地、同く知れる所、改まる事なし。況や、常住を談ずる門には、萬法皆常住なり、身と心と分く事なし。寂滅を談ずる門には、諸法皆寂滅なり、性と相とをわく事なし。然るを、何ぞ身滅心常と云ん、正理に背かざらんや。しかのみならず、生死は即涅槃なりと覺知すべし、未だ生死の外に涅槃を談ずる事なし。況や、心は身を離て常住なりと領解するを以て、生死を離れたる佛智と妄計すと云とも、領解・知覺の心は、即猶ほ生滅して、全常住ならず。是れは、なきにあらずや。

You should know that, in the buddha dharma, from the start, we talk of body and mind as one and nature and mark as not two.[55] This is something known in Sindh in the West and the Land of the East alike, without any deviation. Moreover, in teachings that talk of permanence, the myriad dharmas are all permanent, without distinction between body and mind; and in teachings that talk of quiescence, the dharmas are all quiescent, without distinction between nature and mark. Despite this, how can we say that the body perishes but the mind is constant? Does this not go against reason? Not only that, but we should perceive that birth and death are themselves nirvāṇa; we never talk of nirvāṇa apart from birth and death. Not to mention that, even if, understanding that the mind is free from the body and is permanent, one mistakes that for the buddha wisdom, free from birth and death, the mind that has this understanding and perception would itself still arise and cease and in no sense be permanent. Is this not nonexistent?[56]

[V1:40]

嘗觀すべし、身心一如の旨は、佛法の常に談ずる所なり。然るに、何ぞ此の身の生滅せんとき、心ひとり身を別れて生滅せざらん。若し一如なる時あり、一如ならぬ時あらば、佛説自ら虚妄になりぬべし。又、生死は除くべき法ぞと思へるは、佛法を厭過なる。

We should try to see that the teaching of the unity of body and mind is something always talked about in the buddha dharma. How, then, when the body arises and ceases, could the mind alone separate from the body and not arise or cease? If there are times when they are one and times when they are not one, the Buddha's preaching would become false. Moreover, to think that birth and death are dharmas to be eliminated amounts to the offense of despising the buddha dharma.[57]

---

55 **You should know** (*shiru beshi* 知るべし): This section corresponds to the second half of section 48 in the Gentō text.

56 **Is this not nonexistent?** (*kore wa, naki ni arazu ya* 是れは、なきにあらずや): Presumably, meaning, "this situation could not be." Cf. the Gentō text here: "Is this not ludicrous?" (*kore hakanaki ni arazu ya* これはかなきにあらずや).

57 **Moreover** (*mata* 又): The Gentō text follows this sentence with the rhetorical question, "Shouldn't we be more prudent?" (*tsutsushimazaramu ya* つつしまざらむや).

[V1:41]

佛法の中に、心性大總相の法門と云は、一大法界を籠て、性相をわかず、生滅を云事なし。菩提・涅槃に及まで、心性にあらざるなし。一切諸法・萬象森羅、共に只一心にして、こめず兼いれずと云事なし。此の諸の法門、皆平等一心なり、敢て異違なしと談ずる、即佛家の心性を知れる様子なり。然るを、此の一法に身と心とを分別し、生死と涅槃とをわく事あらんや。既に佛子也、外道の見を語たる狂人の舌の響を、耳に觸るる事なかれ。

We should know that, in the buddha dharma, what is called the dharma gate of the great universal attribute of the nature of the mind collects the entire great dharma realm, without distinguishing nature and attribute, and does not speak of arising and ceasing. There is nothing, even up to bodhi and nirvāṇa that is not the nature of the mind. *All the dharmas, the thicket of myriad forms*, are all just this one mind, with nothing not included and unified. The various dharma gates are all equally the one mind. To talk of there being no differences — this is the sign that the house of the buddhas has understood the nature of the mind. Despite this, how could one differentiate this one dharma into body and mind and distinguish birth and death and nirvāṇa? Since we are children of the Buddha, do not give ear to the sounds of the tongues of crazy people who talk of the views of other paths.

[V1:42] {2:550}

問曰、此の坐禪を純らせん人、必ず戒律を嚴淨すべしや。示曰、持戒梵行は、即ち禪門の規矩なり、佛祖の家風なり。未だ戒を不受、又戒を破れる者、其の分なきにあらず。

Question: Should the person who would exclusively practice seated meditation invariably observe the precepts in strict purity?[58]

Answer: Keeping the precepts and pure practice are the standards for the Zen gate and the house style of the buddhas and ancestors. But it is not the case that those who have not yet received the precepts or who have broken the precepts are disqualified.

[V1:43]

問曰、此の坐禪を勤ん人、更に眞言・止觀の行をかね修せん、妨げ有べからざるか。示曰、在唐の時、宗師に眞訣を聽し因、西天東地の古今に、佛印を正傳せし諸祖、何も、いまだ、しかの如きの行を兼ね修すとはきかず、と謂ひき。誠に、一事をこととせざれば、一智了達する事なし。

58　**Question** (*tōte iwaku* 問曰): This section corresponds to sections 51-52 in the Gentō text.

V1. Talk on Pursuing the Way *Bendōwa* 辨道話 203

Question: Are there no obstacles to someone's performing this seated meditation who engages in dual cultivation with the practices of Shingon or Calming and Contemplation?[59]

Answer: When I was in the Tang, listening to the true arcanum of my teacher, he said that he had never heard of any of the ancestors who directly transmitted the buddha seal in Sindh in the West and the Land of the East, past or present, who engaged in the dual cultivation of such practices. Truly, when one does not devote oneself to one thing, one does not master one wisdom.

[V1:44]

問曰、此の行、在俗の男女もつとむべしや、獨り出家人のみ修するか。示曰、祖師の曰、佛法を會する事、必ずしも男女・貴賎に預るべからず。

Question: Is this practice something that lay men and women should also perform, or is it engaged in solely by those who have left home?[60]

Answer: The ancestral masters say that the understanding of the buddha dharma should not necessarily have anything to do with male or female, noble or base.[61]

[V1:45]

問曰、出家人は、諸緣すみやかに離れて、坐禪辨道に無礙。在俗の繁務は、何にしてか一向に修行して、無爲の佛道に叶はん。示曰、おほよそ、佛祖あはれみの餘り、廣大の慈門を闢き置り。是れ一切衆生を證入せしめんが爲なり、人天を誰れか入らざらん者や。爰以、昔・今を尋に、其證、是れ多し。暫く代宗・順宗の、帝位にして、萬機、いとしげかりし、坐禪辨道して、佛祖の大道、會通す。李相國・防相國、共に輔佐の臣位に侍りて、一天の股肱となりし、坐禪辨道して、佛祖の大道に證入せりき。只志の有り無しに依るべし、身の在家・出家には、よるべからず。又深く事の殊・劣をわきまふる人、自ら信ずる事有り。況や、世務は佛法をさふと思ふ者は、只世中に佛法無しとのみ知りて、佛中に世法無き事を、未だ知らざるなり。近比大宋に、憑相公と云ありき、祖道に長ぜりし大官なり。後に詩を作りて、自を云に曰く、公事之餘喜坐禪、少曾將脇到牀眠、雖然現出宰官相、長老之名四海傳。此れは、官務に隙無き身なれども、佛道に志し深ければ得道せるなり。他を以て我を顧み、昔を以今をかへりみるべし。大宋國には、今の世の國王・大臣・士俗・男女、共に心を祖道にとど

---

59 **Question** (*tōte iwaku* 問曰): This section corresponds to sections 53-54 in the Gentō text.

60 **Question** (*tōte iwaku* 問曰): This section corresponds to sections 55-56 in the Gentō text.

61 **should not necessarily have anything to do with male or female, noble or base** (*kanarazushimo nannyo kisen ni azukaru bekarazu* 必ずしも男女・貴賎に預るべからず): Taking the verb *azukaru* 預る here in the sense *kakawaru* 係る ("be connected with"); cf. the Gentō text, "we should not discriminate between male or female, noble or base" (*nannyo kisen o erabu bekarazu* 男女貴賤をえらぶべからず).

めざるなし。武門・文家、何れも參禪學道を心ざせり。志す者、必ず心地を開明する事多し。是れ世務の佛法を妨げざる、自から知れたり。國家に眞實の佛法弘通すれば、諸佛・諸天無間衛護するが故に、賢士・智臣産れて、王化を助けて太平ならしむるを以て、終に佛法・世法一如に圓通す。庶民、誰か良縁を結ばざらん。又、釋尊の在世には、逆人・邪見、道をえき。祖師の會下には、獵者・樵翁、悟を開く。況や、其の外の人をや。只正師の教道を尋ぬべし。

Question: People who have left home, quickly escaping the various involvements, have no obstacles to pursuing the way in seated meditation; but how can the busy lay person practice single-mindedly and conform to the unconditioned way of the buddhas?[62]

Answer: The buddhas and ancestors, with an overabundance of empathy, have opened this gate of compassion. It was in order to enable all living beings to enter verification; who among the humans and devas could not enter it? Hence, when we inquire into past and present, there are many who have had this verification. For the moment, [we might mention] Daizong and Shunzong, who, while serving as emperors and completely occupied with the myriad affairs of state, pursued the way in seated meditation and understood the great way of the buddhas and ancestors; or State Minister Li and State Minister Fang, who both served in ministerial posts as adjuncts and were the very "arms and legs" of the emperor, and who pursued the way in seated meditation and entered verification of the great way of the buddhas and ancestors.

This must only depend on whether there is or is not the aspiration; it should not depend on whether one's status is that of householder or renunciant. Again, the person who profoundly evaluates the value of things will naturally believe. Not to mention that those who think that worldly duties interfere with the buddha dharma know only that there is no buddha dharma within the worldly but do not yet recognize that there are no worldly dharmas within the buddha [dharma].

Recently, in the Great Song, there was a certain Ministerial Magistrate Feng, a high official advanced in the way of the ancestors. Later, he composed a verse in which he refers to himself, saying,

As official duties allow, I enjoy seated meditation,
Rarely reclining on a bed to sleep.
Though appointed to the Offices of the Secretariat,
My name as an elder is spread across the four seas.

Though he was someone without a break from his government duties, because his aspiration for the way of the buddhas was profound,

---

62 **Question** (*tōte iwaku* 問曰): This section corresponds to sections 57-58 in the Gentō text.

V1. Talk on Pursuing the Way *Bendōwa* 辦道話

he gained the way. We should use him to reflect on ourselves and use the past as a model for the present. In the Land of the Great Song today, the kings of the realm, the great ministers, the nobles, men and women — none fail to turn their minds to the way of the ancestors. Both military men and literati aspire to practice meditation and study the way. Of those who aspire, many are sure to clarify the mind ground. From this, we naturally recognize that worldly duties do not hinder the buddha dharma. When the genuine buddha dharma is spread throughout the realm, because the buddhas and devas constantly protect it, intelligent men and wise ministers arise, and the royal influence brings great peace; on account of this, in the end, the buddha dharma and worldly dharma perfectly merge as one.[63] Who among the populace will not form favorable connections? Moreover, when Śākya, the Honored One, was in the world, transgressive people and those with false views attained the way. Within the assemblies of the ancestral masters, hunters and woodcutters opened awakening, not to mention the other people. We should just seek the teaching of the way of a true master.

[V1:46] {2:551}
問曰、此の行は、今末代惡世にも、修行せば證を得べしや。示曰、教家に名相を事とせるに、尚ほ正・像・末法を分く事なし、修すれば皆得道すと云。況や、此の單傳の正法には、入法出身、同く自家の財珍を受用する也。證の得否は、修せむ者自ら知らん事、用水の人の、冷煖を自らわきまふるが如し。

Question: If one cultivates this practice, can one attain verification even in the present evil world of the final age?[64]

Answer: In the teaching houses, even while focusing on names and forms, it is still said that, in the real teachings of the Great Vehicle, everyone who practices can gain the way, without distinction among the true, semblance, and final dharma. How much more, then, in this uniquely transmitted true dharma, where, in entering the dharma and leaving the body, we all equally enjoy the precious assets of our own house. Whether or not one has attained verification, those who practice know

---

63 **When the genuine buddha dharma is spread throughout the realm** (*kokka ni shinjitsu no buppō guzū sureba* 國家に眞實の佛法弘通すれば): Cf. the Gentō text paralleling this and the following sentence:

> 國家に眞實の佛法弘通すれば、諸佛・諸天ひまなく衞護するがゆえに、王化太平なり、聖化太平なれば、佛法そのちからをうるものなり。

> When the genuine buddha dharma is spread throughout the realm, because the buddhas and devas constantly protect it, the royal influence brings great peace; and, when the sagely influence brings great peace, the buddha dharma gains strength.

64 **Question** (*tōte iwaku* 問曰): This section corresponds to sections 59-60 in the Gentō text.

206 DŌGEN'S *SHŌBŌGENZŌ* VOLUME VII

for themselves, just as people who use water can tell for themselves whether it is cold or hot.

[V1:47] {2:552}

問曰、あるが云く、佛法には、即心是佛の旨を了達しぬるが如きは、口に經典を誦せず、身に佛道を行ぜざれども、敢て佛法に欠けたる所なし。只佛法は元より自己に有りと知る、是を得道の圓成とす。此外更に他人に向て求むべきにあらず、況や、坐禪辨道を煩しく爲や。示曰、此の言、尤はかなし。若汝が言ふが如くならば、心有ん者、誰か此の旨を知る事無らん。知べし、佛法は、正に自他の見を止て學するなり。自己即佛と知るを佛法とせば、釋迦尊、昔し化道に煩しくせんや。暫く古德の妙則以て是を證すべし。

Question: Some say that, in the buddha dharma, those who fully understand the teaching that "*this mind itself is the buddha,*" though they neither recite scriptures with their mouths nor practice the way of the buddhas with their bodies, lack nothing of the buddha dharma.[65] Merely knowing that the buddha dharma is within oneself from the start — this constitutes the perfect completion of gaining the way; aside from this, there is nothing further to seek from others, much less any need to pursue the way in seated meditation.

Answer: These words are completely baseless. If it were as you say, how could anyone with a mind fail to know this teaching were someone to tell it to them? We should recognize that the buddha dharma is to study having quit views of self and other; if knowing that the self is buddha constitutes attaining the way, would Śākya, the Honored One, have bothered long ago to teach the way? Here, let me verify this with a marvelous case of the old worthies.

[V1:48]

昔則禪師と云、法眼禪師の會下にして監院を司どる時に、法眼禪師問て曰く、則監寺、汝我が會に有て幾の時ぞ。則公が云、我れ師の會に侍て既三年を歷たり。禪師の云く、汝は後生なり、何ぞ常に佛法を問はざる。則公曰く、某甲和尚を欺くべからず、曾て青峰禪師の處に有りし時、佛法に置て安樂の處を了達せり。禪師の曰く、汝、いかなる言ばによりてか入る事を得し。則公の云く、某甲曾て青峰に問ひき、如何是學人の自己。青峯の曰、丙丁童子來求火。禪師の曰、好き言ばなり、但し恐は汝得せざらん事を。則公が曰く、丙丁は火に属す、火を以て更に火を求む、自己を以て自己を求むるに似たり、と會せり。禪師の曰、實に知りぬ、汝ぢ不會けり。佛法もし如是ならば、けふ迄でに傳はらじ。此則公、懆悶して即ち立ちぬ。又中路に至りて思ひき、禪師は是天下の知識、又五百人の導師なり、我が非を諫む、定めて長處有らん。歸て懺悔禮謝して問て曰く、如何是學人の自己なる。禪師の曰、丙丁童子來求火。則公、言下に大に佛法を悟りき。

---

65 **Question** (*tōte iwaku* 問曰): This section corresponds to sections 61-62 in the Gentō text.

V1. Talk on Pursuing the Way *Bendōwa* 辨道話   207

Long ago, when a certain Chan Master Ze was serving as the monastic comptroller in the assembly of Chan Master Fayan, Chan Master Fayan asked him, "Comptroller Ze, how long have you been in my assembly?"

The Honorable Ze said, "I've served in the Master's assembly for three years already."

Chan Master said, "You're my junior. Why don't you ever ask me about the buddha dharma?"

The Honorable Ze said, "I shouldn't deceive the Reverend. Previously, when I was with Chan Master Qingfeng, I fully understood what is ease and joy in the buddha dharma."

Chan Master said, "What words enabled you to enter it?"

The Honorable Ze said, "I once asked Qingfeng, 'What is this student's self?' Qingfeng said, '*The bingding youth comes seeking fire.*'"

Fayan said, "Good words. But I'm afraid you didn't understand them."

The Honorable Ze said, "*Bing* and *ding* belong to fire. I understood that seeking fire with fire is like seeking the self with the self."

Chan Master said, "I knew it. You haven't understood it. If the buddha dharma were like this, it would never have come down to us today."

At this, the Honorable Ze was upset and immediately left. On the road, he thought, "The Chan Master is renowned everywhere as a wise friend; moreover, he is a guide for five hundred people. Surely, his warning me of my error has merit."

He returned to the Chan Master, repented, made bows in apology, and asked, "What is this student's self?"

The Chan Master said, "*The bingding youth comes seeking fire.*"

At these words, the Honorable Ze had a great awakening to the buddha dharma.

[V1:49] {2:553}

明に知りぬ、自己佛法の領解を以て、佛法を知れりと云にはあらず、と云事を。若自己解會を佛法とせば、禪師、先の言を以て導びくべからず、又、しかの如く禁べからず。修行の儀則を咨問し、一向に坐禪辨道して、一知半解を留むる事なかれ。諸佛の妙法、其の功、虚かるべきにあらず。

We clearly see here that understanding that the self is the buddha dharma does not mean that one has known the buddha dharma. If understanding the self were the buddha dharma, the Chan Master would not have guided him with the above words, nor would he have admonished him like this. Just inquire of the procedures for practice, single-mindedly pursue the way in seated meditation, and do not stop at a single knowledge and a half understanding. The merit of the wondrous technique of the buddha dharma will not be in vain.

208 DŌGEN'S *SHŌBŌGENZŌ* VOLUME VII

[V1:50]

問曰、乾唐の古今を聞に、或は竹のおとを听て道を悟り、或は花の色を見て心を明むる者あり。況や、釋迦大師は、明星を見し時、道を證し、阿難尊者は、利竿を倒れし處に法を明めしのみにあらず、六代より後、五家の間に、一言半句の下に、心地を明らむる事多し。彼れ等、必ずしも坐禪辦道せる者のみならんや。示曰、古今の際に、見色明心し、聞聲悟道せし當人、共に辦道に擬議量無く、直下第二人無き事を知るべし。

Question: We hear that in the past and present of India and the Tang, there were those who awakened to the way upon hearing the sound of bamboo, or those who clarified the mind upon seeing the color of flowers; not to mention that Great Master Śākyamuni verified the way when he saw the morning star, or that Venerable Ānanda clarified the dharma at the toppling of the flagpole.[66] And not only that but, after the sixth generation, among the five houses, there were many who clarified the mind ground at a single word or half a line. Were they invariably only those who had previously pursued the way in seated meditation?

Answer: We should know that those people who, in past and present, saw the color and clarified the mind or heard sounds and awakened to the way were all, without pondering or conjecturing in their pursuit of the way, right here, without a second person.

[V1:51]

問曰、西天及び神丹國は、人、もとより質直にして、佛法を以て教化するに、いと早く會入す。我が國は、昔より人に仁智少くして、正種つもり難し。況や、此國の出家人は、大國の在家にも猶劣れり。舉世愚にして、心量、狭少也。有爲の功を執して、事相の善をのみ好む。如是族、坐禪すとも、忽に佛法の無上甚深なるを證すべきにあらず、況や。示曰、所謂此の國の人、未だ仁智あまねからず、人又迂曲なり。辟ひ正直の法を示すとも、甘露返て毒となりぬべし。名利には赴き易く、惑執融け難し。然れども、佛法に證入する事、必ずしも人天の世智を以て出世の舟航とするには有らず。佛在世にも、てまりによりて四果を證し、袈裟を偸み、かけて、悟を開きし、共に愚暗の族、擬狂の畜類也。但し、正信の二つなきに助けらるれば、迷を離るる事速也。

Question: In Sindh to the West and in the Land of Cīnasthāna, people are fundamentally straightforward, and, when taught the buddha dharma, they are quick to understand it.[67] In our land, from long ago, the benevolent and wise have been few, and the true seeds have been hard to accumulate. Not to mention that the renunciants of this land are inferior to the householders of the great countries. Our whole world is stupid; our

---

66 **Question** (*tōte iwaku* 問曰): This section corresponds to sections 65-66 in the Gentō text.

67 **Question** (*tōte iwaku* 問曰): This section corresponds to section 67 and the first part of 68 in the Gentō text.

V1. Talk on Pursuing the Way *Bendōwa* 辦道話 209

mentality, narrow and petty. Attached to conditioned merit, we delight only in superficial goods. How could such a people, even if they practice seated meditation, quickly verify the buddha dharma, unsurpassed and most profound?

Answer: As you say, among the people of this kingdom, benevolence and wisdom are not widespread, and the people are disingenuous. Even if we instruct them with the correct, straightforward dharma, the sweet nectar will become a poison. They easily turn toward fame and profit and find it hard to disperse their delusions and attachments. Nevertheless, entering verification of the buddha dharma is not necessarily building a vessel to appear in the world by the worldly wisdom of humans and devas. Even when the Buddha was in the world, both the one who verified the fourth fruit because of a handball and the one who opened awakening by pilfering and donning a *kāṣāya* were foolish and ignorant, deranged beasts. Yet, when they were saved by faith and nothing else, their escape from delusion was quick.

[V1:52] {2:554}

亦、癡老の比丘黙坐せしを見て、設齋の信女、悟りを開きし、これ智によ らず、文によらず、言を不待、かたりを不待。但し、是れ正信に扶られた り。

Again, upon seeing a stupid old bhikṣu sitting silently and offering him a meal, a woman of faith opened an awakening; this was not based on wisdom, not based on texts, did not depend on words, did not depend on explanations: she was just aided by true faith.[68]

[V1:53]

又、釋教の、三千界に弘めらるる事、纔に二千餘年の前後也。剎士の区区 なる、必ずしも仁智の國にあらず、又利智聰明のみあらんや。然れば有れ ども、如來の正法、もとより不思議の大功德力を備へて、時至れば其の剎 土に廣まる。人、まさに正信修行すれば、利鈍を不分、齊しく得道するな り。我が國の人、智解おろかなり、佛法を會すべからずと思事なかれ。依 之退せば、何れの時か佛法修行のみにおもむかん。

Moreover, the spread of the teachings of Śākya across the trichiliocosm has taken barely two thousand some years, more or less. These lands are varied, not necessarily countries of benevolence and wisdom, [their people] also not necessarily sharp witted and clear. While this may be the case, still, when the time comes, the true dharma of the Tathāgata, endowed from the start with the inconceivable power of great merit, spreads throughout these lands. When the people practice with true faith, they equally gain the way, whether they are sharp or dull. Do not think

68 **Again** (*mata* 亦): This section corresponds to the last part of section 68 in the Gentō text.

210
DŌGEN'S *SHŌBŌGENZŌ* VOLUME VII

that, as the understanding of the people of our kingdom is stupid, they cannot understand the buddha dharma. If they regress because of it, will they not at some point devote themselves solely to practice of the buddha dharma?[69]

[V1:54]

大宋國に、張天覺丞相と云人有りき。護法論を作れるに云、縦へ參じて未徹、猶佛種の因を結ぶ、學して未だ不成、尚ほ人天の果を益す。誠に佛種生長の因果、何によりてか修する道を勸めざらん。又、人皆般若の正信豊なれども、承當する事希なり、受用する事今ま正しきならじ。

In the Land of the Great Song, there was a certain Prime Minister Zhang Tianjue.[70] In his *Treatise in Defense of the Dharma*, he said that, inquiring into it without mastering it, "still forms the cause of the buddha seed; studying it without completing it, still enhances the effect of human and deva." Truly, as the cause and effect of growing the buddha seed, why would one not recommend the way of practice? Moreover, although people are all rich in the true faith of prajñā, they rarely accede to it, and their enjoyment of it is not now correct.[71]

* * * * *

---

69 **If they regress because of it** (*kore ni yorite tai seba* 依之退せば): This sentence does not occur in section 69 of the Gentō text.

70 **In the Land of the Great Song** (*Dai Sō koku* 大宋國): Except for its final sentence, this section has no parallel in the Gentō text.

Prime Minister Zhang Tianjue (*Chō Tenkaku jōshō* 張天覺丞相): I.e., Zhang Shangying 張商英 (*Chō Shōei*, 1043-1122). The words attributed to him here represent a loose Japanese rendering of a passage in his *Hufa lun* 護法論 (T.2114.52:641b15-17):

> 故古德云、聞而不信、尚結佛種之因。學而未成、猶益人天之福。

> Therefore, an ancient worthy has said, "Hearing it without believing it still forms the cause of the buddha seed; studying it without completing it still enhances the good fortune of human and deva."

The "ancient worthy" (*gude* 古德) mentioned here may refer to Yongming Yanshou 永明延壽 (904-975), in his *Yongming Zhijiao chanshi weixin jue* 永明智覺禪師唯心訣 (T.2018.48:996c21-22).

71 **Moreover** (*mata* 又): This sentence corresponds roughly to the final lines in section 69 of the Gentō text, which read,

> いはむや、人みな般若の正種ゆたかなり。ただ承當することまれに、受用することいまだしきならし。

> Needless to say, people are all endowed with the true seeds of prajñā; they just rarely accede to it and have yet to enjoy it.

their enjoyment of it is not now correct (*juyū suru koto ima tadashiki naraji* 受用する事今ま正しきならじ): Suggests a confusion with the Gentō text's *juyū suru koto imadashiki narashi* 受用することいまだしきならし).

V1. Talk on Pursuing the Way *Bendōwa* 辨道話 211

[V1:55] {2:555}

先の問答往來し、賓主相交する事妄りがはし。幾か、花なきそらに花をな
さしむる事を得ると云へども、釣を離れて三寸に道を快よくせん人を待つ
のみにあらず。此國、坐禪辨道におきて、未だその宗旨を傳へ知らん。志
さん者、可悲。此故に、異域の見聞を集め、明師の眞訣を記し、參學の願
はんに傳へんとす。此外、叢林の規範、及寺院の格式、いま、しめすにい
とまあらず、又、草草にすべからず。

The preceding back and forth of questions and answers, with its alternation of guest and host, is rather random. I may have managed to create
a fair number of flowers in a flowerless sky, but I am not merely waiting
for someone quick to say something "three inches from the hook."[72] In
this land, the essential point of pursuit of the way in seated meditation
has not been transmitted and understood, and those who aspire [to learn
it] are to be pitied. For this reason, I have collected what I saw and heard
in the foreign regions, recorded the true arcanum of the illumined masters, and sought to convey them to those who wish to study them. Apart
from this, I do not have time here to explain the rules and regulations of
the monastic groves, or the customs and procedures of the temples and
cloisters, which, moreover, should not be treated perfunctorily.

---

72 **waiting for someone quick to say something "three inches from the hook"** (*chō
o hanarete sanzun ni dō o kokoroyoku sen hito o matsu* 釣を離れて三寸に道を快よく
せん人を待つ): I.e., expecting someone to give a profound response. A rare instance
in the "Bendōwa," not found in section 70 of the Gentō text, of language reflecting a
Chan saying — in this case, the words of Chuanzi ("The Boatman") Decheng 船子德
誠 (dates unknown), when Jiashan Shanhui 夾山善會 (805-881) visited his boat. Their
conversation can be found in several Chinese sources (see, e.g., *Jingde chuandeng lu*
景德傳燈錄, T.2076.51:315b24-28; *Zongmen tongyao ji* 宗門統要集, ZTS.1:150c2-6);
here is the version recorded in Dōgen's *shinji Shōbōgenzō* 眞字正法眼藏, (DZZ.5:168-
172, case 90):

師曰、甚處學得来。夾曰、非耳目之所到。師曰、一句合頭語、萬劫繋驢橛。又
問、垂糸千尺、意在深潭。離釣三寸、子何不道。夾擬開口。師便以篙打落水
中。夾纔出水上船、師曰、道道。夾又擬開口。師又打。夾山於是忽然大悟。

The Master [Decheng] said, "Where have you been studying?"
Jia said, "Where eye and ear don't reach."
The Master said, "Words of a single line in accord; a donkey's tethering stake for ten
thousand kalpas."
Again, he asked, "I let down a line a thousand feet; its meaning lies in a deep pool.
You're three inches from the hook. Why don't you say something?"
Jia was about to open his mouth, when the Master hit him with the boat pole, knock-
ing him into the water. When Jia reemerged and climbed back in the boat, the Master
said, "Say something! Say something!"
Again, Jai was about to speak, and again the Master hit him. With that, Jiashan suddenly had a great awakening.

212 · DŌGEN'S *SHŌBŌGENZŌ* VOLUME VII

[V1:56]

凡我朝は、龍海の以東に、所として雲烟遥かなれども、欽明・用明の前
後より、秋方の佛法東漸する、即人の幸なり。しかあるに、名相事緣、
しげく紛て、修行に煩ふべし。此門不然。佛像・經典を不借、依所道場
を無揀。只破衣綴盂を生涯として、青岩白石のほとりに茅を結び、端坐修
練するに、佛向上の大道忽に圓通して、一生參學の大事速かに究竟するも
の也。

In sum, although our kingdom is located east of the dragon seas, far
across the clouds and mist, to the good fortune of its people, since around
the time of Kinmei and Yōmei, the buddha dharma from the autumnal
direction gradually came east.[73] However, matters of names and forms
were seriously confused and must present problems for practice. This
tradition is not like that: it does not make use of buddha images or scriptures; hence, it does not select practice places.[74] While we just lead a life
of torn robes and mended bowls, thatching reed roofs by green crags and
white boulders, as we train ourselves sitting erect, the matter beyond the
buddha is immediately perfected, and the great matter of a lifetime of
study is quickly brought to completion.

[V1:57]

是即、佛佛祖祖單傳し直指して、今に及ぶ。鶏足の遺蹤なるべし、龍牙の
誠敕なるべし。其の坐禪の儀則は、過ぬる嘉禄中、撰集せりし普勧坐禪儀
に依行すべし。

This is what buddha after buddha and ancestor after ancestor uniquely
transmitted and directly indicated reaching us in the present.[75] It is the
admonition of Longya; it is the style bequeathed at Cock's Foot. The
procedures for its seated meditation should be carried out according to
the *Universal Promotion of the Principles of Seated Meditation* that I
composed during the preceding Karoku.

[V1:58]

其佛法を弘通こと、王敕を待べしといへども、再靈山の遺囑をおもへば、
國土は本佛國也、佛法を弘通せむに妨ぐべからず。人は皆佛子なり、誰か
背く者有らん。況や今百萬億刹に現出せる王公相将、皆他生、佛法護持の

73　**In sum** (*ooyoso* 凡): This section corresponds to the first part of section 71 in the
Gentō text.

74　**This tradition is not like that** (*kono mon wa shikarazu* 此門不然): This sentence
does not occur in the Gentō text. The argument here seems to be that the worship of a
particular buddha or scripture leads to institutional division.

75　**This is what buddha after buddha and ancestor after ancestor uniquely transmitted and directly indicated reaching us in the present** (*kore sunawachi, butsubutsu
soso tanden shi jikishi shite, ima ni oyobu* 是即、佛佛祖祖單傳し直指して、今に及
ぶ): This sentence does not occur in the Gentō text. The remainder of the section corresponds to the last part of section 71 in that text.

V1. Talk on Pursuing the Way *Bendōwa* 辨道話 213

願志に引れて生來せる者なり、佛の使いと云べし。然れば即、依・正とも
にふるき佛緣あり、今を初て思べきにあらず。如是の理に、此の短簡を以
て、雲遊萍寄の衲子に流通し、捨邪歸正の宗匠に直指すべし。

While it may be that the propagation of the buddha dharma should await a royal decree, when we recall once more the final bequest on Vulture Peak, the land is originally a buddha land, and there should be no hindrance to disseminating the buddha dharma.[76] The people are all the children of the Buddha; who would turn their back on him? Not to mention that the kings and dukes, magistrates and ministers who now appear in hundreds of myriads of *koṭis* of realms were all reborn led by their vow in other lives to protect the buddha dharma; they may be called the emissaries of the Buddha. Thus, their secondary and primary recompense has ancient connections with the Buddha and should not be thought of as beginning now. Reasoning thus, we should disseminate this brief missive to the patch-robed, like wandering clouds and floating weeds, and point directly for teachers who have abandoned the false and taken refuge in the true.

于時寬喜辛卯中秋日、入宋傳法沙門住觀音導利院道元記
On the mid-autumn day, in the junior metal year of the rabbit, in Kangi [12 September 1231], written by Dōgen of Kannon Dōri Cloister, Śramaṇa who entered the Song and transmitted the dharma[77]

于時元德四年壬申正慶改元十一月七日、於能州洞谷山永光寺知賓寮西窓
書寫畢。旨國記
Copied at the west window of the Guest Reception Quarters of Yōkō Monastery, Mount Tōkoku, Nōshū; seventh day, eleventh month, senior water year of the monkey, the fourth year of Gentoku (renamed the first year of Shōkyō) [25 November 1332], by Shikoku[78]

---

76 **propagation of the buddha dharma** (*buppō o guzū koto* 佛法を弘通こと): This section corresponds roughly to sections 71-72 in the Gentō text.

77 **mid-autumn day** (*chūshū* 中秋): I.e., the Harvest Moon Festival, on the fifteenth of the eighth lunar month. In the MS, the date is accompanied by a note:

御飯朝以來四年後也。

This is four years after his [i.e., Dōgen's] return to this kingdom.

78 **Yōkō Monastery** 永光寺: Founded by Keizan Jōkin 瑩山紹瑾 (1268–1325).

renamed the first year of Shōkyō (*Shōkyō kaigen* 正慶改元): The era name was changed from Gentoku 元德 to Shōkyō 正慶 at the end of the fourth lunar month.

永正十二年乙亥八月廿八日奉記之、以奉報答高祖大和尚之二百六十三
年忌辰、壽雲比丘謹敬記之

*Copied this on the twenty-eighth day, eighth month, junior wood year
of the pig, twelfth year of Eishō [5 October 1515], as an offering in
gratitude to the Most Reverend Eminent Ancestor on his two hundred
sixty-third memorial. Respectfully copied by Bhikṣu Juun*[79]

---

79 The date is accompanied by a note:

當年二百六十三年也。

This year is the two hundred sixty-third year.

Most Reverend Eminent Ancestor (*Kōso daioshō* 高祖大和尚): I.e., Dōgen, who died
in 1252.

Bhikṣu Juun (*Juun biku* 壽雲比丘): I.e., Juun Ryōchin 壽雲良椿 (d. 1516), abbot of
Shōbōji 正法寺. His MS includes the following two appended texts, not reproduced in
Kawamura's edition, that reflect passages in the sixty-chapter *Shōbōgenzō*:

1) Variation on a line in the "Sanji gō" chapter (translated above as T8).

三時業事、一生順現法受業、二生順次生受業、三生順後次受業。

Karma of the three times: first birth [sic], karma experienced in the present; second
birth, karma experienced in the next life; third birth, karma experienced in lives after
the next.

2) Variation on a verse quoted in the "Hotsu bodai shin" chapter (translated above as T4).

發心畢竟二無別、如是二心先心難、自未得度先度他、是故我禮初發心。又、初
發已爲天人師、勝出聲聞及圓覺、如是發心過三界、是故得名最無上。

Bringing forth the mind and the ultimate — the two are without distinction;
But of these two minds, the former mind is more difficult.
One delivers others before one is delivered oneself;
Therefore, I pay obeisance to the initial bringing forth of the mind.

Again,

Once it is brought forth, one is a teacher to devas and humans;
Surpassing the *śrāvakas* and perfectly awakened [sic].
Bringing forth the mind like this surpasses the three realms;
Therefore, it can be called completely unsurpassed.

Treasury of the True Dharma Eye
Variant Text 2

The Inheritance Certificate
Shisho
嗣書

The Inheritance Certificate

Shisho

Introduction

This text, preserved at the Kōjakuji 香積寺, in Hiroshima Prefecture, represents what is thought to have been a draft version of the work of the same title occurring as number 39 of the seventy-five-chapter *Shōbō-genzō* (as well as number 8 of fascicle 2 in the twenty-eight-text collection, and number 16 in the ninety-five-chapter edition). It bears a colophon, identical to the seventy-five-chapter *Shōbōgenzō* text, dating the composition to May of 1241, at Dōgen's Kōshōji.

The Kōjakuji manuscript represents a seventeenth-century copy of a manuscript in Dōgen's own hand once owned by the monastery, which had the holograph cut into twenty-six sheets and distributed to its patrons. Today, fourteen of these fragments have been recovered (as identified in the head notes of the Kawamura edition of the text translated below here).

With a few notable exceptions, the text varies little from the seventy-five-chapter *Shōbōgenzō* version. The annotation of the following translation does not repeat the information provided for that version; rather, it is limited to noting how the sections of the two texts are related and to pointing out their occasional significant differences.

正法眼藏拾遺二
Treasury of the True Dharma Eye
Variant Text 2

嗣書
The Inheritance Certificate
(草案本・香積寺所蔵)
(Draft text, Kōjakuji collection)

{2:557}

観音導利興聖寶林寺

Kannon Dōri Kōshō Hōrin Monastery[1]

[V2:1]

佛佛、かならず佛佛に嗣法し、祖祖、かならず祖祖に嗣法する。これ證契なり、これ單傳なり、このゆえに無上菩提なり。佛にあらざれば、佛を印證するにあたはず、佛の印證をえざれば、佛となることなし。佛にあらずよりは、たれかこれを最尊なりとし、無上なりと印可することあらん。

Buddha after buddha invariably inherits the dharma from buddha after buddha; ancestor after ancestor invariably inherits the dharma from ancestor after ancestor. This is the verification and accord; this is the unique transmission. Therefore, it is unsurpassed bodhi. If one is not a buddha, one cannot certify a buddha; if one does not receive the certification of a buddha, there is no becoming a buddha. Insofar as one is not a buddha, who would deem this as most honored or certify it as unsurpassed?

[V2:2]

佛に印證せらるるに、無師獨悟するなり、無自獨證するなり。このゆえに、佛佛證嗣し祖祖證契すといふなり。この道理のていたらくは、佛佛にあらざるがあきらむべきにあらず、いはんや十地・等覺の所量ならんや。いかにいはんや、經師・論師等の、ゆめにもきかざるところなり。たとひきくとも、きくべからず、佛佛相嗣するがゆえに。

When one receives the certification of a buddha, one awakens alone without a teacher, one awakens alone without a self. Therefore, it is said that buddha after buddha verifies and inherits, ancestor after ancestor

---

1 **Kannon Dōri Kōshō Hōrin Monastery** 観音導利興聖寶林寺: This notice of the site of composition does not occur in the seventy-five-chapter *Shōbōgenzō* text.

verifies and accords. The way this principle really is cannot be clarified if one is not [one among] buddha after buddha; how could it be something measured by those on the ten stages or virtual awakening? How much less is it something that sūtra masters, treatise masters, and the like, hear of even in their dreams. Even if they did hear of it, they would not be able to hear it, for buddha after buddha inherits it.[2]

[V2:3] {2:558}

しるべし、佛道は、佛佛の究盡、佛佛にして佛佛にあらざるときなし。たとえば、石は石に相嗣し、玉は玉に相嗣することあり。又菊も相嗣し、松も印證するに、みな前菊後菊如如なり、前松後松究盡なるがごとし。しかあるをきかざる人、あきらめざるともがらあるは、いはゆる佛佛相傳の道得にあふといえども、いかにいふ道得なりとあやしむにもおよばず。佛佛相嗣し、祖祖證契すといふ領覽あることなし。あはれむべし、佛種族に相似せりといえども、佛子にあらざることを、子佛にあらざることを。

We should know that the way of the buddhas is the exhaustive investigation of buddha after buddha; there is no time that it is not buddha after buddha, as buddha after buddha. It is like, for example, stones inheriting from stones, and jewels inheriting from jewels; like when chrysanthemums inherit from each other, and pines certify each other, the *prior chrysanthemums and later chrysanthemums are all such*, and the *prior pines and later pines are all an exhaustive investigation* [of each other].[3] People who have not heard, those who have not clarified, that this is so, though they may encounter the saying "transmission of buddha after buddha," do not even wonder what this saying means.[4] They have no comprehension that buddha after buddha inherits from each other, and ancestor after ancestor verifies and accords with each other. How pitiful that, though they may resemble the family of the buddha, they are not the children of the buddha, are not child buddhas.

---

2 **for buddha after buddha inherits it** (*butsubutsu sōshi suru ga yue ni* 佛佛相嗣するがゆえに): I.e., only those who inherit it can truly hear it. This phrase occurs in the seventy-five-chapter *Shōbōgenzō* text as the introductory clause of the first sentence in section 3.

3 **prior pines and later pines are all an exhaustive investigation [of each other]** (*zen shō go shō gūjin naru* 前松後松究盡なる): Presumably, meaning that, like buddha after buddha, they perfectly replicate each other. The seventy-five-chapter *Shōbōgenzō* text reads here simply:

前松後松如如なるがごとし。

The prior pines and later pines are all such.

4 **those who have not clarified** (*akiramezaru tomogara aru wa* あきらめざるともがらあるは): Ignoring the final *aru* ある; the seventy-five-chapter *Shōbōgenzō* text reads simply *tomogara wa* ともがらは。

V2. The Inheritance Certificate *Shisho* 嗣書   219

[V2:4]
六祖、あるとき衆にしめしていはく、七佛より慧能にいたるに四十祖あ
り、慧能より七佛にいたるに四十祖あり。

The Sixth Ancestor once addressed the assembly saying, "From the seven buddhas through Huineng, there are forty buddhas; from Huineng through the seven buddhas, there are forty ancestors."

[V2:5]
この道理、あきらかに參究すべし。いはゆる七佛は、過去莊嚴劫に出現せ
るもあり、賢劫に出現せるもあり。しかあるを、四十祖につらぬるは佛道
なり、佛嗣なり。六祖より向上に七佛にいたれば、四十祖の佛嗣なり、七
佛より向上して六祖にいたれば、四十佛の佛嗣なるべし。佛道祖道、かく
のごとし。證契にあらず、佛祖にあらざれば、佛智慧にあらず、祖究盡
にあらざるなり。いはゆる、しばらく四十祖といふは、ちかきをあぐるな
り。深遠に、佛佛あひ嗣法せることの不退不轉なり、不斷不絕なるを、佛
學するなり。その佛儀は、釋迦牟尼佛は、七佛以前に成道すといえども、
ひさしく迦葉佛に嗣法せるなり、降生より三十歳、十二月に成道すといえ
ども、すなはち七佛以前に成道せり、又、迦葉佛は、釋迦牟尼佛に嗣法す
ると、參究するなり。この道理をしらざるには、佛道をあきらめず、佛道
あきらめざれば、佛嗣にあらず。佛嗣といふことは、佛子といふことな
り。

This principle, we should clearly investigate.[5] Of the "seven buddhas," some appeared in the past, Adornment kalpa, some appeared in the Worthy kalpa. Nevertheless, what links the forty ancestors is the way of the buddhas, the inheritance of the buddhas.

When we go beyond the Sixth Ancestor through the seven buddhas, it is the inheritance of the buddhas of forty ancestors; and when we go above the seven buddhas through the Sixth Ancestor, it should be the inheritance of the buddhas of forty buddhas.[6] The way of the buddhas, the way of the ancestors, is like this. If it is not verification and accord, not buddhas and ancestors, then it is not the wisdom of the buddhas, not the exhaustive investigation of the ancestors.[7] That we talk for the moment of "forty ancestors" is just to bring up the ones that are close to us.

---

5 **This principle, we should clearly investigate** (*kono dōri, akiraka ni sankyū su beshi* この道理、あきらかに參究すべし): The first three sentences of this section correspond to section 5 in the seventy-five-chapter *Shōbōgenzō* text.

6 **When we go above the Sixth Ancestor through the seven buddhas** (*Rokuso yori kōjō ni shichi butsu ni itareba* 六祖より向上に七佛にいたれば): This and the following four sentences correspond to section 6 in the seventy-five-chapter *Shōbōgenzō* text.

7 **not the exhaustive investigation of the ancestors** (*so gūjin ni arazaru* 祖究盡にあらざる): The seventy-five-chapter *Shōbōgenzō* text continues here:

佛智慧にあらざれば、佛信受なし、祖究盡にあらざれば、祖證契せず。

220 DŌGEN'S *SHŌBŌGENZŌ* VOLUME VII

It is Buddhist study of [the fact that] the mutual inheritance, profound and far-reaching, of the dharma of buddha after buddha is irreversible and unchanging, uninterrupted and unceasing.[8] That deportment of the buddhas is such that, although Buddha Śākyamuni may have attained the way before the seven buddhas, long after, he inherited the dharma from Buddha Kāśyapa; although he may have attained the way in the twelfth month, thirty years from his descent to birth, he attained the way before the seven buddhas.[9]

Moreover, we investigate the fact that Buddha Kāśyapa inherited the dharma from Buddha Śākyamuni.[10] When we do not know this principle, we have not clarified the way of the buddhas; and, if we have not clarified the way of the buddhas, we are not the heirs of the buddhas. To be an heir of the buddhas means to be a child of the buddhas.

[V2:6] {2:559}

釋迦牟尼佛、あるとき、阿難にとはしむ、過去諸佛は、これたれが弟子なるぞ。釋迦牟尼佛いはく、過去諸佛は、これ我釋迦牟尼佛の弟子なり。

Buddha Śākyamuni was once asked by Ānanda, "Whose disciples were the buddhas of the past?"[11]

Buddha Śākyamuni said, "The buddhas of the past were my, Buddha Śākyamuni's, disciples."

[V2:7]

諸佛の佛儀、かくのごとし。この諸佛に奉覲して、佛嗣を成熟せむ、すなはち佛佛の佛道にてあるべし。

If it is not the wisdom of the buddhas, there is no trust in the buddha; if it is not the exhaustive investigation of the ancestors, the ancestors do not verify and accord.

8   **It is Buddhist study** (*butsugaku suru nari* 佛學するなり): The unexpressed grammatical subject here is probably the Sixth Ancestor's saying above. This and the following sentence parallel section 7 in the seventy-five-chapter *Shōbōgenzō* text.

9   **he attained the way before the seven buddhas** (*shichi butsu izen ni jōdō seri* 七佛以前に成道せり): The seventy-five-chapter *Shōbōgenzō* text reads here:

降生より三十歳、十二月八日に成道すといへども、七佛以前の成道なり、諸佛齊肩同時の成道なり、諸佛以前の成道なり、一切の諸佛より末上の成道なり

Although he may have attained the way on the eighth day of the twelfth month, thirty years from his descent to birth, it was an attainment of the way preceding that of the seven buddhas, an attainment of the way equal to and simultaneous with that of the other buddhas, an attainment of the way preceding that of the other buddhas, an attainment of the way first before all the buddhas.

10   **Moreover** (*mata* 又): The remainder of this section corresponds to section 8 in the seventy-five-chapter *Shōbōgenzō* text.

11   **Buddha Śākyamuni** (*Shakamuni butsu* 釋迦牟尼佛): This section corresponds to section 9 in the seventy-five-chapter *Shōbōgenzō* text.

V2. The Inheritance Certificate *Shisho* 嗣書

The buddha deportment of the buddhas is like this. Attending these buddhas, receiving and fulfilling the buddhas' inheritance — precisely this must be the way of the buddhas of buddha after buddha.[12]

* * * * *

[V2:8]

この佛道、かならず嗣法するとき、さだめて嗣書あり。もし嗣法なく、嗣書なきは、すなはち天然外道なり。佛道、もし嗣法を決定するにあらずよりは、いかでか今日にいたらん。これによりて、佛佛なるには、さだめて佛嗣佛の嗣書あるなり、佛嗣佛の嗣書をうるなり。その嗣書のていたらく、日月星辰を佛嗣しても嗣法すべし、皮肉骨髓を得せしめても嗣法すべし、正法眼藏を附しても嗣法すべし。あるいは袈裟を相嗣し、あるいは拄杖を相嗣し、あるいは松枝を相嗣し、あるいは拂子を相嗣す。あるいは優曇華を相嗣し、あるいは、金襴衣を相嗣す。靸鞋の相嗣あり、竹箆の相嗣あり。

In this way of the buddhas, whenever someone inherits the dharma there is definitely an inheritance certificate. To be without dharma inheritance, without the inheritance certificate — this is an other path of natural occurrence. If there were no determining dharma inheritance in the way of the buddhas, how could it have reached us today? Accordingly, those who are [in the lineage of] buddha after buddha, definitely have inheritance certificates of a buddha inheriting from a buddha, definitely receive inheritance certificates of a buddha inheriting from a buddha. As for the nature of those inheritance certificates, we should inherit the dharma by a buddha inheritance of the sun, moon, and stars; we should inherit the dharma by getting the skin, flesh, bones, and marrow; we should inherit the dharma by a bequest of the treasury of the true dharma eye.[13] Some inherit a *kaṣāya*; some inherit a staff; some inherit a pine branch; some inherit a whisk; some inherit an *udumbara* flower; some inherit a gold brocade robe. There is an inheritance of shoes; there is an inheritance of bamboo staffs.

12　**The buddha deportment of the buddhas** (*shobutsu no butsugi* 諸佛の佛儀): This section corresponds to section 10 in the seventy-five-chapter *Shōbōgenzō* text.

13　**we should inherit the dharma by a bequest of the treasury of the true dharma eye** (*Shōbōgenzō o fushite mo shihō su beshi* 正法眼藏を附しても嗣法すべし): This clause is not found in the corresponding section 11 of the seventy-five-chapter *Shōbōgenzō* text.

222 DŌGEN'S *SHŌBŌGENZŌ* VOLUME VII

[V2:9]

これらの嗣法を相嗣するとき、あるいは指血して書嗣し、あるいは舌血して書嗣す、あるいは油乳をもてかき、嗣法する、ともにこれ嗣書なり。嗣せるもの、得せるもの、ともにこれ佛嗣なり。まことにそれ佛祖となるとき、嗣法かならず現成す。現成すること期せざれどもきたり、もとめざれども嗣得せる佛祖、ままにおほし。嗣法あるは、かならず佛佛祖祖なり。

When these dharma inheritances are inherited, blood from a finger may be used to document the inheritance, or blood from the tongue may be used to document the inheritance; or the dharma inheritance may be written with oil or milk: all of these are inheritance certificates.[14] Both the one who has made the inheritance and the one who has received it are heirs of the buddha. Truly, whenever they become buddhas and ancestors, dharma inheritance always occurs. When it occurs, it comes unanticipated, and there are many buddhas and ancestors who have inherited the dharma although they did not seek it. Those who have dharma inheritance are invariably buddha after buddha and ancestor after ancestor.

* * * * *

[V2:10] {2:560}

第二十八祖、西來よりこのかた、東土には、佛家に嗣法あることをきくなり、嗣法あることをみるなり、それよりさきは、かつていまだきかざりしなり。西天の論師・法師等、およばず、しらざるところなり。あはれむべし、十聖・三賢の境界、およばざるところ、三藏義學の呪術師等、ありとだにもうたがはざるものなり。かなしむべし、道器なる人身をうけて、いたづらに教網にまつはれて透脱の法をしらず、跳出の期を期せざらん。かるがゆえに、學道を、審細にすべき、參究の志氣を、もはらすべきなり。

Ever since the Twenty-eighth Ancestor came from the west, in the Land of the East, the fact that the house of the buddhas has dharma inheritance has been heard, the fact that it has dharma inheritance has been observed.[15] Prior to that, it had never been heard. It is something unreached by, unknown to, the likes of the treatise masters and dharma masters of Sindh in the West. What a pity that it is something unreached in the realm of the ten sages and three worthies, while the masters of spells among the doctrinal scholars of the tripiṭaka, and the like, do not even wonder whether it exists. How sad that, while receiving the human body that is a vessel of the way, being futilely entangled in a web of doctrine, they

---

14 **When these dharma inheritances are inherited** (*korera no shihō o sōshi suru toki* これらの嗣法を相嗣するとき): This section corresponds to section 12 in the seventy-five-chapter *Shōbōgenzō* text.

15 **Ever since the Twenty-eighth Ancestor came from the west** (*dai nijūhachi so, seirai yori kono kata* 第二十八祖、西來よりこのかた): This section corresponds to section 13 in the seventy-five-chapter *Shōbōgenzō* text.

V2. The Inheritance Certificate *Shisho* 嗣書

do not know how to transcend it and have no expectation of a chance to spring forth from it. Therefore, we should study the way with the utmost care and should be single-minded in our resolve to investigate it.

[V2:11]

道元在宋のとき、嗣書を禮拜することをえしに、多般の嗣書あり。そのなかに、惟一西堂とて、天童に掛錫せしは、越上人なり、前住廣福寺の堂頭なり、先師と同郷人なり。先師、つねにいはく、境風は、一西堂に問取すべし。

When Dōgen was in the Song and was able to pay obeisance to inheritance certificates, there were many types of inheritance certificates.[16] Among them was [one shown to me by] the West Hall Weiyi, a person of Yue enrolled at Tiantong, who had formerly served as head of hall of Guangfu Monastery. He was from the same birthplace as my former master. My former master always said, "You should ask West Hall Yi about the customs of the region."

[V2:12]

あるとき、西堂いはく、古蹟の可觀は、人間の珍玩なり、いくばくか見來せる。道元いはく、見來せることなし。ときに西堂いはく、吾那裏に壱軸の古蹟あり、甚麼次第なり、與老兄看。

On one occasion, the West Hall said, "To be able to inspect old calligraphy is one of the rare pleasures of a human. How many have you seen?"

Dōgen said, "I've never seen one."[17]

Whereupon, the West Hall said, "In my place, I have a scroll of old calligraphy, somewhat questionable. *Let me show it to my elder brother.*"

[V2:13]

といひて、携來をみれば、嗣書なり。すなはち、法眼下のにてありけるを、老宿の衣鉢のなかより、えたりけり。惟一長老のにはあらざりけり。かれにかきたりし様は、

His having said that, when I saw what he brought, it was an inheritance certificate.[18] It had been in the lineage of Fayan and had been obtained from among the robe and bowl of an elder. It was not the Senior Weiyi's own. On it was written the following:

16　**When Dōgen was in the Song** (*Dōgen zai Sō no toki* 道元在宋のとき): This section corresponds to section 14 in the seventy-five-chapter *Shōbōgenzō* text.

17　**"I've never seen one"** (*kenrai seru koto nashi* 見來せることなし): The corresponding passage in section 15 of the seventy-five-chapter *Shōbōgenzō* text reads "I've seen only a few" (*kenrai sukunashi* 見來すくなし).

18　**His having said that** (*to iite* といひて): This section corresponds to the second half of section 15 in the seventy-five-chapter *Shōbōgenzō* text.

224 DŌGEN'S *SHŌBŌGENZŌ* VOLUME VII

[V2:14] {2:561}

初祖摩訶迦葉、悟於釋迦牟尼佛、釋迦牟尼佛悟於迦葉佛。

"*The First Ancestor, Mahākāśyapa, was awakened under Buddha Śākyamuni; Buddha Śākyamuni was awakened under Buddha Kāśyapa.*"[19]

[V2:15]

かくのごとくかきたりき。予、これをみしに、正嫡の、かならず正嫡にありけることを、決定す。未曾有の法なり。

It was inscribed like this.[20] Upon seeing it, I became firmly convinced that the direct descendant has invariably been a direct descendant. It is something unprecedented.

[V2:16]

雲門下の嗣書といひて、宗月長老の、天童の首座職に充せりしとき、道元にみせしは、いま嗣書をうる人のつぎかみの師、および西天・東地の佛祖をつらねならべて、そのしたに、嗣書うる人の名字あり。諸佛より直にいまの新祖師の名字につらぬるなり。しかあれば、如來より四十餘代、ともに新嗣の名字へきたれり。たとえば、おのおの新祖にさづけたるがごとし。しかあれば、摩訶迦葉・阿難陀等は、餘門のごとくにつらなれり。

When Elder Zongyue held the position of head seat at Tiantong, he showed Dōgen an inheritance certificate said to be from the Yunmen lineage.[21] The [name of the] master just preceding the recipient of the inheritance certificate was lined up in a row with the buddhas and ancestors of Sindh in the West and the Land of the East, and below those was the name of the recipient of the inheritance certificate. There was a direct connection from the buddhas to the name of the new ancestral master. Thus, it extended from the Tathāgata, through more than forty

---

19 **The First Ancestor, Mahākāśyapa** (*shoso Makakashō* 初祖摩訶迦葉): This section corresponds to the first sentence of section 16 in the seventy-five-chapter *Shōbōgenzō* text.

20 **It was inscribed like this** (*kaku no gotoku kakitariki* かくのごとくかきたりき): This sentence represents the last sentence of section 16 in the seventy-five-chapter *Shōbōgenzō* text. The remaining two sentences here correspond roughly to part of section 17 of the seventy-five-chapter *Shōbōgenzō* text, which reads:

予道元これらを見しに、正嫡の、正嫡に嗣法あることを、決定信受す。未曾見の法なり。佛祖の、冥感して兒孫を護持する時節なり、感激不勝なり。

Upon seeing this, I, Dōgen, became firmly convinced that there is dharma inheritance by a direct descendant from a direct descendant. It was something I had never seen. This was an instance of the buddhas and ancestors using their hidden influence to protect one of their descendants. I was unbearably moved.

21 **When Elder Zongyue held the position of head seat at Tiantong** (*Shūgetsu chōro no, Tendō no shuso shoku ni jū serishi toki* 宗月長老の、天童の首座職に充せりしとき): This section corresponds to section 18 in the seventy-five-chapter *Shōbōgenzō* text.

V2. The Inheritance Certificate *Shisho* 嗣書

generations, down to and including the name of the new heir. It was as if each had bestowed [the transmission] on the new ancestor. Thus, Mahākāśyapa, Ānanda, and the rest, were lined up as in other traditions.

[V2:17]

ときに道元、宗月首座にとふ、和尚、いま五家、宗派をつらぬるに、いささかの同異あり。そのこころいかん。西天より嫡嫡相嗣せらば、あに同異あらんや。宗月いはく、たとひ同異はるかなりといふとも、ただまさに、雲門山の佛はかくのごとし、とならうべし。釋迦老子、なによりてか尊重他なる、悟道によりて尊重なり。雲門大師、なにによりてか尊重他なる、悟道によりて尊重なり。

At the time, Dōgen asked the head seat Zongyue, "Reverend, what is the meaning of the fact that there are slight discrepancies in the delineation of the lineages of the present five houses?[22] If they have been inherited from successor to successor from Sindh in the West, how could there be any discrepancies?"

Zongyue said, "Even were the discrepancies vast, you should just think that the buddhas of Mount Yunmen are like this. For what was old man Śākya honored? He was honored for his awakening to the way. For what was Great Master Yunmen honored? He was honored for his awakening to the way."

[V2:18]

道元、この語をきくに、いささか領覧あり。

Upon hearing these words, Dōgen had a slight understanding.[23]

[V2:19] {2:562}

いま江浙に、大刹の主とあるは、おほく臨濟・雲門・洞山等の嗣法なり。しかあるに、臨濟の遠孫と自稱するやから、ままにくわだつる不是あり。いはく、頂相壱副・法語壱軸を請して、嗣法の標準にそなふ。しかあるに、一類のいぬあり、尊宿のほとりにして法語・頂相等を懇請して、かくし、たくわふることあまたあるに、官家に陪錢し、一院を討得して、住持のときは、法語の師に嗣法せず、當代の名譽あり、攝政に長親附なるものに嗣法するときは、得法をとはず、名譽をむさぼる。かなしむべし、末法惡時、かくのごとくの邪風あふぐことを。かくのごとくのやから、かつていまだ祖佛の道に通達せることなし。

At present, in Jiangzhe, the leaders of the great monasteries mostly have dharma inheritance from Linji, Yunmen, or Dongshan.[24] But a

---

22 **At the time** (*toki ni* ときに): This section corresponds to the question and answer in section 19 in the seventy-five-chapter *Shōbōgenzō* text.

23 **Upon hearing these words** (*kono go o kiku ni* この語をきくに): This line corresponds to the last sentence of section 19 in the seventy-five-chapter *Shōbōgenzō* text.

24 **At present, in Jiangzhe** (*ima Kōsetsu ni* いま江浙に): This section parallels section 20 in the seventy-five-chapter *Shōbōgenzō* text, the last sentence of which reads,

bunch calling themselves distant descendants of Linji occasionally engage in scheming improprieties: that is, asking for a copy of a mortuary portrait or a scroll of dharma words, they provide themselves with a sign of their dharma inheritance. And then there is one kind of dog that, begging in the vicinity of venerables for dharma words, a portrait, or the like, hides them away and builds up a large store of them. Then, he bribes government officials and is granted a cloister; and, when he becomes abbot, instead of inheriting the dharma from the master whose dharma words he has, he inherits the dharma from someone currently famous, someone long and intimately connected with the regency. At that time, there is no question of his having attained the dharma; it is just desire for fame. How lamentable that there blow such corrupt winds in this evil age at the end of the dharma. This type has never penetrated the way of the ancestors and buddhas.

[V2:20]

おほよそ、法語・頂相等をあたふることは、教宗の講師および在家の男女等にもさづけ、投院せる行者等にもゆるすなり。そのむね、諸家の録にあきらかなり。又、その人にあらざるが、みだりに嗣法の證據をのぞむによりて、壱軸の書をもとむることあり。有道のいたむところなりといえども、なまじいに援筆する尊宿あり。古來の書式によらず、いささか師吾のよしをかくなり。近來の法は、ただその師の會にて得力すれば、すなはちかの師を師と嗣法するなり。かつてその師の印をえざれども、ただ入室・上堂に咨參して、長連牀にあるともがら、住院のときは、その師承を擧するにいとまあらざれども、大事打開するとき、その師を師とせるのみおほし。

In general, in the granting of dharma words, mortuary portraits, and such, they are given even to lecturers in the teaching houses, as well as to male and female householders.[25] They are also granted to postulants attached to a cloister, and the like. This point is clear in the records of the various houses. Or, again, an unqualified person, shamelessly desiring proof of dharma inheritance, may seek a scroll of writing; though this may be painful for those who possess the way, there are venerables who reluctantly take up the brush. They do not follow the traditional form of composition but just write a little something to the effect, "the teacher, I . . . ." [The recipients] have never received the teacher's certification, but have merely sought instruction in his room-entering and convocations, while spending time on the long platforms; though, once they become

かくのごとくのやからのなかに、いまだかつて一人として、佛祖の道を夢にも見聞するあらず。

Among this type, there has never been one who saw or heard the way of the buddhas and ancestors even in his dreams.

25 **In general** (*ooyoso* おほよそ): This section corresponds to section 21 in the seventy-five-chapter *Shōbōgenzō* text.

V2. The Inheritance Certificate *Shisho* 嗣書

abbots of cloisters, they have no time to bring up their inheritance from their master, there are many of them who simply regard as their master the master at the time that the great matter was opened.

[V2:21] {2:563}

又、龍門佛眼禪師清遠和尚の遠孫にて、傳藏といふものありき。かの傳藏主、また嗣書を帶せり。嘉定のはじめに、やまふしけるに、郷僧隆禪上座、かの傳藏を看病しけるに、勤勞ありけるによりて、看病を謝せむがために、嗣書をとりいだして、拜せしめけり。みがたきものなり、與儞禮拜いひけり。

Again, there was a person named Canon [Prefect] Zhuan, a distant descendant of Reverend Qingyuan, Chan Master Foyan of Longmen.[26] That Canon Prefect Zhuan also had an inheritance certificate. When he took ill at the beginning of Jiading, our countryman monk, the Senior Seat Ryūzen, had nursed that Canon [Prefect] Zhuan; and, because his efforts had been so diligent, in order to thank him for nursing him, [Zhuan] took out his inheritance certificate and allowed [Ryūzen] to pay obeisance to it, saying, "It's something one rarely gets to see, but *I'll let you pay obeisance to it.*"

[V2:22]

それよりのちハ年ののち、嘉定十六年癸未あきのころ、道元、はじめて天童山に寓直するに、隆禪上座、ねんごろに傳藏主に請して、嗣書を道元にみせしは、その嗣書のかきやう、七佛よりのち臨濟にいたるまで四十五祖をつらねかきて、臨濟よりのちの師は、一圓相をつくりて、そのなかにめぐらして、法諱と花字とをうつし、かけり。新嗣は、おはりに、年號の下頭にかけり。臨濟の尊宿に、かくのごとくの不同ありとしるべし。

After that, eight years later, in the autumn of the junior water year of the sheep, the sixteenth year of Jiading, when Dōgen first lodged at Mount Tiantong, Senior Seat Ryūzen kindly made a request of Canon Prefect Zhuan, who let Dōgen see the inheritance certificate.[27] In the format of the inheritance certificate, it listed in a row the forty-five ancestors from the seven buddhas through Linji; for the masters after Linji, there was a circle with the dharma names and signatures copied around the interior. The new heir was last, written beneath the name of the year. We should realize that there are such differences among [the inheritance certificates of] the venerables of Linji.

---

26 **Again** (*mata* 又): This section corresponds to section 22 in the seventy-five-chapter *Shōbōgenzō* text.

27 **After that, eight years later** (*sore yori nochi hachinen no nochi* それよりのち八年ののち): This section corresponds to section 23 in the seventy-five-chapter *Shōbōgenzō* text.

228 DŌGEN'S *SHŌBŌGENZŌ* VOLUME VII

[V2:23]

先師天童堂頭、ふかく、みだりに嗣法せる人を、いましめき。叢林の中興なり。みずからも、まだらなる袈裟をもちいず。芙蓉山の楷禪師の衲法衣つたはれりといえども、上堂陞座等にもちいず。おほよそ住持職として、まだらなる法衣、かつて一生のうちにかけず。こころある、ものしらざる、ともにほめき。眞箇なりと尊重す。

My former master, Head of Hall of Tiantong, warned against people who improperly got dharma inheritance.[28] [His tenure saw] the revival of the monastery. He himself did not use a patterned *kāṣāya*. Although the patchwork dharma robe of Chan Master Daokai of Mount Furong had come down to him, he did not use it even when ascending to the hall or mounting the seat, and the like. In general, while serving as an abbot, he never once donned a patterned dharma robe throughout his entire life. Both the thoughtful and the ignorant alike praised him. They respected him as authentic.

[V2:24]

先師、上堂するに、つねに諸方をいましめていはく、近來、祖道に名をかれるやから、みだりに法衣を搭し、長髮をこのみ、師號に署せることを出世の舟航とせり。あはれむべし、たれかこれをすくはん。うらむらくは、諸方長老、無道心にして學道せざることを。嗣書・嗣法の因縁をきけるもまれなり。これ、祖道の凌遲なり。

In his convocations, my former master regularly admonished those of all quarters, saying:[29]

In recent times, many of those who borrow the name of the way of the ancestors improperly don dharma robes, like to grow out their hair, and regard signing with the title of master as a vessel for appearance in the world. How pitiful. Who can save them? It is regrettable that the elders in all quarters lack the mind of the way and do not study the way. Those who have heard the circumstances of inheritance certificates and dharma inheritance are also rare. This is the erosion of the way of the ancestors.

[V2:25] {2:564}

かくのごとく、よのつねにいましむるに、天下の長老、うらみず。しかあればすなはち、誠心辨道することあらば、嗣書あることをきくべし。きくことをえ、しることをえば、學道なるべし。

---

28 **My former master, Head of Hall of Tiantong** (*senshi Tendō dōchō* 先師天童堂頭): This section corresponds to section 24 in the seventy-five-chapter *Shōbōgenzō* text, with slight variation.

29 **In his convocations** (*senshi, jōdō suru ni* 先師、上堂するに): This section corresponds to all but the final sentence of section 25 in the seventy-five-chapter *Shōbōgenzō* text, with slight variation.

V2. The Inheritance Certificate *Shisho* 嗣書

When he repeatedly remonstrated in this way, the elders from everywhere did not resent it.[30]

Thus, when there is sincere pursuit of the way, one will surely hear that there are inheritance certificates. And, when one is able to hear that and able to know that, it is surely the study of the way.

* * * * *

[V2:26]

臨濟の嗣書は、まづその名字をかきて、某甲子、われに參ず、とも、わが
會にきたれり、とも、入吾堂奥、とも、嗣吾、ともかきて、ついでのごと
く前代をつらぬるなり。かれも、いささかいひきたれる法訓あり。いはゆ
る宗趣は、嗣は、おはり・はじめに、これただ眞善知識をとぶらふ的旨な
り。臨濟にかけるは、かくのごとくかく、まのあたりみしによりて、しる
すなり。

In Linji inheritance certificates, [the master] first writes his name, then writes, "disciple so-and-so inquired of me," or writes, "joined my community," or writes, "entered the interior of my hall," or writes, "inherited from me," and then lines up the previous generations in order.[31] Those, too, have a few dharma instructions handed down by word of mouth. The import of what they say is that inheritance, in the end and the beginning, comes down to the clear point of visiting a true wise friend. In Linji, they are written like this. Since I have seen one with my own eyes, I present it here.

[V2:27]

了派藏主者、威武人也。今吾子也。德光參侍徑山杲和尚、徑山嗣夾山勤、
勤嗣楊岐演、演嗣海會端、端嗣楊岐會、會嗣慈明圓、圓嗣汾陽昭、昭嗣首
山念、念嗣風穴昭、昭嗣南院顒、顒嗣興化獎、獎是臨濟高祖之長嫡也。

Canon Prefect Liaopai is a person of Weiwu.[32] He is now my offspring. Deguang trained under Reverend Gao of Mount Jing. Jingshan inherited from Qin of Mount Jia. Qin inherited from Yan of Yangqi. Yan inherited from Paiyun Duan of Haihu. Duan inherited from Hui of Yangqi. Hui inherited from Yuan of Ciming. Yuan inherited from Zhao of Fenyang. Zhao inherited from Nian of Mount Shou. Nian inherited

---

30 **When he repeatedly remonstrated in this way** (*kaku no gotoku, yo no tsune ni imashimuru ni* かくのごとく、よのつねにいましむるに): This section corresponds to the final sentence of section 25 and section 26 in the seventy-five-chapter *Shōbōgenzō* text.

31 **In Linji inheritance certificates** (*Rinzai no shisho wa* 臨濟の嗣書は): This section corresponds to section 27 in the seventy-five-chapter *Shōbōgenzō* text.

32 **Canon Prefect Liaopai** (*Ryōha zōsu* 了派藏主): This section corresponds to section 28 in the seventy-five-chapter *Shōbōgenzō* text.

230   DŌGEN'S *SHŌBŌGENZŌ* VOLUME VII

*from Zhao of Fengxue. Zhao inherited from Yong of Nanyuan. Yong
inherited from Jiang of Xinghua. Jiang's inheritance was as the oldest
legitimate heir of the Eminent Ancestor Linji.*

[V2:28]

これは、阿育王山佛照禪師德光、かきて派無際にさづけてありけるを、天
童の住持にてありしとき、小師僧智庚、ひそかにもちきたりて、了然寮に
して道元にみせし。ときに、大宋嘉定十七年甲申正月二十一日、はじめて
これをみる、喜感いくそばくぞ。すなはち佛祖の冥感なり、燒香・禮拜し
て披看に、この嗣書を請出することは、去年七月のころ、師廣都寺、ひそ
かに寂光堂にして、道元にかたれり。

This was written by Deguang, Chan Master Fozhao, of Mount Ayuwang, who conferred it on Pai Wuji.[33] When the latter was abbot of Tiantong, the young monk Zhigeng confidentially brought it and showed it to
Dōgen in the Liaoran quarters. I first saw this on the twenty-first day of
the first month of the senior wood year of the monkey, the seventeenth
year of Jiading in the Great Song. How great was my joy! It was surely
due to the hidden influence of the buddhas and ancestors. Burning incense and making bows, I unrolled and examined it. I had asked that this
inheritance certificate be taken out because, in the seventh month of the
previous year, the Prior Shiguang had told Dōgen about it in private in
the Jiguang Hall.

[V2:29] {2:565}

道元、すなはち都寺にとふ、如今、たれ人かこれを帶持せる。都寺いは
く、堂頭老漢那裏有相似。のちに請出ねんごろにせば、さだめてみするこ
とあらん。

Dōgen asked the Prior, "Who has it now?"[34]

The Prior said, "*It seems to be in the old man head of hall's place.* Later, if you ask him politely to take it out, I'm sure you can see it."

[V2:30]

道元、このことばをききて、喜踊ほねにとほり、もとむるこころ日夜に休
せず。このゆえに、今年ねんごろに小師の僧智庚をかたらひ、一片の心を
なげて請得せりしなり。

After Dōgen heard these words, joy penetrated my bones, and my desire to see it did not let up day or night.[35] Therefore, in the following

---

33 **Deguang, Chan Master Fozhao, of Mount Ayuwang** (*Aikuōzan Busshō zenji Tokkō*
阿育王山佛照禪師德光): This section corresponds to section 29 and the first sentence of
section 30 in the seventy-five-chapter *Shōbōgenzō* text.

34 **Dōgen asked the Prior** (*Dōgen, sunawachi tsūsu in tou* 道元、すなはち都寺にと
ふ): This exchange occurs in section 30 in the seventy-five-chapter *Shōbōgenzō* text.

35   **After Dōgen heard these words** (*Dōgen, kono kotoba o kikite* 道元、このこと

V2. The Inheritance Certificate *Shisho* 嗣書　　231

year, I spoke with the young monk Zhigeng and, with my single-mind-edness, got my request.

[V2:31]

そのかける地は、白絹の表背せるにかく、表紙は、あかき錦なり、軸は、玉なり、長九寸ばかり、闊七尺餘なり、 閑人にはみせず。

The material on which it was written was mounted on white silk.[36] The backing was red brocade; the spindle was jade. The height was just nine inches; the length, more than seven feet. It was not shown to outsiders.

[V2:32]

道元、すなはち智庚を謝す。又即時に堂上に參じて燒香、禮謝無際和尚。ときに無際いはく、遮一段事、少曾見知。今老兄知得、學道之實歸也。

Dōgen thanked Zhigeng.[37] Also, I immediately called upon the head of hall, burned incense, and made a prostration to thank Reverend Wuji. Whereupon, Wuji said, *"This is something that few are able to see for themselves. Now, elder brother, you know of it, and it will be a true refuge in your study of the way."*

[V2:33]

ときに、道元喜感無勝。

At the time, *Dōgen's joy was unbearable.*[38]

[V2:34]

又、寶慶のころ、道元、台山・鴈山等に雲遊するついでに、平田の萬年寺にいたる。住持者福州の元鼒和尚なり。宗鑑長老退院ののち鼒和尚、補す、叢席を一興す。

Also, during the Baoqing era, while Dōgen was wandering to Mount Tai, Mount Yan, and so on, I arrived at the Wannian Monastery of Pingtian.[39] The abbot was Reverend Yuanzi of Fuzhou. After the retirement of Elder Zong-jian, Reverend Yuanzi filled the post and greatly revived the monastic seat.

ばをききて): This section parallels the last two sentences of section 30 in the seventy-five-chapter *Shōbōgenzō* text.

36　**The material on which it was written was mounted on white silk** (*sono kakeru ji wa, hakuken no hyōhai seru ni kaku* そのかける地は、白絹の表背せるにかく): This section parallels the first part of section 31 in the seventy-five-chapter *Shōbōgenzō* text.

37　**Dōgen thanked Zhigeng** (*Dōgen, sunawachi Chikō o shasu* 道元、すなはち智庚を謝す): This section parallels the second part of section 31 in the seventy-five-chapter *Shōbōgenzō* text.

38　**At the time** (*toki ni* ときに): This section corresponds to the final sentence of section 31 in the seventy-five-chapter *Shōbōgenzō* text.

39　**Also, during the Baoqing era** (*mata, Hōkyō no koro* 又、寶慶のころ): This and the following sections through 39 together correspond to section 32 in the seventy-five-chapter *Shōbōgenzō* text.

232 DŌGEN'S *SHŌBŌGENZŌ* VOLUME VII

[V2:35]

人事のついでに、むかしよりの佛祖の家風を往來せしむるに、大潙・仰山の令嗣話を君擧するに、

When I had an interview with him, we conversed about the house styles of the buddhas and ancestors from ancient times; and, when we raised the topic of Dawei and Yangshan's talk on designating an heir,

[V2:36]

長老いはく、曾看嗣書也否。道元いはく、いかでかこれをみん。

The Elder said, "*Have you ever seen my inheritance certificate?*"

Dōgen said, "How could I have seen it?"

[V2:37]

長老、すなはちみづからたちて、嗣書をささげていはく、

The Elder immediately stood up himself, presented the inheritance certificate to me, and said:

[V2:38] {2:566}

這箇は、たとひ親人なりといえども、たとひ侍僧の、としをへたるといえども、これをみせしめず、これすなはち佛祖の法訓なり。しかあれども、元鼒、ひごろ出城して見知府のために在城のとき、一夢を感ずるにいはく、　大梅山法常禪師とおぼしき高僧ありて、梅花一枝をさしあげていはく、

I would not show this even to people close to me, even to an acolyte monk after years of service. This is the rule of the buddhas and ancestors. However, recently, when Yuanzi went out to the city and stayed there to see the prefectural governor, I had a dream, in which an eminent monk I thought was Chan Master Fachang of Mount Damei held out a sprig of plum blossoms and said,

[V2:39]

もし、すでに船舷をこゆる實人あらんには、花をおしむことなかれ、といひて、梅花を、われにあたふ。ときに元鼒、おぼえずして夢中に吟じていはく、未跨船舷、好與三十、しかあるに、不經五日、與老兄相見。いはんや、老兄に、すでに船舷跨來、この嗣書、また梅花綾にかけり。大梅のおしふるところならむ、夢草と符合するゆえにとりいだすなり。老兄、もしわれに嗣法せんことをもとむや、たとひもとむとも、おしむべきにあらず。

"If there is a real person who has 'crossed the gunwales,' do not begrudge him the flowers."

So saying, he gave me the plum blossoms. Without thinking, in the dream, Yuanzi recited the lines, "*Even before you crossed the gunwales, I should have given you thirty blows.*"

V2. The Inheritance Certificate *Shisho* 嗣書 233

And now, *not five days have passed, and I meet my elder brother*. What's more, the elder brother has "crossed the gunwales," and this inheritance certificate is written on plum blossom figured damask. It must be what Damei was teaching me. It is because it matches the plant in my dream that I've brought this out. Do you seek to inherit the dharma from me? Should you seek it, I could not refuse.

[V2:40]

道元、信感おくところなし。嗣書を請すべしといえども、ただ燒香・禮拜して、恭敬供養するのみなり。ときに、燒香侍者法寧といふあり、はじめて嗣書をみるといひき。これは、落地梅綾のしろきにかけり。長九寸餘、闊一尋餘なり。軸子は、黄玉なり、表紙は、錦なり。

Dōgen could not contain his devout emotions.[40] Although I was supposed to request an inheritance certificate, I only offered my respects, merely burning incense and bowing. At the time, there was an incense acolyte named Faning there, who said that it was the first time he had seen the inheritance certificate.

It was written on white damask with a plum pattern.[41] The height was over nine inches; the length was over eight feet. The spindle was yellow jade; the backing was brocade.

---

40 **Dōgen could not contain his devout emotions** (*Dōgen, shinkan oku tokoro nashi* 道元、信感おくところなし): This section corresponds to section 33 in the seventy-five-chapter *Shōbōgenzō* text, which is followed by two sections not included here:

道元ひそかに思惟しき、この一段の事、まことに佛祖の冥資にあらざれば、見聞なほかたし。邊地の愚人として、なんのさいはひありてか數番、これをみる。感涙霑袖。

Dōgen thought to himself, truly without the unseen help of the buddhas and ancestors, it would be hard to experience this event. By what good fortune could an ignorant person from a peripheral land see these several times? Tears of joy wet my sleeves.

ときに維摩室・大舍堂等に、閑寂無人なり。

At the time, the Weimo room, Dasheng hall, and the rest, were silent and empty.

41 **It was written on white damask with a plum pattern** (*kore wa, rakuchi bairyō no shiroki ni kakeri* これは、落地梅綾のしろきにかけり): This and the last two sentences of this section correspond to section 36 in the seventy-five-chapter *Shōbōgenzō* text

234 DŌGEN'S *SHŌBŌGENZŌ* VOLUME VII

[V2:41]

道元、台山より天童にかえる路程に、大梅山護聖寺の旦過に宿するに、大梅祖師きたる、開花せる一枝の梅花をささぐる靈夢を感ず。祖鑑、もとも仰憑するものなり。その一枝花の、縦・横、一尺餘なり。梅花、あに優曇にあらざらんや。道元、在宋のあひだ、歸國ののち、いまだかつて人にかたらず。

On my way back to Tiantong from Mount Tai, Dōgen stayed at the overnight quarters at Husheng Monastery on Mount Damei.[42] There, I experienced a numinous dream, in which the Ancestral Master Damei came and presented me with a sprig of plum blossoms in full bloom. The mirror of the ancestors is a most reliable thing. The diameter of the blossoms on the sprig was more than one foot. How could the plum blossoms be anything but *udumbara*?[43] While Dōgen was in the Song and after my return to this land, I have never spoken of this to anyone.

* * * * *

[V2:42]

いま、わが洞山宗門にかける、臨濟等にかけるにことなり。佛祖の衣裏にかかれりけるを、青原高祖したしく六祖の几前にして、手指より淨血をいだしてかき、正傳せりけるなり。この指血に、六祖の指血を合してかきけると、相傳せり。初祖・二祖のところにも、合血の儀、おこなはれけると、相傳す。これ、吾子參吾、などはかかず、七佛および諸佛の、かきつたえられける嗣書の儀なり。

The writing of inheritance certificates in our present Dongshan lineage differs from their writing in Linji and the rest.[44] What was afixed within the robes of the buddhas and ancestors, the Eminent Ancestor Qingyuan received in direct transmission, personally drawing pure blood from his finger and writing at the desk of Caoxi. Tradition has it that it was written and transmitted by mingling the blood from his finger with the blood from Caoxi's finger. Tradition has it that the rite of mingling blood was carried out in the case of the First Ancestor and Second Ancestor as well. Without writing such things as "my offspring" or "made inquiries

---

42 **On my way back** (*kaeru rotei ni* かえる路程に): This section corresponds to section 37 in the seventy-five-chapter *Shōbōgenzō* text.

43 **How could the plum blossoms be anything but *udumbara*?** (*baika, ani udon ni arazaran ya* 梅花、あに優曇にあらざらんや): The corresponding sentence in section 37 of the seventy-five-chapter *Shōbōgenzō* text is followed by an interesting sentence not included here:

夢中と覺中とおなじく眞實なるべし。

What happens in dreams and in waking must be equally real.

44 **our present Dongshan lineage** (*ima, waga Tōzan shūmon* いま、わが洞山宗門): This section corresponds to section 38 in the seventy-five-chapter *Shōbōgenzō* text.

V2. The Inheritance Certificate *Shisho* 嗣書

of me," this is the procedure for the inheritance certificate written and handed down among the buddhas as well as the seven buddhas.[45]

嗣書

The Inheritance Certificate

仁治二年辛丑春三月二十七日書

Written on the twenty-seventh day of the third month of the junior metal year of the ox, the second year of Ninji [9 May 1241][46]

[V2:43]

先師天童和尚、しめしていはく、諸佛、かならず嗣法あり、いはゆる釋迦牟尼佛者、迦葉佛に嗣法す、迦葉佛は、拘那含牟尼佛に嗣法す、拘那含牟尼佛者、拘留孫佛に嗣法するなり。かくのごとく佛佛相嗣して、いまにおよぶと信受すべし、これ、學佛の道なり。ときに道元まうす、　迦葉佛、入涅槃ののち、釋迦牟尼佛、はじめて出世・成道せり。いはんやまた、賢劫の諸佛、いかにして莊嚴劫の諸佛に嗣法せむ。この道理、いかん。　先師いはく、なんぢがいふところは、聽教の解なり、十聖・三賢等の道なり、佛祖嫡嫡のみちにあらず。わが佛佛相傳の道は、しかあらず。釋迦文佛、まさしく迦葉佛に嗣法せり、とならひきたるなり。釋迦の、嗣法してのちに、迦葉佛は入涅槃すると、學するなり。釋迦佛、もし迦葉佛に嗣法せざらんは、天然外道とおなじかるべし、たれか釋迦佛を信ずるあらん。かくのごとく佛佛相嗣して、いまにおよびきたれるによりて、箇箇佛ともに正嗣なり、つらなるにあらず、あつまれるにあらず、まさにかくのごとく佛佛相嗣すると學するなり。諸阿笈摩教のいふところの劫量・壽量等にかかはるべからず。もし、ひとえに釋迦佛よりおこれり、といはば、わづかに二千餘年なり、ふるきにあらず。相嗣もわづかに四十餘代なり、あらたなる、といひぬべし。この佛嗣は、しかのごとく學するにあらず。釋迦佛は、迦葉佛に嗣法する、と學し、迦葉佛は、釋迦佛に嗣法せり、と學するなり。かくのごとく學するとき、まさに諸佛諸祖の嗣法にてはあるなり。

45　**the procedure for the inheritance certificate written and handed down among the buddhas as well as the seven buddhas** (*shichi butsu oyobi shobutsu no, kakitsutaerarekeru shisho no gi* 七佛および諸佛の、かきつたえられける嗣書の儀): In the seventy-five-chapter *Shōbōgenzō* text, there follows an important additional section not found here:

> しかあればしるべし、曹溪の血氣は、かたじけなく青原の淨血に和合し、青原の淨血、したしく曹溪の親血に和合して、まのあたり印證をうることは、ひとり高祖青原和尚のみなり、餘祖のおよぶところにあらず。この事子をしれるともがらは、佛法はただ青原のみに正傳せる、と道取するなり。

Thus, we should realize that, the lifeblood of Caoxi being graciously mingled with the pure blood of Qingyuan, and the pure blood of Qingyuan being intimately mingled with the parental blood of Caoxi, the personal reception of the seal of verification was only by the Eminent Ancestor Reverend Qingyan alone and was not something achieved by any other ancestors. Those who know the facts of this matter say that the buddha dharma was directly transmitted only to Qingyuan.

46　**Written on the twenty-seventh day** (*nijūshichi nichi sho* 二十七日書): A notice of the date of composition does not appear at this point in the seventy-five-chapter *Shōbōgenzō* text.

236   DŌGEN'S *SHŌBŌGENZŌ* VOLUME VII

My former master, Reverend Tiantong, taught:

The buddhas always have dharma inheritance. That is, Buddha Śākyamuni inherited the dharma from Buddha Kāśyapa; Buddha Kāśyapa inherited the dharma from Buddha Kanakamuni; Buddha Kanakamuni inherited the dharma from Buddha Krakucchanda. We should have faith that buddha after buddha has inherited in this way down to the present. This is the way of studying the buddhas.[47]

At the time, Dōgen said,

Buddha Śākyamuni appeared in the world and attained the way only after Buddha Kāśyapa had entered nirvāṇa.[48] Not to mention, moreover, [the problem of] how the buddhas of the Worthy kalpa could inherit the dharma from the buddhas of the Adornment kalpa. What is the reasoning here?

My former master said,

What you say is the understanding of the heard teachings, the way of the ten sages and three worthies, not the way of successor after successor of buddhas and ancestors.[49] Our way of the transmission by buddha after buddha is not like this. We study that Buddha Śākyamuni did indeed inherit the dharma from Buddha Kāśyapa. We study that Buddha Kāśyapa entered nirvāṇa only after Buddha Śākya inherited the dharma. If Buddha Śākyamuni had not inherited the dharma from Buddha Kāśyapa, it would be the same as an other path of natural occurrence; who would have faith in Buddha Śākya? Because buddha after buddha has inherited in this way reaching down to the present, each and every buddha is a direct heir. They are not lined up; they are not bunched together. We study that truly buddha after buddha inherits in this way. It has nothing to do with the numbers of kalpas or numbers of lifespans discussed in the teachings of the *āgamas*. If we say it occurred only from Buddha Śākya, it is merely two thousand and some years, not very old. The inheritance, too, is a mere forty-some generations and would have to be called something new. This inheritance of the buddha is not studied in this way. We study that Buddha Śākya inherited the dharma from Buddha Kāśyapa; we study that Buddha Kāśyapa inherited the dharma from Buddha Śākya. When we study in this way, this is truly the dharma inheritance of the buddhas and the ancestors.

---

47 **This is the way of studying the buddhas** (*kore, gakubutsu no dō nari* これ、學佛の道なり): Up to this point, this section corresponds to section 40 in the seventy-five-chapter *Shōbōgenzō* text.

48 **At the time, Dōgen said** (*toki ni Dōgen mōsu* ときに道元まうす): Dōgen's question here corresponds to section 41 in the seventy-five-chapter *Shōbōgenzō* text.

49 **My former master said** (*senshi iwaku* 先師いはく): Rujing's answer here corresponds to section 42 in the seventy-five-chapter *Shōbōgenzō* text.

V2. The Inheritance Certificate *Shisho* 嗣書

[V2:44] {2:568}

このとき、道元、はじめて佛祖の嗣法あることを稟受するのみにあらず、
從來の舊窠をも脱落するなり。

It was then that Dōgen not only first accepted that there was a dharma inheritance of the buddhas and ancestors but also sloughed off his past old nest.[50]

于時仁治二年歳次辛丑三月廿七日、観音導利興聖寶林寺、沙門道元記

Recorded at Kannon Dōri Kōshō Hōrin Monastery; twenty-seventh day, third month of the junior metal year of the ox, the second year of Ninji in Japan [9 May 1241], by Śramaṇa Dōgen, who entered the Song and transmitted the dharma

仁治二年辛丑十二月十二日子時書
學人是法受持

Written on the twelfth day of the twelfth month, in the second year of Ninji, the junior metal year of the ox [14 January 1242] Students should keep this dharma[51]

---

50   **It was then** (*kono toki* このとき): This sentence corresponds to section 43 in the seventy-five-chapter *Shōbōgenzō* text.

51   Presumably, a second colophon by Dōgen, for the Kōjakuji holograph; does not occur in the seventy-five-chapter *Shōbōgenzō* text.

Students should keep this dharma (*gakunin zehō juji* 學人是法受持): A tentative translation, reading the Chinese glyphs in Japanese syntax; alternatively read "kept by student Zehō" (an otherwise unknown individual).

Treasury of the True Dharma Eye
Variant Text 3

Beyond the Buddha
Butsu kōjō ji
佛向上事

Beyond the Buddha

Butsu kōjō ji

Introduction

This work represents the first text in fascicle 1 of the twenty-eight-text *Himitsu Shōbōgenzō* collection. Its provenance is quite unclear: it bears no colophon providing date and place of composition, nor a title identifying it as a chapter of the *Shōbōgenzō*. Although it shares the title of number 26 of the seventy-five- and sixty-chapter *Shōbōgenzō* compilations, the content is quite different. Indeed, only the opening section is devoted to the title theme, while the bulk of the work discusses several other topics, seemingly only loosely related to the title or to each other. While some commentators have sought to interpret these latter discussions as elucidating the meaning of "beyond the buddha," their disparate nature has led others to suggest, perhaps more persuasively, that the text represents, not a coherent essay, but a collection of notes, left behind by Dōgen and copied together at some later time under the title of the opening topic.

正法眼藏拾遺三
Treasury of the True Dharma Eye
Variant Text 3

佛向上事
Beyond the Buddha

(「秘密正法眼藏」初冊所收)
(In the first volume of the *Himitsu Shōbōgenzō*)

[V3:1] {2:569}

洞山悟本大師の云、すべからく佛向上の事あることをしるべし。佛向上の事あることをしりて、正に語話の分あるべし。

Great Master Wuben of Dongshan said, "You should know that there is something beyond the buddha.[1] When you know there is something beyond the buddha, you'll truly be in a position to talk."

[V3:2]

語話の分と云は、轉法輪の分なり。まことに佛向上の事をしらざれば、いたづらにとどこほりて、佛向上に透脱することなし。もし透脱せざれば、魔界をこゆることなし。すでに佛におよぶみちをえんより、すみやかに凡夫のきはをいづるなり。そのみち、通達せる人、まれなり。又、しるべからざれば、いひてさしおくべきにはあらず。まことあるこころざしをして、まことにあきらめたる善知識に參學すれば、かならずおよぶところあるなり。このゆえに洞山は、すべからくしるべし、とはをしゆるなり。そのこころのおもはくは、たとへば、佛におよぶ佛は、きのふまちし佛にて、今日の佛はありけると、さとられぬなり。けふのほとけは、けふのみにあらざりけると、佛にしらせゆくを、佛向上の事といふ。このところよりぞ、とくところも、まことある語話にては、とかるるといふは、いまにいたるまでものがれず。語話にてとかることのやまざる、昨日の昨日ながら、ことばにてあるあり。又、向上の事にてしり、向上の事にてきくとき、うることある法輪の、われをことばとして大小をとき、法輪のわれとして、語話の分をあらしむる佛向上の事あり。

---

1   **Great Master Wuben of Dongshan** (*Tōzan Gohon daishi* 洞山悟本大師): I.e., Dongshan Liangjie 洞山良价 (807-869). Reference, in Japanese, to a saying found in the *Jingde chuandeng lu* 景德傳燈錄, as well as Dōgen's *shinji Shōbōgenzō* 眞字正法眼藏; see Supplementary Notes, s.v. "Beyond the buddha." The saying is the title theme of the "Butsu kōjō ji" chapter in the seventy-five-chapter *Shōbōgenzō*.

242 DŌGEN'S *SHŌBŌGENZŌ* VOLUME VII

To "be in a position to talk" means to "be in a position to turn the dharma wheel." Truly, if we do not know something "beyond the buddha," we remain futilely stuck and are not liberated "beyond the buddha." And, if we are not liberated, we do not transcend the realm of Māra. Once we gain the way leading to buddhahood, we quickly leave the limits of the common people. But those who have penetrated this way are rare. Yet, we should not just say that we cannot know it. When, with genuine aspiration, we study with a wise friend who has truly clarified it, we shall inevitably reach it. Therefore, Dongshan taught that we should know it. His point is that, for example, a buddha, reaching buddhahood, does not recognize that today's buddha existed as the buddha expected yesterday.[2] To keep letting the buddha know that today's buddha existed not only today is called something "beyond the buddha." From this point on until now, whatever we say is said as true talk. The speaking of [such] talk does not stop: it is even in what are yesterday's words. Furthermore, when we know it as something "beyond the buddha," when we hear it as something "beyond the buddha," there is something "beyond the buddha" in which the dharma wheel we attained takes us as the words with which to talk of the great and small, and reveals our "position to talk" as the dharma wheel.

* * * * *

[V3:3] {2:570}
佛のときたまはく、佛轉法輪は、聲色の塵にはあらず。

The Buddha said that the Buddha's turning of the dharma wheel is not the dusts of sound and form.[3]

[V3:4]
いくばくのこころは、佛法はもとより、教・行・證ともに、はじめ・をはりにかかはれるにあらず、又、いまにそまざるなり。しかあればすな

---

2 **today's buddha existed as the buddha expected yesterday** (*kinō machishi butsu nite, kyō no butsu wa arikeru* きのふまちし佛にて、今日の佛はありける): Presumably, meaning that buddhahood is present both before and after one becomes a buddha. The following sentence would then seem to mean that what is "beyond the buddha" refers to the ongoing awareness of this presence.

3 **The Buddha said** (*butsu no tokitamawaku* 佛のときたまはく): The term "dusts" (*jin* 塵) is regularly used for the objects of the senses — here, of the ear and eye. The source of this saying, given here in Japanese, is unknown. Its message is reminiscent of a line of verse, quoted by Dōgen in the "Shōbōgenzō busshō" 正法眼藏佛性, that is attributed to Nāgarjuna in the *Jingde chuandeng lu* 景德傳燈錄 (T.2076.51:210b14):

説法無其形、用辯非聲色。
My preaching of the dharma is without any shape;
The explanations, not sound or form.

V3. Beyond the Buddha *Butsu kōjō ji* 佛向上事　　243

はち、佛の聲をしり、佛のことばをならふべし。いはゆるほとけは、その聲、およばざるところなく、およばざるものなし。又、はじめ・おはりにかかはれて、凡夫・二乘・外道等にひとしきにはあらず。聲のうちに成道し、聲のうちにひかりをはなつ。み、よりさきに聲をあげ、み、ののちに聲をきこゆることも、ひとりほとけのみ、そなへたまふ。しかあれば、生死去來の、佛音聲を通ずるあり、風雨水火の、佛音聲をあぐるあり。廚庫山門の、ひろく其聲を開演し、僧堂・佛殿、たかくその聲を重説す。しかのみにあらず、諸法いづれもこの佛音聲のなかばをきかしめ、三界おのおの、この佛音聲の少許をわすれざるなり。たれか若退若出にわづらはん。おのづから錯あり、謬あることなし。おほよそ、ほとけの聲をきくには、みみしてきき、まなこしてもきき、乃至ねぶれるなか、さむるあひだ、六根、いづれも佛音聲をきこえざることなし。又、法界のうちにも、とにも、いづれも、ところの往來にも、往來のいづれも、ところも、佛音聲のなきところは、いかにもあるべからず。ところにもあり、ときにもあり。又、佛音聲は、聲して聲をとき、聲して聲をきくことわりあり。又、ほとけのことばのていたらくとして、聲をはなれてとくことなく、全聲にとかれて、一語・兩句あり、一語・兩句に、全聲きこえざることなし。この聲のところに、つくさず、きはめざることなし。たとひ人にても、たとひ物にても、われは會せざらん、これはつくさざらん、と、のがれんことをもとむる音聲、さらにあるべからず。かくのごとく、佛語、おもひにもよほされてとかるるにはあらず。音聲にとかれて、おもひにてある音聲もあり。半をとき全をとくに、したしからず、あきらかならずといふことなし。百草ともにあきらかなるのみにあらず、祖師のこころもあきらかなり。ことのほとりより、物のきはを究盡せんとすることなし。作よりつたはれて、ことを、をさめんとみだることもなき、すなはち佛の音聲、佛の言語にてはあるなり。

The point of what this says is that the buddha dharma, in its teaching, practice, and verification, essentially has nothing to do with beginning or end and is also not stained by the present.[4] Thus, we should know the Buddha's voice and learn the Buddha's words. There is nowhere that the voice of the Buddha does not reach, nothing that it does not reach. Moreover, it is not the same as that of common people, followers of the two vehicles, and the other paths, involved as they are with beginning and end.[5] Within his voice, the way is attained; within his voice, the light is emitted. To raise the voice before the body, to hear the voice after the body — the Buddha alone is endowed with this.[6] Thus, there is birth and

---

4　**The point of what this says** (*ikubaku no kokoro wa* いくばくのこころは): Following Kawamura's suggestion (DZZ.2:570n) that *ikubaku no* いくばくの ("a few") here is an error for *iiwaku no* いいわくの ("what is said").

5　**common people, followers of the two vehicles, and the other paths** (*bonbu nijō gedō tō* 凡夫・二乘・外道等): I.e., ordinary people, *śrāvakas*, *pratyeka-buddhas*, and non-Buddhist religious. See Supplementary Notes, s.v. "Three vehicles."

6　**To raise the voice before the body, to hear the voice after the body** (*mi, yori saki ni koe o age, mi, no nochi ni koe o kikoyuru koto* み、よりさきに聲をあげ、み、ののちに聲をきこゆること): The expressions "before the body" (*shinsen* 身先 or *shinzen* 身前) and "after the body" (*shingo* 身後) occur several times in the *Shōbōgenzō*; they

244 DŌGEN'S *SHŌBŌGENZŌ* VOLUME VII

death, coming and going, penetrating the voice of the Buddha; there is wind and rain, water and fire, raising the voice of the Buddha. The kitchen and mountain gate widely expound his voice; the saṃgha hall and buddha hall loudly repeat his voice.[7] Not only this: each of the dharmas lets us hear half of this voice of the Buddha; none of the three realms forgets a bit of this voice of the Buddha. Who would worry about "*whether withdrawing or emerging*"?[8] Naturally, it has no mistakes, has no errors.

In sum, when we hear the Buddha's voice, we hear it with our ears, we hear it with our eyes, and so on through the six organs, none of which fails to hear the voice of the Buddha, whether we are asleep or awake. Again, in the places, in whatever back and forth in the back and forth of places, whether within the dharma realm or outside it, there can be no place at all that lacks the voice of the Buddha.[9] It is there in places; it is there in times. Again, there is a principle that the voice of the Buddha talks of the voice with the voice and hears the voice with the voice. Again, as the state of the Buddha's words, never spoken apart from his voice, there is one word or two lines spoken by his whole voice, and in his one word or two lines we cannot fail to hear his whole voice. There is no case of not mastering, not exhaustively understanding this voice. Whether a person or a thing, we should certainly not have a voice that seeks to avoid [this voice], on grounds that we will not understand it, will not master it. The words of the Buddha are not spoken shaped by thoughts in this way. There is also a voice that is thought spoken by a voice. When talking half or talking all, there is nothing remote, nothing unclear: not only are the hundred grasses all clear; the mind of the

---

can mean "before or after this life" or, perhaps in the case of a buddha, "before or after embodiment."

7   **kitchen and mountain gate** (*zuku sanmon* 厨庫山門); **saṃgha hall and buddha hall** (*sōdō butsuden* 僧堂・佛殿): Reminiscent of a saying attributed to Yunmen Wenyan 雲門文偃 (864-949) appearing at *shinji Shōbōgenzō* 眞字正法眼藏, DZZ.5:166, case 81; see Supplementary Notes, s.v. "Saṃgha hall, buddha hall, kitchen, and mountain gate."

8   **"whether withdrawing or emerging"** (*nyaku tai nyaku shutsu* 若退若出): Perhaps recalling a passage, alluded to elsewhere in the *Shōbōgenzō*, in Chapter 16 of the *Lotus Sūtra* (*Miaofa lianhua jing* 妙法蓮華經, T.262.9:42c13-15):

> 如來、如實知見三界之相。無有生死、若退若出。亦無在世及滅度者。非實非虛非如非異。不如三界見於三界。

> The Tathāgata views the marks of the three realms as they really are: there is no birth or death, whether withdrawing or emerging; there is also no existence in the world or extinction; they are neither true nor false, neither the same nor different. He does not view the three realms as [those in] the three realms view them.

9   **places, in whatever back and forth in the back and forth of places** (*tokoro no ōrai ni mo, ōrai no izuremo, tokoro mo* ところの往來にも、往來のいづれも、ところも): A tentative translation of a rather obscure passage, perhaps meaning "in every place, wherever one may go."

V3. Beyond the Buddha *Butsu kōjō ji* 佛向上事 245

Ancestral Master is also clear.[10] That it does not seek exhaustively to investigate the limits of things from their edges, nor mistakenly seek to control things as conveyed from their actions — this is the voice of the Buddha, the words of the Buddha.[11]

* * * * *

[V3:5] {2:571}

學道には、かならずその行として、坐禪をつとむべし。これむかしより、佛佛あいつたへてたえず、いまにもおよぶなり。ほとけとなるに、これをはなれてなるにあらず。ほとけのつたふるところにあれば、人のはかるべきにあらず。はからんといとなむは、學道の式にはあらず。われにおこなはるるにあきらかなることありといへども、われに、はからるるきはの、くらきなし。かくのごとく、はかりつくすきはのなきには、ちからをつくして、はかれりとおもはんも、はかるにはあらず。いたづらにある、むまや、さるの、しづかあらぬのみなり。しかあるに、もし正師、をしへをたれ、佛祖、跡をのこし、修行、あきらかに見成することあれば、ひごろの學道の、なほざりにあらざりけるともしられ、いまの行履の、むなしきにあらざりけるともあきらむるなり。このとき、身心をかくるることなし。これ量にかかはれらんこころばへにては、通ぜんこともかたし。いはんや、いさごをかぞふる人の、夢にもみるべきにはあらず。ただ非思量の坐禪を、兀兀としてありし人のみ、これを辦得せりき。

In the study of the way, we should always engage in seated meditation as its practice. From long ago, this has been transmitted by buddha after buddha without ceasing down to the present. There is no becoming a buddha apart from this. Since it is transmitted by the buddhas, it is not something humans can fathom. To work at fathoming it is not the procedure for studying the way. Even though it may sometimes be clear in our practice of it, the limits we fathom remain obscure. Thus, without fully fathomed limits, we do not clarify it, even though we exhaust our effort

---

10 **not only are the hundred grasses all clear; the mind of the Ancestral Master is also clear** (*hyakusō tomo ni akiraka naru nomi ni arazu, soshi no kokoro mo akiraka nari* 百草ともにあきらかなるのみにあらず、祖師のこころもあきらかなり): The "hundred grasses" (*hyakusō* 百草) is a common term for "all things"; the "Ancestral Master" (*soshi* 祖師) is Bodhidharma. Allusion to a famous expression, best known in Chan literature from its use in a conversation between Layman Pang Yun 龐蘊居士 and his daughter found in Dōgen's *shinji Shōbōgenzō* 眞字正法眼藏 (DZZ.5:168, case 88); see Supplementary Notes, s.v. "Perfectly clear, the tips of the hundred grasses."

11 **it does not seek exhaustively to investigate the limits of things from their edges, nor mistakenly seek to control things as conveyed from their actions** (*koto no hotori yori, mono no kiwa o gūjin sen to suru koto nashi. sa yori tsutawarete, koto o, osamen to midaru koto mo naki* ことのほとりより、物のきはを究盡せんとすることなし。作よりつたはれて、ことを、をさめんとみだることもなき): A tentative translation; perhaps meaning that [while everything is clear in the speech of the Buddha], it is not based on our definitions.

246 DŌGEN'S *SHŌBŌGENZŌ* VOLUME VII

and think that we have clarified it. [Such effort] is fruitless, nothing but the unrest of the horse and monkey.[12] However, if a true master gives us the teaching, the buddhas and ancestors leave us their traces, and our practice is clearly realized, we will know that our regular study of the way has not been idle and will be clear that our present conduct has not been in vain. At this time, there is nothing hiding body and mind. This is difficult to penetrate with a mind concerned with measure.[13] Still less is it seen, even in their dreams, by those who count grains of sand.[14] Only those who have sat solidly in the seated meditation of nonthinking can discern it.[15]

* * * * *

[V3:6] {2:572}

佛道をならふに、しばらく二の様子あり。いはゆる、こころしてならひ、身してならふなり。身してならふ、といふは、坐禪辦道するところに、作佛をもとめざる行佛あり。公案見成するに、身佛もとより作佛にあらず。羅籠ひさしくやぶれぬれば、坐佛さらに作佛をさいず。かくのごとく、身してならふとき、千古萬古、とこしなへにほとけにいり、魔にいるちからあり。進歩退歩に、溝にみち壑にみつ、ひかりをあらしむる、これを父母未生以前の面目といはざらめやは。

In studying the way of the buddhas, there are provisionally two types: studying with the mind and studying with the body.[16] "Studying with the body" means that, where the way is pursued in seated meditation, there is the practice of a buddha that does not seek to make a buddha.[17] In the

---

12 **unrest of the horse and monkey** (*muma ya, saru no, shizuka aranu* むまや、さるの、しづかあらぬ): From the common Buddhist simile that the untrained mind is like a monkey jumping from branch to branch or a horse running wild.

13 **mind concerned with measure** (*ryō ni kakawareran kokorobae* 量にかかはれらんこころばへ): Or, perhaps, "a mind concerned with thinking," if we take *ryō* 量 here as *shiryō* 思量.

14 **those who count grains of sand** (*isago o kazouru hito* いさごをかぞふる人): From the common simile that a fixation on the words of scripture is like counting grains of sand. See Supplementary Notes, s.v. "Counting sand."

15 **only those who have sat solidly in the seated meditation of nonthinking** (*tada hi shiryō no zazen o, gotsugotsu toshite arishi hito* ただ非思量の坐禪を、兀兀としてありし人): Evoking the famous conversation about seated meditation between Yaoshan Wei-yan 藥山惟儼 (751-834) and an unidentified monk that is cited several times in Dōgen's writings and discussed in his "Shōbōgenzō zazen shin" 正法眼藏坐禪箴. See Supplementary Notes, s.v. "Yaoshan's not thinking." The sentence introduces the section to follow.

16 **studying with the mind and studying with the body** (*kokoro shite narau, mi shite narau nari* こころしてならふ、身してならふなり): This twofold division of study is the theme of the "Shōbōgenzō shinjin gakudō" 正法眼藏身心學道. See Supplementary Notes, s.v. "Body and mind." This section parallels section 8 of the "Shōbōgenzō zazen shin" 正法眼藏坐禪箴 (DZZ.1:105), the annotation for which will not be repeated here.

17 **practice of a buddha that does not seek to make a buddha** (*sabutsu o motomezaru gyōbutsu* 作佛をもとめざる行佛): This phrase and the remainder of the passage parallel

V3. Beyond the Buddha *Butsu kōjō ji* 佛向上事 247

realization of the kōan, from the beginning, the embodied buddha is not making a buddha. When the nets and cages are long broken, a seated buddha does not interfere with making a buddha. When we study with the body like this, from a thousand ages, ten thousand ages past, from eternity, we have the power to enter into buddha, to enter into Māra. In *stepping forward and stepping back*, we display a light that fills the ditches and fills the gullies. How could this not be called our "face *before our father and mother were born*"?[18]

[V3:7]
こころしてならふといふは、心といふやうを、あきらむるなり。こころを
あきらむといふに、凡夫・外道・二乗等の心をあきらむるにはあらず、佛
心をあきらむるなり。

"Studying with the mind" means clarifying the state of "mind." "Clarifying the mind" does not mean clarifying the mind of the common person, the followers of other paths, or the two vehicles: it is clarifying the buddha mind.

[V3:8] {2:573}
昔し、僧ありて慧忠國師に問、いかにあるか是古佛の心、と。國師の云、
牆壁瓦礫。

Long ago, there was a monk who asked the National Teacher Huizhong, "What is the mind of the old buddhas?"[19]

The National Teacher said, "Fences, walls, tiles, and pebbles."

Dōgen's comments in the "Shōbōgenzō zazen shin" 正法眼藏坐禪箴 on Yaoshan's saying on seated meditation as "nonthinking."

18 **"face before our father and mother were born"** (*bumo mishō izen no menmoku* 父母未生以前の面目): Also read *fubo mishō*; a classic Zen expression for the true self, sometimes understood as "before your father and mother gave birth"; see Supplementary Notes, s.v. "Before your father and mother were born."

19 **National Teacher Huizhong** (*Echū kokushi* 慧忠國師): I.e., Nanyang Huizhong 南陽慧忠 (d. 775). His famous saying occurs often in Dōgen's writing and is discussed at length in the "Shōbōgenzō kobutsushin" 正法眼藏古佛心. Variants of this conversation occur in several texts. The *Zongmen tongyao ji* 宗門統要集 has the question put, not by "a monk," but by Dongshan Liangjie 洞山良价 (ZTS.1:31c5); the well-known version found in the *Jingde chuandeng lu* 景德傳燈錄 (T.2076.51:438a9) gives the monk's question as, "What is the buddha mind" (*ana ge shi foxin* 阿那箇是佛心), rather than "the old buddha mind."

"What is the mind of the old buddhas?" (*ika ni aru ka kore kobutsu no shin* いかに あるか是古佛の心): Or, perhaps, "mind of an old buddha." Here and below, Dōgen has made a choice in his Japanese rendering of this question to parse the Chinese expression *gufoxin* 古佛心 ("old buddha mind") such that "old" modifies "buddha," rather than "mind." In his "Shōbōgenzō kobutsushin" 正法眼藏古佛心, he plays with both readings.

248 DŌGEN'S *SHŌBŌGENZŌ* VOLUME VII

[V3:9]

いまわれら、しばらく、このことばをきくべし、しづかに、このこころを
ならふべし。佛道をならはんとおもひ、はじめより古佛の心をあきらむる
を、心を以て學道するとは云べし。自ごころは、いたづらに知見解會にほ
こりて、ひとへに思慮分別のみあり。

Now, for a while, we should listen to these words, should quietly study
their meaning. To intend to study the way of the buddhas, and from
the outset to clarify the mind of the old buddhas — this may be called
"studying the way with the mind." One's own mind, foolishly proud of
its knowledge and understanding, is nothing but thinking and discrimination.

[V3:10]

釋迦老子云、是法非思量分別之所能解と。はかりしるべし、みづからに
は、とるべき心なし、古佛には、ならふべき心ろあり。その心をきかんと
するに、牆壁瓦礫のみつべきあり。そのこころを證せんとするに、牆壁瓦
礫の見成するある。しかあるに、この牆壁瓦礫は、人のなすところといへ
ども、法の云爲なり、たれかこれを強爲せん。かくのごとくみるときに、
牆壁瓦礫は、目前の法にあらず、目前の法は、牆壁瓦礫にはあらざるこ
と、あきらけし。

*Old Master Śākya said, "This dharma is not something that can be
understood by thinking or discrimination."*[20]

We should gauge that, in us, there is no mind to be got; in the old
buddhas, there is a mind to be studied.[21] When we seek to ask about
that mind, it is to be seen in the fences, walls, tiles, and pebbles; when
we seek to verify that mind, it appears in the fences, walls, tiles, and
pebbles. Still, while these fences, walls, tiles, and pebbles may be man-
made, they are the words and deeds of the dharma; who could make
them by force?[22] When seen like this, it is clear that fences, walls, tiles,

---

20 **"This dharma is not something that can be understood by thinking or discrimination"** (*ze hō hi shiryō funbetsu shi shonōge* 是法非思量分別之所能解): From the
famous line in the *Lotus Sūtra* (*Miaofa lianhua jing* 妙法蓮華經, T.262.9:7a18-20):

我以無數方便種種因緣譬喻言辭演說諸法。是法非思量分別之所能解。

I use innumerable techniques, and various stories, parables, and figures of speech
to expound the dharmas. This dharma is not something that can be understood by
thinking or discrimination.

21 **there is no mind to be got** (*toru beki shin nashi* とるべき心なし): Perhaps, recalling
the famous line, discussed in the "Shōbōgenzō shin fukatoku" 正法眼藏心不可得, from
the *Diamond Sūtra* (*Jingang bore boluomi jing* 金剛般若波羅蜜經, T.235.8:751b27-28).

過去心不可得、現在心不可得、未來心不可得。

The past mind cannot be got; the present mind cannot be got; the future mind cannot
be got.

22 **they are the words and deeds of the dharma; who could make them by force?**

V3. Beyond the Buddha *Butsu kōjō ji* 佛向上事 249

and pebbles are not the dharmas before our eyes, and the dharmas before our eyes are not fences, walls, tiles, and pebbles.

[V3:11]

おほよそ牆壁瓦礫の這邊、われらが那頭をてらす、われらが這邊、牆壁瓦礫の那頭にてらさるらん。かくのごとく、古佛の心にてある牆壁瓦礫の、光明にても、功徳にても、あきらかにして、かぞへつべきをばかぞへ、しりぬべきをば記取すべきなり。ものをしり、ことをわきまへんにも、凡夫・二乗・外道等には、ならふべからず、古佛の心に、ならふべし。乃至、よる・ひる十二時の日用も、ひとすぢに古佛にならふべきなり。古佛の心のをしふるところ、古佛の心をきくことをえつ。すでに古佛の心をみることをえつるうへは、よくよくならふべきなり。ゆめゆめ、凡夫にそなはれる心のやうにあらんずると、おもふべからず。

In sum, the here of fences, walls, tiles, and pebbles illumines our there; and our here is illumined by the there of the fences, walls, tiles, and pebbles.[23] In this way, we should count what can be counted and remember what can be remembered of the radiance and the virtues of the fences, walls, tiles, and pebbles that are the mind of the old buddhas. When we seek to know things and distinguish facts, we should learn from the mind of the old buddhas, not learn from common people, or followers of the two vehicles, or the other paths. And so on down to, we should learn solely from the old buddhas in our daily lives throughout the twelve times of night and day.[24] We can hear the mind of the old buddhas in the teachings of the mind of the old buddhas; since we have been able to see the mind of the old buddhas, we should learn from it very well. Even in our dreams, we should not think that it is like the mind belonging to the common people.

(*hō no un'i nari, tare ka kore o gōi sen* 法の云爲なり、たれかこれを強爲せん): A usage, seen elsewhere in Dōgen's writing, that contrasts *un'i* 云爲 ("words and deeds") and *gōi* 強爲 (translated here "make by force"); the latter suggests intentional, premeditated action, while the former seems to be used for behavior that occurs naturally or spontaneously.

23　**the here of fences, walls, tiles, and pebbles illumines our there** (*shōheki garyaku no shahen, warera ga natō o terasu* 牆壁瓦礫の這邊、われらが那頭をてらす): Playful phrasing, perhaps meaning something like, "the lowly things of this world illumine our higher selves." On this reading, the following clause might mean something like, "our ordinary selves are illumined by the higher reality of these things (i.e., as the old buddha mind)." See Supplementary Notes, s.v. "Fences, walls, tiles, and pebbles."

24　**daily lives throughout the twelve times of night and day** (*yoru hiru jūni ji no nichiyū* よる・ひる十二時の日用): The day and night as traditionally divided into twelve two-hour periods.

250 DŌGEN'S *SHŌBŌGENZŌ* VOLUME VII

[V3:12] {2:574}

しかあるを、おろかなる輩ら、凡夫の知見をもってあそびて、佛心もかくあらんずるとあやまりて、能知・所知の知を論じ、寂照・靈照の照を談ず。かくのごとくの邪見は、しかしながら放下すべし。ただ古佛の心にてある牆壁瓦礫を、ならふべし。古佛の心より生ぜる牆壁瓦礫にてあれば、能生にかたどりて、しかいふにはあらぬなり。直に動著せずして、古佛の、といふなり。古佛は、いづれもみな、説法も、修行のときも、涅槃のときも、成道のときも、このこころを心とはせり、とならふべし。

However, foolish types, toying with the views of common people and mistakenly thinking that the buddha mind is also like this, discuss the knowing of the knower and the known, and talk about the illumination of "tranquil illumination" and "spiritual illumination."[25] We should completely discard such false views; we should just study the fences, walls, tiles, and pebbles that are the mind of the old buddhas. It is not that we say this because, since they are fences, walls, tiles, and pebbles born from the mind of the old buddhas, they take the form of what gave them birth: directly, without moving, they are called "of the old buddhas."[26] We should study that every one of the old buddhas has taken this mind as their mind when they preach, when they practice, when they enter nirvāṇa, and when they attain the way.

[V3:13]

しかあれば、わが大師釋尊も、これを心とは住持しけり、祖師も、これを心とは保任せりけるなり。牆壁瓦礫、ひとしや、ひとしからずやと、よくよく見るべし。自然、おのづから親切なるところあらば、古佛の心おのづから古佛の心をとくゆえ、かくのごとくなりと、ききならふべし。この心、さとるとき、やむことをえず。ことやむことをえざるゆえに、宗通も説通も、しかしながら、この心にまかせられてあり。行道も戒道も、盡くこの心にまかせられざるなし。古佛のあらゆる説化は、かくのごとくなるべし。これをこころとして、學道するなり、と。

Therefore, our Great Master Śākya maintained this as his mind, and the ancestral masters maintained this as their mind. We should see very well whether fences, walls, tiles, and pebbles are the same or not the

---

25   **illumination of "tranquil illumination" and "spiritual illumination"** (*jakushō reishō no shō* 寂照・靈照の照): Two terms occurring frequently in Chinese Buddhist materials for the inherent radiance of the mind.

26   **directly, without moving, they are called "of the old buddhas"** (*jiki ni dōjaku sezu shite, kobutsu no, to iu nari* 直に動著せずして、古佛の、といふなり): I.e., just as they are in themselves, the fences, walls, tiles, and pebbles are [the mind] of the old buddhas. This usage of *dōjaku sezu* 動著せず ("without moving"), in the sense "just as it is in itself" is found elsewhere in the *Shōbōgenzō*.

V3. Beyond the Buddha *Butsu kōjō ji* 佛向上事 251

same.[27] We should hear and learn that it is like this, because, if there is something with which nature is naturally intimate, the mind of the old buddhas naturally speaks of the mind of the old buddhas.[28] When this mind awakens, it is inevitable.[29] Since it is inevitable, both mastery of the meaning and mastery of its exposition are left completely up to this mind; there is neither a way of practice nor a way of discipline that is not entirely left up to this mind.[30] All the preaching of the old buddhas must be like this: that we study the way with this as the mind.

* * * * *

[V3:14] {2:575}

又、趙州眞際大師、そのかみ南泉に問、いかにあらんかこれ道にてある、と。南泉、しめしていはく、平常の心、これ道なり、と。

Again, Great Master Zhenji of Zhaozhou once asked Nanquan, "What is the way?"[31]

Nanquan replied, "The ordinary mind is the way."

---

27 **the same or not the same** (*hitoshi ya, hitoshikarazu ya* ひとしや、ひとしからずや): Presumably meaning, "the same or not the same as the mind of the Buddha and the ancestral masters."

28 **if there is something with which nature is naturally intimate, the mind of the old buddhas naturally speaks of the mind of the old buddhas** (*jinen, onozukara shinsetsu naru tokoro araba, kobutsu no shin onozukara kobutsu no shin o toku* 自然、おのづから親切なるところあらば、古佛の心おのづから古佛の心をとく): Perhaps meaning something like, "when the things of nature are just themselves, they are the buddha mind revealing itself."

29 **When this mind awakens, it is inevitable** (*kono shin, satoru toki, yamu koto o ezu* この心、さとるとき、やむことをえず): Probably meaning that its "speaking of the mind of the old buddhas" is inevitable.

30 **both mastery of the meaning and mastery of its exposition** (*shūtsū mo settsū mo* 宗通も説通も); **neither a way of practice nor a way of discipline** (*gyōdō mo kaidō mo* 行道も戒道も): The former pair is a common expression for spiritual understanding and its expression, respectively; the latter pair is an unusual combination, perhaps indicating spiritual practices and rules, respectively. Neither pair occurs elsewhere in the *Shōbōgenzō*.

31 **Great Master Zhenji of Zhaozhou** (*Jōshū Shinsai daishi* 趙州眞際大師): I.e., Zhaozhou Congshen 趙州從諗 (778-897), famous disciple of Nanquan Puyuan 南泉普願 (748-835), whom he questions here in Dōgen's Japanese translation. Their conversation is found at *shinji Shōbōgenzō* 眞字正法眼藏, DZZ.5:134, case 19; and see Supplementary Notes, s.v. "Ordinary mind is the way."

[V3:15]

いはくのこころは、よのつねのこころ、これ道なり、といふなり。よのつねの心とならふこと、もともかすかなるべし。身におきても、心におきても、時には、よのつねなり、とならふなり。たとへば、いささかも染汚なく、趣向なきなり。身心におきては、昨日を今日といはず、今日をあすといはず、おこなはず、身を心となさず、心より身におもむかざるなり。かくのごとくなるを、平常心なりとはいふに、平常なる百草の階級とあやまりぬべきあり。ここにとどこほれらんほどは、百草の平常にてあることを、辨肯すべきなり。この平常の心の道にてあるによりて、百草もかれず、くちざるなり。諸佛祖の、よをのがれ、われをわすれて、みちをおこなひきたれりしも、平常にあらざれば、うべからざるなり、行道、おのづから平常なるがゆえに。われらも、従來の世情をなげすてて、すみやかに佛祖のあとをおこなひ、すすみゆくに、よのつねのこころ、これ道にてればとて、おこなはざらんと、おもひし、をもむきもすれば、平常をあやまらんと擬するなるべし。修證はなきにあらず、平常にあらぬはなし、平常にあらぬはなく、染汚せんことはあらじ、となり。

The point of what this says is that our usual mind is the way.[32] Studying it as our usual mind is extremely subtle. It is to study that, whether in the body or in the mind, at times, it is usual.[33] For example, it is without the slightest defilement or pursuit.[34] In body and mind, we do not say that yesterday is today; we do not say that, nor behave as if, today is tomorrow; we do not make the body from the mind; we do not move from the mind to the body. When we say that being like this is "the ordinary mind," we may have mistaken it for a class of the ordinary hundred grasses. As long as we remain stuck here, we should confirm that the

---

32 **The point of what this says is that our usual mind is the way** (*iwaku no kokoro wa, yo no tsune no kokoro, kore dō nari, to iu nari* いはくのこころは、よのつねのこころ、これ道なり、といふなり): Dōgen is here simply translating the Chinese term *pingchang* 平常 (J. *byōjō*; "ordinary") with the Japanese *yo no tsune* よのつね (often written 世の常; "normal," "usual," etc.).

33 **whether in the body or in the mind, at times, it is usual** (*shin ni okitemo, shin ni okitemo, toki ni wa, yo no tsune nari* 身におきても、心におきても、時には、よのつねなり): Or, "at the time, it is usual." Perhaps meaning something like, "whether it be the body or the mind, [the way] is usual in each time." Dōgen may be playing here with the temporal sense of *tsune* 常 ("constant") in the expression *yo no tsune* 世の常.

34 **it is without the slightest defilement or pursuit** (*isasaka mo zenna naku, shukō naki nari* いささかも染汚なく、趣向なきなり): "Without defilement" (*zenna* 染汚) likely evokes the words of Nanyue Huairang 南嶽懷讓 (677-744) that Dōgen will repeat in the last sentence of this section. "Without pursuit" (or "direction"; *shukō* 趣向) may reflect the question and answer that follow immediately after the exchange between Zhaozhou and Nanquan quoted above, in section 14 (as found in the *Jingde chuandeng lu* 景德傳燈錄, T.2076.51:276c15-16):

師曰、還có趣向否。南泉曰。擬向即乖。

The Master [Zhaozhou] asked, "Should we pursue it?"

Nanquan said, "To think to pursue it is to be estranged from it."

V3. Beyond the Buddha *Butsu kōjō ji* 佛向上事 253

hundred grasses are ordinary. Since this ordinary mind is the way, the hundred grasses do not wither and do not rot. The buddhas and ancestors have escaped the world, forgotten themselves, and practiced the way; they could not have done so were it not ordinary, for practice of the way is naturally ordinary. We too, when we have cast aside our previous worldly sentiments and quickly practiced and progressed in the traces of the buddhas and ancestors, thinking that the ordinary mind is the way, may have thought not to practice it, may have doubts that, when we pursue it, we misunderstand the ordinary. "It's not that it lacks practice and verification"; there is nothing that is not ordinary.[35] With nothing that is not ordinary, there is no defilement of it.

[V3:16] {2:576}

むかし、釋迦老子、菩提樹下にして明星をみて、たちまちに悟道す。この ことわりは、一物をも將來せざる道理なり。ひごろは、ほとけ、明星を證 して、いまよりは、明星、ほとけをさとりぬるなり。なにのゆえにか明星 に證せられ、又明星を證する。いはゆる、修證はなきにあらず、染汚せん ことはうべからず、となり。

Long ago, the Old Master Śākya at the foot of the bodhi tree saw the morning star and immediately awakened to the way.[36] The reason for this is the principle of not bringing up any thing.[37] Usually, the Buddha verified the morning star; thereafter, the morning star had awakened to the Buddha. For what reason was he verified by the morning star, or verified the morning star? It was "it's not that it lacks practice and verification, but they can't defile it."[38]

---

35 **"It's not that it lacks practice and verification"** (*shushō wa naki ni arazu* 修證はな きにあらず): From the conversation between the Sixth Ancestor and his disciple Nanyue Huairang 南嶽懷讓 recorded in the *shinji Shōbōgenzō* 眞字正法眼藏 (DZZ.5:178, case 101) and appearing frequently in Dōgen's writing; see Supplementary Notes, s.v. "What thing is it that comes like this?" and "Practice and verification."

36 **morning star** (*myōjō* 明星): I.e., the planet Venus. From the tradition that Prince Siddhārtha became a buddha upon seeing the star rise.

37 **principle of not bringing up any thing** (*ichimotsu o mo shōrai sezaru dōri* 一物を も將來せざる道理): Likely, an allusion to the words of Nanquan in his exchange with Huineng introduced just above, in section 15:

祖云、爾作麼生會。師曰、説似一物即不中。

The Ancestor asked, "How do you understand it?" [i.e., the thing that comes like this]. The Master replied, "To say it's like any thing wouldn't hit it."

38 **"it's not that it lacks practice and verification, but they can't defile it"** (*shushō wa naki ni arazu, zenna sen to wa u bekarazu* 修證はなきにあらず、染汚せんとはうべ からず): From Nanquan's response to Huineng in the dialogue introduced in section 15:

祖曰、還假修證否。師曰、修證即不無、染汚即不得。

The Ancestor said, "Does it [i.e., the thing that comes like this] nevertheless depend on practice and verification?"

254 DŌGEN'S *SHŌBŌGENZŌ* VOLUME VII

* * * * *

[V3:17]

長慶といひし、保福和尚に問、いろをみるは、すなはちこころをみるといふ、また、ふねをみるや。保福云く、みる。長慶の云く、ふねはしばらくおく、いかにあらんかこれ心。保福、ゆびして、ふねをさす。

> The one called Changqing asked Reverend Baofu, "It is said that to see forms is to see the mind.[39] Do you see the boat?"
>
> Baofu said, "I see it."
>
> Changqing said, "Leaving aside the boat for now, what is the mind?"
>
> Baofu pointed at the boat.

[V3:18]

しかあればすなはち、いまのよに、われら學道せんにも、佛祖のこころを論ずることは、かくのごとくあるとしるべし。しかありとしりぬるには、外道・二乗等にはひかれざるなり。諸佛如來、かならず三昧に遊化するとき、これを佛道といふ。このなかに、法のために身をすつるといふことあり。そのふねを、あきらめならふには、佛法といふことを、しるべきなり。佛法といふは、いはゆる、萬法なり、百草なり、諸法なり、三界なり。ほとけとして、これを究盡せざるはなきゆえに、これとしてほとけに究盡せられぬはなし。しかあればすなはち、生をとぶらふに、諸法にあらぬはなし、死をたづねるに、いまだ萬法をはなれず。そのためにすといふも、又この法にてあるべし。このゆえに、爲法捨身のむね、あきらかなり。この生、この死、ひさしく住持しきたれる、他にうけたるにあらず、人をまつことなし。這裏消息として、生はこれ身なり、身は即法なり。しかあれば、生の必ず捨なる、もとより法のためなり。死の捨をわすれざる、いまに法に證せられ、法にあらざらんところに身をすてんともとめん、さらにあるべからざるなり。その捨と云は、かならず身にかうぶりて、まさしく爲法捨身のとき、ひかりをめぐらして證顧するは、爲身捨法にてもあり。いはくのこころは、法みづから聲をあげて宣揚するには、爲

> The Master answered, "It's not that it lacks practice and verification, but it can't be defiled by them."

39 The one called Changqing asked Reverend Baofu (*Chōkei to iishi, Hofuku oshō ni tou* 長慶といひし、保福和尚に問): I.e., Changqing Huileng 長慶慧稜 (854-932) and Baofu Congzhan 保福從展 (d. 928), two disciples of Xuefeng Yicun 雪峰義存 (822-908). Their exchange, given here in Japanese, can be found in the *Jingde chuandeng lu* 景德傳燈錄 (T.2076.51:354c8-10), and in Dōgen's *shinji Shōbōgenzō* 眞字正法眼藏 (DZZ.5:222, case 192):

> 長慶問保福、見色便見心、還見船子麼。福曰、見。師曰、船子且致、作麼生是心。福却指船子。
>
> Changqing asked Baofu, "To see form is to see the mind. Do you see the boat?"
> Fu said, "I see it."
> The Master [Chingqing] said, "Leaving aside the boat for now, what about the mind?"
> Fu pointed at the boat.

V3. Beyond the Buddha *Butsu kōjō ji* 佛向上事   255

身捨法のことばあり、身のおのづから聲をあげて開演するには、爲法捨身
のことばつたはれ、この佛行、ならひきたり、まなびきたれりけることひ
さしきわれらにてもあるなり、としるべし。いま、ゆくすえも退轉のある
べからざる、いまの行に行ぜられて、行のわれにあまらざるなし。

Thus, we should recognize that, in our own study of the way in the present age, there is discussion of the mind of the buddhas and ancestors like this. When we have recognized this, we are not drawn to the other paths or the two vehicles. When the buddhas, the tathāgatas, invariably disport themselves in samādhi, this is called the way of the buddhas. Within this, there is discarding the body for the sake of the dharma. To clarify and study "the boat," we should recognize what is meant by "buddha dharma." "Buddha dharma" means "the myriad dharmas," "the hunded grasses," "all the dharmas," "the three realms." Because there are no buddhas, as buddhas, who fail to investigate them exhaustively, there are none of these, as these, not exhaustively investigated by the buddhas. Thus, when we inquire about birth, there is none that is not all the dharmas; when we ask about death, it is still not apart from the myriad dharmas.[40] We may act for their sake, but that is also this dharma; therefore, the meaning of "*discarding the body for the sake of the dharma*" is clear.[41]

This birth and this death that we have long been maintaining were not received from another, do not depend on other people. As our circumstances here, birth is our body, and our body is itself the dharma; therefore, the invariable discarding of birth is, fundamentally, for the dharma. One who does not forget the discarding of death is immediately verified by the dharma; even should we seek to discard the body where there is no dharma, this could never be. This "discarding" is always received by the body, and precisely when we d*iscard the body for the sake of the dharma*, turning the light around and verifying and reflecting on it, it is also *discarding the dharma for the sake of the body*.[42] The mean-

---

40 **when we inquire about birth** (*shō o toburau ni* 生をとぶらふに): Here and below in this passage, *shō* 生 ("birth") might also be rendered "life."

41 **We may act for their sake, but that is also this dharma** (*sono tame ni su to iu mo, mata kono hō nite aru beshi* そのためにすといふも、又この法にてあるべし): Probably meaning, "we may act for the sake of the dharmas of birth and death, but such action is also the buddha dharma."

"discarding the body for the sake of the dharma" (*i hō sha shin* 爲法捨身): A fixed expression occurring several times in Chinese Buddhist texts and in the *Shōbōgenzō*.

42 **discarding the dharma for the sake of the body** (*i shin sha hō* 爲身捨法): A reversal of the standard phrase found also in the "Shōbōgenzō gyōbutsu iigi" 正法眼藏行佛威儀. A similar pattern occurs in the "Shōbōgenzō jishō zanmai" 正法眼藏自證三昧: "They discard the body for the sake of the dharma" (*ihō shashin* 爲法捨身); "they seek the dharma for the sake of the body" (*ishin guhō* 爲身求法).

ing of what this says is that, when the dharma raises its own voice and proclaims, there are the words "*discarding the dharma for the sake of the body*"; and, when the body raises its own voice and expounds, the words "*discarding the body for the sake of the dharma*" are transmitted. And we should know that we are the ones who have long been studying and learning this buddha practice. Never turning back from it now or in the future, we are practiced by the present practice, and the practice never fails to exceed us.

[V3:19] {2:577}

むかしよりいはゆる、道に達する人は生死をこころにまかす、と。まこと
にしかあるべし、うたがふべきにあらず。このむねあらはるるとき、わが
こころをも知り、わが心をしるとき、此旨をもあらはすなり。又我が身と
云ことをも知り、我身の、あらゆる威儀をも、あきらめならふなり。これ
をならふに、生といひ、死といふことのありやうをも、あきらむる也。こ
れを明るは、あきらむまじかりつるを、よこさまにあきらめけるにはあら
ず。あきらかなるを明るには、かくの如く明めらるると、會すべきなり。

From long ago, it has been said that those who have mastered the way leave birth and death to the mind. Truly, this is so, and we should not doubt it. When the meaning of this has appeared, we also know our own mind; and when we know our own mind, it also reveals the meaning of this. Moreover, we also know what our body is and clarify and learn all deportments of our body. In learning this, we have also clarified the nature of what birth is and what death is. Clarifying this does not mean to have clarified across what had not been clarified; we should understand that we have clarified in this way when we clarify what is clear.

[V3:20]

此旨をあきらむるには、まづ心と云やうをしり、心と云ふやうをきくべき
なり。其様子をきくと云は、云く、萬法は是心なり、としり、三界は唯心
なり、と會するなり。知ると云ひ、會すと云ふをも、萬法と三界とにて、
かくのごとくなりける、となり。しかうしてのちに、生はなににまかせら
るる、死はなににまかせらるると、くはしく撿點すべきなり。撿點しもて
ゆくに、あらはるることわりあり、いはゆる、唯心の活計なり、他の、生
ぜしめけるにあらず、唯心の消息なり、物にひかれけるにあらず。然あれ
ば即ち、生死消息、ただ唯心のまかせられけるなり。故いかんとなれば、
萬法にあらぬ唯心なく、唯心にあらぬ萬法はなし。この生死をはらつて、
唯心にあらぬところにおかましと擬すと云ふとも、即ちなほ唯心にはきら
はるべからず。まことに、萬法にまかするは唯心にまかする、とは、二乗
はしらず、外道は分なし、況や凡夫の、夢にも見る處にてあらんや。しか
あれば、我が身をしることも、我心をしることも、唯心にならひ、萬法に
ならふべし。倉卒にすべからず、審細にすべし。これを、生死をこころに
まかする様子、とは云なり。いたづらに、凡夫のこころにまかせんずるや
うにおもうは、あしし。佛の聖教にも、凡夫の心に生死をまかするとはき

V3. Beyond the Buddha *Butsu kōjō ji* 佛向上事　　257

こえず。又、わが心も、生死のまかせらるるにてあらず、凡夫にはあらざ
ると了知すべし。

In clarifying the meaning of this, we should first know how the mind is, hear how the mind is. To hear how it is means to know that the myriad dharmas are this very mind, to understand that the three realms are only mind.[43] It is [to know] that what is called "knowing" and what is called "understanding," as the myriad dharmas and the three realms, have also been like this. After this, we should investigate in detail to what our birth has been given over, to what our death has been given over. As we go on investigating in detail, a principle becomes apparent: it is the livelihood of "only mind," not born by another, the circumstances of "only mind," not brought out by things. Thus, the circumstances of birth and death are just "only mind" having been given over. What is the reason? There is no "only mind" that is not the myriad dharmas; there are no myriad dharmas that are not "only mind." Even though we might think to dispose of this birth and death and put it somewhere that is not "only mind," we would still not be disliked by "only mind." Truly, that giving oneself over to the myriad dharmas is giving oneself over to "only mind," the worldly, the followers of the two vehicles do not know, and the other paths lack the status [to understand]; how much less then could it be something common people see even in their dreams? Thus, both knowing our own bodies and knowing our own minds should learn from "only mind," we should learn from the myriad dharmas. We should not do it precipitately; we should do it in detail. This is called the state of giving birth and death over to the mind. It is bad to think that this is idly giving them over to the mind of the common person. One does not hear in the sacred teaching of the buddhas of giving birth and death over to the mind of the common person. Moreover, we should recognize that our own minds are also not given over by birth and death, and that we are not common people.

* * * * *

43　**the myriad dharmas are this very mind** (*manbō wa ze shin nari* 萬法は是心な り); **the three realms are only mind** (*sangai wa yui shin nari* 三界は唯心なり): The Chinese version of the latter phrase occurs very often in the Buddhist literature and is the title theme of Dōgen's "Shōbōgenzō sangai yui shin" 正法眼藏三界唯心; see Supplementary Notes, s.v. "The three realms are only mind." The exact Chinese equivalent of the former phrase is not common, though one does often find a similar expression, "the myriad dharmas are only mind" (*manbō yui shin* 萬法唯心). Below in this section, Dōgen will use the expression "only mind" (*yui shin* 唯心) as if it were a compound noun.

258 DŌGEN'S *SHŌBŌGENZŌ* VOLUME VII

[V3:21] {2:578}

佛家に觀世音菩薩あり。是をみぬ人は少なく、是れを知る人はまれなり。
風流を買に錢をもちいず、おもてを見るに、いづれか正・不正。いはんと
しては、身をめぐらして禪牀にのぼり、きかんとしては、手をとりて地面
にたつ。一法にもさへられざる處に、慈眼、我れらをてらす。應と應ぜら
ること、驢の井をみると、井の驢をみるとなり。これをあきらむるに、人
なからん。切忌道著、道著せば、即ち頭角も生ぜん。只色を見に心ろをあ
きらめ、聲をきくに、道をさとるのみなり。こころを明む、と云心は、佛
の心にてあるべし。さとる、と云ふ道は、佛道にてあるべし。佛道のな
か、佛家のうちには、ただ見色明心、聞聲悟道のみあり、さらに一物な
し。もしかくのごとくあらんところは、すでに佛道に、應以此身得度者、
即現此身而爲説法と、とくべし。まことに、現身にせざる説法はなく、説
法にあらぬ得度はあらじ。

In the house of the buddhas, there is Bodhisattva Avalokiteśvara.
Those who have not seen him are few; those who know him are rare. His
elegance does not cost a cent; when we look at his faces, which is the
front and which not?[44] To speak [of him], we turn our bodies round and
mount the meditation platform; to hear him, we take his hand and stand
on the ground.[45] Where unobstructed by even a single dharma, his compassionate eyes illumine us.[46] [His] response and [our] being responded
to are "the donkey looking in the well" and "the well looking at the donkey."[47] There is no one to clarify this. "*It's strictly forbidden to speak; if*

---

44   **His elegance does not cost a cent** (*fūryū o kau ni sen o mochiizu* 風流を買うに錢
をもちいず): Perhaps reflecting the well-known line in the *Xiangyang ge* 襄陽歌, by Li
Bai 李白:

清風朗月不用一錢買，玉山自倒非人推。

The fresh breeze and bright moon do not cost a cent;
The jade mountain topples of itself, without anyone pushing it.

when we look at his faces, which is the front and which not? (*omote o miru ni, izure
ka shō fushō* おもてを見るに、いづれか正・不正): Presumably, a reference to the
eleven-headed version of Avalokiteśvara (*Jūichi men Kannon* 十一面觀音).

45   **To speak [of him], we turn our bodies round and mount the meditation platform** (*iwan to shite wa, mi o megurashite zenshō ni nobori* いはんとしては、身をめぐ
らして禪牀にのぼり): The grammatical subject is unexpressed here and might well be
understood as "he" [the Bodhisattva]: "To speak, he turns his body round and mounts
the meditation platform."

46   **his compassionate eyes illumine us** (*jigen, warera o terasu* 慈眼、我れらをてら
す): Likely a reference to the thousand-armed, thousand-eyed version of the Bodhisattva
(*senju sengen Kannon* 千手千眼觀音).

47   **"the donkey looking in the well" and "the well looking at the donkey"** (*ro no
sei o miru to, sei no ro o miru to* 驢の井をみると、井の驢をみると): From a dialogue,
featuring Caoshan Benzhi 曹山本寂 (840-901) and Senior Seat De 德上座 (dates unknown), recorded in Dōgen's *shinji Shōbōgenzō* 眞字正法眼藏 (DZZ.5:194, case 125);
see Supplementary Notes, s.v. "Like the well looking at the donkey."

V3. Beyond the Buddha *Butsu kōjō ji* 佛向上事 259

you speak, horns will grow on your head."[48]

It is just "clarifying the mind upon seeing forms and awakening to the way upon hearing sounds."[49] The "mind" of "clarifying the mind" is the mind of the buddhas; the "way" of "awakening [to the way]" is the way of the buddhas. In the way of the buddhas, in the house of the buddhas, there is only "*seeing forms and clarifying the mind, hearing sounds and awakening to the way*"; there is nothing beyond this. Where it is like this, surely in the way of the buddhas, we should say, "*To those who would attain deliverance by means of this body, I appear in this body and preach the dharma for them.*"[50] Truly, there is no preaching of the dharma that does not appear in a body; there is no attaining deliverance that is not preaching the dharma.

* * * * *

48   **"It's strictly forbidden to speak; if you speak, horns will grow on your head"** (*sekki dōjaku, dōjaku seba, sunawachi zukaku mo shō zen* 切忌道著、道著せば、即ち頭角も生ぜん): A mix of Chinese and Japanese translation, from a saying attributed to Nanquan Puyuan 南泉普願; see Supplementary Notes, s.v. "Move among different types."

49   **"clarifying the mind upon seeing forms and awakening to the way upon hearing sounds"** (*shiki o miru ni kokoro o akirame, shō o kiku ni, dō o satoru* 色を見に心ろをあきらめ、聲をきくに、道をさとる): Japanese rendering of two phrases that Dōgen will repeat in Chinese just below (*ken shiki myō shin, mon shō go dō* 見色明心、聞聲悟道). In the context of his discussion of the Bodhisattva Avalokiteśvara here, Dōgen may have had in mind a saying of Yunmen Wenyen 雲門文偃 that he mentions in a postscript to the "Shōbōgenzō Kannon" 正法眼藏觀音 chapter (a saying found in Dōgen's *shinji Shōbōgenzō* 眞字正法眼藏, DZZ.5:258, case 257; see also the *Yunmen yulu* 雲門語錄, T.1988.47:554a13-15):

> 擧古云、聞聲悟道見色明心。師云、作麼生是聞聲悟道見色明心。乃云、觀世音菩薩將錢來買餬餅。放下手云、元來秖是饅頭。
>
> Taking up an old saying, [Yunmen] said, "Hearing sounds and understanding the way; seeing forms and clarifying the mind." The Master [Yunmen] said, "What is this 'hearing sounds and understanding the way; seeing forms and clarifying the mind'?" Then he said, "Bodhisattva Observer of the Sounds of the World comes with cash to buy rice cakes." He put down his hand and said, "Basically, they're just dumplings."

50   **"To those who would attain deliverance by means of this body, I appear in this body and preach the dharma for them"** (*ō i shi shin tokudo sha, soku gen shi shin ni i seppō* 應以此身得度者、即現此身而爲説法): From the Avalokiteśvara chapter of the *Lotus Sūtra* (*Miaofa lianhua jing* 妙法蓮華經, T.262.9:57a23ff.), in which it is said that, to those who can attain deliverance through contact with a particular body (a buddha, a *pratyeka-buddha*, a *śrāvaka*, etc.), the Bodhisattva Avalokiteśvara appears as that body and preaches the dharma for them. See Supplementary Notes, s.v. "Manifesting a body to preach the dharma."

[V3:22] {2:579}

ふるき人のいはく、この一印の田地、なんぢにうり、あたふることひさし。然あるを四至界畔、しられざることあり。ひごろは、田地はのこらずあたへしかども、中心にありつる樹子は、いまだあたへざりつるを、いまよりは、樹子をもをしむべからず、といへり。

An ancient has said, "I sold you this paddy field long ago, but you haven't recognized its four border ridges.[51] The field, I always gave without remainder, but the tree that was in the middle, I haven't given you. From now on, I won't begrudge you the tree."

[V3:23]

これを參學するには、この田地をさづけられて、ひさしくなりにけることをわすれざるべし。界畔をたひらかにして、四至あきらかなり。遊戯するところに、ことごとく瑞をなし、祥をなす。まことに、われらにつきにける田地、かくのごとくありける、とおもひあはすべし。

In studying this, we should not forget the fact that it has been a long time since we were given this paddy field. Its border ridges are level, and its four sides are clear. Where we disport ourselves in it, it produces all manner of auspiciousness and good fortune. Truly, we should take into consideration that the field we have had has been like this.

---

51 **An ancient** (*furuki hito* ふるき人): A saying given in Japanese. Though Dōgen's source is uncertain, a similar saying is attributed to Xuedou Zhongxian 雪竇重顯 (980-1052): see *Mingjue chanshi yulu* 明覺禪師語錄 (T.1996.47:679b15-17):

> 一日云、大衆。者一片田地、分付來多時也。爾諸人四至界畔、猶未識在。若要中心一樹子、我也不惜。

> One day, he said, "Members of the great assembly, it's been a long time since I divvied up this rice paddy for you, but people still haven't recognized its four border ridges. If you want the tree in the middle, I won't begrudge it."

Treasury of the True Dharma Eye
Variant Text 4

Washing the Face
Senmen
洗面

Washing the Face

Senmen

INTRODUCTION

This work represents the version of "Senmen" included as number 50 in the sixty-chapter *Shōbōgenzō*. Like the version represented by chapter 50 in the seventy-five-chapter *Shōbōgenzō*, it bears colophons stating that it was presented to the assembly, first in the autumn of 1239 at Kōshōji, and again in the winter of 1243 at Kippōji, in Echizen; it lacks the third colophon found in the seventy-five-chapter *Shōbōgenzō* text, recording an additional presentation in 1250 at Eiheiji — a fact that suggests this text preserves an earlier version of the work.

The two versions are generally parallel in their organization and content but also show many, sometimes quite interesting, differences. Thus, the preservation of this version provides an excellent example of how Dōgen drafted and edited his writing. The annotation of this translation does not repeat information provided in the seventy-five-chapter translation; rather, it is limited to indications of the correspondences between the two versions and the occasional note on material specific to the present text.

正法眼藏拾遺四

Treasury of the True Dharma Eye
Variant Text 4

洗面

Washing the Face

(六十巻本系・洞雲寺本所収)

(Sixty-chapter compilation version, Tōunji text)

[V4:1] {2:580}

釈迦牟尼佛言、以油塗身、澡浴塵穢、著新淨衣、内外倶淨。

Buddha Śākyamuni said:[1]
  Anointing the body with oil,
  He bathes away the dirt;
  Donning a new clean robe,
  Both inside and out are pure.

[V4:2]

しかあればしるべし、身心に香油をぬり、身心の塵を澡浴するは、内外ともにきよきなり、内外ともにきよむるなり。内身・外身をきよむるなり、身内・身外をきよむるなり、心内・心外をきよむるなり。身心内外、みなともに清淨なるがゆえに、内外倶淨の佛道取現成せり。

Thus, we know that to apply scented oils to body and mind, and to bathe away the dust of body and mind are "both inside and out are pure," are purifying both inside and out.[2] They are purifying the inner body and the outer body; they are purifying the inside of the body and the outside of the body; they are purifying the inside of the mind and the outside of the mind. Because the inside and outside of body and mind are both pure, there occurred this saying by the Buddha, "*both inside and out are pure.*"

---

1   **Buddha Śākyamuni** (*Shakamuni butsu* 釋迦牟尼佛): This section corresponds to section 1 of the seventy-five-chapter *Shōbōgenzō* text.

2   **Thus, we know** (*shika areba shiru beshi* しかあればしるべし): This section parallels section 2 of the seventy-five-chapter *Shōbōgenzō* text, but the content is quite different.

[V4:3]

しかあるに、不聞佛經、不參佛道の愚人いはく、澡浴は、みのうへのみ、すすがるにとも、身内に五臓あり、六腑あり、かれらを一一に澡浴せざらんは、清淨といふべからず、しかあれば、あながちに身表を澡浴すべからず。かくのごとくいふは、佛道をしらず、佛説をきかず、佛經にあはず、佛祖嫡嫡の兒孫にあらざるなり。

Nevertheless, stupid people who *have not heard the sūtras of the buddhas and have not studied the way of the buddhas* say that, while bathing may wash just the surface of the body, within the body, there are the five organs and the six viscera, and, if we do not bathe each of those, we will not be pure; therefore, we need not necessarily bathe the surface of the body.[3] Those who talk like this do not know the way of the buddhas, have not heard the preaching of the buddhas, have not encountered the sūtras of the buddhas, and are not the descendants of the line of successors of buddhas and ancestors.

[V4:4]

しばらく照顧すべし、我身の内外、いまだあきらめざるところなり。諸法の性相、いまだあきらめざるとひとし。我身をあきらめざることは、我心をあきらめざらんがごとし。しかあれども、その我心をきよめんとするには、貪・瞋・癡をなからしめんとす、諸斷を習學す。しかありといへども、我心の邊量際斷、いまだむかしよりしらざるところなり。その量、しらざれども、これをきよむる法を學す。所斷に擬する貪・瞋・癡も、その邊表、また不可得なりといへども、かくのごとく修學し、究盡しきたりて成道す。身心一如なるゆゑに、身量もただ五尺・六尺のみにはあらざるなり、五尺・六尺は、五尺・六尺にあらざるべし、處在も、此界他界・盡十方界等の量にかかはるべからず。遮裏是什麼處在、説細説麁のゆゑに、心量もまた思量分別・不思量不分別等にあらず。かくのごとくのゆゑに、身量もきはむべきにあらず、心量もきはむべきにあらず。身量・心量、かくのごとくなるがゆゑに、得恁麼活鱍鱍なり、活鱍鱍地の透脱、かくのごとし。この身心量のごとく、澡浴量も、かくのごとし。この量を量拈して修證する、これ佛祖道なり、ただ計我を實とすべからず。このゆゑに、洗浴してきよめ、塗香してきよむ。身量をことごとくあらふべくは、すなはち洗面これなり。もし、身量ことごとくあらはれずば、澡浴塵穢、内外倶淨の道理、いかにしてか受持せん。まさに一澡浴量の身心量を究盡して清淨するは、佛祖道なり。　一澡浴量に、身心量を究盡清淨ならしむるなり、たとひ四大なりとも、たとひ五蘊なりとも、たとひ不壞性なりとも。四大とは、地・水・火・風なり。五蘊とは、色・受・想・行・識なり。澡浴してさらに清淨の四大五蘊ならしむなり。ただ水をきたしすぎて、そのあとを、清淨なるとのみしるべきにあらず。水、なにとしてか本淨ならん、水、なにとしてか自淨ならん、水、もし自淨なるといはば、塵垢の自淨も、水とひとしかるべし。水の淨・不淨を論ずるにはあらず、香油の淨・不淨をもとむるにあらず、佛祖の修證を參學するなり。もし、塵垢は畢竟じて染汚なり、といはば、水もまた、染汚をなすべし。しかあれども、佛

3　**Nevertheless** (*shika aru ni* しかあるに): Aside from minor variation, this section closely accords with section 3 of the seventy-five-chapter *Shōbōgenzō* text.

V4. Washing the Face *Senmen* 洗面

祖の澡浴を參學修證するなり。あるいは淨水をもて澡浴し、あるいは河水
にいりて澡浴す、あるいは諸法を拈じて澡浴するなり。法を拈じて法をき
よむる法は、ひとり佛祖道のみにあり、外道はしらず、外道にはなきがゆ
えに。もし、愚人のいふがごとくならば、五臓六腑を細塵に抹して、即空
ならしめて、水をもてあらふとも、なほさらに塵中をあらはず、空中をあ
らはざらん。このとき、いかなる法を修してか、内外の清淨を見取せん。
愚兒、いかでか空を澡浴する法をしらん、愚兒、いかでか空を拈じて身心
を澡浴する法をきかん。

We should reflect awhile on the fact that our bodies are something
not yet clarified, just as the nature and marks of the dharmas are not yet
clarified.[4] That we have not clarified our bodies is like our not having
clarified our minds. However, when we try to purify our minds, we train
in the eradications, in order to rid ourselves of greed, anger, and delusion.[5] And this is so even though where the limits of our minds are cut
off is something we have not known from long ago.[6] We do not know
its dimensions, but we study ways to purify it. While the boundaries
of the greed, anger, and delusion to be eradicated are also ungraspable,
having trained in this way and exhaustively investigated them, we attain
the way.

Because body and mind are one, the dimensions of the body are not
merely five feet or six feet; its five feet or six feet must not be five feet or
six feet, and its location should have nothing to do with the dimensions
of *this world or other worlds, or of all the worlds in the ten directions.*
"Where are we here, that we're talking of fine and talking of coarse?"
Therefore, the dimensions of the mind are also not [measured by] *thinking or discriminating, or not thinking or not discriminating.*[7] Because
they are like this, we cannot exhaust the dimensions of the body; we
cannot exhaust the dimensions of the mind. And because the dimensions

4   **We should reflect awhile** (*shibaraku shōko su beshi* しばらく照顧すべし): This
section, while roughly parallel to sections 4 and 5 of the seventy-five-chapter *Shōbōgenzō* text, contains much that is different.

5   **eradications** (*shodan* 諸斷): I.e., practices to eliminate the spiritual defilements.

6   **where the limits of our minds are cut off** (*gashin no henryō saidan* 我心の邊量際
斷): An awkward attempt to render an unusual expression, likely meaning simply "the
limits of our minds."

7   **Therefore, the dimensions of the mind are also not [measured by] thinking or
discriminating, or not thinking or not discriminating** (*yue ni, shinryō mo mata shiryō
funbetsu fushiryō fufunbetsu tō ni arazu* ゆえに、心量もまた思量分別・不思量不分別
等にあらず): Presumably, the argument here is that, because body and mind are one,
and the dimensions of the body are incalculable, the dimensions of the mind are also inconceivable. The expression *no yue ni* のゆえに (rendered here "therefore") might also
be parsed with the preceding sentence, yielding, ". . . its location should have nothing
to do with the dimensions of this world or other worlds, or of all the worlds in the ten
directions; for 'where are we here, that we're talking of fine and talking of course?'"

266   DŌGEN'S *SHŌBŌGENZŌ* VOLUME VII

of the body and the dimensions of the mind are like this, they are thus brisk and lively, and their brisk and lively liberation is like this.[8] Because the dimensions of body and mind are like this, the dimensions of bathing them are also like this. Thinking on and taking up these dimensions, to practice and verify them — this is the way of the buddhas and ancestors.[9] We should not take the imputed self as real.

Therefore, we bathe and purify them, we apply fragrances and purify them. That we should wash all the dimensions of the body — this is "washing the face." If we do not wash all the dimensions of the body, how could we receive and keep the principle of "*He bathes away the dirt . . . Both inside and out are pure*"? Exhaustively to investigate and purify the dimensions of body and mind by the dimensions of a single bathing is the way of the buddhas and ancestors. By the dimensions of a single bathing, the dimensions of body and mind are exhaustively investigated and purified, be they the four elements, be they the five aggregates, be they the undestroyed nature. "The four elements" means earth, water, fire, and wind; "the five aggregates" means form, sensation, perception, formations, and consciousness. By bathing them, they are further turned into the pure four elements and five aggregates. But we should not think that this means simply that they are pure only after water is introduced and washes them. How could water be originally pure? How could water be pure in itself? If water is pure in itself, dirt should be pure in itself, the same as water. It is not a question of the purity or impurity of water; it is not seeking the purity or impurity of scented oils: it is studying the practice and verification of the buddhas and ancestors. If we say that, in the end, dirt is defiled, then water, too, should be defiling. Nevertheless, we study and we practice and verify the bathing [practiced by] the buddhas and ancestors. We use pure water to bathe; we go into river water to bathe; we take up the dharmas to bathe.

---

8   **their brisk and lively liberation is like this** (*kappatsupatchi no tōdatsu, kaku no gotoshi* 活鱍鱍地の透脱、かくのごとし): Taking *kappatsupatchi* 活鱍鱍地 ("brisk and lively") as modifying *tōdatsu* 透脱 ("liberation"); the phrase could also be read "the liberation of [or from] the brisk and lively state is like this." See Supplementary Notes, s.v. "Brisk and lively."

9   **Thinking on and taking up these dimensions** (*kono ryō o ryōnen shite* この量を量 拈して): A tentative translation of the unusual *ryōnen* 量拈, taking *ryō* here in the sense of "thinking" (*shiryō* 思量), from the earlier "thinking or discriminating" (*shiryō funbetsu* 思量分別); might also be taken as *shōryō* 商量 ("to deliberate"). Dōgen is here playing with the glyph *ryō* 量 ("measure"), otherwise rendered throughout this passage as "dimensions." The parallel passage in section 4 of the seventy-five-chapter *Shōbōgenzō* text reads simply, "taking up these dimensions" (*kono ryō o nentoku shite* この量 を拈得して).

V4. Washing the Face *Senmen* 洗面 267

The dharma in which we take up the dharma to purify the dharma is found only in the way of the buddhas and ancestors: the other paths do not know of it, for it does not exist in the other paths.[10] If it were as the stupid people say, then even if we were to grind down the five organs and six viscera to a fine dust, rendering them empty in themselves, and washed them with water, we would still not also be washing inside the dirt or washing inside the emptiness. At this time, what dharma could we practice, such that we would see their purity "inside and out"? How could foolish children know the dharma of bathing emptiness? How could foolish children hear of the dharma that takes up emptiness to bathe body and mind?

[V4:5] {2:582}

いはゆる佛祖道は、沐をもちいてきよむる法あり、このとき、　身心内外・五臓六腑、法界虚空の内外中間、ともにきよきなり。あるいは、香をもちいてきよむることあり、このとき、過・現・當來・因縁行業、ともにきよきなり。あるいは、一句一偈をもちいてきよむることあり、あるいは、一心一念をもちいてきよむることあり。

That is, the way of the buddhas and ancestors has a dharma of purifying by bathing; at this time, body and mind inside and out, the five organs and six viscera, the dharma realm and empty space inside, outside, and in between, are all pure. Or there is purifying by incense; at this time, the deeds that are causes and conditions in past, present, and future are all pure. Or there is purifying by one line or one gāthā; or there is purifying by one mind or one thought.[11]

[V4:6] {2:583}

經云、三沐三薫、身心清淨。しかあれば、身をきよめ、心をきよむるは、かならず一沐しては一薫し、かくのごとくあひつらなれて、三沐三薫するは、佛祖の修證なり。沐は、ゆあびるなり。薫は、香をたきて身體を薫ずるなり。しるべし、沐偈なり、薫句なり、乃至、風雨・水火・草木・日月・星辰にても、澡浴するなり。審細に參徹すべし。

10　**The dharma in which we take up the dharma to purify the dharma** (*hō o nenjite hō o kiyomuru hō* 法を拈じて法をきよむる法): The text from here to the end of this section loosely parallels section 5 in the seventy-five-chapter *Shōbōgenzō* text, which begins, however, with a rather different sentence:

いまだ染汚せざれども澡浴し、すでに大清淨なるにも澡浴する法は、ひとり佛祖道のみに保任せり、外道のしるところにあらず。

The dharma of bathing though not yet defiled and bathing when already completely pure has been maintained only in the way of the buddhas and ancestors; it is not something known by followers of other paths.

11　**Or there is purifying by one line or one gāthā** (*arui wa, ikku ichige o mochiite kiyomuru koto ari* あるいは、一句一偈をもちいてきよむることあり): This sentence does not occur in the parallel section 6 of the seventy-five-chapter *Shōbōgenzō* text.

268 DŌGEN'S *SHŌBŌGENZŌ* VOLUME VII

It is said in a sūtra,[12]

Bathing three times, censing three times;
Body and mind are pure.

Thus, in purifying the body and purifying the mind, we always bathe once and purify once; continuing in this way, "*bathing three times, censing three times*" is the practice and verification of the buddhas and ancestors. "Bathing" is dousing oneself with hot water; "censing" is lighting incense and perfuming the body. We should know it is a bathing gāthā, a censing line; and so on until wind and rain, water and fire, grass and trees, the sun, moon, and stars are bathing.[13] We should investigate this in detail.

[V4:7]

かくのごとくきよむるとき、法界の内外、ともに清淨なり、細塵の色・空ともに清淨なり。しかあれば、身をきよむるは、心をきよむるなり。身心をきよむるは、國土をきよめ、佛道をきよむるなり。清淨の界量、かならず佛道祖道の現成なり。これによりて清淨を超越し、染汚を脱落せり。面をきよむるは擧體をきよむるなり、擧體をきよむるは、諸法をきよむるなり。たとへば、沈香をあらひきよむるに、片片にをりて、あらふべからず、塵塵に抹して、あらふべからず。ただ表面をあらひて淨潔をみるは、佛道の恒規なり、法にかならず内外あらざるなり。このゆえに、淨ならしむれば、渾法ともに、淨を透脱するなり。

When we purify in this way, inside and out of the dharma realm are all pure, and the form and emptiness of the fine dust particles are all pure. Thus, purifying the body is purifying the mind; purifying body and mind is purifying the land and purifying the way of the buddhas. The dimensions of the realm of purity are invariably a manifestation of the way of the buddhas, the way of the ancestors. In accordance with these, we transcend purity and slough off defilement.[14] To purify the face is to purify the whole body; to purify the whole body is to purify the dharmas.

---

12   **a sūtra** (*kyō* 經): This section corresponds roughly to sections 7 and 8 of the seventy-five-chapter *Shōbōgenzō* text, though the last three sentences here do not occur in that text.

13   **it is a bathing gāthā, a censing line** (*mokuge nari kunku nari* 沐偈なり薫句なり): The unexpressed subject ("it") is unclear here; nor is it clear whether we are to take *mokuge* 沐偈 (and, *mutatis mutandis, kunku* 薫句) as "a gāthā of (or for) bathing," or (as is suggested by what follows here) "a gāthā that bathes."

14 **In accordance with these, we transcend purity and slough off defilement** (*kore ni yorite shōjō o chōotsu shi, zenna o datsuraku seri* これによりて清淨を超越し、染汚を脱落せり): This sentence corresponds roughly to the final sentence of section 4 of the seventy-five-chapter *Shōbōgenzō* text:

これによりて修證するに、淨を超越し、不淨を透脱し、非淨・非不淨を脱落するなり。

In practicing and verifying in accordance with these, we transcend purity, we pass beyond impurity, we slough off non-purity and non-impurity.

V4. Washing the Face *Senmen* 洗面 269

For example, when we wash and purify aloes wood incense, we would not break it into pieces and wash it, nor would we grind it into powder and wash it.[15] To see that it is clean simply by washing its surface is the fixed rule of the way of the buddhas. There are no inside and out in the dharma. Therefore, when we purify it, all the dharmas transcend purity.

[V4:8]

三寶を供養する法は、もろもろの香をたてまつらんとては、みづからが手をあらひ、香をとり、淨水をもて香をあらひきよめて、三寶にたてまつるなり。三祇百劫ののち、因圓果滿して、成正覺せんとするときも、てづからみづから袈裟をあらひ、身体をあらふなり。因圓果滿して、最後身の菩薩、ただいま樹下に坐せんとするに、なにのけがれありてか、これこれをのぞかん。しかあれども、身心を洗浴するは、諸佛の法なる道理、よくよく功夫參學すべし。

In the method of making offerings to the three treasures, when we wish to offer any kind of incense, we wash our hands, take the incense, wash and purify it with clean water, and make the offering to the three treasures.[16] After the three *asaṃkhyeya* and one hundred kalpas, when, with *cause perfected and effect completed*, one is to attain right awakening, with one's own hands, one washes the *kāṣāya* and washes the body.[17] When, with *cause perfected and effect completed*, the bodhisattvas in their last bodies are to take their seat beneath the tree, should there be any impurities, they will remove this or that one of them. We should carefully make concentrated effort and study the principle that, nevertheless, bathing body and mind is the dharma of the buddhas.[18]

[V4:9] {2:584}

洗面は、西天竺國よりつたはれて、東震旦國に流通せり。数百歳の佛祖、おこなひきたれるのみにあらず、億千萬劫の前後、あひつたはれり。ただ垢膩をのぞくのみにあらず、これ、佛祖の命脈なり。その體例は、いはく、もしおもてをあらはざれば、禮をうけ、他を禮する、ともに罪をうるなり。自禮も自受すべし、他禮もうるなり。自禮も自受すべし、他禮も他受すべし。かくのごとく、時節ともに間斷あらず。もし洗面せざれば、罪

---

15 **For example** (*tatoeba* たとへば): This example occurs in section 10 of the seventy-five-chapter *Shōbōgenzō* text.

16 **In the method of making offerings to the three treasures** (*sanbō o kuyō suru hō* 三寶を供養する法): This sentence parallels the opening of section 11 in the seventy-five-chapter *Shōbōgenzō* text.

17 **After the three *asaṃkhyeya* and one hundred kalpas** (*sangi hyakkō no nochi* 三祇百劫ののち): I.e., at the very end of the bodhisattva path. This reference to the purifications of the bodhisattva on the eve of buddhahood parallels material in the first part of section 4 of the seventy-five-chapter *Shōbōgenzō* text.

18 **nevertheless** (*shika aredomo* しかあれども): I.e., the buddhas bathe body and mind despite the fact that the bodhisattva has already removed any impurities before becoming a buddha.

をうくるなり。洗面の時節は、あるいは五便、あるいは昧旦をその時節とす。褊衫、あるいは直裰を著しながら、手巾をたづさへて洗面架におもむく。手巾は、一幅のぬのなり、ながさ一丈二尺にすべし。そのいろ、しろかるべからず、しろきは制す。

Washing the face was handed down from the Land of Sindhu in the West and spread in the Land of Cīnasthāna in the East.[19] It has not only been performed for hundreds of years by buddha after buddha and ancestor after ancestor; it has circulated before and after *koṭis* of thousands of myriads of kalpas. It is not only to remove grime and grease; it is the vital artery of the buddhas and ancestors.

It is said of its form that, when one does not wash the face, one incurs an offense both in receiving obeisance and in offering obeisance to another. Our own obeisance, we should receive ourselves, and also receive the obeisance of the other; our own obeisance, we should receive ourselves, and the other's obeisance should be received by the other.[20] In this way, at any time without interruption, when we do not wash the face, we incur an offense.

The time for washing the face may be either the fifth watch or at dawn.[21] Wearing the partial robe or the long robe, we take along a hand cloth and proceed to the face-washing stands. The hand cloth is a single piece of cloth, which should be one *jō* two *shaku* in length. Its color must not be white; white is forbidden.

[V4:10]

三千威儀經云、當用手巾有五事。一者當拭上下頭。二者當用一頭拭手、以一頭拭面。三者不得持拭鼻。四者以用拭膩汚、當即浣之。五者不得拭身體。若澡浴各當自有巾。いはゆる、手巾の半分にはおもてをのごひ、半分には手をのごふべし。はなたりをのごふことなかれ、はなのうちをののご

---

19 **Washing the face was handed down from the Land of Sindhu in the West** (*senmen wa, Saitenjiku koku yori tsutawarete* 洗面は、西天竺國よりつたはれて): The first three sentences of this section parallel section 12 in the seventy-five-chapter *Shōbōgenzō* text.

20 **Our own obeisance, we should receive ourselves** (*jirai mo jiju su beshi* 自禮も自受すべし): The point of this sentence is unclear; perhaps, suggesting that, in offering our respects to another, we are showing respect for ourselves; or, more provocatively, that our bowing to a buddha is a buddha bowing to a buddha. The corresponding sentence in section 13 of the seventy-five-chapter *Shōbōgenzō* text seems more straightforward:

自禮禮他、能禮所禮、性空寂なり。

One's own obeisance and the obeisance of the other, "the one who offers obeisance and the one to whom obeisance is offered — their natures are empty and quiescent."

21 **The time for washing the face** (*senmen no jisetsu* 洗面の時節): This sentence and the remainder this section correspond to sections 14 and 15 in the seventy-five-chapter *Shōbōgenzō* text.

V4. Washing the Face *Senmen* 洗面   271

ふことなかれ、わき・せなか・はら・へそ・もも・はぎを、のごふことな
かれ。

In the *Sūtra of the Three Thousand Rules of Deportment*, it is said,[22]

*There are five points regarding use of the hand cloth. First, wipe us-
ing the top and bottom ends. Second, use one end to wipe the hands
and the other end to wipe the face. Third, do not use to wipe the nose.
Fourth, when soiled from wiping grease, wash immediately. Fifth, do
not use to wipe the body; when bathing, each should have their own
[bath] towel.*

That is to say, we should use half of the hand cloth to wipe the face
and half to wipe the hands. Do not wipe nasal mucus; do not wipe inside
the nose; do not wipe the armpits, back, belly, navel, thighs, or calves.

[V4:11] {2:585}
手巾は、つねにあらふべし。しめれらんをば、つねにほして、かわかすべ
し。　手巾をふたへにをりて、左のひぢにあたりて、そのうへにかく。わ
なにてあるかたを、ほかにたれ、うちにいだく、兩説あり。

The hand cloth should be washed regularly.[23] When it is damp, it
should be aired out and dried regularly. Fold the cloth in two and hang
it over the left arm near the bend of the elbow. Let the looped ends hang
down apart [from the body] or hold them in close [to the body]; there are
two [different] explanations.

[V4:12]
雲堂の洗面所は、後架裏なり。庵裏單寮は、便宜のところにかまふべし。
住持人は、方丈裏にて洗面す。耆年老宿、その居處にしたがひて、便宜の
ところを、洗面架とせり。住持人、もし雲堂に宿せば、後架にて洗面すべ
し。

The place for washing the face by the cloud hall is the rear washstands.[24] In hermitages and individual quarters, it is provided wherever
convenient. The abbot washes his face in the abbot's quarters. For seniors and elders, face-washing stands are provided where convenient
to their residences. When the abbot lodges in the cloud hall, he should
wash his face at the rear washstands.

---

22 ***Sūtra of the Three Thousand Rules of Deportment*** (*Sanzen iigi kyō* 三千威儀經):
This section parallels section 16 and part of 17 in the seventy-five-chapter *Shōbōgenzō*
text.

23 **The hand cloth** (*shukin* 手巾): This section corresponds to material in section 17 of
the seventy-five-chapter *Shōbōgenzō* text.

24 **The place for washing the face by the cloud hall** (*undō no senmen jo* 雲堂の洗面
所): This section corresponds to section 18 of the seventy-five-chapter *Shōbōgenzō* text.

[V4:13]

洗面所にいたりて、手巾のわななるところを、うなじにかく。ふたつのはしを、左右のかたより、まへにひきこして、左右のてにて、おのおの手巾の左右のはしをとりて、左右のわきより、手巾の左右のはしを、うしろへおしやるがごとくして、うしろにて、おのおのひきちがへて、左のはしは右へきたし、右のはしは左にきたして、むねのまへにあたりて、むすぶなり。かくのごとくすれば、褊衫のくびは手巾におほはれ、兩袖は手巾にゆひあげられて、ひぢよりかみにあがりぬるなり。ひぢよりしもは、あらはなり。たとへば、たすきをかけたらんがごとし。

Upon arriving at the face-washing stand, drape the loop in the hand cloth around the nape of the neck, with the two ends pulled forward over the left and right shoulders.[25] With the left and right hands, grasp each end of the cloth and pass the left and right ends of the cloth under the left and right armpits and around to the back. Cross them in the back, so that the left end comes around to the right and the right end comes around to the left, and tie them together in front of the chest. In this way, the collar of the partial robe is covered by the hand cloth, and the sleeves are tied up by the cloth, so as to be raised above the elbows, while below the elbows, the forearms and hands are exposed. It is similar, for example, to wearing a sleeve cord.

[V4:14]

そののち、もし後架ならば、面桶をとりて、かまのほとりゆきて、一桶の湯をとりて、架のうへเにおく。もし餘所ならんは、打湯を面桶にいるるなり。湯をえてのちに、楊枝をかむべし。

After that, if it is at the rear washstands, take a face bucket, go to the area of the cauldrons, get a single bucket of hot water, come back, and place it on the face-washing stand.[26] If it is at some other place, pour the hot water into the face bucket. After getting hot water, you should chew the willow twig.

[V4:15]

華嚴經淨行品云、手執楊枝、當願衆生、心得正法、自然清淨。　晨嚼楊枝、當願衆生、得調伏牙、噬諸煩惱。しるべし、手執楊枝は、教菩薩法なり、晨嚼楊枝は教菩薩法なり。楊枝のながさ、あるいは四指、あるいは八指、あるいは十二指、あるいは十六指なり。

25　**Upon arriving at the face-washing stand** (*senmen jo ni itarite* 洗面所にいたりて): This section corresponds to the first part of section 19 of the seventy-five-chapter *Shōbōgenzō* text.

26　**After that** (*sono nochi* そののち): This section corresponds to the last two sentences of section 19 and the first sentence of section 20 of the seventy-five-chapter *Shōbōgenzō* text.

V4. Washing the Face *Senmen* 洗面　　　273

In the "Pure Practice" chapter of the *Flower Garland Sūtra*, it is said,[27]

Grasping the willow twig,
Pray that living beings
Attain the true dharma in their minds
And are naturally purified.
Chewing the willow twig at daybreak,
Pray that living beings
Attain the teeth of discipline
That bite off the afflictions.

We should know that "*grasping the willow twig*" is a *dharma taught to bodhisattvas*, that "*chewing the willow twig at daybreak*" is a *dharma taught to bodhisattvas*.[28] The length of the willow twig may be four fingers, eight fingers, twelve fingers, or sixteen fingers.

[V4:16] {2:586}

摩訶僧祇律第三十四云、齒木應量用、極長十六指、極短四指。しかあれ
ば、四指よりみじかくすべからず、十六指よりもながくすべからず。ふと
さは、小指のおほきさなり。しかいへども、それよりちひさきも、さまた
げなし。そのかたちは、　小指形なり。一端はふとく、一端はほそし。古
云、如如來指形。ふときかたを、微細にかむなり。

In number 34 of the *Mahāsāṃghika Vinaya*, it is said, "For the tooth stick, use according to proper size: a maximum length of sixteen fingers; a minimum length of four fingers."[29]

We know from this that it should not be shorter than four fingers nor longer than sixteen fingers.[30] The thickness is the size of the little finger, though there is nothing to prevent something thinner. Its shape is that of the little finger: one end thicker, the other end thinner. *Of old it was said,* "*Like the shape of the Tathāgata's finger.*" We chew the thicker end into fine strands.

27　the "**Pure Practice**" **chapter of the *Flower Garland Sūtra*** (*Kegon kyō jōgyō bon* 華嚴經淨行品): This quotation corresponds to sections 21 and 23 of the seventy-five-chapter *Shōbōgenzō* text.

28　**We should know** (*shiru beshi* しるべし): The phrase "a dharma taught to bodhi-sattvas (*kyō bosatsu hō* 教菩薩法) is a fixed expression found in the *Huayan jing* 華嚴經 and other texts; the sentence containing the phrase here does not occur in the seventy-five-chapter *Shōbōgenzō* text. The final sentence here occurs in section 24 of that text.

29　**number 34 of the *Mahāsāṃghika Vinaya*** (*Makasōgi ritsu dai sanjūshi* 摩訶僧祇律第三十四): This quotation corresponds to section 25 of the seventy-five-chapter *Shōbōgenzō* text.

30　**We know** (*shiru beshi* しるべし): This paragraph corresponds to section 26 of the seventy-five-chapter *Shōbōgenzō* text. That version does not include the old saying given here, the source of which is unknown.

274 DŌGEN'S *SHŌBŌGENZŌ* VOLUME VII

[V4:17]

三千威儀經云、嚼頭不得過三分。かむこと、三分をよくよくかみて、はの
うへ、はのうら、みがくがごとくすべし。たびたび、とぎ、みがくがごと
くすべし。はのもとのししのうへ、よくよく、みがき、あらふべし。はの
あひだ、よくよく、かいそろへ、きよからしむべし。三度、したを、こそ
ぐべし。

In the *Sūtra of the Three Thousand Rules of Deportment*, it is said,
"The chewed tip should not exceed three tenths of an inch."[31]

Having thoroughly chewed the three tenths, rub and clean the front
and back of the teeth as if polishing them. We should rub them repeatedly, as if polishing them. We should polish and clean the gums at the base
of the teeth. We should thoroughly scrape and clean between the teeth.
We should scrape the tongue three times.[32]

[V4:18]

三千威儀經云、刮舌有五事。一者不得過三返。二者舌上血出當止。三者不
得大振手、汚僧伽梨衣若足。四者棄楊枝、莫當人道。五者常當屏處。いは
ゆる刮舌みたび、といふは、水をくくみて、舌をこそげて、きよむること
三度するなり、三刮するにはあらず。血のいでんまですべし、といふこと
もあり。血、いでば、やみね、といふ。三刮にあらず、としるべし。

In the *Sūtra of the Three Thousand Rules of Deportment*, it is said,[33]

Regarding scraping the tongue, there are five points. First, do not
exceed three times. Second, stop if the surface of the tongue bleeds.
Third, do not move the hand so much that the *saṃghāti* robe or the
feet are soiled. Fourth, do not dispose of the willow twig where people
walk. Fifth, always do this in a screened-off place.

The "scraping the tongue three times" mentioned here means that fill-
ing the mouth with water and scraping away at the tongue is repeated
three times; it does not mean to make three scrapes. It is also said that
one should continue until it starts to bleed but stop when there is bleed-
ing. We should know that it is not three scrapes.

---

31 ***Sūtra of the Three Thousand Rules of Deportment*** (*Sanzen iigi kyō* 三千威儀經):
The quotation corresponds to section 27 of the seventy-five-chapter *Shōbōgenzō* text; the
remainder of this section parallels section 28.

32 **We should thoroughly scrape and clean between the teeth** (*ha no aida, yokuyoku,
kaisoroe, kiyokarashimu beshi* はのあひだ、よくよく、かいそろへ、きよからしむべ
し): The predicate *kaisoroe* かいそろへ looks like an error for *kakisoroe* かきそろへ; the
seventy-five-chapter *Shōbōgenzō* text reads *yoku kakisoroe kiyoku arau beshi* よくかき
そろえきよくあらふべし ("thoroughly scrape between the teeth and wash them clean").

33 ***Sūtra of the Three Thousand Rules of Deportment*** (*Sanzen iigi kyō* 三千威儀經):
The quotation corresponds to section 29 of the seventy-five-chapter *Shōbōgenzō* text; the
remainder of this section parallels the first part of section 30.

V4. Washing the Face *Senmen* 洗面

[V4:19] {2:587}

三千威儀經云、淨口者、嚼楊枝・漱口・刮舌。又、三千威儀經云、若不嚼
楊枝、若食、若服藥、若飲、得三突古羅罪。しかあれば、諸佛祖ならびに
佛祖兒孫、その眼目のごとくまぼりきたれり、鳥の兩翼のごとく常隨しき
たれり。佛祖を慕古せんとき、楊枝のみを護持すべきなり、これすなはち
佛祖種子なり、佛果上に直道なるべし、西天よりつたはれ、如來より正傳
せり、護持すべし、失墜せざれ。見楊枝は、見佛祖なるべし、逢人なり、
逢自なり。三十二相八十種好の佛儀をみる、透脱の見佛なり、しかあれど
も、ほとけの身心を見究盡するにあらず。楊枝をみる、透脱の見佛なり、
しかあれども、楊枝の内外を見究盡するにあらず。見究盡せざるは一等な
りといふとも、見佛は透脱の見佛なり、よろこぶべし。

In the *Sūtra of the Three Thousand Rules of Deportment*, it is said,
"Purifying the mouth means chewing the willow twig, rinsing the
mouth, and scraping the tongue." Again, it is said in the *Sūtra of the
Three Thousand Rules of Deportment*, "If one does not chew the willow
twig, then, if one eats, takes medicine, or drinks, one incurs three *duṣkṛta*
offenses."[34]

Thus, the buddhas and ancestors, as well as the descendants of the
buddhas and ancestors, have been guarding it, like their own eyes, have
always been keeping it, like the two wings of a bird.[35] When we admire
the ancients, the buddhas and ancestors, we should especially maintain
the willow twig; it is the very seed of the buddhas and ancestors. It is the
direct path of the fruit of buddhahood, handed down from Sindh in the
West, directly transmitted from the Tathāgata. We should maintain it; do
not lose it. Seeing the willow twig is seeing the buddhas and ancestors,

---

34 *Sūtra of the Three Thousand Rules of Deportment* (*Sanzen iigi kyō* 三千威儀經):
The first quotation here occurs in section 29 of the seventy-five-chapter *Shōbōgenzō* text;
the second quotation, which does not occur in that text, is found at *Sanqian weiyi jing* 三
千威儀經, T.1470.24:914a19-20.

duṣkṛta **offenses** (*tokira zai* 突古羅罪): The least serious of five grades of offense (*gohin*
五篇) explained in the vinaya; expiation requires confession before one other monk or
repentance by oneself.

35 **have always been keeping it, like the two wings of a bird** (*tori no ryōyoku no
gotoku jōzui shikitareri* 鳥の兩翼のごとく常隨しきたれり): The direct object here is
likely "the willow twig." The simile of the two wings anticipates the final line of the
quotation from the *Fanwang jing* 梵網經 (T.1484.24:1008a19-20) appearing in section
20, below:

是二時中、此十八種物、常隨其身如鳥二翼。

During these two periods, one should always keep these eighteen kinds of articles
close to one's person, like the two wings of a bird.

This sentence seems to correspond loosely to the last sentence in section 30 of the seventy-five-chapter *Shōbōgenzō* text. The remainder of Dōgen's comments here do not occur
in that text, sections 31-34 of which are devoted to quotation of and comment on the
miracle of the Buddha's willow twig that grew into a giant tree.

meeting a person, meeting oneself.[36] Seeing a buddha's deportment of thirty-two marks and eighty auspicious signs is a liberated seeing of a buddha, yet it is not exhaustively investigating the seeing of the body and mind of a buddha; seeing the willow twig is a liberated seeing of a buddha, yet it is not exhaustively investigating the seeing of the inside and out of the willow twig.[37] Even if the "not exhaustively investigating the seeing" is the same, we should rejoice that seeing a buddha is a liberated seeing of a buddha.

[V4:20]

梵網菩薩戒經云、若佛子、常應二時頭陀、冬夏坐禪、結夏安居、常用楊枝・澡豆・三衣・瓶、鉢・坐具、錫杖・香爐・漉水囊・手巾・刀子・火燧・鑷子・繩子牀・經・律・佛像・菩薩形像。而菩薩行頭陀時、及遊方時、行來百里千里、此十八種物、常隨其身。頭陀者、從正月十五日至三月十五日、八月十五日至十月十五日。是二時中、此十八種物、常隨其身如鳥二翼。

In the *Brahma's Net Bodhisattva Precepts Sūtra*, it is said,[38]

---

36 **Seeing the willow twig is seeing the buddhas and ancestors** (*ken yōji wa, ken busso naru beshi* 見楊枝は、見佛祖なるべし): An almost identical sentence is found in section 37 of the seventy-five-chapter *Shōbōgenzō* text.

meeting a person (*hō nin* 逢人): Possibly, reflecting the words of Sansheng 三聖 and Xinghua 興化, quoted in case 92 of the *shinji Shōbōgenzō* 眞字正法眼藏 (DZZ.5:172) and alluded to elsewhere in the *Shōbōgenzō*:

> 三聖院慧然禪師〈嗣臨濟〉道、我逢人即出、出即不爲人。興化道、我逢人即不出、出即便爲人。
> Chan Master Huiran of the Sansheng Cloister (succeeded Linji) said, "When I meet a person, I come forth; but, when I come forth, I don't benefit the person."
> Xinghua said, "When I meet a person, I don't come forth; but, when I do come forth, I benefit the person."

37 **Seeing a buddha's deportment of thirty-two marks and eighty auspicious signs is a liberated seeing of a buddha** (*sanjūni sō hachijisshu gō no butsugi o miru, tōdatsu no kenbutsu nari* 三十二相八十種好の佛儀をみる、透脱の見佛なり): "Thirty-two marks and eighty auspicious signs" refers to the distinctive properties of a buddha's body.

exhaustively investigating the seeing (*ken gūjin su* 見究盡す): An awkward attempt to render an unusual predicate, presumably, meaning something like, "to see fully." A possible paraphrase of this somewhat obscure passage might read something like the following:

> To be able to see the marks and signs on the body of a buddha represents a higher kind of ("liberated") seeing, but there is more to seeing a buddha than this; similarly, to be able see the willow twig is a higher way of seeing a buddha, but there is more to seeing the willow twig than this. Though in both cases there is more, it is enough to recognize that they are both higher kinds of seeing.

38 *Brahma's Net Bodhisattva Precepts Sūtra* (*Bonmo bosatsu kai kyō* 梵網菩薩戒經): Corresponding to section 35 of the seventy-five-chapter *Shōbōgenzō* text.

V4. Washing the Face *Senmen* 洗面

You children of the Buddha, during the dhūta of the two periods, summer and winter seated meditation, and the summer retreat, you should always use willow twigs, soap, the three robes, a water flask, a bowl, a sitting cloth, a staff, an incense burner, a water filter, a hand cloth, a knife, a flintstone, tweezers, a rope chair, the sūtras, the vinaya, a buddha image, and a bodhisattva image. When bodhisattvas practice the dhūta and when they roam about, whether they travel a hundred miles or a thousand miles, they should always keep these eighteen kinds of articles close to their persons. The dhūta periods are from the fifteenth day of the first month until the fifteenth day of the third month, and from the fifteenth day of the eighth month until the fifteenth day of the tenth month. During these two periods, one should always keep these eighteen kinds of articles close to one's person, like the two wings of a bird.

[V4:21]

この十八種物、ひとつも虧闕すべからず。もし虧闕すれば、鳥の一翼なからんがごとし。たとひ一翼のこれりとも、飛行することあたはじ。しるべし、菩薩の行道もまたかくのごとし、この十八種を二翼とせり。楊枝すでに第一に居せり、もとも具足すべきなり。この楊枝の輕重をあきらめん菩薩、すなはち佛法の輕重をもあきらむべし。いまだあきらめざらんは、佛法もいまだかつてあきらめざるなり。この梵網菩薩戒は、過去・現在・未來の諸佛菩薩の受持しきたるところなるがゆえに、楊枝の出現、また過・現・當に受持しきたれり。

Not a single one of these eighteen kinds of articles should be missing.[39] If any is missing, it would be like a bird lacking a wing: even if one wing remained, it could not fly. You should know that the bodhisattva's practice of the way is also like this: these eighteen kinds of articles are considered the "two wings." Since the willow twig occupies the first position, we should equip ourselves with it above all. Bodhisattvas who clarify the seriousness of the willow twig are surely those who clarify the seriousness of the buddha dharma. Those who have not clarified it have not clarified the buddha dharma either. Because these Brahmā's net bodhisattva precepts are something received and kept by the buddhas and bodhisattvas of past, present, and future, the appearance of the willow twig has also been received and kept in past, present, and future.

---

39 **these eighteen kinds of articles** (*kono jūhasshu motsu* この十八種物): This section largely parallels section 36 of the seventy-five-chapter *Shōbōgenzō* text, but the final sentence here corresponds to section 38 in that text.

278 DŌGEN'S *SHŌBŌGENZŌ* VOLUME VII

[V4:22] {2:588}

禪苑清規云、大乘梵網經、十重・四十八輕、竝須讀誦通利、善知持犯開遮。但依金口聖言、莫擅隨於庸輩。

In the *Rules of Purity for the Chan Park*, it is said,[40]

We should recite and be well versed in all the ten grave and forty-eight lesser precepts of the Mahāyāna *Brahma's Net Sūtra*, knowing what it is to keep or break them, what is permitted and what forbidden. Rely only on the sacred words of the Golden-Mouthed One; do not presume to follow the vulgar crowd.

[V4:23]

しかあるに、大宋國、見在嘉定十六年癸未四月のはじめこれをみるに、天下の僧俗、かつて楊枝の名を、きかず、しらず。楊枝のすがたを、みず、しらず。いはんや嚼楊枝の法を、ゆめにもみたる一箇半箇なし。わづかに口をあらふときは、馬の尾をきりたる、ながさ寸餘なるを、牛の角につけたるものにて、牙歯をあらふのみなり、不淨の器なり、僧家の佛儀にあらず、俗人、なほきらひぬべし。これをもちいるも、萬人に一人なり。しかあれば、天下の僧俗・男女、いづれも二三尺のうちにいて、ものいふとき、口氣はなはだくさし。かぐもの、たへしのぶべからざるがごとし。有道の尊宿と稱し、人天の導師とある、漱口・刮舌の法ありとだにもしらず。口氣はなはだくさく、口のうち、はのうへ、もともけがらはし。これをもて推するに、佛祖の大道、いま陵夷をみるらんこと、いくそばくぞといふことをしらず。蒼波萬里の雲煙に露命ををしまず、異域に道をとぶらふといへども、澆季にうまれあふ、かなしむべし。いくばくの白法か、さきだちて滅没しぬらん。しかあるに、日本一國、朝野の道俗、みな楊枝をもちいる、佛光明を見聞するなり、佛説法を見聞するなり、佛光明の嗣續せるなり、佛祖命の長遠なるなり。よろこぶべし。

Nevertheless, in the Land of the Great Song at present, when I first observed matters at the start of the fourth month of the junior water year of the sheep, the sixteenth year of the Jiading Era, the monks and laity throughout the land had never heard of or known the name of the willow twig. They had never seen and did not know what the willow twig looks like. How much less was there a single person or half a person who had seen even in their dreams the procedure for chewing the willow twig. When they do at least wash out their mouths, they simply use a thing made from horse tail, cut a little more than an inch long and attached to a piece of ox horn, to clean their teeth. It is an impure implement, one that does not conform to the buddha deportment of the monastic order and must be disliked even by the laity. Even those who use this are but one in ten thousand.[41]

---

40 **Rules of Purity for the Chan Park** (*Zennen shingi* 禪苑清規): This section corresponds to section 39 in the seventy-five-chapter *Shōbōgenzō* text.

41 **one in ten thousand** (*mannin ni ichinin* 萬人に一人): To this point, this section loose-

V4. Washing the Face *Senmen* 洗面

279

Therefore, when any of the monks or laity, male or female, speak within two or three feet of you, their breath is extremely malodorous; the smell is virtually unbearable.[42] Even those known as venerables in possession of the way, who have been called teachers of humans and devas, do not know that the procedures for rinsing the mouth and scraping the tongue even exist. Their breath stinks terribly, and the insides of their mouths and surfaces of their teeth are most disgusting. Judging from this, we cannot imagine to what degree we are now witnessing the deterioration of the great way of the buddhas and ancestors. Although we risk our evanescent lives in the clouds and mist of ten thousand miles of deep green waves, and seek the way in foreign lands, how regrettable it is to have been born in a season of decline. How many pure dharmas have already been lost?

Throughout the Land of Japan, however, the religious and laity of court and countryside all use the willow twig.[43] They have experienced the radiance of the Buddha, experienced the Buddha's preaching of the dharma, inherited the radiance of the Buddha, and gained the longevity of lifespan of the buddhas and ancestors. That is something we should rejoice in.

[V4:24] {2:589}

三千威儀經云、用楊枝有五事。一者斷當如度。二者破當如法。三者嚼頭不得過三分。四者疏齒當中三齒。五者當汁澡目用。いま嚼楊枝、漱石の水をもて目をあらふこと、三千威儀經の法なり。楊枝、よくつかひて、牙齒をそろへ、したをこそげて、湯をうがひ、うがひするなり。

In the *Sūtra of the Three Thousand Rules of Deportment*, it is said,[44]

There are five points that pertain to using the willow twig. First, it should be cut to the proper proportions. Second, it should be broken using the proper procedure. Third, in chewing the tip, do not exceed three tenths of an inch. Fourth, in [cleaning] the gaps between teeth, it should be inserted for three bites. Fifth, the sap should be used to rinse the eyes.

Our present practice of chewing the willow twig and using the water with which we rinse the mouth to wash the eyes is a procedure found in

---

ly corresponds to section 41 in the seventy-five-chapter *Shōbōgenzō* text.

42 **Therefore** (*shika areba* しかあれば): This paragraph loosely corresponds to section 42 in the seventy-five-chapter *Shōbōgenzō* text.

43 **Throughout the Land of Japan** (*Nihon ikkoku* 日本一國): This paragraph corresponds to material in section 43 in the seventy-five-chapter *Shōbōgenzō* text.

44 ***Sūtra of the Three Thousand Rules of Deportment*** (*Sanzen iigi kyō* 三千威儀經): This quotation corresponds to section 44 in the seventy-five-chapter *Shōbōgenzō* text; Dōgen's comment following it corresponds to material in section 45 of that text.

the *Sūtra of the Three Thousand Rules of Deportment*.[45] Using the willow twig well, we clean between the teeth, scrape the tongue, and gargle repeatedly with hot water.

[V4:25]

刮舌の法は、楊枝、よくよくつかひてのち、いまはすてんとするとき、なかより二片に擘破して、そのわれたる口邊　、刀口のごとし。これをよこさまにとりて、舌面をこそげては、水をうがひ、うがひをくくみては、擘楊枝にて、こそげ、こそげするなり。血のいづるまでです。牙藥あらば、牙歯につけてあらふべし。水をくくみて、たびたびうがひ、うがひすつべし。うがひを、はきすてんには、面桶のほかに、はきすつべし。楊枝は、たびごとに擘破してすつべし、といへり。

The procedure for scraping the tongue:[46] After thoroughly using the willow twig, when it is to be discarded, we tear it apart into two pieces from the middle, such that the broken edges are like blades. Holding this crosswise, to scrape the tongue, while gargling repeatedly with water, scrape repeatedly with the split willow twig, until blood begins to flow. If we have a tooth medicine, we should clean the teeth with it. Holding the water in the mouth, gargle with it repeatedly. In disposing of the gargle water, spit it out somewhere other than in the face bucket. It is said that the willow twig is to be torn apart and discarded each time.

[V4:26]

經云、破當如法、と。よくよくつかひて、楊枝をすてんには、すてをはりて、彈指三下すべし。華嚴經偈云、澡漱口歯、當願衆生、向淨法門、究竟解脱。

In the *Sūtra*, it says, "It should be broken using the proper procedure."[47]

When we have thoroughly used it, the willow twig is to be discarded; after discarding it, we should snap the fingers three times.[48]

In a gāthā of the *Flower Garland Sūtra*, it is said,[49]

45　**water with which we rinse the mouth** (*sōseki no mizu* 漱石の水): Reading *sōkō* 漱口 for *sōseki* 漱石.

46　**procedure for scraping the tongue** (*katsuzetsu no hō* 刮舌の法): This section corresponds to material in sections 45 and 48 of the seventy-five-chapter *Shōbōgenzō* text.

47　**the *Sūtra*** (*kyō* 經): I.e., the *Sūtra of the Three Thousand Rules of Deportment*; repeating the second of the five rules for use of the willow twig quoted above, section 24.

48　**snap the fingers three times** (*santanji* 三彈指): This advice is found in section 48 of the seventy-five-chapter *Shōbōgenzō* text.

49　**gāthā of the *Flower Garland Sūtra*** (*Kegon kyō ge* 華嚴經偈): This quotation corresponds to section 47 of the seventy-five-chapter *Shōbōgenzō* text. In section 46 of that text, it is recommended that the verse be recited silently while rinsing the mouth.

V4. Washing the Face *Senmen* 洗面

Rinsing out the mouth and teeth,
Pray that living beings
Approach the pure dharma gate
And finally attain liberation.

[V4:27]

つぎに洗面す。両手に湯を掬して、おもてをあらふ。かくのごとく、よくよくあらふあひだ、湯を無度につひやして、面桶のほかに、もらしおとして、はやくうしなふことなかれ。あか、おち、あぶら、のぞこほりぬるまで、あらふなり。　耳のなか、あらふべし、著水不得なるがゆえに。眼裏、あらふべし。著沙不得なるがゆえに。おとがひのした、鼻孔までも、よくよく心のいたらんを度として、あらふべし。あるいは、頭上頂顙までもあらふ、すなはち威儀なり。

Next, do the face-washing.[50] Using both hands, scoop up hot water and wash the face. When washing well like this, do not let the hot water run out too quickly by using an immoderate amount, dripping it outside the face bucket, or spilling it. Wash until the grime is off and the oil removed. We should wash "in the ears"; for "water can't get in." We should wash "in the eyes"; for "sand can't get in." We should wash under the chin, and even the nostrils, as thoroughly as we can. It is also proper deportment to wash as far as the crown of the head.

[V4:28]

つぎに、手巾をもて、おもてをのごふべし。よくよくのごひかわかして、手巾、もとのごとく脱しとりて、ふたつにして、左の臂にかく。雲堂の後架には、公界の拭面あり、それをもちいる。

Next, one should wipe the face with the hand cloth.[51] Having thoroughly wiped and dried [the face], remove the hand cloth, fold it in half, and drape it over the crook of the left arm, as it was to begin with. At the rear washstands of the cloud hall, there are communal face towels; use those.

[V4:29]

洗面のあひだ、桶杓をならし、かまびすしく、おとをなすことなかれ。湯・水を狼藉にして、近邊をぬらすことなかれ。ひそかに觀想すべし、佛祖の威儀面目を相傳して、染汚せしめず、修證する、隨喜懺喜すべし。

While washing the face, do not bang the bucket and ladle, and do not be noisy.[52] Do not get the area wet by splashing the hot and cold water

---

50　**Next, do the face-washing** (*tsugi ni senmen su* つぎに洗面す): This section corresponds to material in section 49 of the seventy-five-chapter *Shōbōgenzō* text, though with considerable differences.

51　**Next** (*tsugi ni* つぎに): This section corresponds to material in section 50 of the seventy-five-chapter *Shōbōgenzō* text, though with considerable differences.

52　**While washing the face** (*senmen no aida* 洗面のあひだ): This section corresponds

282 DŌGEN'S *SHŌBŌGENZŌ* VOLUME VII

about. We should reflect to ourselves that, by personally transmitting the face of the deportment of the buddhas and ancestors, we practice and verify it without creating any defilement, and we should rejoice in and be pleased by that.

[V4:30]

雲堂にあらば、手巾をたづさへて入堂す。輕歩低聲なるべし。

If one is in the cloud hall, take the hand cloth with you when you enter the hall.[53] One should step lightly to keep the sound down.

[V4:31]

耆年宿德の草菴に、かならず洗面架あるべし。あるいは洗面のとき、面藥をもちいる法あり。おほよそ道心辦道のとき、洗面・嚼楊枝おこたらざれ、これ古佛の正法なり。あるいは湯をえざらんところにては、水にても洗面すべし。湯・水すべてえざらんところにては、拭面すべし。そののち禮拜坐禪すべし、受禮・禮他あるべし。本來面目をして淨潔ならしむべし。

In the thatched huts of seniors and elderly worthies, there should always be face-washing stands.[54] When washing the face, there may also be a procedure for using facial ointments.

In sum, when pursuing the way with the mind of the way, do not to be neglectful of washing the face and chewing the willow twig: they are the true dharma of the old buddhas.[55] When hot water is not available, one should wash the face with cold water. When neither hot nor cold water is available, one should rub the face. Only after that should one pay obeisance and sit in meditation, should one receive obeisance and pay obeisance to another. We should purify our original face.

正法眼藏洗面第五十
Treasury of the True Dharma Eye
Washing the Face
Number 50

---

to section 51 of the seventy-five-chapter *Shōbōgenzō* text, though with some differences.

53 **If one is in the cloud hall** (*undō ni araba* 雲堂にあらば): This section corresponds roughly to the last sentence of section 51 of the seventy-five-chapter *Shōbōgenzō* text.

54 **In the thatched huts of seniors and elderly worthies** (*ginen shukutoku no sōan ni* 耆年宿德の草菴に): These two sentences correspond to section 52 of the seventy-five-chapter *Shōbōgenzō* text.

55 **In sum** (*ooyoso* おほよそ): This paragraph roughly parallels section 53 of the seventy-five-chapter *Shōbōgenzō* text.

V4. Washing the Face *Senmen* 洗面

{2:591}

爾時延應元年巳亥十月二十三日、在觀音導利興聖寶林寺示衆

Presented to the assembly at Kannon Dōri Kōshō Hōrin Monastery;
twenty-third day of the tenth month of the junior earth year of the pig,
the first year of En'ō [20 November 1239]

[V4:32]

天竺・震旦國等には、國王・王子、大臣・百官、在家男女、朝野の佰姓、
みな洗面す、神廟等も、あしたごとに洗面するあり。かくのごとく洗面し
て、祖宗を拜し、現在せる父母・師匠を拜す、三界萬靈・十方眞宰をも拜
す、主君をも拜するなり。いまは漁父・樵翁までも、洗面おこたらず。し
かあれども、楊枝はしらず、一得一失なり。日本國は嚼楊枝あり、洗面な
し。いま嚼楊枝・洗面、ともに修證せん、補虧闕の紹隆なり。正傳のうへ
の正傳なるべし、佛祖の照臨なるべし。

In the lands of Sindhu and Cīnasthāna, the kings and princes, great
ministers and high officials, male and female householders, and commoners of court and countryside, all practice face-washing.[56] In their
shrines to the gods as well, there is face-washing every morning. Having
washed the face in this way, they pay obeisance to the ancestors; pay
obeisance to their present father and mother and their ordination teacher;
pay obeisance to the myriad spirits of the three realms and the true lords
of the ten directions; and pay obeisance to the ruler. Nowadays, even
fishermen and woodsmen do not neglect washing the face; however,
they do not know of the willow twig. It is "one gained, one lost." In the
Land of Japan, there is chewing the willow twig, but no face-washing.
Now, our practice and verification of both chewing the willow twig and
washing the face represent a revival that has repaired the deficiency. This
must be a direct transmission on top of a direct transmission; it must be
the illuminating presence of the buddhas and ancestors.

爾時寛元元年癸卯十月二十日、在越州吉峰精舍示衆

Presented to the assembly at Kippō Vihāra, Esshū; twentieth day of the
tenth month of the junior water year of the rabbit, the first year of
Kangen [3 December 1243]

---

56 **In the lands of Sindhu and Cīnasthāna** (*Tenjiku Shintan koku tō ni* 天竺震旦國等
に): This section corresponds roughly to section 54 of the seventy-five-chapter *Shōbōgenzō* text.

于時文明十二庚子年二月初七日、於越州吉田郡志比庄吉祥山永平寺承
陽庵書寫之。比丘光周

*Copied this, in the Jōyō Hermitage, Eihei Monastery, Mount Kichi-
jō, Shihi Estate, Yoshida District, Esshū; seventh day, second month,
senior metal year of the rat, the twelfth year of Bunmei [18 March
1480]. Bhikṣu Kōshū*[57]

---

57 **Bhikṣu Kōshū** (*biku Kōshū* 比丘光周): Fifteenth abbot of Eiheiji (1434–1492?).

Treasury of the True Dharma Eye
Variant Text 5

Extensive Study
Henzan
遍参

Extensive Study

Henzan

INTRODUCTION

This text represents a manuscript held by Eiheiji of chapter 37 of the sixty-chapter *Shōbōgenzō*, a variant version of number 57 of the seventy-five-chapter compilation. The two versions bear colophons with identical information on the date and place of composition: winter of 1243-44, at Yamashibu 禪師峰, in Echizen. It is thought, however, that the present version represents an earlier draft of the "Henzan" chapter, subsequently edited as the seventy-five-chapter *Shōbōgenzō* version. There are quite a few differences between the two texts, but for the most part they are relatively minor.

The translation here does not repeat the annotation of the seventy-five-chapter *Shōbōgenzō* version; rather, it is limited to indicating the parallel sections in the two texts, and to the occasional note on issues specific to this version.

正法眼藏拾遺五
Treasury of the True Dharma Eye
Variant Text 5

遍參
Extensive Study

(六十巻本系・永平寺所蔵一本)
(Sixty-chapter compilation version, Eiheiji collection)

[V5:1] {2:592}

佛祖の大道は、究竟參徹なり、足下無糸去なり、足下雲生なり、華開世界現なり、甜苽徹蔕甜なり、苦苽連根苦なり、甜甜徹蔕甜の參學もあるべし。

The great way of the buddhas and ancestors is study and penetration of the ultimate; it is to "go without a string at your feet"; it is "clouds arose underfoot"; it is "a flower opens, and the world arises"; it is the sweet melon is sweet through to its stem; it is the bitter melon is bitter to its root.[1] There must also be the extensive study of the sweet sweetness is sweet through to the stem.

* * * * *

[V5:2]

玄沙山宗一大師、因雪峰召師云、備頭陀何不遍參去。師云、達磨不來東土、二祖不往西天。雪峰深然之。

Great Master Zongyi of Mount Xuansha was once addressed by Xuefeng, who said, "Bei Dhūta, why don't you go off on an extensive study?"

The Master said, "Dharma didn't come to the Land of East; the Second Ancestor didn't go to Sindh in the West."

Xuefeng deeply approved this.

---

1 **The great way of the buddhas and ancestors** (*busso no daidō* 佛祖の大道): This section varies slightly from section 1 in the seventy-five-chapter *Shōbōgenzō* version.

[V5:3]

いはゆる遍參底の道理は、翻巾斗參なり、聖諦の亦不爲なり、何階級之有なり。

The principle of extensive studying is *the study of a flip*; it is "*don't do even the sacred truths*"; it is "*what stages are there?*"

* * * * *

[V5:4]

南嶽大慧禪師、はじめて曹溪に參ずるに、曹溪いはく、是甚麼物恁麼來。この泥彈子の一著子なるを遍參すること、始終八年なり。

When Chan Master Dahui of Nanyue first visited Caoxi, Caoxi said, "*What thing is it that comes like this?*"[2]

His extensive study of this ball of mud was eight years from start to finish.

[V5:5] {2:593}

末上に遍參するとき、古佛に白してまうさく、懷讓會得、當初來時、和尚接懷讓是甚麼物恁麼來。ちなみに曹溪道、儞作麼生會。ときに大慧まうさく、説似一物即不中。これ、遍參現成なり、八年現成なり。

In the end, when he had extensively studied it, he addressed the old buddha, saying, "*Huairang has understood what the Reverend put to Huairang when I first came: 'What thing is it that comes like this?'*"

Thereupon, *Caoxi said, "How do you understand it?"*

At this point, Dahui said, "*To say it's like any thing wouldn't hit it.*"

This is the realization of extensive study, the realization of eight years.

[V5:6]

曹溪とふ、還假修證否。大慧まうさく、修證不無、染汚即不得。すなはち曹溪いはく、吾亦如是、汝亦如是、乃至西天諸佛諸祖亦如是。これよりさらに八載遍參す。頭正尾正かぞふるに、十五白の遍參なり。

Caoxi asked, "*Then does it depend on practice and verification?*"

Dahui said, "*It's not that it lacks practice and verification, but it can't be defiled by them.*"

Thereupon, Caoxi said, "*I'm also like this, you're also like this, and the buddhas and the ancestors of Sindh in the West are also like this.*"

Thereafter, he spent eight years more in extensive study. True from head to tail, all told it was fifteen autumns of extensive study.

---

2 **Chan Master Dahui of Nanyue** (*Nangaku Daie zenji* 南嶽大慧禪師): This and the following two sections correspond to section 4 in the seventy-five-chapter *Shōbōgenzō* version.

V5. Extensive Study *Henzan* 遍参 289

[V5:7]

恁麼來は、遍参なり。説似一物即不中に、諸佛諸祖を開殿見参する如是を亦す。甚麼物の入畫看に、六十五百千萬億の轉身遍参見を現前せしむ。等閑に入一叢林、出叢林を遍参とするにあらず。

"Coming like this" is extensive study. In "*To say it's like anything wouldn't hit it*," [he] makes "also" the "like this" that "opens the hall and sees the buddhas and ancestors."[3] When "what thing is it" "enters the picture and looks," he reveals the view of extensive study of transforming the body "sixty-five hundreds of thousands of myriads of *koṭis*" of times. He does not take casually "entering a grove" and "leaving a grove" as extensive study.[4]

[V5:8]

いま雪峰道の遍参の宗旨、かならずしも出嶺をすすむるにあらず、玄沙道の達磨不來東土、二祖不往西天の遍参を、助発するなり。たとへば、なんぞ遍参にあらざらん、といはんがごとし。

The essential point of the extensive study spoken of here by Xuefeng does not necessarily recommend his leaving the peak: it helps him in the extensive study of "*Dharma didn't come to the Land of the East; the Second Ancestor didn't go to Sindh in the West*" spoken of by Xuansha.[5] It is, for example, like saying, "How could this not be extensive study?"

---

3 **[he] makes "also" the "like this" that "opens the hall and sees the buddhas and ancestors"** (*shobutsu shoso o kaiden kenzan suru nyoze o yaku su* 諸佛諸祖を開殿見参する如是を亦す): An awkward attempt to render Dōgen's play with the phrase "also like this" (*yaku nyoze* 亦如是) in Caoxi's final comment. Cf. the less tortured version in section 5 of the seventy-five-chapter *Shōbōgenzō* version:

説似一物即不中、諸佛諸祖を開殿参見する、すなはち亦如是遍参なり。

"To say it's like anything wouldn't hit it": to "open the hall and see the buddhas and ancestors" is the extensive study of "also like this."

4 **"entering a grove" and "leaving a grove"** (*nyū ichi sōrin, shutsu ichi sōrin* 入一叢林、出一叢林): The seventy-five-chapter *Shōbōgenzō* version continues here:

全眼睛の参見を遍参とす、打得徹を遍参とす。面皮厚多少を見徹する、すなはち遍参なり。

He takes seeing with the entire eye as extensive study, being able to penetrate it as extensive study. Seeing through the thickness of the skin of the face — this is extensive study.

5 **The essential point of the extensive study spoken of here by Xuefeng** (*ima Seppō dō no henzan no shūshi* いま雪峰道の遍参の宗旨): This section, which returns to the conversation introduced in section 2, above, corresponds to the first part of section 6 in the seventy-five-chapter *Shōbōgenzō* version (which lacks the final sentence here).

[V5:9]

いま玄沙道の達磨不來東土は、來而不來の亂道にあらず、遍參の道理を通達するなり。たとひ、東土の全土、たちまちに極涌して達磨に參侍轉身する遍參ありとも、屋裏の兒孫としては、かへりてこれ遍參を參ずべし。この道は、遍參して雪峰と同參、見取せしむるなり。

Xuansha's saying here, "*Dharma didn't come to the Land of the East*," is not some confused saying about coming or not coming: it penetrates the principle of extensive study.[6] Even if there were an extensive study in which the entire land of the Land of the East were suddenly to gush up, attending on Dharma and transforming the body, as descendants within the house, [we] should still study this [as] extensive study.[7] These words let [us] see [him] extensively studying and studying together with Xuefeng.

[V5:10] {2:594}

二祖不往西天、この不往は、當蓋當なり、足下雲生なり。二祖、もし西天にゆかば、佛法、いま東土にいたるべからず。達磨、もし東土にきたらば、佛法、いま東土に正傳すべからず。不來親曾不來なり、不往無外不往なり。これを動著せば、なにをか遍參とせん。

"*The Second Ancestor didn't go to Sindh in the West*": this "didn't go" is *righter than right*, is "clouds arise underfoot."[8] If the Second Ancestor had gone to Sindh in the West, the buddha dharma would not now have

---

6 **Xuansha's saying here, "Dharma didn't come to the Land of the East"** (*ima Gensha dō no Daruma furai Tōdo* いま玄沙道の達磨不來東土): This section parallels the second part of section 6 in the seventy-five-chapter *Shōbōgenzō* version, but from this point through section 11, below, the two texts show many differences.

it penetrates the principle of extensive study (*henzan no dōri o tsūdatsu suru nari* 遍參の道理を通達するなり): The seventy-five-chapter *Shōbōgenzō* version has here:

> 大地無寸土の道理なり。いはゆる達磨は、命脈一尖なり。

> It is the principle that "the whole earth lacks an inch of ground." "Dharma" here is the tip of the vital artery.

7 **descendants within the house** (*okuri no jison* 屋裏の兒孫): I.e., later members of the lineage of the buddhas and ancestors. From here to the end of the section, the seventy-five-chapter *Shōbōgenzō* version reads:

> 轉身にあらず、さらに語脈の翻身にあらず。不來東土なるゆゑに、東土に見面するなり。東土たとひ佛面祖面相見すとも、來東土にあらず、拈得佛祖失却鼻孔なり。

> This would not be transforming the body, nor would it be flipping the body in the stream of words. Since he "didn't come to the Land of the East," he meets the Land of the East face-to-face. Though the Land of the East encounters buddha faces and ancestor faces, this is not "coming to the Land of the East": it is getting hold of the buddhas and ancestors and losing the nose.

8 **righter than right** (*tō gai tō* 當蓋當): A tentative translation of an uncommon expression with no known precedent in the Chinese Buddhist canon; taking *tō* 當 here in the sense "appropriate," "correct" (though perhaps it could also be understood as "here,

V5. Extensive Study *Henzan* 遍参 291

reached the Land of the East; if Dharma had come to the Land of the East, the buddha dharma would not now have been correctly transmitted to the Land of the East.[9] *"Not coming" is the not coming that is personally once; "not going" is the not going that is without outside.* If you move these, what do we take as extensive study?[10]

---

right here"). This sentence is missing in the seventy-five-chapter *Shōbōgenzō* version, which reads here:

> おほよそ、土は、東西にあらず、東西は土にかかはれず。二祖不往西天は、西天を遍参するには不往西天なり。

> In sum, the "land" is not east or west; east and west have nothing to do with the "land." "The Second Ancestor didn't go to Sindh in the West" is, in extensively studying Sindh in the West, he "didn't go to Sindh in the West."

9 **If the Second Ancestor had gone to Sindh in the West** (*niso, moshi Saiten ni yukaba* 二祖、もし西天にゆかば): The seventy-five-chapter *Shōbōgenzō* version reads here,

> 二祖もし西天にゆかば、一臂落了也。

> If the Second Ancestor had gone to Sindh in the West, one arm would have fallen off.

10 **"Not coming" is the not coming that is personally once; "not going" is the not going that is without outside** (*furai shinzō furai nari, fuō muge fuō nari* 不來親曾不來なり、不往無外不往なり): The significance of the terms *shinzō* 親曾 ("personally once") and *muge* 無外 ("without outside") here is subject to interpretation; perhaps, the sense is "a not coming that is already present"; "a not going that has nowhere else to go." The former term occurs often in the *Shōbōgenzō*, especially in allusion to a line of verse by Tiantong Rujing 天童如淨 (*Rujing heshang yulu* 如淨和尚語録, T.2002A.48:130c7-11):

> 親曾見佛不相瞞。

> He [i.e., Piṇḍola] once personally saw the Buddha; he doesn't deceive.

The latter term occurs less frequently but appears prominently in "Shōbōgenzō sangai yui shin" 正法眼藏三界唯心:

> 諸佛應化法身は、みなこれ三界なり、無外なり。たとへば、如來の無外なるがごとし、牆壁の無外なるがごとし、三界の無外なるがごとく、衆生無外なり

> The response, transformation, and dharma bodies of the buddhas are all the three realms, are without outside. This is like the tathāgatas being without outside, like fences and walls being without outside; just as the three realms are without outside, living beings are without outside.

The seventy-five-chapter *Shōbōgenzō* version replaces this sentence with a greatly expanded passage:

> しばらく二祖なにとしてか西天にゆかざる。いはゆる碧眼の眼睛裏に跳入するゆえに、不往西天なり。もし碧眼裏に跳入せずば、必定して西天にゆくべし。抉出達磨眼睛を遍参とす。西天にゆき東土にきたる、遍参にあらず。天台・南嶽にいたり、五臺・上天にゆくをもて、遍参とするにあらず。四海五湖、もし透脱せざらんは、遍参にあらず。四海五湖に往來するは、四海五湖をして遍参せしめず、路頭を滑ならしむ、脚下を滑ならしむ、ゆえに遍参を打失せしむ。

> Now, why did the Second Ancestor not go to Sindh in the West? Because he jumped into the eye of Blue Eyes, he "didn't go to Sindh in the West." If he had not jumped into Blue Eyes, he would definitely have gone to Sindh in the West. He made gouging out Dharma's eye his extensive study. Going to Sindh in the West or coming to the Land of the East is not extensive study. Going to Tiantai or Nanyue is not extensive study; we do not take going to Wutai or the heavens as extensive study. If we

[V5:11]

しかあれば、雪峰の行履を觑著し、玄沙の先蹤を参究して、遍参して閑遊なかれ。たとへば、遍参は、石頭大底大、石頭小底小なり。石頭をして大参・小参ならしむべし。大底は大底を遍参究するを、遍参といふ、小底は小底を遍参究するを、　遍参といふ。百千萬箇を百千萬頭に参見するは、いまだ遍参にあらず。半語脈裏に百千萬轉身なるを、遍参と究盡するなり。遍参は、たとへば、打地唯打地を遍参とすべし。打地一番、打空一番、打四方八面來を遍参とせず、倶胝唯豎一指を、遍参なりとす、更豎拳頭せば、遍参にあらざらん。爲人もかくのごとくなるべし、爲自もかくのごとくなるべし。

Thus, looking at the conduct of Xuefeng and investigating the traces of Xuansha, make extensive study of them and do not wander idly.[11] Extensive study is, "*the bigness of a stone is big, the smallness of a stone is small.*" We should make the stone a big study, a small study. As for "bigness," extensively studying and investigating bigness is called "extensive study"; as for "smallness," extensively studying and investigating smallness is called "extensive study." To see the hundreds of thousands of myriads in the hundreds of thousands of myriads is not yet extensive study. It is exhaustively investigating extensive study as being the turning of the body hundreds of thousands of myriad times within the flow of half a word. For example, we should take "*Dadi just struck the ground*" as extensive study; we do not take *striking the ground once, striking the sky once, striking the four quarters and eight sides* as extensive study. We take "*Juzhi's just holding up one finger*" as extensive study. If he *then raised his fist*, this would probably not be extensive study.[12] For the sake of the other should be like this; for the sake of oneself should be like this.

$$* \quad * \quad * \quad * \quad *$$

---

have not transcended the four seas and five lakes, it is not extensive study. Coming and going to the four seas and five lakes does not make the four seas and five lakes study extensively: it makes the road slippery; it makes the footing slippery; hence, it makes one lose extensive study.

11   **Thus** (*shika areba* しかあれば): This section roughly parallels section 8 in the seventy-five-chapter *Shōbōgenzō* version, albeit with many differences.

12   **If he then raised his fist** (*kō ju kentō seba* 更豎拳頭せば): This and the following sentence do not occur in the seventy-five-chapter *Shōbōgenzō* version. See Supplementary Notes, s.v. "Fist."

V5. Extensive Study *Henzan* 遍参

[V5:12]

玄沙示衆云、與我釋迦老子同參。時有僧出問、未審、參見甚麼人。師云、
釣魚舩上謝三郎。

> Xuansha addressed the assembly, saying, "Old Master Śākya and I studied together."[13]

> At that time, a monk came forward and asked, "I don't understand. With whom did you study?"

> The Master said, "The Xie's third boy on a fishing boat."

[V5:13] {2:595}

しかあれば、釋迦老子參底の頭正尾正、みずから玄沙老漢と同參なるべ
し。玄沙參底の頭正尾正、したしく釋迦老子と同參す。釋迦老子と玄沙老
漢と、參足・參不足なき、これ遍參の道理なり。釋迦老子は、玄沙老漢と
同參するゆえに、古佛なり、玄沙老漢は、釋迦老子と同參するゆえに、兒
孫なり。この道理、よくよく遍參すべし。

Thus, the studying of Old Master Śākya that is right from head to tail must be himself studying together with Old Man Xuansha.[14] The studying of Xuansha that is right from head to tail is himself intimately studying together with Old Master Śākya. It is Old Master Śākya and Old Man Xuansha studying together. The study of Old Master Śākya and Old Man Xuansha is neither sufficient nor insufficient: this is the principle of extensive study. Because Old Master Śākya studies together with Old Man Xuansha, he is an old buddha; because Old Man Xuansha studies together with Old Master Śākya, he is a descendant. This principle, we should give thorough extensive study.

[V5:14]

釣魚舩上謝三郡、このむね、審細に參學すべし、といふは、釋迦老子と玄
沙老漢と同時同參の時節を、遍參功夫すべし。釣魚舩上謝三郎を參見する
玄沙を、同參すや、いなや。玄沙山上禿頭漢を同參する謝三郎を、同參す
や、いなや。同參・不同參、みづから功夫せしめ、他づから功夫ならしむ
べし。玄沙と釋迦老子と同參を遍參しおはりて、謝三郎と與我と、參見甚
麼人の道理を遍參すべし。もし遍參の道理現在前せざるときは、參自不得

---

13 **Xuansha addressed the assembly** (*Gensha jishu* 玄沙示衆): This quotation parallels section 9 in the seventy-five-chapter *Shōbōgenzō* version.

14 **Thus** (*shika areba* しかあれば): This section corresponds to section 10 in the seventy-five-chapter *Shōbōgenzō* version, which reads at this point:

> 釋迦老子參底の頭正尾正、おのづから釋迦老子と同參なり。玄沙老漢參底の頭
> 正尾正、おのづから玄沙老漢と同參なるゆえに、釋迦老子と玄沙老漢と同參な
> り。

> The studying of Old Master Śākya that is right from head to tail is himself studying together with Old Master Śākya. The studying of Old Man Xuansha that is right from head to tail is himself studying together with Old Man Xuansha; hence, it is Old Master Śākya and Old Man Xuansha studying together.

なり、參他不得なり、參人不得なり、參我不得なり、自釣自上不得なり、未釣先上不得なり。すでに遍參究盡なるには、脱落遍參なり、海枯不見底なり、人死不留心なり。いはゆる海枯といふは、全海枯なり。しかあれども、枯竭しぬるには、不見底なり。不留・早留、ともに人心なり。しかあるに、人死のとき、心不留なり、心不留は、人死なり。かくのごとく、一方の表裏を參究すべきなり。

"*The Xie's third boy on a fishing boat*": the meaning of this, we should study in detail.[15]

That is, we should make concentrated effort at extensive study of the moment when Old Master Śākya and Old Man Xuansha study together at the same time. Do they, or do they not, study together the Xuansha who meets "*the Xie's third boy on a fishing boat*"? Do they or do they not study together the Xie's third boy who studies together with the *baldheaded fellow on Mount Xuansha*? We should have ourselves concentrate, have the other concentrate, on studying together and not studying together. Having extensively studied Xuansha and Old Master Śākya studying together, we should extensively study the principle of "with whom" the Xie's third boy and "I" studied. When the principle of extensive study is not immediately present to us, *study of ourselves is not possible, study of the other is not possible; study of the person is not possible, study of the self is not possible; fishing for oneself and rising by oneself are not possible, rising before being caught is not possible.*

When extensive study has been exhaustively investigated, it is extensive study sloughed off; it is, "*when the ocean dries up, we cannot see the bottom*"; it is, "*when a person dies, he does not leave his mind behind*." "When the ocean dries up" means the entire ocean is dried up. Nevertheless, when the ocean has entirely dried up, "*we cannot see the bottom.*" "Not leaving" and "early leaving" are both the person's mind.[16]

---

15 **"The Xie's third boy on a fishing boat": the meaning of this, we should study in detail** (*chōgyō sen jō Sha sanrō, kono mune, shinsai ni sangaku su beshi* 釣魚舩上謝三郡、このむね、審細に參學すべし): This section parallels sections 11 and 12 in the seventy-five-chapter *Shōbōgenzō* version.

16 **"Not leaving" and "early leaving" are both the person's mind** (*furyū sōryū, tomo ni ninshin nari* 不留・早留、ともに人心なり): The corresponding sentence in the seventy-five-chapter *Shōbōgenzō* version reads, "Not leaving and entirely leaving" (*furyū zenryū* 不留全留). The unusual *sōryū* 早留 ("early leaving") here suggests a play with the expression *ryūshin* 留心 ("leave his mind behind"), a term that normally means "to pay attention," "take heed," etc., as in the well-known saying attributed to Zhaozhou Congshen 趙州從諗 (778-897) (*Jingde chuandeng lu* 景德傳燈錄, T.2076.51:278a5-6):

毘婆尸佛早留心、直至如今不得妙。

The Buddha Vipaśyin early took heed of this, but right up to the present, hasn't got its subtlety.

Dōgen gives a variant of the saying in his *Eihei kōroku* 永平廣錄 (DZZ.4:222, no. 59).

V5. Extensive Study *Henzan* 遍参

Hence, when "the person dies," the mind is "not left behind." "The mind not left behind" is "the person dies." In this way, we should investigate the surface and interior of a single side.

* * * * *

[V5:15] {2:596}
先師天童古佛、あるとき諸方の長老の道舊なる、いたりあつまりて上堂を請するに、上堂云、大道無門、諸方頂顎上跳出、虚空絕路、清凉鼻孔裏入來。恁麼相見、瞿曇賊種、臨濟禍胎。咦、大家顚倒舞春風、驚落杏華飛亂紅。

My former master, the Old Buddha of Tiantong, on one occasion when old associates among the elders from all quarters assembled and request-ed a convocation, *said in his convocation address,*[17]

The great way has no gate;
It springs forth from the crowns in all quarters.
Empty space ends the road;
It enters the nostrils of Qingliang.
Meeting like this,
Gautama's traitorous seed,
Linji's disastrous embryo.
Ii!
Everyone toppled over, dancing in the spring wind;
Startled, the falling apricot blossoms fly in crimson chaos.

[V5:16]
いまの上堂は、先師古佛、ちなみに建康府の清凉寺に住持のとき、諸方の長老きたれり。これらの道舊とは、あるひは賓主とありき、あるひは隣單なりき。かくのごとくの舊友なり、おほからざらめやは。あつまりて上堂を請するときなり。渾無箇話の長老は、いたらず、請せられず、大尊貴なるを、かしづき、請するなるべし。おほよそ先師の遍參は、諸方のきはむべきにあらず。二三百年來は、先師のごとく遍參なる古佛あらざるなり、眞箇の遍參なり。

This convocation address is from the time when my former master, the Old Buddha, was the abbot of the Qingliang Monastery, in the Prefecture of Jiankang, to which the elders from all quarters had come.[18] That these were "old associates" means they had once been guest and host or been neighboring seats. They were thus his old friends; how could they not

---

17 **My former master, the Old Buddha of Tiantong** (*senshi Tendō kobutsu* 先師天童古佛): This quotation corresponds to section 13 in the seventy-five-chapter *Shōbōgenzō* version.

18 **This convocation address** (*ima no jōdō* いまの上堂): This section corresponds to sections 14 and 15 in the seventy-five-chapter *Shōbōgenzō* version.

296   DŌGEN'S *SHŌBŌGENZŌ* VOLUME VII

have been many? It was a time when they had assembled and requested a convocation. Elders completely lacking this talk did not come, did not request [the convocation]. Though themselves great worthies, they attended him and requested [an address].

In general, the extensive study of my former master was not something fulfilled by those from all quarters. In the last two or three hundred years in the Land of the Great Song, there have been no old buddhas with extensive study like my former master; his was true extensive study.

[V5:17]

大道無門は、條條轡なり、汝問趙州轡なり。しかあるを、大道まさに渾身の跳出するに、餘外をもちいず、頂顴上より跳出するなり、鼻孔裏より入來、參學するなり。いまだ頂顴上より跳脱せざるをば、參學人といはず、遍參漢にあらず。いままでも見一知識の風流、聞一頭話の工夫、みなこれよりするなり。いまの去那邊去、來遮裏來、その間隙あらざるがごとくなる、大道の渾體なり。毘盧頂上行は、無諍三昧なり、既得恁麼は、毘盧行なり。跳出の遍參を參徹する、これ胡蘆の胡蘆を跳出する、胡蘆頂顴上を選佛場とせることひさし。命如糸なり、胡蘆遍參胡蘆なり。

"*The great way has no gate*" is each one so, is "*You asked about Zhaozhou, right?*"[19] Still, when the whole body truly springs forth, without using anything else, the great way springs from "the crowns," it enters into "the nostril" and studies. If one has not yet sprung forth from the crown, one is not a person of study, is not a fellow of extensive study.[20]

---

19   **"The great way has no gate" is each one so** (*daidō mumon wa, jōjō nii nari* 大道無門は、條條轡なり): This section corresponds to sections 16 and 18 in the seventy-five-chapter *Shōbōgenzō* version. The unusual expression *jōjō nii* 條條轡, tentatively translated "each one so," also occurs in the "Shōbōgenzō gyōbutsu iigi" 正法眼藏行佛威儀; here, perhaps, meaning, "every instance of the great way is without a gate."

"You asked about Zhaozhou, right?" (*nyo mon Jōshū nii* 汝問趙州轡): From a well-known dialogue between an unidentified monk and Zhaozhou Congshen 趙州從諗, recorded in Dōgen's *shinji Shōbōgenzō* 眞字正法眼藏 (DZZ.5:150, case 46):

趙州因僧問、如何是趙州。師曰、東門南門西門北門。僧曰、不問遮箇。師曰、儞問趙州轡。

Zhaozhou was once asked by a monk, "What is Zhaozhou."
The Master said, "East Gate, South Gate, West Gate, North Gate."
The monk said, "I didn't ask about that."
The Master said, "You asked about Zhaozhou, right?"

The opening sentence of section 16 in the seventy-five-chapter *Shōbōgenzō* version replaces Zhaozhou's question here with a comment on the dialogue by Chan Master Yuantong Xian 圓通僊:

大道無門は、四五千條華柳巷、二三萬座管絃樓なり。

"The great way has no gate" is "four or five thousand lanes of flowers and willows, twenty or thirty thousand pavilions of flutes and zithers."

20   **not a fellow of extensive study** (*henzan kan ni arazu* 遍參漢にあらず): Section 16 of the seventy-five-chapter *Shōbōgenzō* version concludes here with the remark, "We

V5. Extensive Study *Henzan* 遍参

Even up till now, the tradition of seeing a wise friend, the concentrated effort of hearing a saying, have all derived from this.[21] The present *"going over there and coming over here,"* as if there were no gap between them, is the whole body of the great way. "Walking atop the head of Vairocana" is "the unconflicted samādhi." *"Since you have got such a thing"* is Vairocana walking.

Thoroughly to study the extensive study that "springs forth" — this is the bottle gourd springing forth from the bottle gourd; for long, "atop the head" of the bottle gourd has been made the site where the buddha is selected. It is *"his life is like a thread"*; it is *the bottle gourd extensively studying the bottle gourd.*[22]

{2:597}

正法眼藏遍參三十七
Treasury of the Eye of the True Dharma
Extensive Study
Thirty-seven

[Eiheiji MS:]

爾時寛元元年癸卯十一月二十七日、在越宇禪師峰下茅菴示衆
Presented to the assembly at a thatched hermitage below Yamashibu, Etsuu; twenty-seventh day, eleventh month of the junior water year of the rabbit, the first year of Kangen [8 January 1244]

[Tōunji MS:]

同癸卯臘月廿七日書寫之在同菴侍者寮。懷奘
Copied this at the acolyte's quarters of the same hermitage; twenty-seventh day, month of offerings, the same junior water year of the rabbit [7 February 1244]. Ejō

---

should just study with Xuansha the essential point of extensive study" (*henzan no shūshi, tada Gensha ni sangaku su beshi* 遍參の宗旨、ただ玄沙に參學すべし). This is followed by a short section, missing here, citing famous examples of extensive study by Chan masters of the Tang dynasty.

21 **Even up till now** (*ima made mo* いままでも): This sentence does not occur in the seventy-five-chapter *Shōbōgenzō* version, which begins its section 18 with the sentence:

遍參は、ただ祇管打坐、身心脱落なり。

Extensive study is simply "just sitting" with "body and mind sloughed off."

22 **the bottle gourd extensively studying the bottle gourd** (*korō henzan korō* 胡蘆遍參胡蘆): The seventy-five-chapter text ends with the additional sentence:

一莖草を建立するを、遍參とせるのみなり。

We have merely set up "one blade of grass" and taken it as extensive study.

Treasury of the True Dharma Eye
Variant Text 6

Great Awakening
Daigo
大悟

Great Awakening

Daigo

Introduction

This text is not included in any extant compilation of the *Shōbōgenzō* and seems to have remained largely unknown in the Sōtō tradition. Rather, it was preserved in the Ōsu Bunko 大須文庫 collection of the Shingon temple Shinpukuji 真福寺, in Nagoya, where it was only discovered in 1979. The manuscript is undated but identifies its place of composition as Kōshōji, Dōgen's residence from 1236 to 1243. The content is thought to represent an early draft of the "Daigo" text that occurs as number 10 of the seventy-five-chapter *Shōbōgenzō*, a work bearing colophons dated early spring 1242 at Kōshōji and spring 1244 at Kippōji. That text differs considerably from this earlier version, focusing as it does on just three of the several sayings on great awakening that we find here.

The translation follows Kawamura's edition, including his interpolation (marked by chevrons) of glyphs illegible in the manuscript. The annotation directs readers to parallel material in the seventy-five-chapter *Shōbōgenzō* text, where additional relevant notes can be found.

正法眼藏拾遺六
Treasury of the True Dharma Eye
Variant Text 6

大悟
Great Awakening

(草案本・真福寺所藏)
(Draft text, Shinpukuji Collection)

觀音導利興聖寶林寺
Kannon Dōri Kōshō Hōrin Monastery

[V6:1] {2:598}

佛佛の大道、つたはること綿密なり、功業、現成なること、平展なり。このゆへに、大悟あり、不悟あり、省悟あり、失悟あり。ともにこれ佛祖、あるときは抛却し、あるときは把定するところなり。抛却、および把定にあら＜ず＞、泥團の形段も現成せり。

The great way of buddha after buddha is handed down meticulously; their meritorious deeds are manifested openly.[1] Therefore, there is great awakening; there is not awakening; there is reflective awakening; there is losing awaking. They are all what the buddhas and ancestors sometimes throw away, sometimes hold tight; they also manifest the shape of the mud ball, neither thrown away nor held tight.[2]

---

1 **The great way of buddha after buddha** (*butsubutsu no daidō* 佛佛の大道): This and the following section loosely parallel the seventy-five-chapter *Shōbōgenzō* text, section 1.

2 **they also manifest the shape of the mud ball, neither thrown away nor held tight** (*hōkyaku, oyobi hajō ni ara[zu], deidan no gyōdan mo genjō seri* 抛却、および把定にあら＜ず＞、泥團の形段も現成せり): A tentative translation, perhaps meaning that the various types of awakening express the ordinary deluded state just as it is. The term "mud ball" (*deidan* 泥團), typically referring to the state of delusion, is best known from the expression "a guy who plays around with a mud ball" (*nong ni tuan han* 弄泥團漢), used in Chan literature for someone who wastes his time "fiddling around" with meaningless thoughts or activities.

[V6:2]

しるべし、大悟<より>、諸佛諸祖は恁麼來なり。ゆへに、大悟<は>、佛祖の邊際にかかはれるにあらざるなり。

We should know that it is from great awakening that the buddhas and ancestors "come like this."[3] Therefore, it is not that great awakening has anything to do with the boundaries of the buddhas and ancestors.[4]

[V6:3]

しかあるに、あるいは、生知あり、といふ、いはゆる生じて生をしるなり。學而知者あり、といふ、學して生をしるなり。佛智者あり、といふ、無師智者あり、といふとも、三擧に回去する、行履の條條なり。

Still, it is said there are "those who know at birth": that is, they know birth upon being born.[5] It is said there are "those who know from study": they know birth from studying it. While it is said there are "those with buddha knowledge" or said there are "those who know without a master," they are instances of the conduct of returning when it is raised the third time.[6]

---

3 **"come like this"** (*inmo rai* 恁麼來): Recalling the famous conversation, much loved by Dōgen, between the Sixth Ancestor, Huineng 六祖慧能, and Nanyue Huairang 南嶽懷讓, which begins,

祖曰、從什麼處來。師曰、嵩山安國師恁麼來。祖曰、是什麼物恁麼來。
The Ancestor asked, "Where are you coming from?"
The Master said, "I'm coming from the National Teacher An on Mount Song."
The Ancestor said, "What thing is it that comes like this?"

For the version of the dialogue given in Dōgen's *shinji Shōbōgenzō* 眞字正法眼藏 (DZZ.5:178, case 101), see Supplementary Notes, s.v. "What thing is it that comes like this?"

4 **it is not that great awakening has anything to do with the boundaries of the buddhas and ancestors** (*daigo [wa], busso no henzai ni kakawareru ni arazaru nari* 大悟<は>、佛祖の邊際にかかはれるにあらざるなり): Cf. the seventy-five-chapter *Shōbōgenzō* text, section 1:

佛祖は大悟の邊際を跳出し。
The buddhas and ancestors spring off from the boundaries of great awakening.

5 **Still, it is said there are "those who know at birth"** (*shikaaru ni, arui wa, shōchi ari, to iu* しかあるに、あるいは、生知あり、といふ): This section loosely parallels section 2 of the seventy-five-chapter *Shōbōgenzō* text.

6 **they are instances of the conduct of returning when it is raised the third time** (*sanko ni kaiko suru, anri no jōjō nari* 三擧に回去する、行履の條條なり): The sense is uncertain and the translation tentative. The interpretation assumes an allusion to the highest type of person described by Yunmen 雲門 in section 31, below. This phrase does not occur in the seventy-five-chapter *Shōbōgenzō* text.

V6. Great Awakening *Daigo* 大悟　　　　303

[V6:4] {2:599}

生知あれば、生悟あるべし。佛祖すでに調御丈夫とあるに、みな生悟＜なるを＞拈來せるがゆへに、學道＜に＞大悟する、生悟なるべし、學悟する、生悟なるべし。學悟なるがゆへに、いま三界を擧して大悟し、四大＜を擧＞して大悟とし、諸佛を擧して大悟＜し＞、諸法＜を＞擧して大悟し、諸緣を擧し＜て大＞悟しきたれること、いますなはち正當恁麼時なり。

Since there is knowing at birth, there must be awakening at birth.[7] The buddhas and ancestors, being tamers of persons, because they have all taken up what is awakening at birth, in studying the way, their greatly awakening is awakening at birth, their awakening by study is awakening at birth. Because they are awakened by study, now is the very time in which they have been taking up the three realms and greatly awakening, taking up the four elements and greatly awakening, taking up the buddhas and greatly awakening, taking up the dharmas and greatly awakening, taking up conditions and greatly awakening.

[V6:5]

このゆへに、臨濟院の慧照大師いはく、盡大地覓に一人として不悟者難得。

Therefore, Great Master Huizhao of Linji Cloister said, "In all the whole earth, it's hard to find a single person who's unawakened."[8]

[V6:6]

しかれば、盡地にあらゆるは、不悟者にはあらざるべし。悟を齊限とせむともがらは、休歇＜す＞べし、悟、これ齊限にあらざるがゆへに。不悟者、かならずしも悟者にあらず。悟のうへにも、さらに進一歩するに、朝到西天、暮到唐土あるなり。十聖・三賢、等覺・妙覺等は、ひとへに待悟＜爲＞則なるのみなり。かれらに悟なし＜と＞い＜は＞ず、待悟するのみなり。

Therefore, on all the earth, none is an unawakened person. Those who would limit awakening should stop; for awakening is not limited. The unawakened person is not necessarily an awakened person. Advancing a step beyond awakening, there is, *in the morning, going to Sindh in the*

7　**Since there is knowing at birth** (*shōchi areba* 生知あれば): This section parallels sections 3 and 4 of the seventy-five-chapter *Shōbōgenzō* text, the latter of which gives a more polished version of the awkward last sentence here.

8　**Great Master Huizhao of Linji Cloister** (*Rinzai in no Eshō daiji* 臨濟院の慧照大師): I.e., Linji Yixuan 臨済義玄 (d. 866). This quotation parallels section 5 of the seventy-five-chapter *Shōbōgenzō* text. There, Linji's words are given as:

大唐國裏、覓一人不悟者難得。

In the Land of the Great Tang, it's hard to find a single person who's unawakened.

West; in the evening, going to the Land of the Tang.[9] The ten sages and three worthies, the virtually awakened and the wondrously awakened, all just make awaiting awakening the norm.[10] We do not say they lack awakening; [they] just await awakening.

[V6:7]

しるべし、盡地に不＜悟＞者なきがゆへに、待悟は齊限なるのみなり。＜待＞悟の齊限なる、待悟帶累することを辭せずといへども、待悟に親切ならず。をほ＜よ＞そ、大悟は、不拘小節なり。

We should know that, because there are no unawakened people on all the earth, awaiting awakening is limited.[11] Even though this may not state the fact that awaiting awakening is limited, or that awaiting awakening is troubling, it is not intimate with awaiting awakening. In sum, "great awakening *doesn't bother with trifling matters.*"[12]

[V6:8]

曹谿のいはく、大悟は不拘小節。又、永嘉眞覺大師のいはく、大象は不遊於兎徑と。

Caoxi said, "The great awakening *doesn't bother with trifling matters.*"[13] Again, Great Master Zhenjue of Yongjia said, "The great elephant *doesn't follow rabbit tracks.*"

---

9   **in the morning, going to Sindh in the West; in the evening, going to the Land of the Tang** (*chō tō Saiten, bo tō Tōdo* 朝到西天、暮到唐土): Variant of a fairly common expression in Chan texts for the pedagogic dexterity of the accomplished master. The second clause occurs more often as, "in the evening, returning to the Land of the Tang" (*bo ki Tōdo* 暮歸唐土).

10   **The ten sages and three worthies, the virtually awakened and the wondrously awakened** (*jisshō sanken, tōgaku myōgaku tō* 十聖・三賢、等覺・妙覺等): I.e., those on the various stages of the bodhisattva path.

make waiting for awakening the norm (*tai go [i] soku* 待悟＜爲＞則): An expression also found in Dōgen's *Eihei kōroku* 永平廣錄 and in section 17 of the seventy-five-chapter *Shōbōgenzō* text. See Supplementary Notes, s.v. "Await awakening."

11   **because there are no unawakened people on all the earth, awaiting awakening is limited** (*jinchi ni fu[go]sha naki ga yue ni, taigo wa saigen naru nomi nari* 盡地に不＜悟＞者なきがゆへに、待悟は齊限なるのみなり): I.e., the lack of unawakened people restricts [the value of (?)] "awaiting awakening."

12   **"great awakening does not bother with trifling matters"** (*daigo wa, fukō shōsetsu* 大悟は、不拘小節): A saying that Dōgen ascribes to Huineng in the following section.

13   **Caoxi** (*Sōkei* 曹谿): Also written 曹溪. I.e., the Sixth Ancestor, Huineng 慧能. The source for the attribution of this saying to Huineng is unclear. Rather, this and the following quotation are both usually attributed to the Sixth Ancestor's follower Yongjia Xuanjue 永嘉玄覺 (d. 723), in his famous poem, the *Zhengdao ge* 證道歌 (T.2014.48:396c27):

大象不遊於兎徑。大悟不拘於小節。

The great elephant doesn't follow rabbit tracks;

The great awakening doesn't bother with trifling matters.

V6. Great Awakening *Daigo* 大悟   305

[V6:9] {2:600}

大悟不拘於＜小＞節、いはゆる小節は、報化佛顯なり、等覺・妙覺、始覺・本覺、有覺・無覺等なり、法身＜有＞病・法身無病等なり、佛向上・佛邊求等なり、無始無終・有始有終等なり、すなはち、大悟なり、といふにあらず。

"*The great awakening doesn't bother with trifling matters.*" "Trifling matters" are *the appearance of the buddhas of recompense and transformation;* they are *virtual awakening and wondrous awakening, initial awakening and original awakening, having awakening and lacking awakening, and the like;* they are "*the dharma body is sick*" and "*the dharma body is not sick,*" and the like; they are "*beyond the buddha*" and "*searching in the vicinity of the Buddha,*" and the like; they are *lacking beginning and end and having beginning and end, and the like* — these are not said to be the great awakening.[14]

[V6:10]

盡＜界＞に＜不＞悟者をもとむるに難得なり、と道取＜する＞なり。しかあれば、前程に大悟のあるべから＜ざ＞るにはあらず。不悟者とならむことは、いまだしきなり。進一步も盡地なり、退一步も盡地なり、步一步も盡地なり、步獨步盡地なるべし。

He says it is hard to find an unawakened person in the entire world.[15] Thus, it is not that there will be no great awakening in the future: there has not yet been [anyone] becoming an unawakened person.[16] Advancing one pace is all the earth; retreating one pace is all the earth; pacing one pace is all the earth; pacing the solitary pace is all the earth.

---

14 **"the dharma body is sick"** (*hosshin [u] byō* 法身＜有＞病): Variation on a Zen phrase, as in the saying, "the dharma body is sick, the form body is troubled" (*hosshin byō shikishin fuan* 法身病色身不安) (see, e.g., *Xutang heshang yulu* 虛堂和尚語錄, T.2000.47:996c17).

"searching in the vicinity of the Buddha" (*buppen gu* 佛邊求): Perhaps reflecting the line of verse by Chan Master Jiashan Shanhui 夾山善會禪師 (805-881) (*Jingde chuandeng lu* 景德傳燈錄, T.2076.51:324a18):

勞持生死法、唯向佛邊求

If you're troubled to keep the dharmas of life and death,
Just look for them in the vicinity of the Buddha.

For the contrast drawn in Chan texts between "what is in the vicinity of the buddha" (*buppen ji* 佛邊事) and "what lies beyond the buddha" (*butsu kōjō ji* 佛向上事), see Supplementary Notes, s.v. "Beyond the buddha."

15 **He says** (*dōshu [suru]* 道取＜する＞): This section loosely parallels section 7 of the seventy-five-chapter *Shōbōgenzō* text.

16 **it is not that there will be no great awakening in the future** (*zentei ni daigo no aru bekara[za]ru ni wa arazu* 前程に大悟のあるべから＜ざ＞るにはあらず): Presumably, an ironic reassurance that there is still hope for an unawakened person.

306 DŌGEN'S *SHŌBŌGENZŌ* VOLUME VII

* * * * *

[V6:11]

京兆華嚴寺休靜禪師に僧問、大悟底人却迷時如何、師云、破鏡不＜重＞照、落華難上樹。

> Chan Master Xiujing of the Huayan Monastery in Jingzhao was asked by a monk, "What about when the person of great awakening reverts to delusion?"[17]
>
> The Master said, "The broken mirror doesn't reflect again; the fallen flower can't climb the tree."

[V6:12]

この道理、しづかに悟取すべし。百億身を究盡しても悟取し、換面回＜頭＞しても悟取し、十千界を經歴しても悟取すべし、直趣萬年にも悟取すべし、一念にも悟取し、毫忽にも悟取すべし。

We should quietly awaken to the rationale of this. We should awaken to it though we exhaustively investigate hundreds of *koṭis* of lives; we should awaken to it though we change the face and turn the head, awaken to it though we pass through ten thousand realms; we should awaken to it even when *directly proceeding ten thousand years*; we should awaken to it even in a single thought, awaken to it even in a hair's breadth.[18]

[V6:13]

しばらく師の宗旨の＜＞と摸索せむとするに、さきより摸索すべき僧問あり。そのこころは、この問話僧は、參飽叢林の雲衲なるべし。

When we would grope a bit for . . . of what the Master means, we should first grope for what he was "asked by a monk."[19] The meaning of this is that the monk who asked this must have been one robed in clouds and sleeved in mist who has studied his fill in the grove.[20]

17　**Chan Master Xiujing of the Huayan Monastery in Jingzhao** (*Keichō Kegonji Kyūjō zenji* 京兆華嚴寺休靜禪師): I.e., Huayan Xiujing 華嚴休靜 (dates unknown), disciple of Dongshan Liangjie 洞山良价 (807-869). This quotation parallels section 8 of the seventy-five-chapter *Shōbōgenzō* text.

18　**directly proceeding ten thousand years** (*jiki shu bannen* 直趣萬年): Perhaps a variant of (or a copyist error for) the homophonous 直須萬年 ("surely take ten thousand years"), as in the saying, found in the *shinji Shōbōgenzō* 眞字正法眼藏 (DZZ.5:166, case 85) and elsewhere the *Shōbōgenzō*, attributed to Shishuang Chingzhu 石霜慶諸 (807-888); see Supplementary Notes, s.v. "It would surely take ten thousand years."

19　**When we would grope a bit for . . . of what the Master means** (*shibaraku shi no shūshi no . . . to mosaku semu to suru ni* しばらく師の宗旨の＜＞と摸索せむとするに): Several glyphs in this clause are illegible. This section parallels section 9 of the seventy-five-chapter *Shōbōgenzō* text.

20　**one robed in clouds and sleeved in mist who has studied his fill in the grove** (*san-*

V6. Great Awakening *Daigo* 大悟   307

[V6:14]

しかあるに、大悟底人却迷時如何、と問取するに、華嚴きらはず、叢林わ
らはぬ、すなはち問ふべきを問し、ならひきたれるを露胆するなるべし。
これをもて參究するに、佛佛祖祖の家風・道業には、大悟底人却迷を單傳
の懷業とせり。

Moreover, when he asks, "*What about when the person of great awakening reverts to delusion?*" Huayan does not disapprove nor the members of the grove disparage it; that is, he asks what should be asked and
courageously shows what he has learned.[21] When we investigate with
this, in the house style and work of the way of buddha after buddha and
ancestor after ancestor, "*the person of great awakening reverting to delusion*" is taken as a cherished deed uniquely transmitted.[22]

[V6:15] {2:601}

いま、西天より傳來せると自稱する經師・論師の立せる家門には、大悟・
大覺・却迷とはいわず。大悟・大覺の前程、いまだその落處の＜種草＞に
なるをしらず。ゆへに、大迷の以前、＜知る＞なし、大悟のをはりをしら
ず。大迷のはじめ＜を＞しらざるがゆへに、大悟をもしらず、大迷をも＜
し＞らざるなり。ゆへにそこばくの謗法となる。永嘉いはく、欲得不招無
間業、莫謗如來正法輪なり。

Now, in the houses established by the sūtra masters and treatise masters
claiming to have transmitted them from Sindh in the West, they do not
speak of "great awakening" or "great awareness" or "reverting to delusion." They have not understood that the state prior to "great awakening"
or "great awareness" forms the seedling of the conclusion.[23] Therefore,
they lack understanding of what is before great delusion and do not understand the end of great awakening. Because they do not understand the
beginning of great delusion, they do not understand great awakening nor
understand great delusion. Therefore, they commit many denigrations

---

pō sōrin no unnō 參飽叢林の雲衲): I.e., a well-trained monk. "Robed in clouds" (*unnō*
雲衲) is a literary expression for the itinerant monk; akin to the more common "clouds
and water" (*unsui* 雲水). "The grove" (*sōrin* 叢林) is the monastic institution.

21   **Moreover** (*shikaaru ni* しかあるに): This section has some parallel in section 10 of
the seventy-five-chapter *Shōbōgenzō* text.

22   **cherished deed uniquely transmitted** (*tanden no egō* 單傳の懷業): Presumably,
meaning something like "inner acts [i.e., thinking] passed down [by the buddhas and
ancestors]."

23   **They have not understood that the state prior to "great awakening" or "great
awareness" forms the seedling of the conclusion** (*daigo daikaku no zentei, imada sono
rakusho no [shusō] ni naru o shirazu* 大悟・大覺の前程、いまだその落處の＜種草＞
になるをしらず): Presumably, meaning they do not realize that the state of delusion represents the prior condition for awakening. "Great awareness" here and below represents
daikaku 大覺, a term usually (and better) rendered by "great awakening"; the English is
intended simply to distinguish it here from *daigo* 大悟.

of the dharma. Yongjia has said, "*If you don't wish to invite unremitting karma, don't denigrate the true dharma wheel of the Tathāgata.*"[24]

[V6:16]

經師・論師等、みだりに迷覺一如のことばに醉狂せるは、あるいはいふ、永劫に迷妄してさらに出離解脱すべからず、迷悟一如なり、と。あるいはいふ、生なし、佛なし、かるがゆへに迷悟不二なり。あるいはいふ、無覺なり、本覺なるがゆへに無迷なり、本來清淨なるがゆへに。あるいはいふ、迷も菩提なり、覺も菩提なり。あるいはいふ、作用に迷悟＜は＞あれども、體性に迷悟なし。かくのごとくの頻族は、世界に稻麻竹葦なり。しかあれども、佛佛祖祖の家業を正聞せる種草にはあらざるなり。

The sūtra masters and treatise masters, recklessly drunk on the words "delusion and awakening are one," say that we are deluded for eternal kalpas and will not escape to liberation; [hence,] delusion and awakening are one. Or they say that there are no living beings and no buddhas; therefore, delusion and awakening are not two. Or they say that we have no awakening, for we have original awakening; we have no delusion, for we are fundamentally pure. Or they say that delusion is bodhi and awakening is bodhi. Or they say that, while there are delusion and awakening in function, there are no delusion or awakening in essence. Such gangs are ubiquitous, like "rice, hemp, bamboo, and reeds" in the world.[25] Nevertheless, they are not seedlings who have heard the truth of the family enterprise of buddha after buddha and ancestor after ancestor.

[V6:17]

いま、僧の問處を搜尋して、佛の家業を辦究せむとするに、大悟底人却迷時如何と問すれば、大悟底人迷時＜な＞り、とはとはず、なる、とはとわず。又、大悟もあり、とはとわず、なし、ととわず、却迷あり、とはとわず、なし、とはとわず、大悟底人却迷時如何と＜と＞ふなり、と動着せず、參究すべし。動著すれば、拄杖三十なり。

Now, when we look into what the monk asked and pursue the family enterprise of the buddhas, when he asks, "*What about when the person of great awakening reverts to delusion?*" he does not ask about whether there is or is not a time when the person of great awakening is deluded.[26] Again, he does not ask whether there is or is not great awakening; he does not ask whether there is or is not reverting to delusion. He asks,

---

24 **Yongjia** (*Yōka* 永嘉): I.e., Yongjia Xuanjue 永嘉玄覺 (d. 723), in his *Zhengdao ge* 證道歌 (T.2014.48:396b27).

25 **"rice, hemp, bamboo, and reeds"** (*tō ma chiku i* 稻麻竹葦): I.e., dense and profuse; a simile from Kumārajīva's translation of the *Lotus Sūtra*; see Supplementary Notes.

26 **he does not ask about whether there is or is not a time when the person of great awakening is deluded** (*daigo tei nin mei ji [na]ri, to wa towazu, naru, to wa towazu* 大悟底人却迷時＜な＞り、とはとはず、なる、とはとわず): Reading *nari* なり as *ari* あり and *naru* なる as *nashi* なし, in accord with the sentence following.

V6. Great Awakening *Daigo* 大悟

309

"*What about when the person of great awakening reverts to delusion?*"
We should investigate this, without moving it; should we move it, it is
thirty blows of the staff.

[V6:18] {2:602}

又、大悟却迷といふとき、大悟の破滅して大迷は出現する、とはいわざる
なり、この宗旨、審細にすべし。しるべし、大悟たとひ却迷すといふと
も、すなはち大悟＜の＞迷なり。天魔・外道の認ずる大悟なるべからず、
却迷なるべからず、大悟却迷なり。十聖・三賢の認ずる二三にあらず、
いはゆる、千迷萬迷は大悟却迷なり、と參學するなり。大迷＜の＞千發萬
發、たとひ大地なりとも、不悟者難得なるべし。この道は、外道のしるに
あらず、ただ佛道のみにあり。

Again, when he says that "*great awakening reverts to delusion,*" he is
not saying that great awakening is destroyed and great delusion appears.
We should [study] the meaning of this in detail. We should recognize
that, though great awakening may revert to delusion, it is the delusion
of great awakening. It is not the great awakening, not the reversion to
delusion, recognized by the Deva Māra and the other paths; it is "*great
awakening reverts to delusion.*" It is not two or three recognized by the
ten sages and three worthies; we study that a thousand delusions, a myriad delusions, are "*great awakening reverting to delusion.*" Even if a
thousand occurrences, a myriad occurrences, of great delusion are the
whole earth, "*it's hard to find a person who's unawakened.*" This saying
is not known to the other paths; it is only in the way of the buddhas.

[V6:19]

しかあればすなはち、却迷は不悟にあらず、大悟は盡地なるべし。却迷と
問する宗旨、これを單傳せる問旨は、大悟底人却迷悟如何といはむがごと
し。問頭、かくのごとく問取すといえども、問法にも、かくのごとく聽取
するなり。聲現のときも、かくのごとく現前するなり。修行辨道にも、か
くのごとく辨道するなり。

Thus, reverting to delusion is not unawakened, and great awakening
is all the earth. The significance of asking of "reverting to delusion" is
like saying that the question that has uniquely transmitted this is, "*what
about when the person of great awakening reverts to delusion?*" Though
the question may be asked in this way, in asking about the buddha dharma as well, we hear it like this.[27] When the voice occurs, it appears before us like this. In practicing and pursuing the way as well, we pursue
the way like this.

27　**in asking about the buddha dharma as well, we hear it like this** (*monpō ni mo,
kaku no gotoku chōshu suru* 問法にも、かくのごとく聽取する): Presumably, meaning
that the specific question about "reverting to delusion" is a way of questioning the buddha dharma more generally. Hence, the following two sentences would mean something
like, "this is how such questioning sounds, and this is how we train in Buddhism."

310 DŌGEN'S *SHŌBŌGENZŌ* VOLUME VII

[V6:20]

しかればすなはち、不悟にあらざれども、大悟す、不迷なりといえども、大悟するなり。しるべし、まどひを旋轉＜して＞さとりとするにあらず、不悟にあらざれども大悟あり。さとりを磨抹してまどひとするにあらず、大悟底人却迷如何なり。相即にあらず、無罣礙にあらざるなり。

Thus, though it is not unawakened, it greatly awakens; though it may be undeluded, it greatly awakens. It is not that it turns delusion into awakening: although it is unawakened, it has a great awakening. It is not that it polishes awakening and makes it delusion: it is "*what about when the person of great awakening reverts to delusion?*" It is not mutual identity; it is not unobstructed.

[V6:21]

師いはく、破鏡不重照。

The Master said, "*The broken mirror doesn't reflect again.*"

[V6:22]

この祗對をきくにも、佛佛祖祖の＜勳＞業を用著すべし。いはゆる、大悟却迷、と問取するに、破鏡不重照、と祗對あれば、鏡は悟なるべし、不重照は却迷しぬれば、さらに大悟なるべからず、まどひなるべし。鏡、すでに破しては、照、かさねてきたるべからざるがごとし。もしかくのごとく會取し問取せむは、佛法にあらず。いはゆる、破鏡不重照、と祗對せむことは、＜如何＞是佛、と問來せむにも、恁麼祗對すべし、如何是祖師西來意、と問來せむにも、祗對は恁麼なり。あるいは、水は冷暖にあらず、水は濕乾にあらず、といはむがごとし。又、あるいは、古鏡不重照、といはむがごとし。ただ不重照といふ、照なし、といはず、照きたる、といはず、照さりぬ、といはず。しかあれば、この祗對、大悟底人却迷あるべし、といふにあらず、なかるべし、といふにあらず、問不是、といふにあらざるなり。

When we hear this answer as well, we should employ the meritorious acts of buddha after buddha and ancestor after ancestor. That is, when asked about "*great awakening reverting to delusion,*" when he answers, "*the broken mirror doesn't reflect again,*" then the "mirror" must be "awakening"; and "doesn't reflect again," since it has "reverted to delusion," must be a "delusion" that will not again be "great awakening." It is as if the mirror having broken, the reflection will not have come again. To understand, to question, like this is not the buddha dharma. That is, the answer, "*the broken mirror doesn't reflect again*" — he should also answer like this when asked, "what is a buddha?"; when asked, "*what is the intention of the Ancestral Master coming from the west?*" the answer should be like this. Or it is like saying, "water is neither cold nor hot; water is neither wet nor dry."[28] Or, again, it is like saying, "*the old mirror*

---

28 **"water is neither cold nor hot; water is neither wet nor dry"** (*mizu wa reidan ni*

V6. Great Awakening *Daigo* 大悟 311

doesn't reflect again." To say simply, "it doesn't reflect again," is not saying that it does not reflect; it is not saying that it has been reflecting; it is not saying that the reflection has gone. Thus, this answer is not saying that there is "*the person of great awakening reverting to delusion,*" not saying that there is not, not saying that the question is wrong.

[V6:23] {2:603}

落華難上樹、といふをも、枝を辭しきたり庭に落在しぬれば、上樹しがたし、といえると會取しつべし、しかにはあらざるなり。たとへば、飛花難上樹、とも道得し、開花難上枝、とも道取し、春花難上空、とも道取せるごとし。この宗旨を、大悟・却迷に辨究しもてゆくべし。開花かならずしも上枝にあらず、春花かならずし＜も＞上山にあらず、ただこれ、花の時の花なり、花開の開なり。をのれより化城する帶累なし、ゆへに徧界不曾藏なり。他に染汚せらるる、彩色なし、ゆへに演出大藏教なり。

He says, "*The fallen flower can't climb the tree.*" This will have been understood to be saying that, since it has abandoned the branch and fallen to the garden, it cannot climb up the tree. But it is not so. It is like saying, "*the flying flowers can't climb the tree,*" or saying, "*the open flowers can't climb to the branch,*" or saying, "*the spring flowers can't climb to the sky.*" We should investigate the meaning of this in terms of "great awakening" and "reverting to delusion." The open flower is not necessarily on a branch; the spring flower is not necessarily on the mountain: it is just the flower at the time of the flower, the opening of the flower opening. It has no trouble from conjuring its own city; therefore, "*in the realms everywhere, it has never been hidden.*"[29] It has no stain from being defiled by another; therefore, it is "*expounding the teaching of the great treasury.*"[30]

---

arazu, mizu wa shikkan ni arazu 水は冷暖にあらず、水は濕乾にあらず): Reminiscent of a line in the "Shōbōgenzō sansui kyō" 正法眼藏山水經:

水は強弱にあらず、濕乾にあらず、動靜にあらず、冷暖にあらず、有無にあらず、迷悟にあらざるなり。

Water is neither strong nor weak, neither wet nor dry, neither moving nor still, neither cold nor hot, neither being nor non-being, neither delusion nor awakening.

29　**It has no trouble from conjuring its own city** (*onore yori kejō suru tairui nashi* をのれより化城する帶累なし): Allusion to the famous metaphor in Chapter 7 of the *Lotus Sūtra* (*Miaofa lianhua jing* 妙法蓮華經, T.262.9:22a18ff), in which a caravan leader conjures an oasis city on the desert as a resting place for his weary travelers. The metaphor is intended to explain why the Buddha teaches nirvāṇa for the arhats if there is only the one vehicle leading to buddhahood.

"in the realms everywhere, it has never been hidden" (*henkai fu zō zō* 徧界不曾藏): A popular saying attributed to Chan Master Shishuang Qingzhu 石霜慶諸 recorded in the *shinji Shōbōgenzō* 眞字正法眼藏 (DZZ.5:157-158, case 58); see Supplementary Notes.

30　**"expounding the teaching of the great treasury"** (*enshutsu daizō kyō* 演出大藏教): Suggestive of a saying attributed to Touzi Datong 投子大同 (819-914) (see, e.g. *Jingde chuandeng lu* 景德傳燈錄, T.2076.51:319a24-26):

312　DŌGEN'S *SHŌBŌGENZŌ* VOLUME VII

* * * * *

[V6:24]

龍牙山道和尚いはく、無中得悟。

Reverend Dao of Mount Longya said, "*Attaining awakening within nothingness.*"[31]

[V6:25]

この道よくよく七通八達あるべし。無中の道取する、むしろ、こころなからむや。宗旨＜あ＞るべくは、道聲現ずべし。無中は、無内にあらず、無外にあらざるべし。中、かならずしも當ならむや、中、かならずしも心ならむや。三際、斷ずべし、萬根、枝すべし。これを、偏正に旋擧することなかれ、これを、邊表に錯認することなかれ。未至なるによりて無といふ、といはざる、無遺なるを無といふ、といはざれ。萬根、ともに拔群することあらば、彼彼の無、すなはち待悟なるべし、三際、をなじく坐斷することあらば、此此の無、まさに得なるべし。有時とま＜た＞ず、有形とまたず、有緣といはず、有地といはず、有始といはず、有來といはず、有變・有化といはず、有成・有見といはず。ただ無中得悟といえるがゆへに、仙家步曆は、俗塵に混ぜず、佛道の得悟、これ無中なるのみなり。

We should have fully "seven penetrations and eight masteries" of these words. How could the saying of "within nothingness" be more thoughtless? For it to have meaning it should manifest the voice of the way.[32] "Within nothingness" is not inside nothingness; it is not outside nothingness. Is "within" necessarily present? Is "within" necessarily the mind? The three junctures should be cut off; the ten thousand roots should be scattered.[33] Do not turn this round within the inclined and upright; do

---

僧問、大藏教中還有奇特事也無。師曰、演出大藏教。

A monk asked, "Are there really any weird events in the teaching of the great treasury?"

The Master said, "Expounding the teaching of the great treasury."

31　**Reverend Dao of Mount Longya** (*Ryūgesan Dō oshō* 龍牙山道和尚): Neither the person nor the source of this saying is known. If, as has been suggested, the glyph *dō* 道 here is an error for *ton* 遁, the person in question is likely Longya Judon 龍牙居遁 (835-923), cited elsewhere in the *Shōbōgenzō*.

32　**it should manifest the voice of the way** (*dōshō genzu beshi* 道聲現ずべし): Perhaps reflecting a passage, cited elsewhere in the *Shōbōgenzō*, in the *Lotus Sūtra* (*Miaofa lianhua jing* 妙法蓮華經, T.262.9:18c20-21):

我等今者、眞是聲聞、以佛道聲、令一切聞。

Now, we

Are truly *śrāvakas*,

Who cause all to hear

The voice of the way of the buddhas.

33　**the ten thousand roots should be scattered** (*mankon, shi su beshi* 萬根、枝すべし): The translation is tentative; perhaps suggesting freedom from the myriad things

V6. Great Awakening *Daigo* 大悟 313

not misjudge this within boundaries.[34] Do not say that it is called "nothingness" because it has not arrived; do not say that its lacking remains is called "nothingness." If the ten thousand roots are all surpassed, those "nothingnesses" will be "awaiting awakening"; if the three junctures are all cut off, these "nothingnesses" will be "attaining."[35] It is not a matter of "there being a time"; it is not a matter of "there being a shape"; he does not speak of "there being conditions"; he does not speak of "a realm of being"; he does not speak of "there being a beginning"; he does not speak of "there being a coming"; he does not speak of "there being a change" or "there being a transformation"; he does not speak of "there being an accomplishment" or "there being an appearance."[36] Because he says only *attaining awakening within nothingness*," the walk of the sage is not dirtied by the dust of the world; the attainment of awakening on the way of the buddhas is only "within nothingness."

(*banbutsu* 萬物). See the phrase just below, "if the ten thousand roots are all surpassed" (*mankon, tomo ni batsugun suru koto araba* 萬根、ともに拔群することあらば).

34 **Do not turn this round within the inclined and upright** (*kore o, henshō ni senko suru koto nakare* これを、偏正に旋擧することなかれ): The terms "inclined and upright" (*henshō* 偏正) recall their use for "relative" and "absolute" in Zen discourse on the five ranks (*go'i* 五位), for which, see Supplementary Notes, s.v. "Five ranks." The unusual term *senko* 旋擧 ("turn and raise," perhaps in the sense "consider") occurs again below, section 27, but not elsewhere in the *Shōbōgenzō*.

35 **those "nothingnesses"** (*hihi no mu* 彼彼の無); **these "nothingnesses"** (*shishi no mu* 此此の無): More literally, "that and that nothingness," "this and this nothingness"; a play with "this and that" (*hishi* 彼此). The two clauses here comment on the terms "attaining awakening" in the quotation.

"awaiting awakening" (*taigo* 待悟): Perhaps a copyist's error for "attaining awakening" (*tokugo* 得悟).

36 **It is not a matter of "there being a time"** (*uji to ma[ta]zu* 有時とま＜た＞ず): This clause begins a sentence in which Dōgen plays with the glyph *u* 有 ("existence," "being"), the opposite of the "nonexistence" (*mu* 無) in the quotation. The translation seeks, rather awkwardly, to preserve something of this play, even at the expense of the usual meanings of the terms involved. Thus, "there being a time" renders *uji* 有時 ("sometimes"); "there being a shape" renders *ugyō* 有形 ("having shape"); "there being conditions" renders *u'en* 有緣 ("conditioned"); "realm of being" renders *uchi* 有地, here, likely a playful opposite of "realm of nothingness" (*mu sho'u chi* 無處有地); "there being a beginning" (*ushi* 有始) and "there being a coming" (*urai* 有來) represent what is likely a play on "from beginningless time" (*mushirai* 無始來); "there being a change" (*uhen* 有變) and "there being a transformation" (*uke* 有化) bisect the compound *henka* 變化 ("transformation"); and, finally, "there being an accomplishment" (*ujō* 有成; "completion") and "there being an appearance" (*uken* 有見; "visible"; also "having views"; "view of existence") are here likely playing on *genjō* 見成 ("realization," "manifestation," etc.).

[V6:26] {2:604}

しかあればすなはち、二祖、禮拜依位而立するに、傳法藏す、悟なし、と
せず。阿難・二祖のために大悟せる、雪山の大悟せざるにあらず、木石の
大悟せざるにあらず、大悟の三拜あり、大悟得髓あるのみなり。頭頭知、
了了知、たれかこれを、盡地にあらずといはむ、三祖・四祖・五祖等、み
なかくのごとし。大悟あるときは、人道あり、天道あるときは、大悟ある
のみなり、見明星悟道は、見明星道得なり。

Thus, when the Second Ancestor *made a bow and stood in place*, he
received transmission of the dharma treasury; this is not taken as lacking
awakening.[37] Ānanda and the Second Ancestor had the great awakening;
the Snowy Mountains do not fail to have the great awakening; the trees
and rocks do not fail to have the great awakening. The great awakening
simply has the three bows; the great awakening simply "gets the marrow." *Knowing every single thing, knowing all about it* — who would
say these are not all the earth? The Third Ancestor, Fourth Ancestor, and
Fifth Ancestor were all like this. When there is great awakening, there
is the human path; when there is the deva path, there is just the great
awakening. "*Seeing the dawn star and awakening to the way*" is *seeing
the dawn star and saying it*.[38]

[V6:27]

青原・南嶽の、六祖に正傳する、佛佛祖祖の大悟を正傳せるのみなり。
青原は、聖諦不爲、の階級のみにして、さらに身前身後の大悟なし。南
嶽は、説似一物即不中、の會得のみにして、大悟・不悟の染汚にかかはれ
ず。＜もし＞大悟を旋擧すること、道得現前すべし、會得現前すべし、こ
れを不悟の祖佛といふべし、大悟の道得とならふべし。

Qingyuan and Nanyue receiving direct transmission from the Sixth
Ancestor was simply the direct transmission of the great awakening of
buddha after buddha and ancestor after ancestor.[39] Qingyuan was simply
at the stage of "*not doing even the sacred truths*" and had no further great

---

37 **the Second Ancestor made a bow and stood in place** (*niso, raihai ei ni ryū suru*
二祖、禮拜依位而立する): From the famous account of the transmission of the lineage
from Bodhidharma to Huike 慧可, in which the latter demonstrates that he has "gotten
the marrow" of the First Ancestor's teaching by silently bowing. This section has some
parallel in section 14 of the seventy-five-chapter *Shōbōgenzō* text.

38 **"Seeing the dawn star and awakening to the way"** (*ken myōjō godō* 見明星悟
道): A fixed phrase for the awakening of the Buddha upon seeing the rise of Venus in the
dawn sky. The following "seeing the dawn star and saying it" (*ken myōjō dōtoku* 見明
星道得) introduces sayings (*dōtoku* 道得) of the two disciples of the Sixth Ancestor in
the following section — and suggests an interesting identification of the experience of
awakening with the verbal expression of it.

39 **Qingyuan and Nanyue** (*Seigen Nangaku* 青原・南嶽): I.e., Qingyuan Xingsi 青原
行思 (d. 740) and Nanyue Huairang 南嶽懷讓 (677-744), the two chief disciples of the
Sixth Ancestor.

V6. Great Awakening *Daigo* 大悟   315

awakening before the body or after the body.[40] Nanyue simply attained the understanding of "*to say it's like any thing doesn't hit it*" and had nothing to do with the defilements of great awakening or not awakening.[41] Turning round the great awakening, a saying should appear, an understanding should appear. These should be called the unawakened buddhas and ancestors and should be studied as the sayings of great awakening.

[V6:28] {2:605}

しかあればมすなはち、大悟・不悟・失悟等は、身前にもあり、身後にもあり、同修身にもあり、生前にもあり、生後にもあり、同修生にもあり、父母未生以前にもあり、徧界未曾藏にもあり。他人の、わがために大悟するあり、わが、他人のために大悟するあり、他人の、他人のために大悟するといふ、さらにこれ自己の、自己のために大悟するなるあらむ。

Thus, great awakening, not awakening, losing awakening, and the rest, are before the body, are after the body, are practicing together with the body, are before birth, are after birth, are practicing together with birth, are *before your father and mother were born*, are *in the realms everywhere, it has never been hidden*.[42] There is others having the great awakening for us; there is our having the great awakening for others; there is others having the great awakening for others — these will further be the self having the great awakening for the self.

---

40 **"not doing even the sacred truths"** (*shōtai fu i* 聖諦不爲): From the words of Nanyue to the Sixth Ancestor (see, e.g., *Jingde chuandeng lu* 景德傳燈錄, T.2076.51:240a19-21):

後聞曹溪法席乃往參禮。問曰。當何所務即不落階級。祖曰。汝曾作什麼。師曰。聖諦亦不爲。祖曰。落何階級。曰聖諦尚不爲。何階級之有。祖深器之。

> Later, upon hearing of the dharma seat at Caoxi, he [i.e., Nanyue] went and paid his respects. He asked, "What business would avoid falling down the stages?"
> The Ancestor said, "How do you understand it?"
> The Master said, "Don't do even the sacred truths."
> The Ancestor said, "What stage will you fall to?"
> He said, "If you don't do even the sacred truths, what stages are there?" The Ancestor deeply respected him.

before the body or after the body (*shinzen shingo* 身前身後): I.e., in previous or subsequent lives.

41 **"to say it's like any thing doesn't hit it"** (*setsuji ichimotsu soku fuchū* 說似一物即不中): From the words of Nanyue in response to the Sixth Ancestor's question of what it is that comes like this. From the anecdote alluded to in section 2, above.

42 **before your father and mother were born** (*bumo mishō izen* 父母未生以前): Also read *fubo mishō izen*. A classic Zen expression for the true self; sometimes understood as "before your father and mother gave birth." See Supplementary Notes, s.v. "Before your father and mother were born."

in the realms everywhere, it has never been hidden (*henkai mi zō zō* 徧界未曾藏): Slight variation on the Chan expression introduced above, section 23.

316 DŌGEN'S *SHŌBŌGENZŌ* VOLUME VII

[V6:29]
雪山の、雪山のために大悟するあらむ、木石の、木石のために大悟するあらむ。しかあれば、諸佛の大悟は、衆生のために大悟するがゆへに、衆生の大悟なるべし。衆生の大悟は、諸佛の大悟を大悟べし、前後といふことなかれ。いまの大悟は、をのれにあらず、他にあらず。住して、心識にかかはれず、さりて、境界にへだてらるるあらず。もし、とどまりて自身に處在せば、いかでか保任せむ、さりて他境にあらず、又いかにしてか住持せむ、きたるにあらざれども、塡溝塞壑なり、さるにあらざれども、切忌隨它覓なり。

   Likely, there are the Snowy Mountains having a great awakening for the Snowy Mountains; likely, there are trees and rocks having a great awakening for trees and rocks.[43] Hence, because the buddhas have the great awakening for living beings, it is the great awakening of living beings. The great awakening of living beings should be the great awakening to the great awakening of the buddhas; do not say it comes before or after. The present great awakening is neither one's own nor another's. Abiding, it has nothing to do with mind or consciousness; departing, it is not separated by perceptual objects. When stopping, it is located in one's own body; how can we take care of it? When departing, it is another's object; how can we maintain it? It has not come; yet "*it fills the ditches and clogs the gullies.*" It has not gone; yet "*seeking it from another is strictly prohibited.*"

[V6:30]
現前大宋國諸山に住せり杜撰のやから、おほく佛佛祖祖家業を正傳せざる、ともにをもはく、四果の、手まりにより、しかのごとく大悟もあらむずる、とおもひて、いたづらに死漢を學して、遠來の賓語を攬待せむとす。脱落なる大悟の、いま不失なると保任不著なり、未逢道得なるがゆへなり。いまは、かくのごとくの飯袋子のみなり。さらに一箇半箇の粥飯なし。又、いたづらに枯木死灰の〈爲偁〉、をしふ。佛祖の怨家なり、いくばくか祖師の大道を廢せしむる。いたづらに貪名愛利のやから、大利の主となれるによりてなり。雲水の道をふさぐ、大罪といひぬべし。

   At present, a bunch of illiterates running the various mountains in the Land of the Great Song, most of whom do not directly transmit the family enterprise of buddha after buddha and ancestor after ancestor, thinking that there could not be such a great awakening in which the fourth fruit was based on a handball, futilely study the dead guys and try to collect their honored words from afar.[44] They are not able to accept that

---

43 **Likely, there are the Snowy Mountains having a great awakening for the Snowy Mountains** (*Sessen no, Sessen no tame ni daigo suru aramu* 雪山の、雪山のために大悟するあらむ): This section parallels parts of section 14 of the seventy-five-chapter *Shōbōgenzō* text.

44 **various mountains** (*shozan* 諸山): Also read *shosan*. A term for the major Buddhist monasteries.

V6. Great Awakening *Daigo* 大悟   317

the great awakening that is sloughing off is not now lost, for they have never encountered a saying. Nowadays, it is nothing but such rice bags; there is not one or a half serving of gruel or rice.[45] Moreover, they foolishly teach association with the dried-up trees and dead ashes.[46] They are the enemies of the buddhas and ancestors; how often have they caused the ruin of the great way of the ancestral masters? It is due to a bunch who foolishly covet fame and love profit having become the heads of the great monasteries. It has to be called a great offense that blocks the way of clouds and water.

* * * * *

[V6:31] {2:606}

雲門示衆云、擧するに三種の人あり。因説得悟、一人は、因喚得テ悟、一人は見擧便回去、儞道、便回去ノ意作麼生、師云、也好與三十棒なり。

Yunmen addressed the assembly, saying, "In raising [a topic], there are three types of people: [one] *attains awakening because of talk*; one *attains awakening because of calling*; one *sees it raised and immediately returns.*[47] *Tell me,* what's the meaning of 'immediately returns'?"

The Master [Yunmen] said, "I should give you thirty blows."

---

the fourth fruit was based on a handball (*shika no, temari ni yori* 四果の、手まりにより): Allusion to the story of an old monk who became an arhat, the fourth and final stage in the traditional *śravaka* path, when hit by a ball. The story, which is also alluded to in Dōgen's "Bendōwa" 辨道話, can be found in the *Saṃyukta-ratna-piṭaka-sūtra* (*Zabaozang jing* 雜寶藏經, T.203.4:494a22-b29).

dead guys (*shikan* 死漢): Dimwits; roughly synonymous with the "dried-up trees and dead ashes" introduced just below in this section.

45   **rice bags** (*han taisu* 飯袋子): I.e., monks who are good for nothing but eating.

46   **they foolishly teach association with the dried-up trees and dead ashes** (*itazura ni koboku shikai no [i go], oshiu* いたづらに枯木死灰の＜爲侶＞、をしふ): I.e., advocate joining those who practice mental quiescence; following Kawamura's reconstruction of the illegible text as *i go* 爲侶, or *tomo taru*. See Supplementary Notes, s.v. "Dried-up tree."

47   **Yunmen addressed the assembly** (*Unmon jishu* 雲門示衆): Mixed Japanese/Chinese rendering of a passage found at *Yunmen Kuangzhen chanshi guanglu* 雲門匡眞禪師廣錄, T.1988.47:557b18-20:

舉三種人。一人因説得悟。一人因喚得悟。第三人見舉便迴去。爾道、便迴去意作麼生。復云、也好與三十棒。

In raising [a topic], there are three types of people: "one attains awakening because of talk; one attains awakening because of calling; the third sees it raised and immediately returns. Tell me, what's the meaning of 'immediately returns'?" Again, he said, "I should give you thirty blows."

[V6:32]

いはゆる、説によりて得吾あり、といふは、參究すべき審細あり。それ説といふ道理、いかにあるべきぞ。しばらく、説取行不得底、の説を學すべし、行取説不得底、の行を學すべし。行取するところに、説不得底の道理あり。しかれば、その説、たとひ眼耳親切にあらず、をよび身心の親切にあらずといふとも、因説はかならず悟なるべきなり、因説の、かならず悟なるがゆへに、得吾なるなり。説の因、すでに現成するには、前後の際を參究する、＜か＞ならず因をもちいるべし、説をもちいるべし。悟這邊も恁麼なり、悟那邊も恁麼なり、悟向上も恁麼なり。

There are details to be investigated in his saying that there is [one who] attains awakening because of talk: what is the principle of "talk"? We should study for a while the "talk" of "*talk of what can't be practiced*," study for a while the "practice" of "*practice what can't be talked of.*"[48] In what is practiced lies the principle of "what can't be talked of." Thus, although that talk may not be intimate with eye and ear, nor intimate with body and mind, "because of talk" is invariably awakening; because "because of talk" is invariably awakening, one "attains awakening." Since the "because" of "talk" has occurred, the investigation of the times of before and after should always employ "because," should always employ "talk."[49] This side of awakening is like this; that side of awakening is like this; beyond awakening is like this.

[V6:33]

因喚得悟、といふ。悟、かならず喚によるなり、喚、それ悟をつかうか。ゆへにこの喚、かならずしも主人公にも、をよぼさるるにあらざるなり。この喚、はじめあれば、大悟、始あり、大悟、始あれば、自己、始あり、自己、始あらば、自己、をはりあり、大悟、をはりあり、因、をはりあるなり。をはりは、平常にならうべし、いはゆる這頭を喚來せるなり。はじめは吾常にならふ、這頭を喚來するなり。大悟、いまだ人をやぶらず、人、いまだ大悟を染汚することなし、大悟さらに大悟を罣礙することなきものなり。

He says that one "*attains awakening because of calling.*" Awakening is invariably because of calling; does the calling itself use awakening? Therefore, this calling is not necessarily being called by the one in

---

48 **"talk of what can't be practiced"** (*sesshu gyō futoku tei* 説取行不得底); **"practice what can't be talked of"** (*gyōshu setsu futoku tei* 行取説不得底): From the words of Dongshan Liangjie 洞山良价 (e.g., at *Liandeng huiyao* 聯燈會要, ZZ.136:549b14; see also *shinji Shōbōgenzō* 眞字正法眼藏, DZZ.5:164, case 77).

49 **Since the "because" of "talk" has occurred, the investigation of the times of before and after should always employ "because," should always employ "talk"** (*setsu no in, sudeni genjō suru ni wa, zengo no sai o sankyū suru, [ka]narazu in o mochiiru beshi, setsu o mochiiru beshi* 説の因、すでに現成するには、前後の際を參究する、＜か＞ならず因をもちいるべし、説をもちいるべし): I.e., in order to understand the states before and after the great awakening, one must understand what is meant by the terms "because" and "talk" in Yunmen's use of them.

V6. Great Awakening *Daigo* 大悟   319

charge. Since this calling has a beginning, great awakening has a beginning; since great awakening has a beginning, the self has a beginning; since the self has a beginning, the self has an ending, the great awakening has an ending, and "because" has an ending. The ending should accord with the ordinary: it has called forth this side; the beginning accords with my usual; it calls forth this side.[50] The great awakening never breaks down the person; the person never defiles the great awakening. The great awakening is surely not something that obstructs the great awakening.

* * * * *

[V6:34] {2:607}
黄龍南禪師の云、花綻柳開、鳥語官官たり、水の聲の潺潺たり、是非名利、都不相關なり。しるべし、古來佛祖は、是非・名利なげすてきたり、かかはれずといふことを。

Chan Master Nan of Huanglong said,[51]

The blossoms burst, the willows bud;
The birds cry guanguan;
The water sounds chanchan.
Right and wrong, fame and profit —
Have nothing to do with them.

We should know that, since ancient times, the buddhas and ancestors have been casting aside right and wrong, fame and profit, and having nothing to do with them.

---

50 **The ending should accord with the ordinary** (*owari wa, byōjō ni narau beshi* を はりは、平常にならうべし); **the beginning accords with my usual** (*hajime wa go jō ni narau* はじめは吾常にならふ): Perhaps, meaning that, while awakening has a beginning and ending, it conforms to what is ordinary, or constant. The term *byōjō* ("ordinary") may here invoke the "mind" in the famous saying, "the ordinary mind is the way" (*byōjō shin ze dō* 平常心是道); if this is the case, the odd expression *go jō* 吾常 ("my usual") may reflect an unusual variant of this saying occurring in the *Shōbōgenzō busshō* 正法眼藏佛性 (DZZ.1:14): "My ordinary mind is the way" (*go jō shin ze dō* 吾常心是道).

it has called forth this side (*shatō o kanrai seru nari* 這頭を喚來せるなり): Perhaps, meaning that "great awakening" "calls" "the self" — or summons the "person" (*hito* 人) of the following sentence.

51 **Chan Master Nan of Huanglong** (*Ōryū Nan zenji* 黄龍南禪師): I.e., Huanglong Huinan 黄龍慧南 (1002-1069); a mixed Chinese/Japanese version of a line in a letter in the *Huanglongshan Nan chanshi shuchi ji* 黄龍山南禪師書尺集 (ZT.2 [*Soroku bu* 祖錄 部 1]: *Ōryū shoseki shū* 黄龍書尺集 8, "Yo Shin zentetsu" 與晉禪姪 13-14).

320 DŌGEN'S *SHŌBŌGENZŌ* VOLUME VII

[V6:35]

又、師弟の住院をいましむるに云、夫住持者、弘道得具因緣、內明佛法機、外赴群生望、若不然者、保持至理消息機緣、竹戶ノ第堂、靜坐塵埃ノ外、松床木枕、困眠風月之中、以煙霞水石暢其情、去名利是非忘其念、未能如是、宜在知非。

Again, admonishing a younger abbot of cloister, he said,[52]

The abbot spreads his sayings and acquires conditions. Within, he illumines the workings of the buddha dharma; without, he attends to the hopes of living beings. Otherwise, maintaining the ultimate principle and suspending connections, in the reed hall of his bamboo quarters, he sits quietly beyond the dust; on the wooden pillow of his pine bed, he sleeps amidst the breezes and moonlight.[53] Keeping to the hazy waters and rocks, he's at ease with his feelings; sending off fame and profit, right and wrong, he's forgotten such thoughts. If he hasn't been able to be like this, he'd better recognize his error.

[V6:36]

しかあれば、しりぬ、是非・名利は、先來より、大聖ともにいましめきたる處なり。

Thus, we know that, from long ago, right and wrong, fame and profit, were something the great sages have been warning against.

[V6:37]

しかるに、大宋國、いま名利の臭皮袋、をほく雲水の主人となれるゆへに、好聲をきく人すくなしと。いはむや、<赤>人をみる人、ををからむや。ゆへに、大悟の名、すべてきかず、佛祖の道、すでに廢せるがごとし。佛祖のいかなるべきと、しれるものまれなり。あはれむべし、大悟は、小量としらず、大悟は、たいりやうとしらず。大悟の、大悟をやぶる、長短にくらし。大悟の大悟を見成する、<七八>に未道得なり。大悟より大悟の生長する<と>しらず、大道に大悟を負載せると學せざるともがらををく、名字を佛祖の家門にかけたる運窮なり。

Yet, in the Land of the Great Song, because stinking skin bags of fame and profit have often become the heads of the monks, there are few who hear a welcome voice, much less are there many who see a genuine person.[54] Therefore, they never hear the term "great awakening," and it is as if the way of the buddhas and ancestors had gone completely to

---

52 **Again, admonishing a younger abbot of cloister** (*mata, shitei no jūin o imashimuru ni* 又、師弟の住院をいましむるに): Continuing to quote (with slight variation) from the *Huanglongshan Nan chanshi shuchi ji* 黃龍山南禪師書尺集 (ZT.2 [*Soroku bu* 祖錄部 1]: *Ōryū shoseki shū* 黃龍書尺集 2, "Yo sutei jari" 與師弟闍黎 9-11).

53 **reed hall** (*daidō* 第堂): Reading *bō* 茅 for *dai* 第, after the source text.

54 **genuine person** (*sekinin* 赤人): Literally, "red, or naked, person"; the translation takes *seki* 赤 here as "sincere," "authentic," as in *sekishin* 赤心.

V6. Great Awakening *Daigo* 大悟

ruin. Those who know what the buddhas and ancestors should be are rare. What a pity: they do not know great awakening as small; they do not know great awakening as large. They are largely unaware that great awakening breaks up great awakening; they are mostly unable to say that great awakening manifests great awakening. Those who do not know that great awakening grows from great awakening and fail to study that great awakening is carried by great awakening are many. It is an extreme misfortune that has attached words and letters to the household of the buddhas and ancestors.

* * * * *

[V6:38] {2:608}

舒州投子山義青禪師、曾謁浮山圓鑑禪師遠和尚。稍經三載、遠一日問師云、外道問佛、不問有言。不問無言、世尊默＜ス如何＞。師擬スルニ開口、遠以手掩師口。師於此大悟遂作禮。遠云、汝妙悟玄機耶。師云、設有妙悟、也須吐却。

Chan Master Yiqing of Mount Touzi in Shuzhou visited Reverend Yuan, Chan Master Yuanjian of Fushan.[55] *Eventually, after three years, Yuan asked the Master, "A follower of an other path asked the Buddha, 'I don't ask about the spoken, and I don't ask about the unspoken.' The World-Honored One was silent. What about this?"*

As the Master went to open his mouth, *Yuan covered his mouth with his hand. At this, the Master had a great awakening and bowed. Yuan said, "Did you have a wondrous awakening to the dark workings?"*

The Master said, "Even if there is a wondrous awakening, we should spit it out."

[V6:39]

師の悟則、あきらめ、參究すべし。口をおおはれて大悟する、なきにあらず。たとひ、日ごろよ＜り＞大悟なりといへども、大悟するなり、たとひ、向＜來＞より大悟なしといふとも、大悟するなり。大悟、いまだ他人の手裏にありとも、大悟＜する＞なり、大悟、いまだ毫忽地あらはれずとも、大大悟するなり。大悟、たとひ盡大地也とも、大悟するなり、たとひ盡大道なりとも、大悟＜するなり＞。大悟、たとひ盡大悟なりとも、大悟する＜なり＞、大悟、たとひ盡自己なりとも、大悟するなり、大悟、たとひ不悟なり＜とも＞、大悟するなり。

We should clarify and investigate the case of the Master's awakening. It is not that there is no great awakening with the mouth covered. Even

---

55　**Chan Master Yiqing of Mount Touzi in Shuzhou** (*Jōshū Tōsuzan Gisei zenji* 舒州投子山義青禪師): I.e., Touzi Gisei 投子義青 (1032-1083). His conversation with Fushan Fayuan 浮山法遠 (991-1067) can be found, e.g., at *Liandeng huiyao* 聯燈會要, ZZ.136:912b14-18.

322 DŌGEN'S *SHŌBŌGENZŌ* VOLUME VII

though it may be a great awakening from these days, it greatly awakens; even though it may be a great awakening from the past, it greatly awakens. Even if the great awakening is still in the hand of another, it greatly awakens; even if a hair's breadth of great awakening hasn't appeared, it greatly, greatly awakens. Even if great awakening is all the whole earth, it greatly awakens; even if it is the entire great way, it greatly awakens. Even if great awakening is the entire great awakening, it greatly awakens; even if great awakening is the entire self, it greatly awakens. Even if great awakening is not awakening, it greatly awakens.

[V6:40] {2:609}

しかあれば、今、師の道取する設有妙悟也須吐却の道、いかに道取するとかせむ。用著するか、用著せざるか。大悟は、吐却の葛藤にまかすべし、吐却は、大悟の葛藤とせるのみなり。向上道は、即未名大悟也。

So, how does he say the saying said here by the Master, "*Even if there is a wondrous awakening, we should spit it out*"?[56] Does he use it? Does he not use it? The great awakening, he should leave to the entanglement of "spit it out"; "spit it out, he simply took as the entanglement of 'great awakening.'" A higher saying is, "*It's not called 'great awakening.'*"

* * * * *

[V6:41]

先師、よのつねに衆にしめしていはく、參禪者心身脱落也、不是待悟爲則。

My former master always addressed the assembly, saying, "*Studying Chan is mind and body sloughed off.*[57] *It does not take awaiting awakening as the norm.*"

[V6:42]

この道得は、上堂の時は、法堂の上にしてしめす、十方の雲水、あつまりきく。小參の時は、寝堂<裏にして>道す、諸方衲子、みなきくところなり。夜間は、雲堂裏にして拳頭と同時に霹靂す。睡者も聞、不睡者も聞。夜裏も道す、日裏も道す。しかあれども、<智音>まれなり、爲問すくなし。

This saying was delivered in the dharma hall, on the occasion of convocations, with monks from the ten directions assembled to hear it. It was said in his private quarters, at the time of the small convocations,

---

56 **how does he say** (*ika ni dōshu suru to ka semu* いかに道取するとかせむ): The grammatical subject is unexpressed here and in the sentences to follow. The translation assumes it is Yiqing throughout, but it might alternatively be taken as "we."

57 **My former master** (*senshi* 先師): I.e., Tiantong Rujing 天童如淨 (1162-1227). Variation on a saying appearing several times in the *Shōbōgenzō*.

V6. Great Awakening *Daigo* 大悟

heard by monks from all quarters. At evening meditation, in the cloud hall, the thunder sounded together with the blows of his fists.[58] It was heard by those asleep, heard by those not asleep. It was said at night, said in the day. Nevertheless, those who knew the voice were rare and none questioned it.

[V6:43]

いはゆる、參禪<者>、といふは、佛佛祖道なり。參禪の言、< >者なるがゆへに、恁麼いふなり。

The "studying Zen" he speaks of is the way of the ancestors and buddha after buddha. He says this because the words "studying Zen" are ...[59]

[V6:44]

心身脱落は、脱落心身なり。脱落の脱落しきたれるがゆえに、身心脱落なり。これ、大小・廣狭の邊際にあらず。ここをもて、不是待悟爲則なり。

"*Mind and body sloughed off*" is *sloughing off mind and body*. Because sloughing off has been sloughing off, it is "*body and mind sloughed off.*" This is not within the confines of great or small, broad or narrow. This is "*not taking awaiting awakening as the norm.*"

[V6:45]

待悟といふは、大悟を所期として學道することなかれ。大悟を所期とすれば、所期の悟と親切ならざるのみにあらず、大悟、いくばくか所期にわづらはむ。學道すでに大悟にいたらむとき、大悟、はじめにかかはれ、學道、ついに大悟に際斷せられぬるがごとし。もし待悟爲則せば、すでに大悟現成せむよりのちは、學道すべからざるか。恁麼の見解は、佛道の行履なり、恁麼の行履<は>、佛頭の關捩、諸佛の大道にあらず。古佛の授記しきたれるところ、夢なり未見在<者なるべし>。

"Awaiting awakening" means do not study with the expectation of a great awakening. When we expect great awakening, it is not only that we do not become intimate with the awakening we expect, but how many expectations will trouble the great awakening? When our study of the way reaches great awakening, in the beginning we get involved in the great awakening, and our study of the way seems to have been cut off from great awakening. If we "*take awaiting awakening as the norm,*" after great awakening has appeared, should we no longer study the way? Such a view is not conduct on the way of the buddhas; such conduct is not the pivot at the head of the buddhas, not the great way of the bud-

---

58 **the thunder sounded together with the blows of his fists** (*kentō to dōji ni byakuryaku su* 拳頭と同時に霹靂す): Reflecting a line from a verse by Rujing, alluded to elsewhere in the *Shōbōgenzō*; see Supplementary Notes, s.v. "Fist."

59 **because the words "studying Zen" are . . .** (*sanzen no gon . . . wa naru ga yue ni* 參禪の言< >者なるがゆへに): the ellipsis is illegible in the manuscript.

324   DŌGEN'S *SHŌBŌGENZŌ* VOLUME VII

dhas.[60] What has been predicted by the old buddhas, they will not see, be it in their dreams.[61]

[V6:46] {2:610}

大悟は、生と同生するなり、大悟は、死と同死するなり。諸佛と同現成し、祖師と同西來するなり。栢樹と同成佛し、虚空と同參落地し、牆壁と同心なり、百草と同根なり、と參學すべきなり。しるべし、大悟すでに現成するに、しるべし、大悟を罣礙せざる道理なり。

The great awakening is born together with birth; the great awakening dies together with death. It appears together with the buddhas; it comes from the west together with the Ancestral Master.[62] We should study that it attains buddhahood together with the cypress tree; it studies falling on the ground together with empty space.[63] It is the same mind as fences and walls, the same root as the hundred grasses.[64] When great awakening

---

60 **Such a view is not conduct on the way of the buddhas; such conduct is not the pivot at the head of the buddhas, not the great way of the buddhas** (*inmo no kenge wa, butsudō no anri nari, inmo no anri [wa], buttō no kanrei, shobutsu no daidō ni arazu* 恁麼の見解は、佛道の行履なり、恁麼の行履＜は＞、佛頭の關捩、諸佛の大道にあらず): A sentence difficult to parse; the translation tries to read the final negative copula as governing both clauses. The odd "pivot at the head of the buddhas" (*buttō no kanrei* 佛頭の關捩) seems to be a play on the common "higher pivot" (*jōtō kanrei* 上頭關捩, or *kōjō kanreisu* 向上關捩子). See Supplementary Notes, s.v. "Pivot."

61 **What has been predicted by the old buddhas** (*kobutsu no juki shikitareru tokoro* 古佛の授記しきたれるところ): Presumably, a reference to predictions of the supreme awakening of buddhahood.

62 **it comes from the west together with the Ancestral Master** (*soshi to dō seirai suru nari* 祖師と同西來するなり): A reference to the advent of Bodhidharma in China. See Supplementary Notes, s.v. "Coming from the west."

63 **it attains buddhahood together with the cypress tree; it studies falling on the ground together with empty space** (*hakuju to dō jōbutsu shi, kokū to dōsan rakuchi shi* 栢樹と同成佛し、虚空と同參落地し): Allusion to a dialogue between Zhaozhou Congshen 趙州從諗 (778-897) and a monk (found at *Zhaozhou lu* 趙州錄 ZZ.118.321b14-16 and elsewhere). Here is the version discussed by Dōgen in his "Shōbōgenzō hakujushi" 正法眼藏柏樹子:

> 大師有僧問、柏樹還有佛性也無。大師云、有。僧曰、柏樹幾時成佛。大師云、待虚空落地。僧曰、虚空幾時落地。大師云、待柏樹子成佛。
>
> The Great Master was asked by a monk, "Does the cypress tree have the buddha nature or not?"
> The Great Master said, "It does."
> The monk said, "When does the cypress attain buddhahood?"
> The Great Master said, "Wait till empty space falls on the ground."
> The monk said, "When does empty space fall on the ground?"
> The Great Master said, "Wait till the cypress tree attains buddhahood."

Compare Supplementary Notes, s.v. "Cypress tree at the front of the garden."

64 **the same mind as fences and walls** (*shō heki to dōshin nari* 牆壁と同心なり): Allusion to the famous definition of the buddha mind, first attributed to Nanyang Huizhong

V6. Great Awakening *Daigo* 大悟   325

surely appears, we should recognize that it is the principle that it does not obstruct great awakening.

[V6:47]

しかるを、いま、人、をほく大悟を擧して、學道＜の究竟＞の寶所と錯認＜しけ＞る、あはれむべし、いくばくか、究竟の寶所は大悟のみにあらざることを蹉過する、捨父逃逝なるべし。大悟を所期として、これよりのちは卜度なからむとをもふは、經師・論師等の錯解なり。もし大悟を究竟とせば、草も究竟所なるべし、木も究竟所なるべし、承言も究竟所なるべし、會宗も究竟所なるべきなり。しかあれば、大悟を究竟所なりと認ずることなかれ。もしかくのごとくあらば、佛法、いかでか今日にいたらむ。佛法の今日到來することは、大悟を究竟とせず、大悟を爲則とせざるによりてなり。しかもかくのごとくありといふとも、この大悟、さらに佛量を拈來して度量するには、えざるなり、法量を拈來して度量するには、えざるなり。臨濟等、わづかに盡地をみるに、不悟＜の＞者不可得なるをみるといえども、大悟の＜盡＞地のみにあらざる道理、いまだ道得せざる。すでに道得せずば、たれか爲聞をゆるさむ。盡大地不見一箇不悟者、の言を、悟也不可得なるべし、不悟也未見得なるべし。これ、脱落大悟の道理、いまだ道得せざるによりてなり。ひさしく大悟盡地なる行履を＜もて＞行履せる一隅なり。のちに、半臨濟あり＜て＞、その道得を代道せむことを＜ゆ＞るすべし。＜し＞かればすなはち、先師道の、脱落身心、不＜是＞待悟爲則、を參學すべし。大悟、たとひ明頭來すとも、さらに明頭打なるべし、大悟、たとひ暗頭來すとも、さらに暗頭打なるべし。

Nevertheless, it is lamentable that many people today have mistakenly held up great awakening as the treasure store of the ultimate of the study of the way. How often have they missed the fact that the treasure store of the ultimate is not merely great awakening? It is "*forsaking one's father and running away.*"[65] To make great awakening an expectation and think that we cannot speculate about what will happen from here is the mistaken understanding of the sūtra masters and treatise masters. If we make great awakening the ultimate, then grass should also be the ultimate, trees should be the ultimate, "receiving the words" should be the ultimate, "understanding the sense" should be the ultimate.[66] Hence, do not acknowledge great awakening as the ultimate. If it had been like that, the buddha dharma would not have reached the present day. That

---

南陽慧忠 (d. 775). See Supplementary Notes, s.v. "Fences, walls, tiles, and pebbles."

65   **"forsaking one's father and running away"** (*shafu tōzei* 捨父逃逝): A phrase from the parable of the prodigal son (*gūji* 窮子) that appears in the *Lotus Sūtra* (*Miaofa lianhua jing* 妙法蓮華經, T.262.9:16b26, 17c14).

66   **"receiving the words"** (*shō gon* 承言); **"understanding the sense"** (*e shū* 會宗): After lines from the famous poem *Cantong qi* 參同契, by Shitou Xiqian 石頭希遷 (700-790) (*Jingde chuandeng lu* 景德傳燈錄, T.2076.51:459b18-19):

承言須會宗。勿自立規矩。
Receiving the words, understand their sense;
Don't set up standards of your own.

the buddha dharma has reached the present day is due to its not taking great awakening as the ultimate, not taking it as the norm.

Nevertheless, while this may be so, the great awakening cannot be gauged by taking up the measure of the Buddha, cannot be gauged by taking up the measure of the dharma. Someone like Linji may look merely at all the earth and see that he "*can't find an unawakened person*," but he never spoke of the principle that great awakening is not only all the earth.[67] And, since he has not spoken of it, who would listen to him? The words, "*in all the whole earth, we do not see a single unawakened person*," should be "*we cannot get awakening*," should be "*we cannot get nonawakening*." This is because he has not spoken of the principle of sloughing off great awakening. It is one corner, long practiced, of the conduct that is all the earth of great awakening. Later, if there is a half Linji, we should let him say that in his stead. Thus, we should study the saying of my former master that "[studying Zen is] sloughing off body and mind and not taking awaiting awakening as the norm." Great awakening, though "the bright comes," should further be "the bright does it"; great awakening, though "the dark comes," should further be "the dark does it."[68]

* * * * *

[V6:48] {2:611}

京兆米胡和尚、令僧問仰山、今時ノ人還假悟否。仰山云、悟即不無、爭奈落第二頭何。僧回擧似米胡、深肯之。

Reverend Mihu of Jingzhao had a monk ask Yangshan, "People of the present time, do they still avail themselves of awakening?"[69]

---

67 **"can't find an unawakened person"** (*fugo [no] mono fukatoku* 不悟＜の＞者不可得): Variation on Linji's saying quoted in section 5, above: "it's hard to find a single person who's unawakened."

68 **Great awakening, though "the bright comes," should further be "the bright does it"; great awakening, though "the dark comes," should further be "the dark does it"** (*daigo, tatoi meitō rai su tomo, sara ni meitō ta naru beshi, daigo, tatoi antō rai su tomo, sara ni antō ta naru beshi* 大悟、たとひ明頭來すとも、さらに明頭打なるべし、大悟、たとひ暗頭來すとも、さらに暗頭打なるべし): Tentative translation of terms drawn from the notoriously enigmatic saying of the monk Puhua 普化 (dates unknown), recorded in the *Linji lu* 臨濟錄 (T.1985.47:503b20-21):

明頭來明頭打。暗頭來暗頭打。

When the bright comes, the bright does it. When the dark comes, the dark does it.

69 **Reverend Mihu of Jingzhao** (*Keichō Beiko oshō* 京兆米胡和尚): A disciple of Weishan Lingyou 潙山靈祐 (771-853), also known simply as Reverend Mi 米和尚, dates unknown. This quotation parallels section 15 of the seventy-five-chapter *Shōbōgenzō* text.

V6. Great Awakening *Daigo* 大悟

Yangshan said, "It's not that they lack awakening, but how can they help falling into the second rate?"

The monk returned and presented this to Mihu, who deeply assented to it.

[V6:49]

今時人者、三世諸佛なり。ゆへに、今時人、これ今時人也。這頭に現成し、那頭に現成する、ともに今時の人也。

"*People of the present time*" are the buddhas of the three times.[70] Therefore, people of the present time *are people of the present time*. Both those who appear on this side and those who appear on that side are "people of the present time."

[V6:50]

假悟不とは、さとりをもちいるや、といふなり。しかのごとくいふ、宗旨かくれざるあれども、＜經論＞の學者ききがたしと。いはゆる今時人は、今は作麼生なるぞ、時は作麼生なるぞ、人は作麼生なるぞ、著眼看すべし。甚處＜來＞なるぞ、那裏去なるぞ。たとひ頭正なりとも、かならず尾正なるべからず、一條鐵なるべからず、かくのごとく聞著すべし。榜樣擬著すべきににたれども、意頭の知少なるに蹉過せしむるなり。

"Do they *avail themselves of awakening?*" means "do they make use of awakening?" The meaning of such a saying is not hidden, but the scholars of the sūtras and treatises find it hard to understand. In "people of the present time," what do we make of "the present"? What do we make of "time"? What do we make of "people"? We should try looking at this. Where are they coming from? Have they gone over there? They may be right from the head but not necessarily right to the tail, not necessarily one strip of iron.[71] We should hear it like this. While it seems we should figure out the standard, we let it pass for paucity of knowledge of the reason.[72]

---

70 **"People of the present time"** (*konji nin sha* 今時人者): This section loosely parallels section 16 of the seventy-five-chapter *Shōbōgenzō* text.

71 **They may be right from the head but not necessarily right to the tail** (*tatoi zushin nari tomo, kanarazu bishin naru bekarazu* たとひ頭正なりとも、かならず尾正なるべからず): From the expression "right from head to tail" (*zushin bishin* 頭正尾正). "One strip of iron" (*ichijō tetsu* 一條鐵) is a common expression for "a single unity"; see Supplementary Notes, s.v. "One strip of iron." The grammatical subject here is unexpressed; the translation assumes it to be "people of the present time."

72 **While it seems we should figure out the standard, we let it pass for paucity of knowledge of the reason** (*bōyō gijaku su beki ni nitaredomo, itō no chishō naru ni shaka seshimuru nari* 榜樣擬著すべきににたれども、意頭の知少なるに蹉過せしむるなり): A tentative translation of a sentence the sense of which is uncertain; perhaps meaning that we do not understand enough about "people of the present time" to figure out what it really means. The verb *gijaku* 擬著 ("to figure out") may be an error for the

328 DŌGEN'S *SHŌBŌGENZŌ* VOLUME VII

[V6:51] {2:612}

還假悟否は、さとりをかるやいなや、となり。しかあれば、さとり、在る
にあらず、悟、なきにあらず、さとりは本末是にあらず、さとり、舊新に
あらず、假べからず、さとるにあらず、かるべきにあらず。さとりは、佛
にあらず、さとりは〈吾〉にあらざる宗旨あり。

"*Do they still avail themselves of awakening?*" means "do they borrow awakening?"[73] Hence, it is not that awakening exists nor that it does
not exist. Awakening is not right from start to finish; awakening is not
new or old and should not be borrowed; it does not awaken and is not
to be borrowed. There is a point that awakening is not the buddha, that
awakening is not the self.

[V6:52]

仰山いはく、悟即不無、爭奈落第二頭何。

Yangshan said, "*It's not that they don't have awakening, but they can't
help falling into the second rate.*"

[V6:53]

その宗旨は、さとりは不無なり、とは、さとりは無にあらず、しかあれど
も第二頭にをつるなり。さとりは有にあらず、しかあれども第二頭にをち
ざるごときなり。第二頭にをつることにてあれば、さとらざらむとにはあ
らざるなり。しかあれば、さとり、第二頭〈に〉をちずと學すべからず。
さとるといへども、かならずをつるなり。第二頭にをつるといえども、か
ならずさとるなり。もししかあれば、すなはち第二頭より向上は、これ第
一頭なりとにあらず、第三頭のあるにあらざるなり。

The point of this is that awakening is not nonexistent — i.e., awakening is not nothing, but it falls into the second rate. Awakening is not exis-
tent, but it seems it does not fall into the second rate. It is not that, since
it falls into the second rate, we ought not awaken. Hence, we should not
study that awakening does not fall into the second rate: it may awaken,
but it invariably falls. Though it falls into the second rate, it invariably
awakens. It is not saying that, in that case, beyond the second rate is the
first rate, and it is not that there is a third rate.

[V6:54]

このさとりは、未落のときにも第二頭にあり、當悟にも第二頭に落在せ
り、のちも第二頭にあるべきなり。その鋒鎧、かくるることなし。逢人す
れども、顛倒せず。

---

homophonous *gijaku* 疑著 ("to doubt"). Neither *itō* 意頭 ("reason") nor *chishō* 知少
("paucity of knowledge") occur elsewhere in the *Shōbōgenzō*.

73　**"Do they still avail themselves of awakening?"** (*kan ke go hi* 還假悟否): This
section loosely parallels materials in section 18 of the seventy-five-chapter *Shōbōgenzō*
text.

V6. Great Awakening *Daigo* 大悟　　329

Awakening is second-rate even when it has not yet fallen. It has fallen into the second rate at the time of awakening and will also be second-rate thereafter. Its blade and armor are not hidden.[74] Though it meets a person, it does not topple over.

[V6:55]

しかるを、大悟は起首あれども、末上さらにあらざるとみだりがはしくするは、佛道にあらず。大悟は向上あり、大悟は末上にもあり。たとへば着衣とひとしく、たとへば喫飯とひとしく、たとへば磨甎のごとし、たとへば磨鏡のごとし。作鏡も大悟にあり、作甎＜も＞大悟にあり。鼻孔の、上脣にのすることを参究すべきなり。いづれのところかこれ上脣。いはゆる鼻孔の所在なり。しあればすなはち、大悟、たとひ大道を悟盡すとも、なをこれ暫時の伎倆なり。

Nevertheless, while great awakening has a beginning, foolishly to take it as having no subsequent ending is not the way of the buddhas. Great awakening has a beyond; great awakening has an ending. It is like wearing clothes, like taking meals; it is like polishing a tile, like polishing a mirror.[75] Making a mirror is great awakening; making a tile is great awakening. We should investigate the fact that the nose rides on the upper lip.[76] Where is this upper lip? It is where the nose is. Thus, even though great awakening completely awakens to the great way, it is still a temporary device.

[V6:56]

大悟さらに大悟する、ゆへに大悟頭白あり、大悟頭黒あり。

Great awakening further greatly awakens; therefore, there is great awakening's head is white, great awakening's head is black.[77]

74　**Its blade and armor are not hidden** (*sono hōgai, kakururu koto nashi* その鋒鎧、かくるることなし): The point of this and the following sentence is uncertain, and the translation is tentative.

75　**wearing clothes** (*jakue* 著衣); **taking meals** (*kippan* 喫飯): From the fixed expression "wearing clothes and taking meals" (*jakue kippan* 著衣喫飯), used metonymically for "everyday life."

polishing a tile (*ma sen* 磨甎): From the famous story, often cited by Dōgen, in which Nanyue Huairang 南嶽懷讓 likens the practice of seated meditation in order to make a buddha to polishing a clay tile in order to make a mirror; see Supplementary Notes, s.v. "Nanyue polishes a tile."

76　**the nose rides on the upper lip** (*bikū no, jōshin ni nosuru* 鼻孔の、上脣にのする): From the saying *bikong da shangchun* 鼻孔搭上脣, somewhat akin to English "as plain as the nose on your face." See Supplementary Notes, s.v. "Nose."

77　**there is great awakening's head is white, great awakening's head is black** (*daigo tō haku ari, daigo tō koku ari* 大悟頭白あり、大悟頭黒あり): A variant version of the final line of the seventy-five-chapter *Shōbōgenzō* text, section 19.

Treasury of the True Dharma Eye
Variant Text 7

Karma of the Three Times
Sanji gō
三時業

Karma of the Three Times

Sanji gō

INTRODUCTION

This work represents number 8 in the sixty-chapter *Shōbōgenzō*. It was included as number 83 in the 1815 Honzan edition, before the version of "Sanji gō" in the twelve-chapter compilation was available. Like that text, of which it is thought to be an earlier draft, it is undated; unlike that text, it bears a colophon indicating that it was copied by Ejō at Eiheiji in the spring of 1253, a few months before its author's death.

Though much in the two versions is identical, this work is somewhat shorter than the twelve-chapter *Shōbōgenzō* text and lacks, most notably, the sustained criticism of Chan Master Changsha Jingcen 長沙景岑 found near the end of that text. The annotation of this translation does not repeat information provided for the twelve-chapter *Shōbōgenzō* text; rather, it is limited to indications of the correspondences between the two versions and the occasional note on material specific to the present text.

正法眼藏拾遺七
Treasury of the True Dharma Eye
Variant Text 7

三時業
Karma of the Three Times

(六十卷本系・洞雲寺本所収)

(Sixty-chapter compilation version, Tōunji text)

[V7:1] {2:614}

第十九祖鳩摩羅多尊者、至中天竺國。有大士、名闍夜多。問曰、我家父母、素信三寶。而嘗縈疾療、凡所營事、皆不如意。而我隣家、久爲旃陀羅行、而身常勇健、所作和合。彼何幸、而我何辜。尊者曰、何足疑乎。且善惡之報、有三時焉。凡人但見仁夭、暴壽、逆吉、義凶、便謂亡因果虚罪福。殊不知、影響相隨、毫釐靡忒、縱經百千萬劫、亦不磨滅。時闍夜多、聞是語已、頓釋所疑。

When the Nineteenth Ancestor, Venerable Kumāralāta, went to a land of Central Sindhu, there was a great one named Jayata who asked him, "In my family, my father and mother always had faith in the three treasures, yet they suffered from sickness, and all their undertakings went amiss.[1] The family next door to us, however, while they had long worked as caṇḍāla, were always strong and fit, and whatever they did went well. Why are they so fortunate, and what is our crime?"

The Venerable said, "What is there to doubt? The recompense for good and evil exists through the three times. The common people, seeing only that the benevolent die young, while the violent live long, the treasonous have good fortune, while the righteous have misfortune, think that cause and effect do not exist, and evils and blessings are void. They are completely ignorant of the fact that the shadow and the echo follow without a hair's breadth of variation. Even over a hundred thousand myriad kalpas, they will not be erased."

After Jayata heard these words, his doubts were immediately resolved.

---

1 **The Nineteenth Ancestor, Venerable Kumāralāta** (*dai jūkyū so Kumorata sonja* 第十九祖鳩摩羅多尊者): This and the following two sections correspond almost exactly to sections 1-3 of the twelve-chapter *Shōbōgenzō* text.

334 DŌGEN'S *SHŌBŌGENZŌ* VOLUME VII

[V7:2]

鳩摩羅多尊者は、如來より第十九代の附法なり。如來、まのあたり名字を記しまします。ただ釋尊一佛の法をあきらめ、正傳せるのみにあらず、かねて、三世の諸佛の法をも、曉了せり。

Venerable Kumāralāta was vouchsafed the dharma in the nineteenth generation after the Tathāgata. The Tathāgata himself prophesied his name. He not only clarified and directly transmitted the dharma of one Buddha, Śākyamuni, he also fully comprehended the dharma of the buddhas of the three times.

[V7:3]

闍夜多尊者、いまの問をまうけしよりのち、鳩摩羅多尊者にしたがひて、如來の正法を修習し、つひに第二十代の祖師となれり。これもまた、世尊はるかに、第二十祖は闍夜多なるべし、と記しましませり。しかあればすなはち、佛法の批判、もともかくのごとくの祖師の所判のごとく、習學すべし。いまのよに、因果をしらず、業報をあきらめず、三世をしらず、善惡をわきまへざる邪見のともがらに群すべからず。

After Jayata asked this question, he practiced the true dharma of the Tathāgata under Kumāralāta and eventually became the ancestral master of the twentieth generation. Here, too, the World-Honored One had prophesied long ago that the twentieth ancestor would be Jayata. Hence, we should learn that our judgments of the buddha dharma are to be just like such a decision by the Ancestral Master. We should not associate with those who, ignorant of cause and effect in the present period, unclear about actions and their consequences, ignorant of the three times, hold a false view that fails to differentiate good from evil.

[V7:4] {2:615}

いはゆる、善惡之報有三時焉、といふは、

"*The recompense for good and evil exists through the three times*" refers to:[2]

[V7:5]

三時 一者順現法受。二者順次生受。三者順後次受。

The "three times": [karma] (1) experienced in the present; (2) experienced in the next life; (3) experienced in lives after the next.

---

2 **"The recompense for good and evil"** (*zen'aku shi hō* 善惡之報): Sections 4-6 here correspond to section 4 of the twelve-chapter *Shōbōgenzō* text.

V7. Karma of the Three Times *Sanji gō* 三時業

[V7:6]

これを三時といふ。佛祖の道を修習するには、その最初より、この三時の業報の理をならひあきらむるなり。しかあらざれば、おほくあやまりて邪見に墮するなり。ただ邪見に墮するのみにあらず、惡道におちて、長時の苦をうく。續善根せざるあひだは、おほくの功德をうしなひ、菩提の道、ひさしくさはりあり、をしからざらめや。この三時の業は、善惡にわたるなり。

These are called the "three times." In practicing the way of the buddhas and ancestors, from the outset, we learn and clarify the principle of actions and consequences over these three times. Where this is not the case, many are mistaken and fall into false views. Not only do they fall into false views, but they fall into the evil paths and suffer for a long time. So long as they do not maintain their good roots, they lose much of their merit and long have obstacles on the path to bodhi. How regrettable! The actions of these three times include both good and evil.

* * * * *

[V7:7]

第一順現法受業者、謂、若業此生造作增長、即於此生受異熟果、是名順現法受業。

Of the first, "karma experienced in the present," it is said,[3]

When the karma is performed and develops in this life, and its ripened fruit is experienced in this life, it is called "karma experienced in the present."

[V7:8]

いはく、人ありて、あるいは善にもあれ、あるいは惡にもあれ、この生につくりて、すなはちこの生にその報をうくるを、順現法受業といふ。

That is, when a person performs [an act] in this life, be it good or evil, and receives the recompense in this life, it is called "karma experienced in the present."

[V7:9]

惡をつくりて此生にうけたる例、

An example of doing evil and receiving [the consequences] in this life:

---

3 **"karma experienced in the present"** (*jungen hō jugō* 順現法受業): This and the following two sections correspond to sections 5-7 of the twelve-chapter *Shōbōgenzō* text.

[V7:10] {2:616}

曾有採樵者、入山遭雪、迷失途路。時會日暮、雪深寒凍、將死不久。即前入一蒙密林中、乃見一羆。先在林內、形色青紺、眼如雙炬。其人惶恐、分當失命、此實菩薩、現受羆身。見其憂恐、尋慰諭言、汝今勿怖、父母於子或有異心、吾今於汝終無惡意。即前捧取、將入窟中、温煖其身、令蘇息已、取諸根果、勸隨所食。恐令不消、抱持而臥。如是恩養、經於六日。至第七日、天晴路現。人有歸心、羆既知已、復取甘果、飽而餞之、送至林外、慇懃告別。人跪謝曰、何以報。羆言、我今不須餘報、但如比日我護汝身、汝於我命、亦願如是。其人敬諾。担樵而下山、逢二猟師、問曰、山中見何蟲獸。樵人答曰、我亦不見餘獸、唯見一羆。獵師求請、能示我不。樵人答曰、若能與三分之二、吾當示汝。獵師依許。相與俱行、竟害羆命、分肉爲三。樵人兩手欲取羆肉、惡業力故、雙臂俱落。如珠縷斷、如截藕根。獵師危忙、驚問所以。樵人恥愧、具述委曲。是二獵師、責樵人曰、他既於汝有此大恩、汝今何忍行斯惡逆。怪哉、汝身何不糜爛。於是獵師共其肉施僧伽藍。時僧上座、得妙願智、即時入定、觀是何肉、即知是與一切衆生作利樂者、大菩薩肉。尋時出定、以此事白衆。衆聞驚歎、共取香薪、焚燒其肉、收其餘骨、起窣堵婆、禮拜供養。如是惡業、待相續、或度相續、方受其果。

There was once a woodcutter who, having entered the mountains and encountering a snowstorm, became disoriented and lost his way.[4] Time passed, and the sun set; the snow was deep, it was bitter cold, and he was on the verge of death. Upon entering a dense grove, he came upon a bear that had long been living in the grove. Its body was a dark blue; its eyes, like twin torches. The man was terrified that he was about to lose his life; but this was in fact a bodhisattva that had manifested in the body of a bear. Seeing his fear, it reassured him, saying, "Do not be afraid. Parents may be disloyal to their child, but I will never think of harming you."

Then it approached and grasped him, brought him into a cave, and warmed him. After it had revived him, it brought him roots and fruits, urging him to eat all he could. Concerned that his chill was not thawed, it embraced him and lay down. For six days, it cared for him like this. On the seventh day, the weather cleared, and the path appeared. The man wished to return; and the bear, realizing this, again brought him sweet fruits and fed him as a parting gift. Accompanying him to edge of the grove, it bade him a polite farewell. The man kneeled and thanked it, saying, "How can I repay you?"

The bear said, "I don't need any repayment. I only ask that, just as I have protected your body these last days, you will do the same for my life." The man politely agreed.

---

4   **There was once a woodcutter** (*sō u saishō sha* 曾有採樵者): This section corresponds to sections 8 and 9 of the twelve-chapter *Shōbōgenzō* text.

V7. Karma of the Three Times *Sanji gō* 三時業　　　337

Bearing his wood and descending the mountain, he met two hunters, who asked him, "What beasts have you seen in the mountains?"

The woodcutter replied, "I haven't seen any beasts except a bear."

The hunters asked him, "Can you show us?"

The woodcutter replied, "If you give me two-thirds, I'll show you."

The hunters agreed, and they went together. Eventually, they took the bear's life and divided its meat into three. When the woodcutter went to take the bear meat with his two hands, by the force of his evil deed, both his arms fell off, like pearls from a severed string, like lotus roots cut off. The hunters were panic-stricken; alarmed, they asked the reason. The woodcutter, ashamed, related in full the details. The two hunters reproached the woodcutter, saying, "It showed you such great kindness; how could you commit such treachery? It's strange that your entire body didn't decompose."

Thereupon, the hunters both donated their meat to a saṃghārāma. At the time, the senior seat of the monastery had attained the wondrous wisdom that knows at will. He immediately entered into meditation and saw what meat it was, realizing that it was the flesh of a great bodhisattva who offered benefit and joy to all living beings. Immediately emerging from meditation, he reported this to the assembly. Hearing it, the assembly was amazed. Collecting fragrant kindling, they cremated the flesh. Collecting the remaining bones, they erected a stūpa and paid obeisance and made offerings to it.

One who commits an evil deed such as this will surely experience its fruit, whether in the ensuing continuum or a continuum beyond.

[V7:11] {2:617}

かくのごとくなるを、惡業の順現報受業となづく。おほよそ恩をえては、報をこころざすべし。他に恩しては、報をもとむることなかれ。いまも恩ある人を逆害をくはへんとせん、その惡業、かならずうくべきなり。衆生、ながくいまの樵人のこころなかれ。林外にして告別するには、いかがしてこの恩を謝すべき、といふといへども、やまのふもとに獵師にあうては、二分の肉をむさぼる。貪欲にひかれて、大恩所を害す。在家・出家、ながくこの不知恩のこころなかれ。惡業力のきるところ、兩手を斷ずること、刀劒のきるよりもはやし。

Cases such as this are called "karma experienced in the present" for an evil action.[5] In general, when receiving a kindness, we should aim to repay it; but, in being kind to another, do not seek repayment. As in the present case, one who would betray and harm a person who has shown kindness will inevitably experience the evil karma. May living beings

---

5 **Cases such as this** (*kaku no gotoku naru* かくのごとくなる): Sections 11-16 here correspond to sections 10-15 of the twelve-chapter *Shōbōgenzō* text.

338 DŌGEN'S *SHŌBŌGENZŌ* VOLUME VII

never have the mind of this woodcutter! In bidding farewell at the edge
of the grove, he asked how he could thank [the bear] for its kindness;
yet, on meeting the hunters at the foot of the mountain, he craved two
parts of its meat. Drawn by this craving, he harmed one who had shown
him great kindness. May householders and renunciants never have this
mind that does not recognize kindness! The cutting of his two arms by
the power of his evil karma was faster than cutting by a sword.

[V7:12]
この生に善をつくりて、順現法受に、善報をえたる例、

An example of doing good and receiving good recompense in this life:

[V7:13]
昔健馱羅國迦膩色迦王、有一黄門、恆監内事。暫出城外見有群牛數盈五
百、來入城内。問驅牛者、此是何牛。答言、此牛將去其種。於是黄門即自
思惟、我宿惡業、受不男身。今應以財救此牛難。遂償其債、悉令得脱。善
業力故、令此黄門即復男身。深生慶悦、尋還城内、侍立宫門、附使啓王、
請入奉覲。王令喚入、怪問所由。於是黄門具奏上事。王聞驚喜、厚賜珍
財、轉授高官、令知外事。如是善業、要待相續、或度相續、方受其果。

*Long ago, in the Land of Gandhāra under King Kaniṣka, there was a
eunuch who permanently served as overseer of internal affairs. Once,
when he was outside the city, he saw a herd of fully five hundred oxen
coming into the city. He asked the herdsman, "What are these oxen
for?"*

He replied, "These oxen are going to be castrated."

*At this, the eunuch thought to himself, "Due to my past evil deeds,
I have received this non-male body. Now, I should use my wealth to
rescue these oxen from their misfortune."*

*He thereupon redeemed them and had them all released. By the power
of this good deed, the eunuch immediately recovered his male body.
Overjoyed, he returned to the city. At the palace gate, he dispatched
a messenger to the king requesting an audience. The king had him
summoned and, thinking [his request] strange, asked him the reason.
Thereupon, the eunuch reported the above incident in full. The king
was delighted; he lavished him with precious gifts, promoted him to
high rank, and put him in charge of external affairs.*

*One who commits a good deed such as this will surely experience its
fruit, whether in the ensuing continuum or a continuum beyond.*

V7. Karma of the Three Times *Sanji gō* 三時業

[V7:14]

あきらかにしりぬ、牛畜の身、をしむべきにあらざれども、すくふ人、善果をうく。いはんや恩田をうやまひ、徳田をうやまひ、もろもろの善を修せんをや。かくのごとくなるを、善の順現法受業となづく。善により悪によりて、かくのごとくのことおほかれど、つくしあぐるにいとまあらず。

We see clearly here that, while the body of an ox is not something to prize, the person who comes to its rescue experiences a good fruit. How much more so one who practices various good deeds honoring the fields of kindness or the fields of merit. Such cases are called good "karma experienced in the present." Although there are many such cases, both of good and of evil, there is no time here to give them all.

* * * * *

[V7:15] {2:618}

第二順次生受業者、謂、若業此生造作増長、於第二生受異熟果、是名順次生受業。

Of the second, "karma experienced in the next life," it is said,
When the karma is performed and develops in this life, and its ripened fruit is experienced in the next life, it is called "karma experienced in the next life."

[V7:16]

いはく、もし人ありて、この生に五無間業をつくれる、かならず順次生に地獄におつるなり。順次生とは、この生の、つぎの生なり。餘のつみは、順次生に地獄におつるもあり、また順後次受のひくべきあれば、順次生に地獄におちず、順後業となることもあり。この五無間業は、さだめて順次生受業に地獄におつるなり。順次生、また第二生とも、これをいふなり。

That is, when a person commits the five deeds of the uninterrupted hell, he or she necessarily falls into that hell in the next life. "The next life" refers to the life after this life. There are other offenses for which one falls into hell in the next life; there are also cases in which, when it [is karma that] involves experience in lives after the next, instead of falling into a great hell in the next life, it becomes karma of subsequent lives. These five deeds of the uninterrupted hell are invariably "karma experienced in the next life," for which one falls into the hell. "The next life" is also referred to as "the second life."

340 DŌGEN'S *SHŌBŌGENZŌ* VOLUME VII

[V7:17]

五無間業といふは、一殺父。二殺母。三殺阿羅漢。四出佛身血。五破法輪僧。これを五無間業となづく、また五逆罪となづく。はじめの三は、殺生なり、第四は、殺生の加行なり。如来は、いかにも人にころされさせたまはず、ただ身血をいだすを逆とす。中夭なきは、最後身菩薩・覩史多天一生所繋菩薩・北洲・樹提伽・佛醫なり。第五破僧罪は、虚誑語なり。この五逆、かならず順次生受業に地獄におつるなり。

The five deeds of the uninterrupted hell:[6] (1) killing one's father; (2) killing one's mother; (3) killing an arhat; (4) spilling the blood of a buddha's body; (5) disrupting the saṃgha of the dharma wheel.

These are called "the five deeds of the uninterrupted hell"; they are also called "the five heinous offenses." The first three are the taking of life; the fourth is the precursor to taking life: a tathāgata is by no means killed by anyone, but merely causing him to bleed is considered a heinous offense.[7] Those who do not experience premature death are bodhisattvas in their final bodies, bodhisattvas bound to one more life in Tuṣita Heaven, those in the Northern Continent, Jyotiṣka, and the Buddha's physician.[8] The fifth [offense], disrupting the saṃgha, is false speech. These five heinous offenses are invariably karma experienced in the next life, for which one falls into hell.

[V7:18]

提婆達多は、この五無間業のなかに三をつくれり。いはく、蓮華色比丘尼をうちころす。この比丘尼、大阿羅漢なり。これを殺阿羅漢罪とす。盤石をなげて、世尊をうちころしたてまつらんとす、盤石、とくに山神にさへられて、くだけぬ、そのくだけ、ほとばしりて、如來の足指にあたれり、

---

6 **five deeds of the uninterrupted hell** (*go muken gō* 五無間業): This list corresponds to section 16 of the twelve-chapter *Shōbōgenzō* text. The remainder of this section, however, differs markedly from section 17 of that text — the exception being the last sentence here, which parallels the first sentence of that section.

7 **precursor to taking life** (*sesshō no kegyō* 殺生の加行): Taking *kegyō* 加行 in the sense of a preliminary action — presumably, in the sense that wounding is "preliminary" to killing.

8 **Those who do not experience premature death** (*chūyō naki* 中夭なき): These and other such fortunates are listed in the *Jushe lun song shu lun ben* 倶舍論頌疏論本, by Yuanhui 圓暉 (fl. 8th c.), T.1823.41:885a2-11.

Northern Continent (*Hokushū* 北洲): I.e., Uttarakuru (*Hokkuroshū* 北倶盧洲), the continent lying to the north of Mount Sumeru in Buddhist cosmology, whose inhabitants enjoy a lifespan of a thousand years; see Supplementary Notes, s.v. "Four Continents."

Jyotiṣka (*Judaika* 樹提伽): The wealthy householder who avoided death at the hands of Ajātaśatru by becoming a bhikṣu, as predicted by the Buddha.

the Buddha's physician (*butsu i* 佛醫): The famous physician Jīvaka (Giba 耆婆), who was rescued from death as an infant and went on to serve as physician to King Bimbisāra and the Buddha.

V7. Karma of the Three Times *Sanji gō* 三時業 341

足指やぶれ、血、まさにいづ。これ、出佛身血罪なり。初學愚鈍の比丘五
百人をかたらひて、伽耶山頂にゆきて、別羯磨をつくる、これ、破僧罪な
り。この三逆罪によりて、阿鼻地獄におちぬ。いまに無間の苦をうく。四
佛の提婆達多、なほ阿鼻にあり。

Devadatta committed three of these five deeds of the uninterrupted hell.[9] That is, he killed the Bhikṣuṇī Utpalavarṇā. This *bhikṣuṇī* was a great arhat. This represents the offense of killing an arhat. He sought to kill the World-Honored One by throwing a rock at him; the rock, blocked by a mountain deity, shattered, and the fragments scattered, striking the Tathāgata's toes, injuring them, and spilling his blood. This is the offense of spilling the blood of a buddha's body. He convinced five hundred ignorant new bhikṣus to go with him to Mount Gajaśīrṣa to form a separate karma; this is the offense of disrupting the saṃgha.[10] On account of these three heinous offenses, he fell into the *avīci* hell, and even now experiences uninterrupted suffering. There are Devadattas under four buddhas in *avīci*.

[V7:19] {2:619}

倶伽離比丘、この生に、舍利弗・目犍連を謗するに、無根波羅夷の法をも
てす。世尊みづから、いさめましす、梵王きたりて、制すれどもやま
ず。二尊者を謗して、地獄におちぬ。

In this life, Bhikṣu Kokālika slandered Śāriputra and Maudgalyāyana, groundlessly accusing them of a *pārājika* offense.[11] Although the World-Honored One admonished him, and the Brahmā King came and suppressed him, he did not stop. He slandered the two venerables and fell into hell.

[V7:20]

四禪比丘、臨命終のときに、謗佛せしによりて、　阿鼻地獄におつ。かく
のごとくなるを、順次生受業となづく。

Because the bhikṣu of the fourth dhyāna slandered the Buddha as he approached the end of his life, he fell into the *avīci* hell.[12] Such a case is called "karma experienced in the next life."

---

9 **Devadatta** (*Daibadatta* 提婆達多): The treatment of Devadatta is much expanded in the twelve-chapter *Shōbōgenzō* text, extending from section 17 through the first sentence of 23.

10 **separate karma** (*betsu konma* 別羯磨): I.e, a ritually distinct clerical order, another saṃgha.

11 **Bhikṣu Kokālika** (*Kukari biku* 倶伽離比丘): This section parallels material in section 23 of the twelve-chapter *Shōbōgenzō* text.

12 **bhikṣu of the fourth dhyāna** (*shizen biku* 四禪比丘): This section corresponds to section 24 of the twelve-chapter *Shōbōgenzō* text, sections 25 and 26 of which provide a discussion, lacking here, of the meaning of "uninterrupted" (*mugen* 無間).

342 · DŌGEN'S *SHŌBŌGENZŌ* VOLUME VII

* * * * *

[V7:21]

第三順後次受業者、謂、若業此生造作增長、隨第三生、或隨第四生、或復過此、雖百千劫、受異熟果、是名順後次受業。

Of the third, "karma experienced in a life after the next," it is said,[13]

When the karma is produced and developed in this life, and its ripened fruit is experienced in the third life, or in the fourth life, or after these, even after a hundred thousand kalpas, it is called "karma experienced in a life after the next."

[V7:22]

いはく、人ありて、この生に、あるいは善にもあれ、あるいは惡にもあれ、造作しをはれりといへども、あるいは第三生、あるいは第四生、乃至百千生のあひだにも、善惡の業を感ずるを、順後次受業となづく。菩薩の三祇劫の功德、おほく順後次受業なり。かくのごとくの道理、しらざるがごときは、行者、おほく疑心をいだく。いまの闍夜多尊者の、在家のときのごとし。もし鳩摩羅多尊者にあはずば、そのうたがひとけがたからむ。行者、もし思惟、それ善なれば、惡、すなはち滅す。それ、惡思惟すれば、善、すみやかに滅するなり。

That is, while a person may complete an act, be it good or evil, in this life, he or she will experience the good or evil karma in the third life or in the fourth life or even during as many as a hundred thousand lives — this is called "karma experienced in a life after the next." The merit of the bodhisattva's three *asaṃkhyeya* kalpas is mostly karma experienced in a life after the next. When they do not recognize this truth, practitioners often harbor doubts. Such was the case here with Venerable Jayata when he was a householder. Had he not encountered Venerable Kumāralāta, his doubts would have been difficult to overcome.

When the practitioner's thoughts are good, evil will quickly disappear; when he or she has evil thoughts, good will quickly disappear.

[V7:23] {2:620}

室羅筏國昔有二人、一恆修善、一常作惡。修善行者、於一身中、恆修善行、未嘗作惡。作惡行者、於一身中、常作惡行、未嘗修善。修善行者、臨命終時、順後次受惡業力故、欻有地獄中有現前。便作是念、我一身中、恆修善行、未嘗作惡、應生天趣、何因緣有此中有現前。遂起念言、我定應有順後次受惡業今熟故、此地獄中有現前。即自憶念一身已來所修善業、深生歡喜。由勝善思現在前故、地獄中有、即便隱歿、天趣中有、欻爾現前。從此命終、生於天上。

---

13 **"karma experienced in a life after the next"** (*jun goji ju gō* 順後次受業): From this section through section 26, our text closely parallels sections 27-32 of the twelve-chapter *Shōbōgenzō* text.

V7. Karma of the Three Times *Sanji gō* 三時業 343

Long ago in the Land of Śrāvastī, there were two people, one who always did good, and one who always did evil. The one who practiced good deeds throughout his life constantly practiced good deeds and never did evil; the one who did evil deeds throughout his life always did evil deeds and never practiced good. When the one who practiced good deeds was approaching the end of his life, because of the power of bad karma experienced in a life after the next, there suddenly appeared before him his intermediate state in a hell. Thereupon, he had this thought, "Throughout this life, I have constantly practiced good deeds, never doing evil; I should be born in a heaven. Why is this intermediate state appearing before me?" He then gave rise to the thought, "Surely, it must be because karma experienced in a life after the next has now matured that this intermediate state in hell has appeared before me." He reflected on the good deeds he had done throughout his life and felt profound joy; and, due to the appearance of this excellent good thought, the intermediate state in hell vanished, and an intermediate state in heaven suddenly appeared before him. When his life ended, he was born in a heaven.

[V7:24]
この恆修善行のひと、順後次後の、さだめてうくべきが、わが身にありけるとおもふのみにあらず、さらにすすみておもはく、一身の修善もまた、さだめてのちにうくべし。ふかく歡喜す、とはこれなり。この憶念、まことなるがゆえに、地獄の中有すなはちかくれて、天趣の中有たちまちに現前して、いのち、をはりて、天上にむまる。この人、もし惡人ならば、命終のとき、地獄の中有現前せば、おもふべし、われ一身の修善、その功德なし、善惡あらむには、いかでかわれ地獄の中有をみん。このとき、因果を撥無し、三寶を毀謗せん。もしかくのごとくならば、すなはち命終し、地獄におつべし。かくのごとくならざるによりて、天上にうまるるなり。この道理、あきらめしるべし。

This person who had constantly done good deeds not only thought that he was surely to experience what is experienced in a life after the next, but went on to think that the good he had practiced throughout his life would also surely be experienced thereafter; his feeling "profound joy" refers to this.[14] Because this reflection was a true one, the intermediate state in hell disappeared, an intermediate state in heaven suddenly appeared before him, and, when his life ended, he was born in a heaven. Had this person been an evil person, when his life ended and an intermediate state in hell appeared before him, he would have thought, "The good I practiced throughout my life produced no merit; if good and evil exist, why do I see an intermediate state in a hell?" At this time, he would

---

14　**what is experienced in a life after the next** (*jungo jigo* 順後次後): Reading *jungo jiju* 順後次受.

344 DŌGEN'S *SHŌBŌGENZŌ* VOLUME VII

be denying cause and effect and disparaging the three treasures. Had this been the case, his life would have ended forthwith, and he would have fallen into a hell. Because this was not the case, he was born in a heaven. We should clearly recognize this truth.

[V7:25] {2:621}

作惡行者、臨命終時、順後次受善業力故、歘有天趣中有現前。便作是念、我一身中、常作惡行、未嘗修善、應生地獄、何緣有此中有現前。遂起邪見、撥無善惡及異熟果。邪見力故、天趣中有、尋即隱歿、地獄中有、歘爾現前。從此命終、生於地獄。

> When the one who had done evil deeds was approaching the end of his life, because of the power of the good karma experienced in a life after the next, there suddenly appeared before him his intermediate state in a heaven. Thereupon, he had this thought, "Throughout this life, I have always done evil, never practicing good; I should be born in a hell. Why is this intermediate state appearing before me?" He then gave rise to a false view that denied good and evil as well as their ripened fruits. By the power of this false view, the intermediate state in heaven immediately died out, and an intermediate state in hell suddenly appeared before him. When his life ended, he was born in a hell.

[V7:26]

この人、いけるほど、つねに惡をつくり、さらに一善を修せざるのみにあらず、命終のとき、天趣の中有の現前せるをみて、順後次受をしらず。われ一生のあひだ、惡をつくれりといへども、天趣にむまれんとす、はかりしりぬ、さらに善惡なかりけり。かくのごとく善惡を撥無する邪見力のゆえに、天趣の中有たちまちに隱歿して、地獄の中有すみやかに現前し、いのち、をはりて、地獄におつ。これは邪見のゆえに、天趣の中有、かくるるなり。

Not only had this person throughout his entire life always committed evil and never performed a single good deed, but, seeing the appearance of his intermediate state in a heaven, he failed to recognize it as [karma] experienced in a life after the next. [Seeing that] although he had committed evil his entire life, he was about to be born in a heaven, he concluded that there was no good or evil. Because of the power of his false view that denied good and evil in this way, the intermediate state of heaven immediately died out, an intermediate state of hell quickly appeared, and, when his life ended, he fell into a hell. Here, the intermediate state of heaven vanished because of a false view.

V7. Karma of the Three Times *Sanji gō* 三時業

[V7:27]

しかあればすなはち、行者かならず邪見なることなかれ。いかなるか邪見、いかなるか正見と、かたちをつくすまで學習すべし。まづ因果を撥無し、佛法僧を毀謗し、三世および解脱を撥無する、ともにこれ邪見なり。まさにしるべし、今生のわが身、ふたつなし、みつなし。いたづらに邪見におちて、むなしく惡業感得せん、をしからざらむや。惡をつくりながら惡にあらずとおもひ、惡の報あるべからずと邪思惟するによりて、惡報の感得せざるにはあらず。

Thus, practitioners must never hold false views.[15] What are false views and what correct views — we should study this for as long as we live. First of all, denying cause and effect, denigrating buddha, dharma, and saṃgha, denying the three times and liberation — these are all false views. We should recognize that we do not have two or three selves in this life. What a waste, then, foolishly to fall into false views and meaninglessly suffer evil karma. By believing while committing evil that it is not evil and falsely thinking that there will be no evil recompense, we cannot but suffer the evil recompense.

* * * * *

[V7:28] {2:622}

皓月供奉、問長沙景岑和尚、古德云、了即業障本來空、未了應須償宿債。只如師子尊者・二祖大師、爲什麼得償債去。長沙云、大德不識本來空。彼云、如何是本來空。長沙云、業障是。又問、如何是業障。長沙云、本來空是。彼無語。長沙便示一偈云、假有元非有、假滅亦非無、涅槃償債義、一生更無殊。

The officiant Haoyue asked Reverend Jingcen of Changsha, "A worthy of old has said,

> *If you've understood, the karmic hindrances are fundamentally empty;*
> *If you haven't understood, you have to repay your outstanding debts.*[16]

How then could those like the Worthy Siṃha and the Great Master, the Second Ancestor, have repaid their debts?"

Changsha said, "The Most Virtuous One has not understood 'fundamental emptiness.'"

Haoyue said, "What is 'fundamental emptiness'?"

---

15 **Thus** (*shika areba sunawachi* しかあればすなはち): This section corresponds to the last two sentences of section 32 and the first part of section 33 of the twelve-chapter *Shōbōgenzō* text.

16 **The officiant Haoyue** (*Kōgetsu gubu* 皓月供奉): This section corresponds to section 34 of the twelve-chapter *Shōbōgenzō* text.

346 DŌGEN'S *SHŌBŌGENZŌ* VOLUME VII

Changsha said, "It's 'the karmic hindrances.'"

Haoyue asked again, "What are 'the karmic hindrances'?"

Changsha said, "They're 'fundamental emptiness.'"

Haoyue said nothing. Changsha then presented a gāthā:

> *Nominal existence is from the start not existence;*
> *And nominal extinction is also not extinction.*
> *Nirvāṇa and repayment of debts*
> *Are of one nature, without any difference.*

[V7:29]

長沙の答は答にあらず、鳩摩羅多の、闍夜多にしめす道理なし。しるべ
し、業障のむねをしらざるなり。仏祖の兒孫、修證辨道するには、まづか
ならずこの三時の業をあきらめしらむこと、鳩摩羅多尊者のごとくなるべ
し。すでにこれ祖宗の業なり、廢怠すべからず。このほか不定業あり、ま
た八種の業あること、ひろく参學すべし。いまだこの業報の道理あきらめ
ざらむともがら、みだりに人天の導師と稱することなかれ。

Changsha's answer was not an answer; it lacks the principle that Kumāralāta taught to Jayata.[17] We should understand that he does not understand the meaning of the "karmic hindrances."

In practicing and verifying and pursuing the way, descendants of the
buddhas and ancestors should first of all clarify the karma of the three
times, as did Kumāralāta.[18] Since it is the karma of our ancestors, we
should not neglect it. In addition, we should study extensively that there
are the eight types of karma of indeterminate karma and the rest. Do not
rashly name as the teachers of humans and devas those who have not
clarified the principle of actions and their consequences.

[V7:30]

かの三時の惡業報、かならず感ずべしといえども、懺悔するがごときは、
重を轉じて輕受せしむ、また滅罪清淨ならしむるなり。善業また、隨喜す
ればいよいよ増長するなり。これみな作業の黑白にまかせたり。

Although we are sure to experience that recompense of evil karma in
the three times, those who repent transform serious [offenses] to minor
[recompense] or extinguish offenses and purify them.[19] And, good kar-

---

17 **Changsha's answer** (*Chōsha no kotae* 長沙の答): The criticism of Changsha here is
much expanded in the twelve-chapter *Shōbōgenzō* text, over sections 35-38.

18 **In practicing and verifying and pursuing the way** (*shushō bendō suru ni* 修證
辨道するに): The remainder of this section corresponds roughly to section 39 of the
twelve-chapter *Shōbōgenzō* text.

19 **that recompense of evil karma in the three times** (*kano sanji no akugōppō* かの
三時の惡業報): This section corresponds to material in section 41 of the twelve-chapter
Shōbōgenzō text

V7. Karma of the Three Times *Sanji gō* 三時業 347

ma, if we rejoice in it, increases. This all depends on whether "the karma you have done" is "black or white."[20]

[V7:31]

世尊言、假令經百劫、所作業不亡、因緣會遇時、果報還自受。汝等當知、若純黑業、得純黑異熟、若純白業、得純白異熟。若黑白業、得雜異熟。是故應離純黑及黑白雜業、當勤修學純白之業。時諸大衆、聞佛説已、歡喜信受。

The World-Honored One said,[21]

> *Though you pass through a hundred kalpas,*
> *The karma you have done will not disappear:*
> *When causes and conditions come together,*
> *You will naturally experience the fruits of your deeds.*

> *You should know that, if your deeds are pure black, you will get pure black ripened fruits; if your deeds are pure white, you will get pure white ripened fruits; if your deeds are black and white, you will get mixed ripened fruits. Therefore, you should avoid pure black, as well as black and white, deeds and should strive to practice pure white deeds.*

> *At that time, the great assembly, having heard the Buddha's speech, rejoiced, believed, and accepted it.*

正法眼藏三時業第八
Treasury of the True Dharma Eye
Karma of the Three Times
Number 8

{2:623}

建長五年癸丑三月九日、在於永平寺之首座寮書寫之。懷奘
Copied this in the Head Seat's Quarters of Eiheiji; the ninth day of the third month of the junior water year of the ox, the fifth year of Kenchō [8 April, 1253]. Ejō[22]

---

20 **"the karma you have done" is "black or white"** (*sagō no kokubyaku* 作業の黒白): Introducing the Buddha's words in the next section.

21 **The World-Honored One** (*Seson* 世尊): This section parallels section 40 of the twelve-chapter *Shōbōgenzō* text.

22 This colophon is not found in the twelve-chapter *Shōbōgenzō* text. Like that text, this sixty-chapter *Shōbōgenzō* version lacks a colophon by Dōgen.

The Sōtō Zen Text Project *Shōbōgenzō*

Volume I
The Seventy-five-Chapter Compilation, Part 1

1. The Realized Kōan *Genjō kōan* 現成公案
2. Mahā-prajñā-pāramitā *Maka hannya haramitsu* 摩訶般若波羅蜜
3. Buddha Nature *Busshō* 佛性
4. Studying the Way with Body and Mind *Shinjin gakudō* 身心學道
5. This Mind Itself Is the Buddha *Soku shin ze butsu* 即心是佛
6. Deportment of the Practicing Buddha *Gyōbutsu iigi* 行佛威儀
7. One Bright Pearl *Ikka myōju* 一顆明珠
8. The Mind Cannot Be Got *Shin fukatoku* 心不可得
9. The Old Buddha Mind *Kobutsushin* 古佛心
10. Great Awakening *Daigo* 大悟
11. Principles of Seated Meditation *Zazen gi* 坐禪儀
12. Needle of Seated Meditation *Zazen shin* 坐禪箴
13. Ocean Seal Samādhi *Kaiin zanmai* 海印三昧
14. Sky Flowers *Kūge* 空華
15. Radiance *Kōmyō* 光明

Volume II
The Seventy-five-Chapter Compilation, Part 2

16A. Sustained Practice, Part 1 *Gyōji jō* 行持上
16B. Sustained Practice, Part 2 *Gyōji ge* 行持下
17. Such *Inmo* 恁麼
18. Avalokiteśvara *Kannon* 觀音
19. The Old Mirror *Kokyō* 古鏡
20. Sometimes *Uji* 有時
21. Prediction *Juki* 授記
22. Full Function *Zenki* 全機
23. The Moon *Tsuki* 都機
24. Painted Cake *Gabyō* 畫餅
25. Sound of the Stream, Form of the Mountain *Keisei sanshoku* 谿聲山色
26. Beyond the Buddha *Butsu kōjō ji* 佛向上事
27. Talking of a Dream within a Dream *Muchū setsumu* 夢中説夢
28. Making a Bow and Getting the Marrow *Raihai tokuzui* 禮拜得髓
29. The Mountains and Waters Sūtra *Sansui kyō* 山水經
30. Sūtra Reading *Kankin* 看經

Volume III
The Seventy-five-Chapter Compilation, Part 3

31. Do No Evil *Shoaku makusa* 諸惡莫作
32. Transmitting the Robe *Den'e* 傳衣
33. Sayings *Dōtoku* 道得
34. The Teachings of the Buddhas *Bukkyō* 佛教
35. Spiritual Powers *Jinzū* 神通
36. The Arhat *Arakan* 阿羅漢

37. Spring and Autumn *Shunjū* 春秋
38. Tangled Vines *Kattō* 葛藤
39. The Inheritance Certificate *Shisho* 嗣書
40. The Cypress Tree *Hakujushi* 柏樹子
41. The Three Realms Are Only Mind *Sangai yui shin* 三界唯心
42. Talking of the Mind, Talking of the Nature *Sesshin sesshō* 説心説性
43. The Real Marks of the Dharmas *Shohō jissō* 諸法實相
44. The Way of the Buddhas *Butsudō* 佛道
45. Secret Words *Mitsugo* 密語

Volume IV
The Seventy-five-Chapter Compilation, Part 4

46. The Insentient Preach the Dharma *Mujō seppō* 無情説法
47. Sūtras of the Buddhas *Bukkyō* 佛經
48. Dharma Nature *Hosshō* 法性
49. Dhāraṇī *Darani* 陀羅尼
50. Washing the Face *Senmen* 洗面
51. Face-to-Face Conferral *Menju* 面授
52. Buddhas and Ancestors *Busso* 佛祖
53. Plum Blossoms *Baika* 梅華
54. Washing and Purifying *Senjō* 洗淨
55. The Ten Directions *Jippō* 十方
56. Seeing Buddha *Kenbutsu* 見佛
57. Extensive Study *Henzan* 遍參
58. The Eye *Ganzei* 眼睛
59. Everyday Matters *Kajō* 家常
60. The Thirty-seven Factors of Bodhi *Sanjūshichi hon bodai bunpō* 三十七品菩提分法

Volume V
The Seventy-five-Chapter Compilation, Part 5

61. Song of the Dragon *Ryūgin* 龍吟
62. The Intention of the Ancestral Master's Coming from the West
     Soshi seirai i 祖師西來意
63. Bringing Forth the Mind of Bodhi *Hotsu bodai shin* 發菩提心
64. The Udumbara Blossom *Udonge* 優曇華
65. The Entire Body of the Tathāgata *Nyorai zenshin* 如來全身
66. The King of Samādhis Samādhi *Zanmai ō zanmai* 三昧王三昧
67. Turning the Dharma Wheel *Ten hōrin* 轉法輪
68. Great Practice *Dai shugyō* 大修行
69. The Samādhi of Self Verification *Jishō zanmai* 自證三昧
70. Empty Space *Kokū* 虛空
71. The Pātra Bowl *Hou* 鉢盂
72. The Retreat *Ango* 安居
73. Reading Other Minds *Tashin tsū* 他心通
74. The King Requests Saindhava *Ō saku sendaba* 王索仙陀婆
75. Leaving Home *Shukke* 出家

Volume VI
The Twelve-Chapter Compilation

T1. The Merit of Leaving Home *Shukke kudoku* 出家功德
T2. Receiving the Precepts *Jukai* 受戒
T3. The Merit of the Kāṣāya *Kesa kudoku* 袈裟功德
T4. Bringing Forth the Mind of Bodhi *Hotsu bodai shin* 發菩提心
T5. Offerings to the Buddhas *Kuyō shobutsu* 供養諸佛
T6. Refuge in the Treasures of Buddha, Dharma, and Saṃgha
    Kie buppōsōbō 歸依佛法僧寶
T7. Deep Faith in Cause and Effect *Jinshin inga* 深信因果
T8. Karma of the Three Times *Sanjigō* 三時業
T9. Four Horses *Shime* 四馬
T10. The Bhikṣu of the Fourth Dhyāna *Shizen biku* 四禪比丘
T11. One Hundred Eight Gateways to the Illumination of the Dharma
    Ippyakuhachi hōmyōmon 一百八法明門
T12. The Eight Understandings of the Great Person *Hachi dainin gaku* 八大人覺

Volume VII
Supplementary Chapters, Variant Texts

Supplementary Chapters

S1. Talk on Pursuing the Way *Bendōwa* 辦道話
S2. Procedures for the Hall of Gathered Clouds *Jūundō shiki* 重雲堂式
S3. The *Lotus* Turns the *Lotus* *Hokke ten Hokke* 法華轉法華
S4. The Mind Cannot Be Got *Shin fukatoku* 心不可得
S5. The Four Attractions of the Bodhisattva *Bodaisatta shishōbō* 菩提薩埵四攝法
S6. Instructions to the Administration Cloister *Ji kuin mon* 示庫院文
S7. Only Buddhas with Buddhas *Yui butsu yo butsu* 唯佛與佛
S8. Birth and Death *Shōji* 生死
S9. The Way of the Buddhas *Butsudō* 佛道 (*Dōshin* 道心)

Variant Texts

V1. Talk on Pursuing the Way *Bendōwa* 辦道話
V2. The Inheritance Certificate *Shisho* 嗣書
V3. Beyond the Buddha *Butsu kōjō ji* 佛向上事
V4. Washing the Face *Senmen* 洗面
V5. Extensive Study *Henzan* 遍參
V6. Great Awakening *Daigo* 大悟
V7. Karma of the Three Times *Sanji gō* 三時業

Volume VIII

Introduction
Appendices
Supplementary Notes
Works Cited